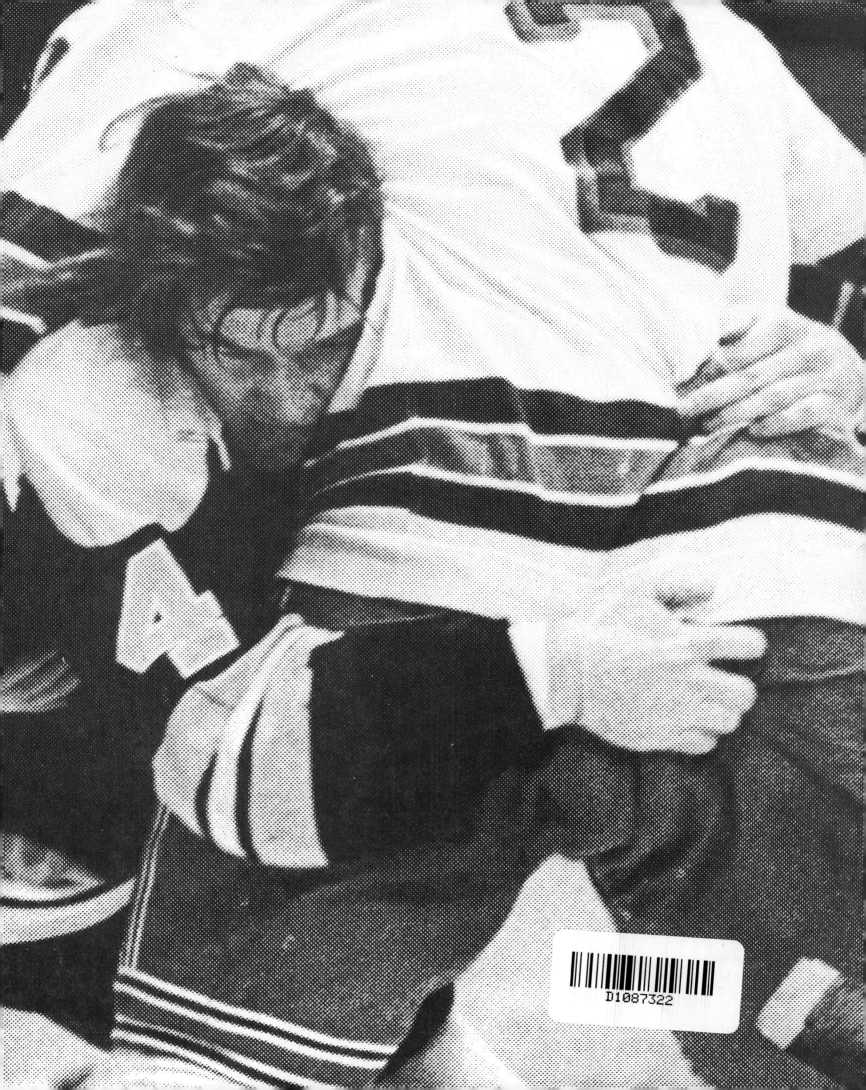

GREAT BOOK OF
HOCKEY

MORE THAN 100 YEARS OF FIRE ON ICE

WRITTEN BY STAN AND SHIRLEY FISCHLER

PUBLICATIONS INTERNATIONAL, LTD.

Stan Fischler, the dean of North American hockey writers, has authored more than 60 books in his distinguished career. His hockey best-sellers include **Slapshot, Hammer, Grapes,** and **Bobby Orr and the Big, Bad Bruins.** He has contributed to such noted publications as **Sports Illustrated, Inside Sports, The Sporting News, The New York Times,** and **Newsweek.** Mr. Fischler has also worked extensively in sports broadcasting.

Shirley Fischler has teamed with her husband on such books as **The Hockey Encyclopedia** and **The Best, the Worst, and Most Unusual in Sports,** a best-seller. Mrs. Fischler was one of the first women in sports broadcasting, serving as a color commentator for the New England Whalers in 1973-74. The Fischlers currently reside in New York City.

Morgan Hughes served as a consultant for the **Great Book of Hockey.** Mr Hughes has written for such publications as **GOAL, Hockey Scene, The Sporting News,** and **Inside Sports.** He currently resides in St. Paul, Minnesota.

CONTENTS

BRACE YOURSELF

THE SPORT OF HOCKEY IS NOT ALWAYS
FUN AND GAMES. THOUGH THE
NHL HAS FEATURED BRILLIANT
SHOOTERS LIKE THE ROCKET AND
GREAT SKATERS LIKE THE ROADRUNNER,
IT HAS ALSO HAD A PLACE FOR THE
BONE-CRUSHERS: TERRIBLE TED,
THE HAMMER, AND DIRTY BERTIE.
SO AS YOU SKATE THROUGH
THE GREAT BOOK OF HOCKEY,
FEEL FREE TO REVEL IN THE
ARTISTRY OF THE LAFLEURS AND
GRETZKYS. BUT BEWARE:
A TERRIBLE TED
MAY BE HEADED YOUR WAY.

WHOSE GAME IS IT?

The Brits, Irish, Dutch, and even the Micmacs all claim hockey as their game.

Though hockey's origins were quite humble, the game developed into an organized sport in the 1870s. The Winnipeg Victorias (*above*) were formed in the 1890s and became the pride of Western Canada.

THE EARLY YEARS

For almost as long as the game of ice hockey has existed, people have argued as to where and by whom the game was first played.

In the early 1900s, Micmac Indians living in Nova Scotia claimed to have played the earliest version of the Canadian sport. *The Dictionary of the Language of the Micmac Indians,* published in 1888, described an ice game called "oochamkunutk," which was played with "a bat or stick." Later, in 1894, *Legends of the Micmacs* referred to an Indian ice game allegedly called "Alchamadijik" or "hurley" (the hurley being the "hockey" stick). Hurley, however, was an old Irish field game introduced into the area by Irish immigrants, who came to work on the Shubenacadie Canal near Dartmouth, Nova Scotia, in 1831.

The Indians' claim was supported by local white men, including novelist Thomas H. Raddall; Ted Graham, a Dartmouth speedskater in the 1880s; and soldiers from the nearby British garrison. All of these men remembered playing a "scrub game" with the Micmacs on frozen ponds and lakes.

"We played with the Indians," said Graham in 1943, "who would play in moccasins or wood skates. They could run like moose on the ice and were very rough in their style of play."

Although the Indians of Canada have been credited with inventing the field game "lacrosse," descendants of the first white settlers in Canada claim that ice hockey originated in Europe. First, they point to 17th-century Dutch paintings that depict a game being played on ice with sticks and skates.

Next, they point out that "shinny"— which unorganized hockey is often called— is directly related to field hockey ("shinning to your side" refers to the field hockey rule of always playing right-handed). And field hockey was imported to Canada from Great Britain and transposed to ice almost immediately. Even hurley, they hasten to point out, originated in Ireland and was introduced to the Indians.

So who really invented the game of hockey? Despite all of the speculation and all of the historical research, nobody really knows for sure. The probability is that in any country where the winters were cold and icy ponds and rivers were safe for skating, some form of ice hockey was created and played—by white man and Indian alike.

What can be proven is that the sport of ice hockey as we know it today evolved in the Dominion of Canada, and that the first recorded occurrence of organized indoor ice hockey took place in Montreal on March 3, 1875, in Victoria Skating Rink.

Lord Stanley Awards Cup to Hockey Champs

1 8 7 5 - 1 9 1 7

The organizer of that first publicized game in Montreal was a man from Halifax, Nova Scotia. James Creighton (1850-1930) played the ice game of hurley discussed above. When a local exhibition of ice lacrosse proved to be a failure with the public, Creighton proposed ice hockey instead, and even ordered sticks to be shipped from Halifax to Montreal. "Prior to that year," said Creighton's friend Henry Joseph in a 1936 interview, "I had never seen a hockey stick around Montreal, nor seen hurley or shinny played on skates."

The game was played with nine-man sides on a surface that measured 80 feet by 204 feet. *The (Montreal) Gazette* reported that "in order to spare the heads and nerves of the spectators, a flat, circular piece of wood" was used instead of the usual rubber ball. This was undoubtedly the precursor to the modern puck.

Hockey's first indoor organized presentation ended in a 2-1 victory for Creighton's team, and significantly enough, also ended with the first recorded account of a hockey fight! "A disgraceful sight took place,"

complained a wire despatch of Kingston's *Daily British Whig* from Montreal. "Shins and heads were battered, benches smashed, and the lady spectators fled in confusion."

The following year, 1876, Creighton's team played the Victoria rink team to a 1-1 tie under "Hockey Association" rules (referring to field hockey rules that had been established in England a year earlier). This contest was significant because the published report of the game referred to the object being struck with sticks as a "puck" for the first time.

▲ **By the 1890s, large Canadian cities began building indoor ice rinks. One of the classiest was Montreal's Victoria rink. Notice the absence of side boards.**

 The 1891 Ottawa Hockey Club, champion of the new OHA, was led by P.D. Ross (fourth from right), who later became Trustee of the Stanley Cup and publisher of the Ottawa Journal.

Creighton was a member of an exclusive Montreal men's organization, the Metropolitan Club. In 1877, this club played an exhibition game against another select group, the St. James Club, with the first published ice hockey rules. There were only seven rules and only the word "ice" distinguished the rules from those of field hockey.

According to "Rule Two," the contest would be an "onside" game, meaning there would be no forward passing: "a player must always be on his own side of the ball." The face-off (or "bully," as it was then called in field hockey) was the same as on the field. It required that the facing centermen bang their sticks together before attempting to control the puck.

Soon there were three ice hockey teams in Montreal, as well as one in Quebec City. Ice hockey was also being played outdoors in Kingston. In 1883, Montreal held a winter carnival and decided that "the novel game of hockey" would be featured in the festival. From Montreal, the Victoria and McGill University teams entered the contest; the Quebec City team joined too. The rules for the series said the teams would carry seven men per side and play two 30-minute periods with ten minutes between periods.

This was the first printed mention of an official playing time for ice hockey. McGill emerged the victor of the first "championship" series in ice hockey.

The annual carnival became the breeding ground of what would become modern Canadian ice hockey. By 1886, it was a four-team contest in which sticks could be of any length, but no more than three inches wide. The puck would be one inch thick, three inches in diameter, and made of vulcanized rubber—the very description of pucks used today.

In June of 1888, Queen Victoria appointed Sir Frederick Arthur Stanley to be Governor General of

Fred Waghorne

HISTORY OF THE FACE-OFF

The face-off became part of hockey at the turn of the century, thanks to referee Fred Waghorne. Waghorne knew from personal experience that many a referee was dissatisfied with the old manner of facing off. In the old method, the puck was placed on the ice by the ref, who then had to make certain each center was lined up correctly and fairly. This often led to sticks in tender areas of the ref's anatomy.

Waghorne debuted his new face-off method in 1900. Waghorne thought it would be best to just drop the puck, "allowing them to do as they darn well pleased," he said. So he did exactly that in a contest in southwestern Ontario and "didn't receive a single squawk from either players or fans."

The next winter, Waghorne was allowed to use the innovation in a National Hockey Association game at Almonte, and it has been a part of hockey ever since.

In the late 19th century, the Montreal Athletic Association's team was known as the Winged Wheelers. Its insignia was later copied by the Detroit Red Wings.

Lord Stanley of Preston, sixth Governor General of Canada, donated a silver cup to Canada's amateur championship team in 1893. The Stanley Cup now is awarded annually to the NHL playoff champion.

The 1896 Stanley Cup champion Montreal Victorias featured an early rushing defenseman, captain Mike Grant *(front row, second from left)*. The Victorias captured Stanley Cups in four straight seasons (1895-98).

Captain of the Montreal Shamrocks, Harry Trihey led his club to two Stanley Cups (1899 and 1900). In one Stanley Cup game against Quebec, Trihey knocked home ten goals.

The Dutch are most often credited with the invention of the true ice skate. An early version, circa 1869, is shown here.

Canada, and soon the 48-year-old sports enthusiast embarked for the Canadian capital city of Ottawa with his wife, eight sons, and two daughters. The significance of their arrival in Canada was soon felt, as the family attended the Montreal Winter Carnival during their first winter there and became instant avid hockey fans.

Soon three of Stanley's sons— Edward, Victor, and Arthur—were playing for a Government House five-man hockey club. The Stanley clan and parliamentary friends were instrumental in developing ice hockey in Ottawa, and soon there was a four-team league there. By November of 1890, the Governor General's oldest son, Arthur, further spread the game by forming the Hockey Association of Ontario (soon to be called the OHA).

On March 18, 1892, Lord Kilcoursie—Frederic Rudolph Lambert—spoke at a banquet honoring the OHA champion Ottawa club. He read a personal letter from Governor Stanley: "There does not appear to be any 'outward or visible sign' of the championship at present, and considering the interest that hockey matches now elicit and the importance of having the games fairly played under generally recognized rules, I am willing to give a cup that shall be annually held by the winning club."

Captain Charles Colville, aide to Lord Stanley, purchased a gold-lined silver cup on a trip to England, spending the then-costly sum of ten guineas, or slightly less than $50. The trophy would be awarded annually to the amateur champions of Canada.

In 1893, with Lord Stanley watching, Ottawa easily defeated all four visiting Quebec teams, but later lost two of four matches in Montreal and Quebec. Montreal AAA, the league champion, became the first winner of what was then called "the Lord Stanley Challenge Trophy."

Montreal AAA went on to win the Cup again in 1894. But in 1895, it lost the league title to the Montreal Victorias, and then received an outside challenge from Queen's University. Montreal agreed to play Queen's, but this presented very confusing

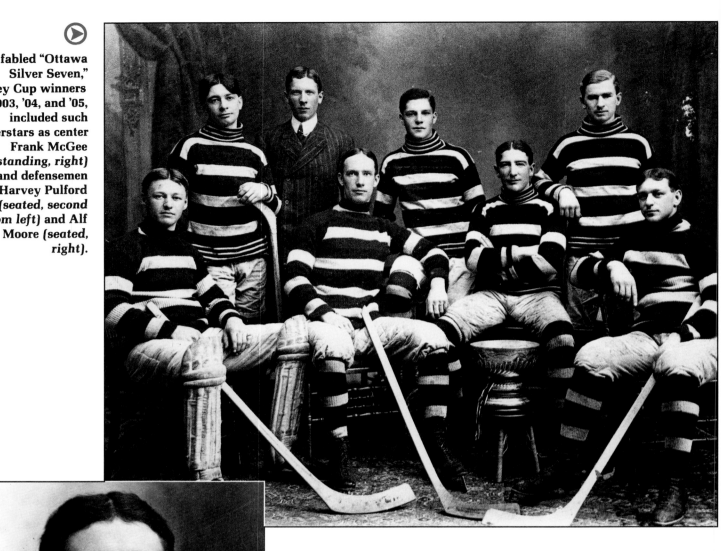

 The fabled "Ottawa Silver Seven," Stanley Cup winners in 1903, '04, and '05, included such superstars as center Frank McGee (standing, right) and defensemen Harvey Pulford (seated, second from left) and Alf Moore (seated, right).

Hall of Famer Alf Smith, a right wing with the Cup-winning Ottawa clubs of 1904 and 1905, was the oldest of seven hockey-playing brothers. Smith was notorious for his less-than-gentlemanly play.

possibilities: If Montreal AAA lost to Queen's, the Cup would leave the league; but if Montreal AAA defeated Queen's, the Victorias would be the team to have their names engraved on the Stanley Cup, since they had won the league title already! Montreal AAA handily defeated the challenger 5-1, and the Montreal Victorias became the Stanley Cup champions by default.

The Montreal Victorias would be a powerhouse in ice hockey for several years, winning the Stanley Cup for four consecutive seasons, 1895-98. It was in 1896, however, that the Victorias met an interesting challenge from the far west of Canada—and from another team sporting the name Victorias.

As the railroad spread across Canada, the city of Winnipeg, Manitoba, became the major terminus for the Canadian Pacific Railroad. Consequently, the town grew rapidly from a tiny hamlet of 200 souls to 25,000 by 1890, when the city's first organized hockey club, the Victorias, was formed. Soon there was a second club, and by 1893 hockey was so prevalent in Manitoba that the Victorias traveled east for a series of exhibition games against the established Quebec and Ontario clubs.

While the Victorias proved no match for the Easterners, they did bring with them several innovations that were soon adopted by Quebec and Ontario

players. For one thing, they had changed the "face" in hockey, from the old field hockey version known as the "bully." In a bully, two players faced each other, then banged their sticks together three times before attempting to hit the puck lying on the ice. Winnipeggers instead placed the puck on the ice and faced each other with sticks poised; but then, upon a signal from the referee, they would simply go after the puck.

Another innovation from Winnipeg was the introduction of goalie pads— the Winnipeg goaler sported cricket pads. Although some players in the East had stuffed items down their stockings for a primitive form of padding, the use of cricket pads on the goaltender was unheard of. However, the pads were quickly imitated by Eastern netminders. Finally, the Winnipeg forwards introduced an underhand or "scoop" shot, now known as the wrist shot, into Ontario hockey.

After their exhibition tour in 1893, Winnipeg virtually disappeared from the Eastern hockey scene—until 1896, when the Winnipeg Victorias challenged the Montreal Victorias. The Stanley Cup challenge match was played in February of 1896, and Winnipeg astounded the Eastern hockey establishment by defeating Montreal 2-0.

The Cup did not spend long in the Wild West, however, as the Montreal club—league champions in 1896—*again* challenged Winnipeg after the close of the regular season. The game was played in Winnipeg in December, 1896, and was reportedly the greatest sporting event in the history of Manitoba, with seats allegedly selling for the incredible price of $12!

It appeared that Winnipeg would again defeat the East, as it was leading 4-2 at halftime. But the Montreal team, featuring the unique end-to-end rushes of defenseman Mike Grant, finally tied the game and ultimately won in the last few moments, on a goal by Ernie McLea. The Montreal Victorias would successfully face a challenge from the Ottawa Capitals in 1897 and win the Cup again in 1898, unchallenged.

Ice hockey by this time was a seven-man game: the goaler, three forwards, a rover (who switched from defense to offense, as the play required), and the point and cover point (the defense included the cover point in front of the point, rather than side by side as they are today).

The so-called "Quebec" version of onside play (no forward passing) was now universal. All players were now allowed to lift the puck when taking shots. And goaltenders were not

This Dawson City game was played on a rink next to a frozen river. It featured the Northwest Mounted Police versus the Dawson City Citizens and took place during the winter of 1900.

RUSSELL BOWIE

Russell Bowie, who toiled at center ice for the turn-of-the-century Victorias, has been called by hard-line oldtimers the greatest pivotman to play the game. A quick glance at Bowie's stats shows that he was indeed the Phil Esposito of his day. Throughout his ten seasons with Winnipeg, from 1899-1908, he amassed 234 goals in 80 games—almost three goals per game!

In 1907, Bowie scored eight goals in one game. Twice he scored seven times in a game, and five times he totaled six goals in a contest. Bowie led the league in scoring for five years and was a perennial All-Star.

Bowie remained an amateur throughout his career, although there were allegations that he had accepted a retainer from the professional Montreal Wanderers in 1907. However, he was finally cleared. While the Wanderers went on to win a string of championships, the Victorias, starring Russell Bowie, never drank Stanley Cup champagne.

The 1899 Montreal Shamrocks clinched their CAHL title against the perennial favorite, the Montreal Victorias. The Shamrocks won it on a goal by captain Harry Trihey (seated, center).

Harry "Rat" Westwick began his career as a goalie, but soon switched to rover. Westwick, a member of the "Ottawa Silver Seven," scored 24 goals in just 13 games in 1905.

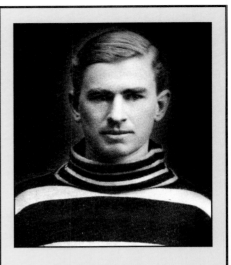

FRANK McGEE

There are those who still insist that Frank McGee, star of the legendary Ottawa Silver Seven, was the greatest player of all time. It's a pretty good argument. A center and rover (rover was the seventh position), McGee was a lightning-fast skater who could stick-handle and shoot with the very best of them. McGee led the Silver Seven to three straight Stanley Cups during his brief career.

McGee scored better than three goals per game in the 23 regular-season contests he appeared in, but even more incredible were his Stanley Cup statistics. In 22 Cup games, Frank scored 63 goals, including an amazing 14-goal game against Dawson City in 1905! An equally dazzling footnote to these astronomical numbers is that Frank had lost an eye prior to his playing days with Ottawa.

But just as his handicap didn't prevent McGee's hockey heroics, neither did it deter him from military service when World War I broke out in Europe. McGee enlisted for overseas action and was killed in France in 1916. Deservedly, he is a member of the Hockey Hall of Fame.

---

allowed to drop to the ice when making saves and could, in fact, be penalized if they did so.

The first recorded ice hockey game between Canada and the United States took place as early as 1886 (between Montreal AAA and Burlington, Vermont). However, the ice game that first spread through the United States was "ice polo," probably an imported variation of the old "rickets" game that had been played in the Canadian Maritimes. Ice polo was a five-man game—with a goaltender, one guard, and three forwards—and was played with a rubber ball. Several American ice polo teams played exhibition games

with Canadian hockey clubs during the 1890s. However, the Americans proved no match in the Canadian version and were soon adapting their game into ice hockey.

The year 1895 saw a record number of encounters between Canadian and U.S. teams. In February 1895, the Winnipeg Victorias visited Minneapolis, Minnesota, and soundly defeated an American conglomeration of ice polo and football players 11-2. Almost simultaneously, a U.S. ice polo club from Illinois played a series of games in Ontario. The Illinois clan mustered only one victory and a tie in 11 games, but brought with them a

new feature—a cage hockey goal (ice hockey goals had been just two posts embedded in the ice).

Only two weeks later, the Quebec Hockey Club traveled south to Baltimore, Maryland, to participate in the first international series ever played on artificial ice. The Baltimore club was defeated 5-2 and 6-1 on consecutive nights. Local journalists criticized the hometown team for lack of team play and the inability to lift the puck as the Canadians did. Interestingly, the Quebec club was led by an American goaltender, Frank Stocking. The Quebec team toured New York and Washington, D.C., before returning north.

Finally, in December 1895, the Queen's University ice hockey club played in New York against Yale University, trouncing the Elis 3-0. Queen's also introduced the game in Pittsburgh, Pennsylvania, that same season. A year later in 1896, two Montreal teams—AAA and the Shamrocks—played a series in New York City, and from that point on New York sports fans became enamored with ice hockey. Soon the Big Apple had four amateur clubs: the New York Hockey Club, the New York Athletic Club, the Crescent Athletic Club of Brooklyn, and the St. Nicholas Skating Club.

By 1902, the Intercollegiate Hockey League had been formed in the States, with Columbia, Dartmouth, Harvard, Princeton, and Yale as members. In the early 1900s, the St. Nicholas Club and Princeton University both featured the talents of an American rover, Hobart "Hobey" Baker. Baker, who some say was the greatest American player ever, was an aviator in World War I and was killed in a plane crash one month after the Armistice.

By the mid-1890s, there were rumors that ice hockey players were actually being paid to perform. Traditionally a "gentlemen's" sport, ice hockey had been strictly an amateur game, and the rumors of payment caused great controversy in Canada.

In 1897 and 1898, a club in Berlin, Ontario, was accused of having players "who received remuneration for their services." Although the accusations were never proven, it is significant that the Berlin team carried on its roster a player named John Liddell Macdonald Gibson. Gibson left amateur hockey for the Detroit College of Medicine and established a dental practice in Houghton, Michigan in 1901.

In 1904, Gibson, with financial backers and the owners of several regional hockey clubs, formed the International Hockey League, the sport's first officially professional league. Although many players in Canada had been receiving money regularly by this time, they still played

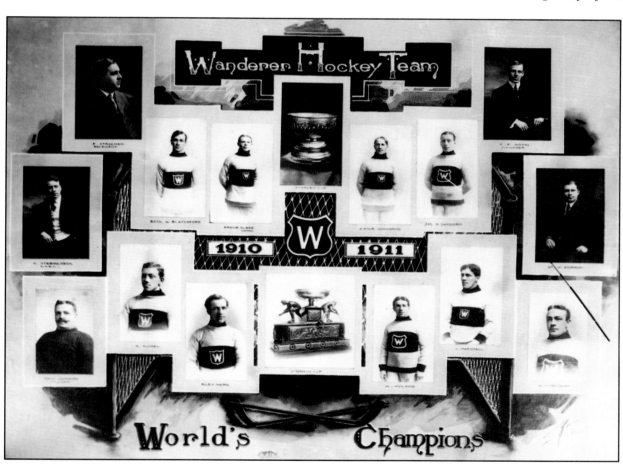

World's Champions

The Montreal Wanderers were champions of the new NHA, taking home the league's first O'Brien Trophy. The 1910 Wanderers also defeated Ottawa for the Stanley Cup.

Field hockey sticks gradually evolved into the common hockey sticks we know today. Shown here are two Winnipeg Victorias sticks from the 1890s.

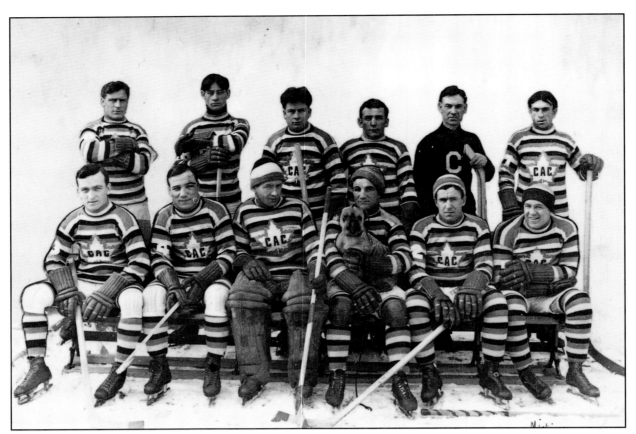

With the talents of Newsy Lalonde and Didier Pitre, the 1912-13 Montreal Canadiens led the NHA at the season's halfway mark. However, the team stumbled in the second half and finished next to last.

Hall of Fame defenseman Art Ross (shown here as an Ottawa Senator) was not only a talented player but the inventor of the "official Art Ross goal net" and a builder of the Boston Bruins.

Though the baseball, football, and basketball have changed significantly over the years, the puck has remained basically the same. This puck marks Toronto's 1900 OHA championship.

in what were officially designated "amateur" leagues. The new IHL consisted of teams from Portage Lake, Michigan; Laurium, Michigan; Houghton, Michigan; Sault Ste. Marie, Michigan; Sault Ste. Marie, Ontario; and Pittsburgh. Ottawa-born star Hod Stuart coached and captained the new Laurium "Calumets," who won the first IHL title.

While publicly acknowledged professionalism was underway in the United States, ice hockey in Canada was also changing. The Amateur Hockey Association of Canada became the Canadian Amateur Hockey League (CAHL) in 1899, and the Victorias' hold

on the Stanley Cup was broken by another Montreal team—the Shamrocks, who won in 1899 and 1900.

Records were being set and broken, and the game's first "superstars" began to emerge. In a Stanley Cup game on February 4, 1899, the Shamrocks' Harry Trihey scored ten goals vs. Quebec, setting an individual Stanley Cup scoring record that has not been, nor likely ever will be, broken. A few days later, the Vics tromped Ottawa in Montreal by a score of 16-0, another hard-to-beat record.

In 1900, the CAHL adopted the use of goal nets, and the wearing of hockey gloves became common. Also, players

continued to strap primitive shin guards on the outside of their stockings. The Shamrocks were called upon that year to face two challenges to the Cup: from Winnipeg in midseason and from the Halifax Crescents after the regular season. As always, the series against Winnipeg was close, exciting, and well attended, while the contests against the Crescents went almost unnoticed. Regardless, the Shamrocks defeated both of their foes to win the Cup.

The Ottawa Senators were the easy winners of the regular season in 1901, but it was the Shamrocks and Winnipeg Vics who met for the Stanley

Cup. The Vics beat the Shamrocks in two straight games. The series was significant for several reasons: the games drew record crowds (4,000 at the first game, in Winnipeg), made record monies ($2,700 in gate receipts for the second game alone), and one of the Winnipeg forwards, Dan Bain, wore a mask throughout the first game! This must have really startled his opponents, as he led the scoring with three goals.

A revitalized Montreal AAA team won the regular season in 1902 and met the Vics in a three-game series. The larger, more aggressive Winnipeg squad won the first contest 1-0, but the Montreal forwards swarmed Winnipeg's net in the second contest and blanked the Vics 5-0. In the third game, Montreal scored two goals early and then spent almost the entire game doggedly trying to hang on to its lead. For their efforts, Montreal players earned the nickname "Little Men of Iron."

In 1903, a powerful Ottawa Senators team defeated defending Cup champion Montreal, then trounced a challenger—the Rat Portage Thistles—in two games. This Ottawa club—with Art Moore and Harvey Pulford on defense, Dave Suddy and Billy Gilmour as forwards, and Frank McGee at center—would win three straight Stanley Cups and form the nucleus of the fabled "Ottawa Silver Seven."

On December 5, 1903, the Federal Amateur Hockey League was formed by several disgruntled senior team owners who had tried unsuccessfully to get into the CAHL. The four original teams were Cornwall, the Wanderers, the Capitals, and the Nationals. In the middle of the regular season, the Ottawa Senators withdrew from the CAHL and joined the FAHL. The Wanderers were the easy winners of the regular season in the new FAHL, thereby earning the chance to challenge Ottawa for the Cup—

CYCLONE TAYLOR

Fred "Cyclone" Taylor was a talented, high-scoring rover/center-man who played nine seasons with the Vancouver Millionaires of the PCHA. His reputation as a scorer, however, was earned back east.

Fred Taylor earned the handle "Cyclone" with the 1908 and 1909 Ottawa squads, scoring 17 goals in 21 games and helping the Senators to the 1909 Stanley Cup. The following year, the newly formed Renfrew club vied for Taylor's services and, after much heated discussion and threats of litigation, Taylor jumped to Renfrew.

Quite naturally, contests between Renfrew and Ottawa took on warlike dimensions, with Taylor being scorned as a traitor in his old hometown. It didn't help matters when, on a bet, Cyclone brashly announced that in the two teams' first meeting, he would skate backward through the entire Ottawa squad and score a goal.

Taylor did, in fact, skate backward for "about five yards" before lifting a blistering backhander into the Ottawa cage. Soon, Cyclone Taylor stories abounded all the way to Medicine Hat and back.

The 1913 Stanley Cup-winning Quebec Bulldogs were a star-studded group, boasting future Hall of Famers Tommy Smith (front row, left), Joe Malone (front row, center), and "Bad" Joe Hall (front row, third from right).

The original Stanley Cup, as donated by Lord Stanley of Preston in 1893. Captain Charles Colville, an aide to Lord Stanley, bought the cup on a trip to England. He paid ten guineas, or about $50.

HOBEY BAKER

Improbable as it may seem, one of the most respected hockey players in Canada before World War I was Hobey Baker, an American who never played professionally and never played for a Canadian team.

Born in a small Pennsylvania town, Baker learned to skate effortlessly and stick-handle with remarkable finesse. Hobey first played organized hockey in Concord, New Hampshire, at St. Paul's School. By 1910, he was at Princeton where he captained his team to two intercollegiate titles. (He also kicked a field goal in football that earned the Tigers a tie with Yale.)

In the Ross Cup series in Montreal against the Montreal Stars, he led his amateur St. Nicholas (New York City) team to victory, and the press commented in astonishment: "Uncle Sam has the cheek to develop a first-class hockey player—who wasn't born in Montreal!"

Baker died in 1918, testing a plane as a combat pilot in the United States Armed Forces. He was posthumously inducted into the Hockey Hall of Fame.

 After 21 years of Stanley Cup play, the city of Toronto finally claimed the Lord's mug. The 1914 Toronto Blueshirts fought off challenges from Victoria and the Canadiens to win the prize.

Early ice hockey games were all played outdoors. As evidenced here, participants played with field hockey sticks and wore the minimum amount of equipment.

unsuccessfully, however. In fact, in the 1903-04 season, Ottawa took on four challengers for the Cup and defeated them all.

In January 1905, the Ottawa Silver Seven met the challenge of a Yukon Territory team from Dawson City. It was significant because the Yukon team had to travel 4,000 miles (by dog sled, ship, and train!) at a cost of $3,000 to face Ottawa—only to be the hapless victims in a record-setting Stanley Cup Series. The Ottawa Senators crushed Dawson City 9-2 in Game One. That was bad enough. But then the Senators massacred the Yukoners 23-2 in Game Two, with the incredible Frank McGee scoring 14

goals! The fact that Ottawa later defeated Rat Portage to retain the Cup was highly anticlimactic.

In 1906, the CAHL combined with Ottawa and the Wanderers of the FAHL to form a new league: the Eastern Canada Amateur Hockey Association (ECAHA). And although Ottawa successfully met an early challenge to the Cup from Queen's College, it eventually lost to the Montreal Wanderers in a two-game, total-goals series.

By 1907, Canadian hockey had to face the growing reality of professionalism. But it did so, at least in the ECAHA, by simply allowing amateurs and professionals to play

together, as long as the owners made written declarations before the start of each season as to which players were pros and which were not.

The 1907-08 season was a constant panoply of off-ice battles over professionalism and of on-ice bloodbaths, culminating in the tragic death of FAHL player Bud McCourt, who died after being badly cut by Charles Masson. Masson was eventually tried on charges of manslaughter; but when the possibility arose that McCourt had actually been struck by another player, Masson was acquitted. Nonetheless, hockey had suffered its first fatality due to the direct result of on-ice violence.

Professionalism took over the highest levels of Canadian hockey by the 1908-09 season, at which time the ECAHA voted to drop the word "amateur" from its name and become the ECHA. Coincidentally, the Ontario Professional Hockey League (OPHL) began its first season of operation.

By 1910, the Trustees of the Stanley Cup were forced to deal with the problem of "ringers." Almost the entire Edmonton team—which unsuccessfully challenged the Wanderers the previous year—had consisted of players who had been with other teams during the regular season. The Trustees issued a proclamation stating that all Cup teams had to be composed of players who had been with the team during the regular season, and any roster changes had to be approved by the Cup Committee.

Meanwhile, the various leagues were once again playing musical chairs and changing names faster than a speeding puck. The ECHA was voted out of existence to become the CHA, while, simultaneously, the National Hockey Association (NHA) was formed. By January of 1910, the CHA died, leaving only the NHA and the OPHL.

The 1910-11 season saw the game change from two 30-minute periods to three 20-minute periods—the version we have today. More importantly, the players threatened to strike and form their own league unless owners agreed to pay larger salaries. The owners refused "to be dictated to by their employees," and a massive defection appeared imminent—that is, until the rebelling players discovered that they would be unable to get any rinks in which to play!

The 1911-12 season included several additional changes: two teams from Toronto were admitted to the NHA; the position of rover was finally eliminated, making hockey a six-man game per side; and it was decided that players would wear numbers on their sweaters.

The biggest surprise of the season, though, came when brothers Lester and Frank Patrick—both of whom had starred in the East—formed a rival

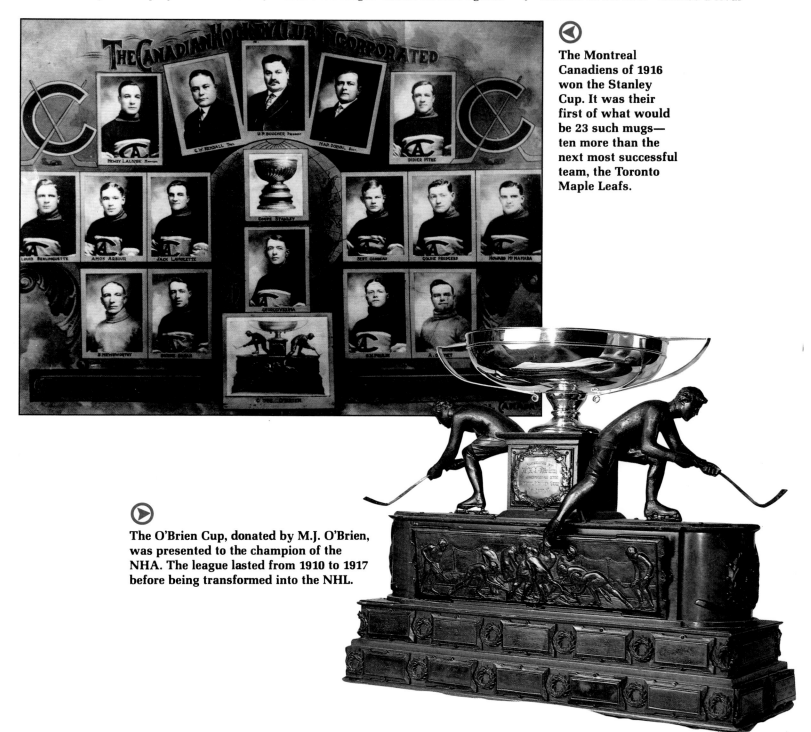

The Montreal Canadiens of 1916 won the Stanley Cup. It was their first of what would be 23 such mugs— ten more than the next most successful team, the Toronto Maple Leafs.

The O'Brien Cup, donated by M.J. O'Brien, was presented to the champion of the NHA. The league lasted from 1910 to 1917 before being transformed into the NHL.

West Coast league called the Pacific Coast Hockey Association (PCHA), which would continue the tradition of seven-man hockey. Meanwhile, a strong Quebec Bulldog team won the Stanley Cup that year and successfully defended its title in 1912-13.

In the 1913-14 season, the modern face-off—in which the puck is dropped instead of placed on the ice—was adopted; the (still unofficial) recording of assists commenced; and goaltenders were still fined if they left their feet or otherwise dropped to the ice to stop a shot. The NHA and PCHA decided to hold an annual five-game series for the Stanley Cup, to be played alternately in the East and West. The Toronto Blueshirts won the inaugural Cup.

The 1914-15 season witnessed another unsuccessful attempt by the players to form a rival league. Both the 1911 and 1914 insurrections were led by Art Ross, a superb player and the man who later developed the "Art Ross" goalie net. The NHA and PCHA both were filled with genuine stars, including Ross, Didier Pitre, Fred "Cyclone" Taylor, Joe Hall, and the Cleghorn brothers (Sprague and Odie), and many of them felt that their annual stipends were woefully inadequate. But again, the players gave in and hockey continued.

In 1914-15, for the first time ever, a Stanley Cup finals series was held in the Far West, as the Vancouver Millionaires defeated Ottawa for the league title. The PCHA also committed the ultimate heresy that year by including the first American team—the Portland Rosebuds.

In 1915-16, the PCHA introduced a second American team—the Seattle Millionaires. Meanwhile, the Montreal Canadiens—the traditionally "French" team in Montreal (as opposed to the predominantly English-speaking Wanderers)—won the Stanley Cup.

Although the Great War had been underway in Europe for almost two

Hall of Famer Jack Marshall played for numerous teams in the early 1900s and was part of five Stanley Cup winners. Marshall managed and played for the Cup-winning Toronto Blueshirts of 1914.

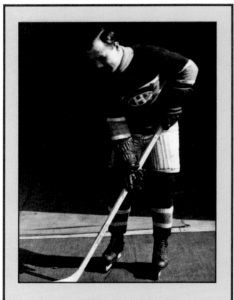

NEWSY LALONDE

Edouard "Newsy" Lalonde was one of the toughest and most controversial figures to skate in pro hockey. He was a member of the original Montreal Canadiens and a legend in his time.

Lalonde, nicknamed "Newsy" because he once worked in a newsprint plant, was one of the roughest players in the game. His clashes with "Bad" Joe Hall were studies in jungle brutality, but Newsy didn't reserve his venom for Hall.

On December 22, 1912, the Canadiens played their hometown rivals, the Wanderers, in an exhibition game. Midway into the game, Lalonde slammed Wanderer Odie Cleghorn into the boards with such force that Odie's teammate and brother, Sprague, charged across the rink and smashed Newsy across the forehead with his stick. The blow just barely missed Lalonde's eye and he required 12 stitches to close the gaping wound.

For the infraction, Sprague was suspended for just one game.

years, it wasn't until the summer of 1916 that large numbers of Canada's professional hockey players began to "join up" and disappear into the trenches. By the beginning of the 1916-17 season, several former stars had lost their lives, including the incredible scorer of the Ottawa Silver Seven, Frank McGee.

There were so many hockey players in military uniform by then that the NHA voted to include the 228th Battalion team as a member for that campaign. The military club, loaded with former NHA and PCHA stars, looked like the class of the league for the first half of the season. However, it ultimately had to withdraw when the unit was shipped overseas in February 1917.

In March of 1917, the battle for the Stanley Cup took place between the defending Montreal Canadiens and the Seattle Millionaires. Game One in Seattle was played with Western rules (where they still employed the rover in the classic seven-man game); nevertheless, the powerful Canadiens won the game 8-4. Game Two was played with Eastern rules but, ironically, Seattle beat Montreal 6-1. Seattle took the series in four games to become the first American team to win the Stanley Cup.

Lord Stanley's original provision for the Cup, that it be a challenge cup and that it be held by the champion team of the Dominion of Canada, had been totally thrown out. But another of his provisions, that the Cup be awarded by the Trustees' absolute decision, became the ultimate criterion.

Hockey began as a gentleman's game with few rules and no equipment. By now it had become a full-fledged professional sport, replete with complicated rules and more and more equipment. Nevertheless, in the years 1917-29, it would change even further and faster than it had in the 42 years since that fateful game in 1875.

◀ In 1917, the Seattle Metropolitans of the PCHL became the first United States team ever to win the Stanley Cup. They would never win another.

▶ The *bleu, blanc, et rouge* of today's Montreal Canadiens uniforms is a far cry from the team's 1910-11 and 1911-12 jerseys, which are shown here.

THE NHL GROWS UP

Between 1917 and 1929,
the NHL fights off its rival
leagues and expands
to ten teams.

POSITIVELY
NO FAST SKATI
ALLOWED

Boston emerged as a
power in the late 1920s,
thanks to the
goaltending of the
brilliant Tiny
Thompson *(left)* and
the coaching of the
legendary Art Ross
(right), who managed
the team until 1954.

1917-1929

In late November of 1917, a meeting of the National Hockey Association was held in Montreal's Windsor Hotel, attended by representatives from the Montreal Canadiens, Montreal Wanderers, Quebec Bulldogs, Ottawa Senators, and Toronto Arenas. At that meeting, representatives decided to form a new league, which would be called the National Hockey League (NHL), and the course of professional hockey in North America was changed for all time—largely because of one man!

Edward J. Livingstone had been granted two Toronto franchises a few years earlier, but it seemed that Eddie Livingstone had a personality and style of operation that rubbed people the wrong way—from other owners to his own players. By the fall of 1917, it was apparent that the other owners would do anything to ensure that Livingstone would not be involved with a franchise. Thus, they created a new league, making sure old Eddie wasn't part of it.

By the time the new NHL began its 1917-18 schedule on December 19, 1917, there were four clubs in the new league: the two Montreal teams, Ottawa, and Toronto. Quebec had dropped out of the new league.

The first season of the fledgling league did not look auspicious. The Montreal Arena burned down early in the season and the Montreal Wanderers, four-time winners of the Stanley Cup, were forced to disband. The Montreal Canadiens finished the season in the Jubilee rink, but the new league had become a tiny three-team operation. The entire sport, as well as the nation, had been decimated by World War I.

Yet, from its less-than-noble birth in 1917, the NHL would survive the Great War as well as its own internecine squabbles. By the end of the Roaring '20s, it would grow into a ten-team operation, boasting American and Canadian divisions. Moreover, the shape and execution of the game would change almost immediately.

In its first season, the NHL finally allowed goaltenders to drop to their knees or fall to the ice in order to make a save. The new rule came about largely because Ottawa's star goalie, Clint Benedict, had persisted for several seasons in dropping to the ice, causing constant stoppages of play.

In the 1918-19 season, the NHL revolutionized the game by introducing the two blue lines, 20 feet from center ice. This created three playing zones and allowed forward passing in the 40-foot neutral, or center, ice area. Suddenly, by painting two lines on the ice surface, the sport had switched from the original "onside" game played in Montreal in 1875 (meaning a player had to be lateral to or behind the puck when it was passed) to an "offside" game. The game had been transformed from a sport of stick-handling to a game of passing.

Malone Knocks Home 44 in NHL's Inaugural Season

1917 - 18

As the NHL began, the directors of the new league chose to retain the constitution and playing rules of the NHA, almost to the letter. The group elected Frank Calder, who had been the secretary of the NHA, to be president/secretary of the NHL.

The Canadiens won the first half-season title, led by the scoring of Joe Malone, who had been acquired from Quebec when the Bulldogs folded. Malone's 44 goals gave him his second straight scoring title and set a record that would stand for some years. But despite Malone's prowess, Montreal slipped to the basement in the second half, and the Toronto Arenas took the crown.

The first NHL playoff was a mere two-game affair consisting of just two teams—the first-half winner (Montreal) vs. the second-half winner (Toronto). In the opener in Toronto, Canadiens Bert Corbeau and Newsy Lalonde combined for three goals, despite spending much of their time in the penalty box for fighting. However, Toronto held the rest of the Montreal squad scoreless—including Malone—and won the game 7-3. Toronto got three tallies from Harry Meeking and another from Art Ross, his first in professional hockey.

Game Two was played in Montreal. Lalonde again scored twice but also garnered several costly penalties for the Canadiens. Montreal won the game 4-3, but since the series was based on total goals, Toronto won the playoff ten goals to seven.

Meanwhile, the PCHL also had its problems and discontinued operation of its Spokane franchise, leaving a three-team league of Seattle, Vancouver, and Portland. Since a split

 In 1917-18, Canadien Joe Malone scored 44 goals in just 20 games. At that pace, he would have scored 172 goals with today's 80-game schedule. Malone remains the only player in NHL history to average two-plus goals per game.

 Before the Maple Leafs left an indelible imprint on pro hockey, several important Toronto teams preceded them. One of the best was the Toronto Arenas, winners of the 1918 Stanley Cup. The Arenas defeated Vancouver for the mug.

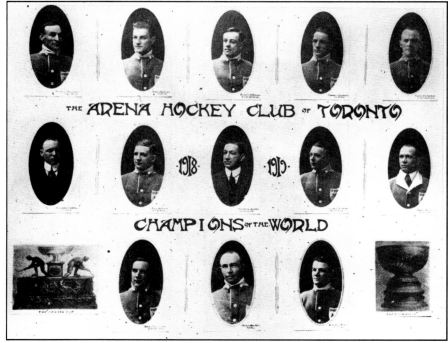

schedule would have meant an unbalanced schedule, it was decided to have a full-season format, with the first- and second-place teams meeting in a playoff after the regular season.

Seattle started slowly but took over the lead by midseason and never relinquished it. Vancouver placed second, sparked by the 32 goals of Fred "Cyclone" Taylor (who won the league scoring title) and backed by the goaltending of Hugh Lehman.

Seattle chose to have the total-goals, two-game playoff begin in Vancouver, so that it could have the home-ice advantage for the final game. The teams battled to a 2-2 draw in regulation time and, because of the total-goals format, no overtime was played. Despite being favored to take the second match at home, Seattle failed to penetrate the impermeable wall that was goalie Lehman. The Vancouver Millionaires defeated the Seattle Metropolitans by a goal.

Now fans geared up for the best-of-five Stanley Cup match: Toronto of the NHL vs. Vancouver of the PCHL.

As in previous years, the games of the Stanley Cup final series alternated between Eastern and Western rules, with the major differences being the use of the seventh man and the forward pass in the PCHL. The series was played in Toronto and opened on March 20, 1918, under Eastern rules. Toronto got two goals each from Alf Skinner and Reg Noble, taking the opener 5-3.

But the Arenas seemed to have difficulty with the PCHL's forward pass rule in Game Two. Although Skinner scored three goals, Vancouver winger Mickey MacKay also scored three goals and his squad won the

CLINT BENEDICT

The consensus down through the years points to the legendary Georges Vezina as the first great goalkeeper of pro hockey. However, a bit more investigation reveals that Clint Benedict had a better overall goals-against average. He was also singularly responsible for introducing the practice of flopping to the ice to stop a shot. And on top of that, he was one of the first goalies to use a face mask.

Believe it or not, prior to 1918, it was a penalty for the goalie to leave his feet in order to block the puck. Benedict would have none of this nonsense and, rather than call a penalty on the maverick netminder every few minutes, the league capitulated and changed the rule.

Benedict was in goal on four Stanley Cup winners during his 18-year career, winning the centerpiece three times with the Ottawa Senators and once with the Montreal sextet near the end of his playing days. A flamboyant showman, Benedict is a member of the Hockey Hall of Fame.

Nicknamed "Cannonball," Didier Pitre played the position of rover when hockey was still a seven-man game. He later played as a right wing with the Canadiens from 1917-23.

Today, the NHL's rookie of the year receives the Calder Memorial Trophy, named after Frank Calder. Originally secretary of the NHA, Calder was named the NHL's first president.

game 6-4 to tie the series. In Game Three, the Millionaires seemed stunned by the aggressive play of the Easterners, probably because they wore virtually no protective gear by comparison, and Toronto won the contest 6-3.

It was apparent that both teams were having difficulty playing under their opponent's rules. Vancouver scored eight times in Game Four and extracted another stellar performance from goalie Lehman, winning the game 8-1 and tying the series two games apiece.

By Game Five, it seemed that Vancouver had finally adapted to Eastern rules, taking an early lead on a goal from Taylor. But the Arenas persevered and won the decisive game 2-1 on goals by Skinner and Corbett Denneny. Toronto was crowned Stanley Cup champion.

Despite Toronto's Cup victory, the NHL's inaugural season was hardly auspicious. The Montreal Wanderers' rink burned down, forcing the team to disband. The NHL was now just a three team outfit—icing Toronto, Ottawa, and the Canadiens—and would remain as such in 1918-19.

Reg Noble, a member of the Arenas' Cup-winning team of 1918, finished the season with 28 goals, third best in the NHL.

In the early days, some stars hand-made their sticks to their artistic tastes. This fancy model belonged to Cyclone Taylor.

Before tubular skates were invented, players wore a skate that consisted of a boot attached to a blade. Here is an "advanced" version, which featured an all-steel construction. It became popular after World War I.

Flu Bug Kills Hall,
Cancels Stanley Cup Series

1918-19

In the fall of 1918, Eddie Livingstone made an abortive attempt to resurrect the NHA, claiming that he had enough shares or votes to do so. However, the other former NHA shareholders walked out on him and the NHA was finally dead.

At the NHL meeting on November 9, Frank Calder was re-elected president, this time for a five-year term. Since Quebec failed to declare its intentions for the season, the league remained a three-team confederation. The league also adopted the PCHL's forward passing rule, introducing the blue lines mentioned earlier.

The only other major rule change involved penalties: For minor infractions, substitutions would not be allowed until the penalized player had served three minutes; for major fouls, no substitutions would be allowed for five minutes; and for match penalties, there would be no substitutions for the remainder of the game.

The Stanley Cup-winning Toronto team was dismal, dropping six of its first seven games, while the Canadiens clinched the first half of the season. Ottawa then went on a tear with a 7-1 record to win the second-half title.

The playoffs had been changed from the total-goals, two-game format to a best-of-seven series, and Montreal dominated Ottawa almost throughout. The Canadiens won the first game 8-4 and followed with victories of 5-3 and 6-3. It looked as though the Montreal squad, managed by the high-scoring Newsy Lalonde, would sweep the series. But Ottawa star Frank Nighbor finally returned from urgent family business and sparked the Senators to a lone victory in Game Four, 6-3. As the teams returned to Montreal for Game Five, the Canadiens gave the home crowd a 4-2 victory to win the series.

In the PCHL, the Portland Rosebuds were suspended for the season and the Victoria Aristocrats, led by Lester Patrick, were reactivated with Portland's players. Lester's younger brother, Frank, was elected president of the league for his sixth term. Also, a deferred penalty system was adopted,

In 1918-19, Canadien Odie Cleghorn led the NHL with 24 goals. He later played for the NHL's Pittsburgh Pirates.

Pictured is the colorful jersey of Hap Holmes, a standout goalie for the Seattle Metropolitans.

ensuring six men and a goalie on the ice at all times.

The Vancouver Millionaires won the regular-season title by one game. Cyclone Taylor garnered the scoring title with 23 goals, supposedly giving an exhibition of skating backward toward the goal during one game. The rivalry between Seattle and Vancouver had taken on violent proportions, and in a game on February 26, Seattle tough guy Cully Wilson broke the jaw of talented Vancouver rover Mickey MacKay, which proved to be the demise of the Millionaires. Seattle trounced Vancouver 6-1 in Game One of the playoffs, and even though the Millionaires recovered enough to win the second contest 4-1, Seattle took the series on goals. Seattle then went on to face the Canadiens for the Stanley Cup.

In the finals, each team again struggled to win by the other guy's rules, and Seattle took Games One and Three (7-0 and 7-2) playing PCHL-style to lead the series 2-1. Game Four has been described by some as the greatest hockey game ever played on the West Coast, as the game was called a draw at 0-0 after an hour and 40 minutes of overtime. Goalies Georges Vezina of Montreal and Hap Holmes of Seattle stole the show.

Fate would now intervene, causing the strangest finale ever in a Stanley Cup playoff. In Game Five, Seattle took an early three-goal lead, but Montreal recovered to tie the game 3-3. At 15:51 of overtime, left winger Jack McDonald beat Holmes to give *Les Habs* the victory and tying the series at two games to two.

But during the match, Montreal's "Bad" Joe Hall left the ice, sick. Hall ended up in the hospital in the throes of the influenza bug that had become epidemic in North America. A sixth game to determine the series had been scheduled, but by this time half of the players on each team were stricken with the disease. On April 5, Joe Hall died, the series was canceled, and for the first—and only—time in Stanley Cup history, no winner was declared.

▲ **Mickey MacKay starred for the Vancouver Millionaires in 1918-19, but he got knocked out of the playoffs when Seattle thug Cully Wilson broke his jaw.**

1918-19

Best Record
Ottawa (12-6-0)

Stanley Cup Finals
Montreal 2
Seattle 2

Leading Scorer
Newsy Lalonde (23/9/32)

▲ **Frank Nighbor was one hockey's best two-way centers. In 13 years with Ottawa, he walked off with one Hart Trophy, two Lady Byngs, and four Stanley Cups.**

BAD JOE HALL

Bad" Joe Hall was born in England, but learned his tough brand of hockey in western Canada. He first achieved distinction in Houghton, Michigan, in 1905 and 1906, playing in the blood-thirsty International Pro League. Friends of Hall said he wasn't as "bad" as his nickname indicated.

"He wasn't mean, despite what a lot of people said about him," said teammate Joe Malone. "He certainly liked to deal out a heavy check and he was always ready to take it as well as dish it out."

In the 1918-1919 season—at the time of a world-wide influenza epidemic—Hall's Canadiens challenged Seattle for the Cup. Midway through the series, Hall was rushed to the hospital, stricken with the flu. Immediately after the game, several other Canadiens were bedded with influenza but none as bad as Hall.

With the series tied at two apiece, an attempt was made to finish the playoff for the Stanley Cup. The Canadiens requested permission to "borrow" players from Victoria, but Seattle declined the bid and the playoff was canceled without a winner.

Six days after he had stumbled off the ice, Hall died of influenza. For the first—and only—time in Stanley Cup history, no Cup was awarded.

Hard to Tell Who's Who
as Players Swap Sweaters

1919-20

After two seasons of dormancy, the Quebec Bulldogs were resurrected by the NHL and their players, dispersed throughout the league, were returned to Quebec. Unfortunately, several of them—notably Tom Smith, Ed Carpenter, Dave Ritchie, and Jack McDonald—were considerably past their prime, and even the talents of Joe Malone and Harry Mummery couldn't make the club a contender.

The Montreal Canadiens moved to their new Mount Royal Arena, the Toronto club changed its name to the St. Patricks, and the league decided on a 24-game split schedule.

By this time, the traffic of players defecting back and forth between the PCHL and the NHL was enormous. For 1919-20, Jack Adams jumped from Toronto to the PCHL and was joined by other stars such as Alf Skinner and Rusty Crawford. On the other hand, the PCHL finally soured on the rough play of Cully Wilson and banned him, whereupon he jumped to Toronto.

Malone shone on a truly bad Quebec Bulldog club. On January 31 against Toronto, he set an NHL record by scoring seven tallies in one game. He then almost tied his own record on the last day of the season, as he scored six times against Ottawa. Malone garnered his second scoring title in three years, but Quebec won only four games during the entire season.

Ottawa was a hockey hotbed dating back to the 19th century. The Ottawa Senators proved to be an early NHL power, winning four Stanley Cups. Their first as an NHL team came in 1920.

Ottawa goalie Clint Benedict led the NHL with five shutouts (no other NHL goaler had any that season!) and a 2.67 goals-against average.

World War I had ended and after several seasons of sagging gates, the NHL was gratified to see larger crowds watching hockey. On February 21, the St. Pats-Senators game in Toronto drew a record crowd of 8,500.

No NHL playoff was needed in 1919-1920 since Ottawa won both halves of the split schedule. The Senators met the Seattle Millionaires in the Stanley Cup championship. Seattle had won the PCHL playoffs against second-place Vancouver largely because of the goal-scoring binges of Frank Foyston.

When Seattle arrived in the East for the Stanley Cup finals, there was an immediate dilemma: Everyone thought that the Millionaires' red, white, and green uniforms looked too much like the Senators' red, white, and black costumes. Finally, Ottawa graciously agreed to wear white sweaters. Ottawa also ignored the fact that ace defenseman Bernie Morris was in the Seattle lineup; Morris had not played one regular-season or playoff game for the West Coast club. The Patrick brothers were up to their old tricks of adding "ringers" to their lineups.

But nothing helped the Millionaires—even playing Games Two and Four by Western rules—as Ottawa won the Cup in five games, blowing out Seattle 6-1 in Game Five. Ottawa was bolstered by the goal-scoring prowess of Frank Nighbor and the outstanding goaltending of Benedict, who posted a shutout in Game Two.

1919-20

Best Record
Ottawa (19-5-0)

Stanley Cup Finals
Ottawa 3
Seattle 2

Leading Scorer
Joe Malone (39/6/45)

Cy Denneny

CORBETT AND CY DENNENY

Long before the Espositos, hockey welcomed another great brother act—the Dennenys. Corbett and his brother Cy both started their stellar hockey careers with the Toronto Shamrocks in 1915.

The Shamrocks soon folded and the Denneny brothers were signed by the Toronto Arenas, skating on a line centered by Duke Keats. This awesome threesome accounted for 66 goals during the 1916 season, tops in the league for scoring by a single line.

Corbett—a forward who could play either center or left wing—enjoyed his best years with Toronto, when he pivoted a line with Reg Noble and Babe Dye. Cy's best years, however, were with the Ottawa Senators.

A rough-'n'-tumble player despite his small stature, Cy was sometimes cast into an enforcer's role. His Senators teammate, Harry "Punch" Broadbent, was a tough cop on the beat as well, and when this duo was paired together, they were gleefully referred to as the "Gold Dust Twins."

Cy skated for five Stanley Cup teams in his long career, four with the Senators and the fifth with the 1928-29 Bruins. He was a fantastic scoring machine (with 246 goals in 326 games), and although he led the league only once in total points, he finished fourth or better for ten consecutive years.

⊙ **Offensive defenseman Harry Cameron.**

⊙ **Early day scoring whiz Tommy Smith.**

⊙ **Gloves worn by Seattle center Frank Foyston.**

Senators Liquidate the Millionaires, Win Cup

1920-21

Quebec had been so dismal the previous season that the team was allowed to fold for a second and final time. NHL Prexy Frank Calder announced that the team had been purchased by Percy Thompson and would be transferred to Hamilton, Ontario. Thompson was aware, however, that he had little chance of putting together a viable club with the same personnel the Bulldogs had previously assembled, so he put out an urgent call for help from the NHL.

Interestingly, this had also happened in 1917, when the owner of the Montreal Wanderers, Sam Lichtenhein, had appealed to the league—in vain—for players. Shunned by his fellow league owners, Lichtenhein folded the club shortly thereafter when the arena burned. A few years older and wiser, the owners realized that the league might fold if it didn't help the new Hamilton franchise.

Toronto responded by giving Hamilton Goldie Prodgers, Joe Matte, and Cecil "Babe" Dye; Montreal contributed Billy Couture. On the motley crew that had been the Quebec Bulldogs, Joe Malone remained the only star.

The new team promptly blanked the Canadiens in the season opener 5-0, as Babe Dye scored two goals. Toronto immediately demanded the return of Dye and instead shipped Mickey Roach to Hamilton. Dye went on to score the most goals in the league that season with 35, although Canadien Newsy Lalonde won the scoring title with 41 points.

Ultimately, Hamilton finished the season in the NHL cellar, while first-half winner Ottawa defeated second-half champ Toronto (with two

Frank Frederickson debuted with the PCHL's Victoria club in 1921. He later starred on several NHL teams.

Montreal Canadiens goalie Georges Vezina wore these humble skates. Unlike today's goalie skates, the old-time models offered virtually no protection.

shutouts) in the NHL playoffs. Senators goaltender Clint Benedict again led the league with a 3.13 GAA and two shutouts.

Meanwhile, the PCHL remained a three-team league, with Vancouver, Seattle, and Victoria as its only members. Victoria signed Olympic star Frank Frederickson after it lost its first three games. On March 4, the Victoria Aristocrats held a "Moose Johnson Night" honoring their veteran defenseman, who was reputed to have the longest reach in all of hockey. On that same night, the Millionaires played Seattle to a tie. That tie ended up costing Seattle the league title. Vancouver then proceeded to trounce the Millionaires in the PCHL playoffs, outscoring them 13-2, for the right to face Ottawa in the Stanley Cup finals.

Ottawa trekked to Vancouver and took with it Sprague Cleghorn, who had played 13 games with Toronto!

The first game opened before 11,000 fans, the largest crowd up to that time ever to witness a hockey game in Canada. The two teams split the first four games, drawing huge crowds (Vancouver turned away more than 2,000 fans for Game Four). All four games were about as intense as you could get, with three contests being decided by one goal.

The Millionaires put up a good fight in Game Five. Alf Skinner put Vancouver in the lead in the first period, but Jack Darragh tied it for Ottawa early in the second. Darragh then won the game—and the Cup—for Ottawa when he converted a pass from Cy Denneny only moments later.

The game was notable for its roughness—Vancouver's Lloyd Cook and Senators Eddie Gerard and Cleghorn received match penalties. Also, Cyclone Taylor made his final appearance on the ice for the PCHL.

Leo Dandurand

THE THREE MUSKETEERS

It is quite possible that there would not be a Montreal Canadiens hockey club today if it were not for "The Three Musketeers"—an off-ice triumvirate that included Leo Dandurand, Joe Cattarinich, and Louis Letourreau.

A French Canadian sportsman, Dandurand was a partner with Cattarinich and Letourreau in a Cleveland racetrack when the Canadiens were put on the auction block in October 1921. The Musketeers were unable to attend the auction in Montreal, but Dandurand strongly desired to obtain the hockey team. He had his friend, Cecil Hart, stand in and bid as high as possible for the Canadiens.

At the auction, Hart found himself competing with two men: Tom Duggan, who was representing both himself and the Mount Royal Arena Company; and NHL President Frank Calder, who was representing an Ottawa group.

The bidding quickly reached $10,000 for *Les Canadiens*. But Hart, after making a phone call to Dandurand, offered $11,000. Duggan and Calder looked at each other and conceded the decision to Hart, who ran out and phoned back Dandurand with the news.

The investment paid off immediately because the Canadiens collected a $20,000 profit the first year the trio owned the team. The club is now worth more than $100 million.

The 1921 Ottawa Senators boasted some of hockey's top players, including goalie Clint Benedict, defenseman Eddie Gerard, and forwards Frank Nighbor and Cy Denneny.

Jack Darragh toiled for Ottawa for 13 seasons until his death in 1924. Darragh knocked in the Cup-winning goal for Ottawa in the 1921 Stanley Cup finals.

Ernie "Moose" Johnson was reported to have the longest reach in hockey. He was one of the game's first great defensemen.

Toronto Wins the Mug
Under Other Guy's Rules

1 9 2 1 - 2 2

With the Roaring '20s fully underway, the NHL adopted several major changes for the 1921-22 season. Following Frank Patrick's lead in the PCHL, the league abandoned the split schedule with first- and second-half champions. Instead, the NHL instituted a full schedule with the first- and second-place teams meeting in a playoff for the NHL title.

Furthermore, goalies were allowed to pass the puck forward up to their own blue line, overtime was limited to 20 minutes, and minor penalties were reduced from three minutes to two. Patrick, meanwhile, introduced the penalty shot in the PCHL, allowing shooters to skate in alone on netminders as compensation for certain infractions.

Also, a third major professional league—the Western Canada Hockey League (WCHL)—was formed, comprised of Calgary, Regina, Saskatoon, and Edmonton. The new league chose to play six-man hockey, like the NHL, eliminating the position of rover.

Dotted with former NHA, PCHL, and NHL players, the new league appeared strong, with the exception of the Saskatoon Shieks. The Shieks were moved to Moose Jaw in February (unfortunately without any improvement). Edmonton's Duke Keats, a former NHAer, won the WCHL scoring title, while his teammate, Hal Winkler, had the best average among WCHL goalies (2.4 goals-against average and one shutout).

Edmonton was an easy winner for the league title, but was upset by second-place Regina in the league playoffs. Regina then challenged the PCHL winner (Vancouver) to a playoff for the right to face the NHL title winner in the Stanley Cup finals. After Regina surprised everyone by beating Vancouver 2-1 in the opening contest, Vancouver ultimately won the two-game, total-goals series by blanking Regina 4-0 in the finale.

In the NHL, George Kennedy, one of the original owners and founders of the Canadiens, died. His widow sold the club to Messrs. Joe Cattarinich and Leo Dandurand (for the sum of $11,000).

▲ **After becoming part-owner of the Habs in 1921-22, Leo Dandurand (*right*) pulled off the NHL's first blockbuster trade. He swapped three players to Hamilton for Sprague Cleghorn and Billy Couture.**

Dandurand wanted the services of Sprague Cleghorn, who had been assigned by the league to Hamilton. In order to get Cleghorn, Montreal put together the first major, multiple-player trade in NHL history. The Canadiens sent defenseman Harry Mummery and wingers Amos Arbour and big, bad Cully Wilson to Hamilton for backliners Billy Couture and Cleghorn.

The trade reunited Sprague with his brother Odie, and the two staged several scoring sprees for the Canadiens. On January 14, they each scored four goals against the hapless Hamilton team; less than two weeks later, they combined for six in a game against Ottawa. But Sprague was known as much for his toughness as for his scoring, and on February 1 he undertook to destroy the entire Ottawa squad on his own. He sliced Eddie Gerard and Cy Denneny and then bulldozed Frank Nighbor—all of whom missed the next two games with injuries!

For all of the scoring and battering, Montreal finished behind Toronto and Ottawa in the regular season. Ottawa was distinguished by the record-setting Harry "Punch" Broadbent, who tallied at least one goal in 16 consecutive games and won the NHL scoring title with 32 goals and 46 points. Toronto then upset the Senators in the total-goals playoff, winning Game One 5-4 and standing off the Senators 0-0 in Game Two.

Vancouver, after defeating Seattle of the PCHL and Regina of the WCHL, met Toronto for the Stanley Cup. Vancouver arrived in Toronto with the addition of two ringers from Victoria—Eddie Oatman and Lester Patrick.

In the finals, each team won two of the first four games, all by the other team's league rules! Vancouver opened the series by defeating the St. Patricks 4-3 on March 17 (St. Patrick's Day!) under Eastern rules. Toronto squeaked by the Millionaires 2-1 in Game Two. After swapping shutout wins in Games Three and Four, Toronto defeated Vancouver 5-1, playing with its own league's Eastern rules, and won the Stanley Cup. Toronto's Babe Dye scored nine goals during the playoffs.

Duke Keats was the star of the WCHL in 1921-22, its debut season. Keats led the league in scoring and sparked Edmonton to a first-place finish. He joined the Blackhawks in 1927-28.

In 1921-22, Ottawa's Harry "Punch" Broadbent scored goals in 16 straight games—still an NHL record. He led the league in goals with 32.

1921-22

Best Record
Ottawa (14-8-2)

Stanley Cup Finals
Toronto 3
Vancouver 2

Leading Scorer
Punch Broadbent
(32/14/46)

THE LOAN OF EDDIE GERARD

Eddie Gerard, defensive player par excellence, was afforded his highest compliment as a player while skating for the 1922 Toronto St. Pats in their Stanley Cup series against the Vancouver Millionaires.

Normally, Eddie was a brilliant forward/defenseman for the Ottawa Senators. But when St. Pat ace defenseman Harry Cameron tore up his shoulder during the crucial series, an urgent SOS went out to Gerard to man Cameron's spot on the Toronto blue line. Personnel loans such as these were commonplace in the early days of hockey, providing you secured an okay from your opponents.

As primitive as the rules of the day were, so must have been the sports media, because Vancouver's usually wily Lester Patrick saw no harm in the 11th-hour replacement. However, after one game of Gerard's puck-hawking and bodychecks, Lester gave the thumbs down to Gerard's stand-in act.

It was too late for Vancouver, though, and the Gerard-led St. Pats rolled to the Cup. Eddie played on three other Cup winners with his own Senators before retiring in 1923. He remained in hockey as a coach and manager and is a member of the Hockey Hall of Fame.

Benedict and Ottawa Best the West, Take the Cup

1922-23

The great Newsy Lalonde had staged a one-player walkout against the Canadiens in 1921-22, and the differences between Lalonde and Montreal were never really resolved. The Canadiens then dealt their aging star to Saskatoon in the WCHL for a tiny left winger named Aurel Joliat (5'6"), who would surprise the pundits by skating to an outstanding 16-year career in the NHL.

The Canadiens then sent Bert Corbeau and Edmond Bouchard to Hamilton for Joe Malone, whose illustrious career was winding down to a finish. And Toronto sent Corbett Denneny to Vancouver for the inimitable Jack Adams. After the trading frenzy, the NHL voted to allow interleague trading only after players were offered to all the teams in their respective leagues.

For the fifth consecutive season, Ottawa goaltender Clint Benedict topped NHL goalies, with a 2.25 GAA and four shutouts in 24 games. Toronto's Babe Dye won the scoring title with 37 points (on 26 goals), and Ottawa won the regular-season title.

Probably the most significant event in the 1922-23 season occurred off the ice and behind the scenes. In March of 1923, a young Canadian named Foster Hewitt sat in a jerry-built glass booth in Toronto's Mutual Street Arena and performed the first radio broadcast of a hockey game.

Ottawa faced Montreal in the league playoffs and won the first game 2-0, though the Canadiens defense badly mauled the Senators in the process. After Ottawa's Cy Denneny scored a goal in the second period, Billy Couture ambushed him from behind, giving Denneny a concussion and cuts requiring several stitches. Then, near the end of the game, Montreal's Sprague Cleghorn, who had been trading shots with Ottawa defenseman Lionel Hitchman, crosschecked Hitchman in the face, knocking him cold. When Cleghorn was banished from the game, the enraged Montreal home crowd started a riot, even attacking the referee.

Canadiens owner Leo Dandurand was so mortified at the behavior of his defensive stars that he suspended them before the league decided to do it. Couture and Cleghorn did not appear in Game Two against Ottawa, and it was assumed that Montreal would be unable to win without their blue-line

The 1922-23 Montreal Canadiens were eliminated from the playoffs by the Ottawa Senators, but had a marvelous squad nonetheless. Georges Vezina (*center, with pads*) was one of the NHL's best goalies.

stars. But, of course, Ottawa wasn't in much better shape since Hitchman and Denneny were so maimed that they hardly appeared in the game. Still, it was Denneny who scored the Senators' single goal to give them the winning goal total for the series.

In the PCHL, officials finally decided to abandon the position of rover. The league also decided—largely because of the "Katie Bar the Door" technique developed by the Ottawa Senators—to limit the number of players who could play defense at any time to three. Moreover, the league decided to have an interlocking schedule with the WCHL. And Vancouver changed its name from Millionaires to Maroons.

Victoria's Frank Frederickson led the PCHL in scoring by a wide margin, with 41 goals in 30 games, and the great Hugh Lehman led goalies with a 2.40 GAA and four shutouts. Although Seattle got off to an early lead, Vancouver ultimately won the PCHL title. Vancouver then won a playoff series against Victoria.

Edmonton again led the WCHL, and this time it didn't blow it in the playoffs. Edmonton defeated the

second-place Regina Caps in the playoff, outscoring the Caps 4-3 in two games. The Eskimos then had to sit and wait for the outcome of the Ottawa-Vancouver series.

Vancouver was heavily favored to beat the Senators. Ottawa arrived on the West Coast severely battered and bruised due to the injuries to Hitchman and Denneny, as well as the loss of Jack Darragh.

In Game One, the teams battled scoreless for 55 minutes until Punch Broadbent won it for Ottawa. In Game Two, Ottawa suffered more injuries: Benedict was hit in the mouth by a puck, Eddie Gerard was badly shaken and had a cut foot, and the newly recovered Denneny injured his elbow! Nonetheless, the Ottawa team persevered. After dropping the second game 4-1, it then defeated the Maroons 3-2 and 5-1.

Facing Edmonton in a best-of-three series, the Ottawa club was inspired, winning the first game 2-1 on goals from Hitchman and Denneny and Game Two 1-0 on a tally by Broadbent. The PCHL president said the 1923 Ottawa Senators were the best team he had ever seen.

1922-23

Best Record
Ottawa (14-9-1)

Stanley Cup Finals
Ottawa 2
Edmonton 0

Leading Scorer
Babe Dye (26/11/37)

SPRAGUE CLEGHORN

Sprague Cleghorn was a Montreal native and a big, capable leader. "He was a product of a rough neighborhood," said the late Bobby Hewitson, then curator of hockey's Hall of Fame, "where everything you got you had to fight for. And he played hockey the same way."

Anyone who doubted Cleghorn's toughness should have been in the Ottawa rink on February 1, 1922. Sprague had played three years for the Senators and saw no reason why the Ottawa sextet had dealt him to Montreal. Cleghorn hated Senators management, and on this night he took out his hostility on his former Senators teammates.

Cleghorn's actions are described vividly in *The Trail of the Stanley Cup* by Charles L. Coleman: "A vicious swing at Eddie Gerard cut him over the eye for five stitches. Nighbor was charged and, in falling, damaged his elbow. A butt end for Cy Denneny required several stitches over the eye and some in his nose. This worked out to a match foul and a $15 fine for Sprague. The Ottawa police offered to arrest Cleghorn for assault. Referee Lou Marsh said in his report that he considered Sprague and his brother Odie a disgrace to the game."

Despite his mean streak, Sprague was considered one of the game's greatest players.

This dashing group of Ottawa Senators won the Cup in 1923, despite serious injuries.

The *Regina (Saskatchewan) Morning Leader* details one of hockey's first radio broadcasts.

Nighbor Wins First Hart; Denneny Falls Down Well

1 9 2 3 - 2 4

In 1924, Dr. David Hart, father of Cecil Hart, a manager/coach of the Montreal Canadiens, donated a trophy to the NHL. Called the Hart Trophy, it was to be awarded to the most valuable player in the league. Thus was created the first trophy for which individual players could compete (the scoring champion did not yet receive a trophy).

At a meeting called in Toronto on February 9, 1924, the NHL accepted the Hart Trophy. It also voted to expand the league for the 1924-25 season by granting a franchise to Boston.

Frank Nighbor of Ottawa, a smooth-skating center, would win the first Hart Trophy, edging out boisterous Montreal defenseman Sprague Cleghorn by one vote. It was astounding that two men

so completely different could be competing for an MVP award.

In fact, Cleghorn's rough play caused so much concern that league officials convened a special meeting in the middle of the 1923-24 season; they discussed the accusations that Sprague was hitting players with deliberate intent to injure. A spearing incident against Cy Denneny was mentioned, and someone even accused Cleghorn of "having something sharp on the end of his stick." Somehow, incredibly, the league dismissed the charges against Cleghorn. Sprague obliged in the very next game by charging Ottawa's Lionel Hitchman violently into the boards. He earned a one-game suspension.

Despite the predations of Cleghorn,

Denneny won the NHL scoring race with 23 points on 22 goals—even though he fell down a well. It seems that the Ottawa club got snowbound overnight on a train from Montreal to Ottawa and Denneny, who was walking around outside looking for food, fell down a well. Luckily, he was found and rescued in time for the train to make it to Ottawa a day late. The Senators also won the regular-season title.

Georges Vezina, the tiny Canadiens goalie they called the "Chicoutimi Cucumber," led the league with a 2.00 average and three shutouts. Vezina then led the Canadiens past the Senators in the total-goals playoff 5-2. More significantly, the Canadiens introduced a youngster named Howie Morenz,

▲ **Howie Morenz was known for his raw speed and his winning attitude. He debuted with Montreal in 1923-24.**

◄ **The Hart Trophy, which debuted in 1923-24, is awarded to the NHL's most valuable player.**

nicknamed the "Stratford Streak." Morenz would soon become the darling of the Montreal crowd, thrilling his fans for more than a decade.

In the PCHL, it was decided that the goalers' pads should not exceed 12 inches in width. The Victoria team changed its name to the Cougars. And Seattle managed to win the regular-season title after dropping eight straight games at one point. Mickey MacKay of Vancouver scored a league-leading 23 goals, while his teammate in goal, Hugh Lehman, had the PCHL's best goals-against average at 2.70.

Calgary won the title in the WCHL, Saskatoon's Bill Cook was the leading scorer with 26 goals, and Regina goaltender Red McCusker led the league with his 2.2 GAA.

The NHL playoffs opened in Montreal on a bad ice surface, and Montreal defeated Ottawa 1-0 on a goal by rookie Morenz. Montreal was even more imposing in Game Two, as Morenz, Aurel Joliat, and Bill Boucher combined for four goals.

Montreal then declared itself the defender of the Stanley Cup, since it had beaten Ottawa, the previous year's winner. Montreal owner Leo Dandurand demanded that the PCHL and WCHL play their playoffs and send the winner back to Montreal. Frank Patrick insisted that *both* Western winners were to come East, as per an agreement with the NHL that had been inked in 1922. It was finally decided that one Western team would earn a bye into the Cup finals via a three-game series between the winners of the two Western leagues.

Calgary defeated Regina in the WCHL playoff, while Vancouver eliminated Seattle in the PCHL. Calgary next bested Vancouver in a three-game set, earning the bye into the finals. Vancouver and Calgary then headed to Quebec to face Montreal.

The Canadiens then easily defeated Vancouver in the semifinals, 3-2 and 2-1. Montreal followed suit in the finals by holding Calgary to a lone goal, winning 6-1 and 3-0. Dandurand had won his Stanley Cup after all.

1923-24

Best Record
Ottawa
(16-8-0)

Stanley Cup Finals
Montreal C. 2
Calgary 0

Leading Scorer
Cy Denneny
(22/1/23)

Hart Trophy
Frank Nighbor
(10/3/13)

BABE DYE

A right winger with limitless potential, Cecil "Babe" Dye was one of the hardest shooters in NHL history. Dye first unleashed his wicked shot during the 1921-22 season, when he debuted with Toronto.

In his rookie season, the Babe played magnificently, scoring 30 goals in 24 games to finish second in the league in scoring. Dye continued to sparkle in Toronto, scoring 26 goals in 22 games during 1922-23. Thanks to Babe's league-high 38 goals in 29 games, Toronto finished a close second to Hamilton in the 1924-25 race.

Dye's last season in Toronto was 1925-26 when he scored 18 goals. However, he was traded to Chicago the following year, scoring 25 times for the Blackhawks. His swan song was played in 1928-29, when the Babe played briefly and ingloriously for the New York Americans (one goal in 42 games).

Dye finished with one of the most disparate goals-per-assists ratios in NHL history. In his career, Babe tallied 200 goals but only 41 assists.

Though they finished the 1923-24 season at a modest 13-11-0, the Canadiens stormed to the Stanley Cup.

Georges Vezina, the Canadiens' legendary goalie, led the NHL in GAA in 1923-24 with a 2.00 mark.

The Ottawa Senators, who won the Cup in 1922-23, proudly donned these uniforms in 1923-24.

NHL Expands to Six, Welcomes Bruins and Maroons

1 9 2 4 - 2 5

Although the NHL had definitely decided to grant a franchise to the city of Boston back in February of 1924, the league met in October of the same year to consider further expansion. A second franchise in Montreal, the Maroons, was officially granted, and it was determined that a team would open in New York City the following year.

With the addition of the Boston Bruins and Montreal Maroons in 1924-25, the league decided to expand the schedule from 24 to 30 games—a change that would trigger a player strike near the end of the season. At the center of the problem was a Hamilton goal-scorer, Reg Green. Hamilton won the regular-season

campaign and, under a new playoff system, was scheduled to meet the winner of a series between the second- and third-place teams.

Green, acting as spokesperson for the entire Hamilton team, protested, pointing out that everyone had signed a contract for a 24-game schedule. Having already played six games beyond what they had contracted for, the players were now being asked to play extra games for no extra pay. Green and his teammates demanded $200 more to play the winner of the Toronto-Montreal series.

NHL President Frank Calder refused to consider the demands of the strikers, and instead declared that the

winner of the Toronto-Montreal series would represent the NHL in the Stanley Cup playoffs. The Hamilton players were officially suspended on April 17, 1925—and fined $200!

The new Bruins opened the season well, beating the Maroons, but then proceeded to drop 11 straight games. The Maroons opened their new arena, the Montreal Forum, by losing to the crosstown rival Canadiens. Boston only won five more games in the season and the Maroons did not do much better, with a 9-19-2 record.

Toronto's Babe Dye won the scoring title with 44 points (on 38 goals). Georges Vezina took goaltending honors with a 1.87 average and five

Jack Walker played 12 years of West Coast hockey before joining Detroit of the NHL in 1926. In 1924-25, he helped the Victoria Cougars to a Stanley Cup.

Hamilton's Billy Burch won the Hart Trophy in 1924-25, then moved to New York to become an American.

In 1924-25, the Canadiens replaced their "C-H" insignia with this version. The globe signified they were world champs.

shutouts, and Hamilton's Billy Burch won the Hart Trophy. Lady Byng, wife of Canada's Governor General, donated a new award for the player "who best combines sportsmanship with effective play." Frank Nighbor, winner of the Hart the year previous, was the first recipient of the Lady Byng Trophy.

The Montreal Canadiens beat the Toronto St. Pats 3-2 and 2-0 in the league semifinals and, because of the suspension of Hamilton, advanced to the Stanley Cup finals.

On the West Coast, the PCHL, in existence since 1912, was in deep financial trouble. And when the Seattle franchise folded, so did the league. Vancouver and Victoria then applied for and were given franchises in the WCHL, which then arranged a 30-game schedule and a playoff system similar to the NHL's. One of the players who would become a legend in the NHL as a defenseman, Eddie Shore, started the season with Regina as a forward.

Calgary gained a bye into the league finals by defeating Regina on the last game of the regular season. The WCHL semifinals featured the Saskatoon Crescents, with Newsy Lalonde and the Cook Brothers, against the third-place Victoria Cougars, who had the talents of veteran Jack Walker and Icelander Frank Frederickson. Victoria won the opener at home 3-1, then tied the second 3-3 to win the playoff on total goals. Gathering momentum with each game, the Cougars then faced Calgary, tying the first game 1-1 and winning the WCHL finals with a 2-0 shutout.

The Stanley Cup finals, featuring two teams that had placed third in their leagues, were decided in only four games. Victoria beat Montreal in the first two (with four goals from Walker), lost the third (as Howie Morenz scored three times), and won the decisive fourth game on two goals Walker set up for Frederickson.

Victoria thus captured the Stanley Cup. It would be the last time a non-NHL team would have that honor.

Lady Byng, Baron Byng

THE LADY BYNG

Lady Byng, wife of Canada's governor-general at the time, Baron Byng of Vimy, became an avid hockey fan. She particularly admired clean play and, in 1925, presented a trophy "to the player adjudged to have exhibited the best type of sportsmanship and gentlemanly conduct combined with a high standard of playing ability." The first recipient was Frank Nighbor of Ottawa, who won the trophy two years in a row.

After Frank Boucher of the Rangers won the award seven times in eight seasons, Lady Byng gave Boucher the trophy to keep. She then donated another trophy in her name in 1936. Lady Byng died in 1949 after which the NHL presented a new trophy, changing the name to Lady Byng Memorial Trophy.

Only Boucher has won the trophy more than four times. Red Kelly took the honor exactly four times, and Bobby Bauer, Alex Delvecchio, and Mike Bossy each won it on three occasions.

A strong Toronto St. Pats team featured defenseman Hap Day (back row, fourth from left), who later became coach of the Leafs.

The Victoria Cougars, one of the great Western hockey teams, won the Cup in 1925. They were managed by Lester Patrick.

WESTERN CHAMPIONS 1924-25   WORLD CHAMPIONS 1924-25

LESTER PATRICK

VICTORIA COUGARS

W.C.H.L. CUP   STANLEY CUP

NHL Stands Alone as Western League Closes Shop

1 9 2 5 - 2 6

In 1925-26, the Hamilton Tigers were sold to a group of New York investors for $75,000 and the team, to be called the Americans, would play at the new Madison Square Garden arena. Another U.S. franchise was granted, this one in Pittsburgh; Odie Cleghorn, on the NHL Board of Governors, represented the new Pirates.

Rule changes for the season included a delayed penalty rule; this meant each team would have a minimum of four players on the ice at all times. Following the evolution of rules in the PCHL, only two men would be allowed to remain behind a team's blue line after the puck had left the defensive zone. Also, a face-off would be called for "ragging" the puck unless the offending team was shorthanded. Only team captains would be allowed to talk to referees. Goalie pads were to be no more than 12 inches wide. And finally, the league would now play a 36-game season. The modern game of hockey

was emerging with each passing year.

The Amerks opened at Madison Square Garden to an unheard of crowd of 17,000 fans, while Pittsburgh spoiled Montreal's home opener by winning 1-0. But the Canadiens suffered far more than a single-game loss that night, as their superb veteran goalie, Georges Vezina—who had never missed a game in almost 15 years—collapsed on the ice with a high fever. Vezina, suffering from tuberculosis, would never play again, and died only four months later.

New faces were rapidly replacing old stars. The Maroons had a rookie, Nels Stewart, who could play both center and defense. Stewart took the league scoring title with 42 points (34 goals) and also won the Hart Trophy. In Ottawa, goalie Alex Connell achieved an astounding 1.17 GAA and a record 15 shutouts, a feat likely never to be repeated. Frank Nighbor won the Lady Byng a second time.

Manned largely with players from the United States Amateur League, the Pittsburgh Pirates did surprisingly well, finishing third behind Ottawa and the Maroons. The quick line changes of Cleghorn kept fresh legs on the ice at all times—and no doubt confused the opponent too. The Boston Bruins, who tied for the league lead in goals scored (92), finished fourth. New York finished fifth and, surprisingly, two "old" clubs—Toronto and the Canadiens—brought up the rear.

Fresh legs couldn't help Pittsburgh against the Maroons in the playoffs, as Montreal won the two-game, total-goals series 6-4. Regular-season champion Ottawa was then favored to defeat Montreal in the league finals. However, the Maroons held the Senators to a tie in Game One and squeaked by Ottawa with a single goal from Babe Siebert in Game Two and earned the right to represent the NHL in the fight for the Stanley Cup.

Meanwhile, in the far West, major-league professional hockey was not faring well. Regina's franchise was moved to Portland and the name Canada was dropped from the league title, making it the Western Hockey League. But a floundering league by any other name still flounders, and the WHL would fold after the 1925-26 season.

In the league's final season, Bill Cook of Saskatoon and Dick Irvin of Portland tied for the scoring title with 31 goals apiece, while a kid named Eddie Shore helped Edmonton win the regular-season title. The Victoria Cougars, again a third-place finisher in the regular season, recaptured their Cup-winning form of the previous year and eliminated Saskatoon and Edmonton in the WHL playoffs. Victoria faced the Montreal Maroons in the Cup finals.

The Maroons completely shut down the Victoria offense for the first two games, winning with 3-0 scores. Then Victoria, on the verge of elimination, came back strong in Game Three, winning 3-2. Montreal again overwhelmed the Cougars in Game Four, as Stewart scored two goals in a 2-0 shutout, and the Maroons were the winners of the 1926 Stanley Cup.

This would be the last appearance of a non-NHL club in Cup competition.

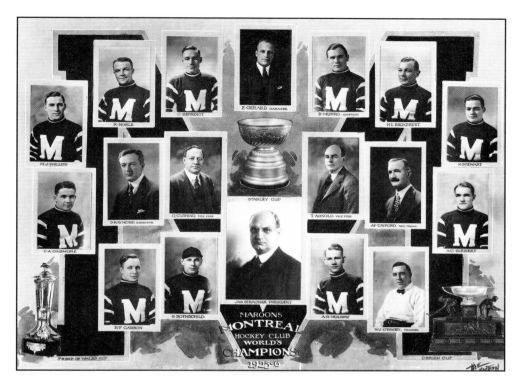

⬆ **Though lesser known than the Canadiens, Montreal's Maroons won the Stanley Cup in 1926. Clint Benedict starred in goal.**

1925-26

Best Record
Ottawa
(24-8-4)

Stanley Cup Finals
Montreal M. 3
Victoria 1

Leading Scorer
Nels Stewart
(34/8/42)

Hart Trophy
Nels Stewart

Lady Byng Trophy
Frank Nighbor

◀ **New York bootlegger "Big" Bill Dwyer bought the Hamilton Tigers in 1925 and moved the team to Manhattan. The New York Americans were aptly named the "Star-Spangled Skaters."**

⬆ **In 1925-26, Nels Stewart captured the Hart and led the league in scoring (34 goals).**

TAFFY ABEL

Bunyanesque Clarence "Taffy" Abel, imported from Minneapolis' minor-league club in 1926 along with Ivan "Ching" Johnson, was one of the original members of the New York Rangers.

Built like a skating dirigible, Taffy played three full seasons with the Rangers before being traded to Chicago. He was the first U.S.-born skater in the NHL.

Abel, a native of Sault Ste. Marie, Michigan, played five full seasons with the Blackhawks, all of them alongside lilliputian Harold "Mush" March. Together they developed an astonishing Mutt-and-Jeff routine.

It worked this way: Abel would carry the puck over the enemy blue line with the tiny March following close behind. Once Taffy was about ten feet inside the opponent's defensive zone, he would pass the puck to March and skate toward the net, spreading himself out as wide as possible. March would then fire the puck through an opening in Abel's legs.

Business is Boomin';
League Expands to Ten Teams
1926-27

What many call the Roaring '20s is often called the Golden Age of Sport. It was not a misnomer. Ty Cobb, Babe Ruth, and Lou Gehrig delighted baseball fans; Red Grange brought football into the American limelight; and the great Jack Dempsey ruled the boxing ring. Hockey would simply do, briefly, what all the other major sports were doing: expand and dazzle a growing audience.

In the spring of 1926, franchises were awarded to the Madison Square Garden Corporation of New York, as well as to groups in Chicago and Detroit. For 1926-27, the NHL would be a ten-team league, and the governors decided to lengthen the schedule to 44 games and create two divisions. The Canadian Division included the

Canadiens, Maroons, Toronto, Ottawa, and the New York Americans; while the American Division was comprised of Pittsburgh, Boston and the three new clubs—New York Rangers, Detroit Cougars, and Chicago Blackhawks.

In order to staff the newly expanded league, the NHL made a deal with the folding Western circuit, purchasing entire rosters for $25,000 per club. The Cook brothers, Bill and Bun, ended up in New York City, as Conn Smythe assembled the New York Rangers. The Cooks would unite with center Frank Boucher to form one of the finest lines the NHL ever produced. Meanwhile, two Franks—Foyston and Frederickson—landed in Detroit; Dick Irvin and Mickey MacKay went to Chicago; and the great Eddie Shore

went to the Boston Bruins.

In Montreal, the Canadiens donated a new trophy to the league in memory of their late, great goalie, Georges Vezina. The Vezina Trophy would be awarded to the team allowing the fewest goals in the regular season. The team would then present the trophy to the goaltender who played the most games for that team in the regular season.

Before the new season could open, Smythe had a major disagreement with the Rangers' majority owner, Col. John Hammond, who wanted to purchase Babe Dye. Smythe argued that Dye was past his prime. Hammond wouldn't let Smythe tell him what to do and promptly fired him. (Incidentally, Dye ended up in Chicago, where he led the Hawks with

25 goals.) Smythe returned to his hometown of Toronto, where he raised $160,000 and bought the basement-dwelling St. Pats team on February 15, 1927. Smythe promptly renamed the team the Maple Leafs and a dynastic franchise was born.

Lester Patrick, a pre-NHL star and one of the founders of the PCHL, was brought in to manage the New York Rangers. The "Silver Fox," as he was called, would mold another dynasty in Madison Square Garden, largely from the nucleus assembled by Smythe.

Canadien center Howie Morenz won the 1927 Canadian Division scoring title with 32 points (25 goals), while Bill Cook of the Rangers won the American Division title with 37 points (33 goals). Herb Gardiner of the Canadiens was awarded the Hart Trophy, while Billy Burch of the New York Americans won the Lady Byng. The first winner of the Vezina Trophy was the Canadiens' own goalie, George Hainsworth, with a GAA of 1.52 and 14 shutouts.

Ottawa won the Canadian Division title with 30 wins and 64 points—six points ahead of the second-place Canadiens. The Maroons were third, the Americans fourth, and the new Maple Leafs couldn't get out of the basement. The Rangers topped the American Division with a 25-13-6 record, followed by Boston (at a mediocre 21-20-3), Chicago, Pittsburgh, and Detroit.

The playoff system had been changed: The first-place team of each division would receive an initial bye, while the second- and third-place clubs would meet in a two-game, total-goals series. The winner of that series would meet the regular-season division winner to determine the division champion. Finally, the two division champions would meet in a best-of-five series to determine the winner of the Stanley Cup.

Ottawa and Boston emerged from the initial rounds to meet in the Stanley Cup finals. The two teams battled to a scoreless double-overtime thriller in Game One, but the Senators then stuck it to the Bruins. In the next three contests, Ottawa won two games and tied another to capture the series in four games. It was the last time the Senators won the Stanley Cup.

GEORGE HAINSWORTH

Few experts believed that George Hainsworth, an English Canadian who stood at only 5'6", could successfully follow the act of his distinguished French predecessor, Georges Vezina, in the Montreal Canadiens goal during the mid-1920s. Furthermore, at 31 years of age, Hainsworth seemed to be approaching the end, rather than the beginning, of his major-league career.

Yet, Hainsworth proved a worthy successor to Vezina. In his first season, 1926-27, he played every one of the 44 games on the Canadiens' schedule, and finished the season with a goals-against average of 1.52 (tops in the NHL) along with 14 shutouts.

Little by little, the Canadiens' fans warmed up to Hainsworth. He won the Vezina Trophy as best goalie, first in 1926-27, again in the 1927-28 season with a remarkable 1.09 goals-against average, and finally in 1928-29, this time allowing only 43 goals in 44 games for a 0.98 mark. Hainsworth played ten full seasons in the NHL, finally retiring at age 41.

Hainsworth was elected to the Hall of Fame in 1961.

1926-27
Best Record
Ottawa
(30-10-4)
Stanley Cup Finals
Ottawa 2
Boston 0
Leading Scorer
Bill Cook
(33/4/37)
Hart Trophy
Herb Gardiner
(6/6/12)
Vezina Trophy
George Hainsworth
Lady Byng Trophy
Billy Burch

Although the NHL expanded into the U.S. during the late 1920s, Canadian teams still dominated. The Ottawa Senators won the Cup in 1927.

Eddie Shore, arguably the greatest defenseman of all time, made his NHL debut in 1926-27 with the Bruins.

Before coaching, Dick Irvin starred briefly for Chicago. He retired after suffering a skull fracture.

Coach Patrick Laces 'Em Up, Sparks Rangers to Cup

1 9 2 7 - 2 8

The NHL was learning rapidly that fans loved to see a fast game of hockey, preferably with as much scoring as possible. In 1926-27, the league expanded the neutral zone by moving the blue lines 60 feet from each goal line. Then in 1927-28, in order to encourage offense, they voted to allow forward passing in the defensive and neutral zones and to limit goalies' pads from 12 to ten inches in width.

The league also decided that teams would change ends after each period, that home teams would be given the choice of goals to defend at the start of a game, and that the Art Ross goal net would be the official net of the NHL. Also, hockey sticks were limited to 53 inches from heel of blade to end of handle. And minor penalties would be issued if a non-goalie deliberately picked up the puck while it was in play, or if a player deliberately shot the puck out of play.

The 1927-28 season would be distinguished by the first American expansion team winning the Stanley

Winners of The Stanley Cup
World's Championship
1927-28

Col. John S. Hammond-Pres.   Ching Johnson-Defence   Lorne Chabot-Goal   Taffy Abel-Defence   Tex Rickard-Dir.
Patsy Callighen-Defence   Lester Patrick - Mgr-Coach   Bill Cook-Capt-Forward   Alex Gray-Forward
Harry Westerby-Trainer   Bun Cook-Forward   Paul Thompson-Forward   Murray Murdock-Forward
Bill Boyd-Forward   Leo Bourgault-Defence   Frank Boucher-Forward   Richard Hext-Dir.

The 1927-28 Rangers were the first team to bring a Stanley Cup to New York. The Blueshirts were spearheaded by the line of Frank Boucher and Bill and Bun Cook, who each finished in the top ten in scoring. Boucher tallied 23 goals, Bill knocked in 18, and Bun rang up 14.

In certain respects, hockey during the 1920s was still a rather primitive sport. Hall of Fame referee Bobby Hewitson had to use these bells to signal infractions during a game. The bells were a precursor to today's whistles.

Cup—and by the "Curse of Muldoon."

Pete Muldoon had been hired to coach the new Chicago Blackhawks for the 1926-27 season, and the club had performed admirably, finishing third in the American Division and making the playoffs. The team scored the most goals in the NHL that year (115); unfortunately, it also allowed the most (116).

Still, Muldoon was stunned when Hawks owner "Major" Fred McLaughlin fired him at the start of the 1927-28 campaign. In fact, Muldoon was allegedly so incensed that he turned to McLaughlin before storming out of Major's office and boomed, "You'll see. I'll make sure you never win an NHL title!"

Prophesy? Curse? Everyone knows such things don't exist. And yet, it would be 40 years before the Chicago Blackhawks would win an NHL title. Perhaps the statute of limitations runs out on curses.

In any case, Muldoon's successors did worse than Pete had done. Barney Stanley and Hugh Lehman split the coaching duties, but the Hawks won only seven games, bringing up the rear of the American Division, which was topped by Boston. New York Rangers center Frank Boucher topped the scoring charts in that division (35 points) and won the Lady Byng Trophy too.

In the Canadian Division, the Montreal Canadiens finished first, while Howie Morenz won both the

James Norris

▲ **In 1927-28, Ottawa's Alex Connell pitched six straight shutouts.**

1927-28

Best Record
Montreal C.
(26-11-7)

Stanley Cup Finals
New York R. 3
Montreal M. 2

Leading Scorer
Howie Morenz
(33/18/51)

Hart Trophy
Howie Morenz

Vezina Trophy
George Hainsworth

Lady Byng Trophy
Frank Boucher

The Rangers featured one of the NHL's top checkers in Ching Johnson. Johnson was a rock-solid defenseman for New York for 11 seasons.

REVIVAL OF THE RED WINGS

Professional hockey in the Detroit area dates back to 1926, when a Detroit syndicate purchased the Victoria (British Columbia) Cougars of the Western Hockey League and moved the club to the Motor City. Playing their home games in nearby Windsor, the team finished in the league cellar in its first year.

By the 1927-28 season, things were looking up. Ten-year NHL star Jack Adams began his illustrious 36-year career with Detroit as manager and coach. The team moved into the gleaming new Olympia Stadium on the night of November 22, 1927, and with a new leader and a new home, the Cougars played .500 hockey and finished in fourth place in the American Division. But success in the late '20s was only moderate. In the 1930-31 season, a change of nickname to "Falcons" failed to improve their fourth-place finish.

Meanwhile in Chicago, industrialist James Norris operated the semipro Chicago Shamrocks, but was itching to own an NHL franchise. Informed that the Detroit franchise was about to fold, Norris successfully bid on and purchased both the hockey team and Olympia Stadium.

The 1933-34 season saw the "new look" Norris franchise under Jack Adams win the division championship—the first of 15 division titles. In 1935-36, they won their first of seven Stanley Cups.

scoring title (51 points on 33 goals) and the Hart Trophy. George Hainsworth, with a 1.09 goals-against average, won the Vezina a second straight time, even though he couldn't match Ottawa's Alex Connell. Connell set a record with six straight shutouts and 446 minutes and nine seconds of scoreless hockey.

The Rangers, in only their second season of play, eliminated Pittsburgh and Boston to make the Stanley Cup finals. There they faced the Montreal Maroons, who had erased Ottawa and the Canadiens from contention.

Montreal blanked the Rangers in the first game 2-0.

In the second period of Game Two, Nels Stewart snapped a shot directly into the eye of Ranger goalie Lorne Chabot, who was unable to continue. Lester Patrick asked the manager of the Maroons, Eddie Gerard, if the Rangers could use Connell in the nets, since the Ottawa netminder was in the stands watching the game. Gerard said no. Patrick then asked if he could use a minor leaguer who was also in attendance. Again, Gerard said no.

Patrick retired to the Rangers'

dressing room completely frustrated. Centerman Boucher jokingly suggested that the 44-year-old Patrick take over in goal. Much to his amazement, Lester seriously pondered the remark and finally said, "I'll do it."

Incredibly, Patrick made 18 saves, allowed only one goal, and the Rangers won the game in overtime. After losing Game Three 2-0, the Rangers came back to win Game Four 1-0 on a goal by Boucher. New York won Game Five 2-1 on two more goals by Boucher, and the Rangers thus won their first Stanley Cup.

Detroit's first NHL team came about in 1926, when the Victoria Cougars of the WHL moved to the Motor City. The 1927-28 edition featured goalie Hap Holmes (wearing pads) and coach Jack Adams (wearing suit). They finished their second season at 19-19-6.

Although he had never been a goaltender, Rangers manager Lester Patrick filled in for the injured Lorne Chabot during Game Two of the 1928 Stanley Cup finals. Patrick won the contest 2-1 in overtime, helping his team to the world championship.

FRANK BOUCHER

One of the classiest players in NHL history, Frank Boucher first gained acclaim as a member of the Royal Canadian Mounted Police, then as a sparkling Ranger on the "A" Line with the Cook brothers, Bill and Bun.

Many scintillating skaters played on that first Ranger team, but none captured the imagination of the Garden crowd like the brothers Cook and Frank Boucher. They moved with the grace of figure skaters and passed the puck with radar-like accuracy. Bill was the crackerjack shot, Bun had the brawn, and Boucher had all the class in the world.

Wrote Dink Carroll of *The (Montreal) Gazette*: "(Boucher) would take the puck away from the enemy with the guile and smoothness of a con man picking the pockets of yokels at a country fair, then whisking it past the enemy goaltender or slipping it to Bill or Bun."

Without question, Boucher was the cleanest player ever to lace on a pair of skates in the NHL. He won the Lady Byng Trophy so many times—seven in eight seasons—the league finally gave it to him in perpetuity and a new Lady Byng Trophy was struck.

Goals Are Scarce; Hainsworth Blanks Half His Foes

1 9 2 8 - 2 9

Still searching for greater offense, the league permitted forward passing in the defensive and neutral zones and into the attacking zone—as long as the receiver was in the neutral zone when the pass was initiated. No forward passing was allowed in the attacking zone. A minor penalty would also be assessed to any player who delayed the game by passing the puck back into his defensive zone. Overtime was limited to one ten-minute period without the sudden-death provision; if the game was still tied, a draw would be called.

The irony was that the league was looking to juice up the offense and succeeded instead in creating a goaltender's bonanza. In Montreal, the diminutive George Hainsworth set a record so astronomical that it's chances of ever being surpassed are virtually nil. Hainsworth notched 22 shutouts in 44 games! The paltry 43 goals he allowed gave him a goals-against average of only 0.98. Even poor Charlie Gardiner, who suffered 44 games in the nets for the lowly Chicago Blackhawks (7-29-8), had a sterling 1.93 average.

On December 22, 1928, Hainsworth delivered one of his shutouts at home against Ottawa while two gentlemen— one French Canadian and the other English-speaking—conducted the first Montreal radio broadcasts of a hockey game. However, management feared that a blow-by-blow of a game would cause people to stay at home and listen

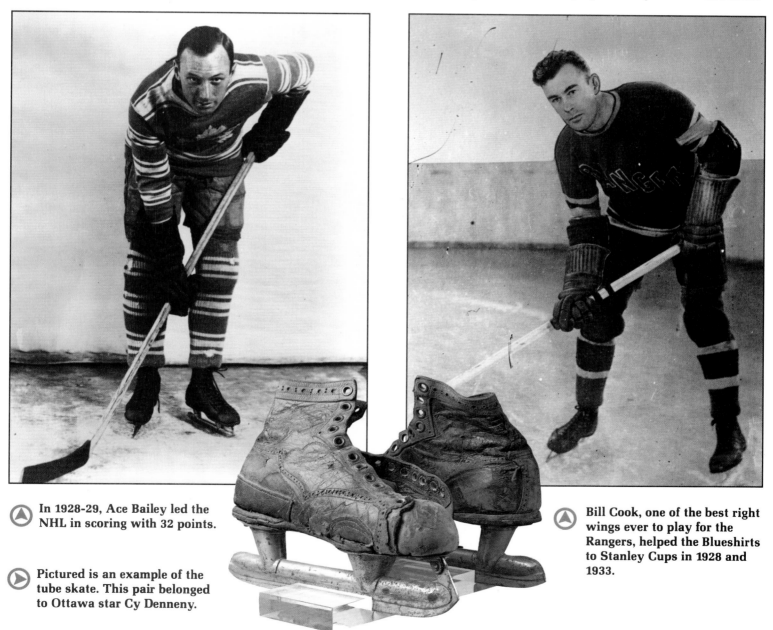

In 1928-29, Ace Bailey led the NHL in scoring with 32 points.

Pictured is an example of the tube skate. This pair belonged to Ottawa star Cy Denneny.

Bill Cook, one of the best right wings ever to play for the Rangers, helped the Blueshirts to Stanley Cups in 1928 and 1933.

instead of coming to watch. Therefore, CJAD's Author Dupont and Elmer Ferguson (who did the English cast) were restricted to a third-period summary and a post-game rundown.

The 1928-29 season was a year of streaks. Boston went 13 games without a loss, before losing to Toronto on February 2. At the other extreme, Chicago went 15 games without a win, before beating Detroit on February 5. And the Canadiens went 17 games without a loss, before losing to Toronto on February 23.

Les Habitants proceeded to go off on another tear, however, playing the last eight games of the season without a loss and finishing first in the Canadian Division. The Canadiens finished nine points ahead of the Amerks, who had surprised the whole league by heading the division for most of the season. One of the reasons for the Americans' surprising performance was the goaltending of Roy Worters, who received the Hart Trophy for his efforts.

Toronto's Ace Bailey took scoring honors in the Canadian Division with a mere 22 goals and 32 points (remember, Joe Malone once scored 44 goals in fewer games). Meanwhile, Cooper Carson of Detroit, with only 18 goals and 27 points, led the American Division. Frank Boucher was awarded the second of the seven Lady Byngs he would win, though his Rangers were forced out of first place by a hot Boston team late in the season.

The Bruins didn't have any players

The 1929 Stanley Cup champion Boston Bruins featured a powerful defense, led by Eddie Shore *(front row, third from left)*, and a productive offense, led by Dit Clapper *(back row, fourth from left)*.

Roy "Shrimp" Worters joined the Americans in 1928-29 and helped turn the team around. With a 1.21 goals-against average, Worters led the once-hapless Amerks into the playoffs. For his efforts, he was awarded the Hart Trophy.

1928-29

Best Record
Montreal C.
(22-7-15)

Stanley Cup Finals
Boston 2
New York R. 0

Leading Scorer
Ace Bailey
(22/10/32)

Hart Trophy
Roy Worters
(1.21 GAA)

Vezina Trophy
George Hainsworth

Lady Byng Trophy
Frank Boucher

In 1928-29, tiny George Hainsworth, only 5'6", achieved one of the biggest feats ever by a goalie. In 44 games, Hainsworth notched 22 shutouts and posted a goals-against average of 0.98. He captured his third straight Vezina.

Frank Boucher was one of the cleanest players ever. Boucher won so many Lady Byng Trophies (seven) that Lady Byng gave him the prize in perpetuity. She then struck another trophy for other players. Boucher was a generous player too. In 1928-29, he led the NHL with 16 assists.

KING CLANCY

Some good old Irish luck intruded to help Maple Leafs manager Conn Smythe obtain one of the most colorful characters hockey has known, Francis "King" Clancy, whose ancestors lived among the peat bogs and rich grassy fields of Ireland.

Frank developed an indefatigable spirit, which was embellished by his natural hockey talent. Despite his small size (5'9"), he starred for the Ottawa Senators throughout the 1920s.

Clancy played on four Stanley Cup winners and appeared to be a fixture in Canada's capital city. Then the Great Depression began, and by the time the 1930-31 season approached, the Ottawa management needed money fast. There was only one thing to do: peddle a star to a wealthier club. And the most attractive star on the club was none other than Clancy.

Toronto's Smythe bought Clancy from Ottawa for $35,000 and threw in two extra players, Art Smith and Eric Pettinger, who were worth a total of $15,000 on the NHL market. Clancy cost Smythe $50,000 but he proved to be worth every penny of it, as he soon led Toronto to a Stanley Cup. Clancy later became an NHL referee and ultimately a vice-president of the Maple Leafs.

with more than 23 points, but their defense was nearly as impenetrable as the Canadiens'. Beantown rookie goalie Cecil Thompson notched 12 shutouts in 44 games. His goals-against average was a measly 1.18.

The NHL once again changed the playoff system. This time the first-, second-, and third-place teams would play their counterparts in the other division. The winners of the series between second-place teams and the series between the third-place teams would then face off. That winner would advance to the Stanley Cup finals against the winner of the first-

place teams' series.

First, Toronto eliminated Detroit in the battle of the third-place teams, and the Rangers clobbered the Americans in two straight to win the battle of the second-place clubs. The Rangers then proceeded to thump Toronto and earn a berth in the Stanley Cup finals. Boston defeated the Canadiens in the battle of first-place teams, and thus met the Rangers in the final series. This was the first time two American teams faced each other in the Stanley Cup finals.

Designated a best-of-three series, Boston didn't need the third game.

Bruins goalie Thompson proved impassable in Game One, winning 2-0 (Thompson's third shutout in five playoff games). Thompson yielded only one goal to New York's Butch Keeling in Game Two, which Boston won 2-1. Boston thus won its first Stanley Cup.

Unfortunately, the Great Depression arrived and the '20s not only stopped roaring but came to a screeching halt. Symptoms of the Depression had already begun, as Ottawa struggled all season with sagging attendance. And Ottawa wasn't the only team with smaller audiences and financial woes.

CHAPTER
3

COPING WITH
THE DEPRESSION

**The NHL struggles
through the 1930s, losing
three teams and many
precious bucks.**

Red Dutton *(right)* and the New York Americans barely survived the Great Depression. Toronto fared much better, thanks to the Kid Line of *(left to right)* Charlie Conacher, Joe Primeau, and Busher Jackson.

THE 1930s

The Great Depression struck the United States and Canada just as the NHL began maturing into a major professional league. Because of the economic upheaval, the circuit down-sized from a two-division, ten-team organization to a one-division, seven-team league.

The NHL's hockey lords also made a major rule change. They had become disenchanted with the overly defensive play caused by the game's limited passing rules, so they decided to open up the game. Beginning with the 1929-30 season, the ice would be divided into three zones—offensive, neutral, and defensive—and forward passing would be permitted in each of the three zones. However, passing from one player to another in a different zone would not be allowed.

The idea, of course, was to eliminate the often dull, low-scoring game that had resulted in many shutouts. League owners seemed aware that Americans liked action, and they wanted their game to appeal to a wider audience in the United States.

Already, two American teams established themselves as dominant forces. The Boston Bruins, led by Eddie Shore, and the New York Rangers, paced by the Cook Brothers and Frank Boucher, each had Stanley Cups on their shelves. Many hoped that Chicago, with its massive new Stadium, and Detroit, boasting the beautiful Olympia rink, would follow suit.

However, the Depression fiscally wounded several league members, in some cases fatally. In 1930, the Pittsburgh franchise was moved to Philadelphia but soon failed there. Once a hockey hotbed, Ottawa lamented the demise of its once-proud Senators. St. Louis had a brief sojourn in the league before dropping out, and by 1938 even the Montreal Maroons deep-sixed for good.

In 1938-39, the NHL returned to the single division format, now with only seven teams: the Canadiens, Maple Leafs, Bruins, Red Wings, Blackhawks, Rangers, and Americans. As the Depression wore on, it became clear that at least one other team would be claimed. Eventually, that team would be the Amerks.

Ironically, the quality of play never wavered and, in fact, improved during the 1930s. "There were so few jobs elsewhere," recalled Frank Selke Sr., "that we had a great pool of young men wanting to earn a living as hockey players."

The decade began with *Les Canadiens* as hockey's dominant team, but the Red Wings came closest to a dynasty by winning consecutive Stanley Cups in 1936 and 1937. Detroit was supplanted by the Bruins, whose Stanley Cup win in 1938 signaled the growth of one of the NHL's most powerful teams. However, as the decade ended, storm clouds were forming over Europe and another world-wide force would alter the game.

Boston Goes 38-5-1
But Loses When It Counts

1929-30

The NHL's new rules produced the desired effect—pleasing just about everyone but the goaltenders. Ralph "Cooney" Weiland of the Bruins notched an astonishing 43 goals and 30 assists in 44 games. It was all the more remarkable considering that a year earlier Irvine "Ace" Bailey of the Maple Leafs led in scoring with 22 goals and 32 points. Weiland had more than

doubled the figure!

Boston's offense was abetted by Aubrey "Dit" Clapper, who finished second in goal-scoring with 41 and third in points with 61—one point behind the Rangers' crafty center, Frank Boucher. Boucher, who centered the still-effective forward line with Bill Cook and Fred "Bun" Cook, was establishing himself as the cleanest

effective player in NHL history. He won the Lady Byng Trophy for the third year in a row.

Some historians argue that the 1929-30 Bruins were the best team of the pre-World War II era, if not of all time, and the arithmetic supports that argument. In a 44-game schedule, Boston went 38-5-1. Their 77-point total put them an arresting 30 points

Brothers Bill Cook *(left)* and Bun Cook *(right)* combined with Frank Boucher to form the greatest line in Rangers history. Boucher was the center, Bill the right wing, Bun the left wing. In 1929-30, the three enjoyed their best season ever as they combined for 79 goals. Nevertheless, the Rangers suffered poor defense and finished at .500.

Known as the "Little Giant," Aurel Joliat weighed in at 140 pounds and played with the Canadiens from 1922-38. In 1929-30, Joliat and linemate Howie Morenz led a high-scoring Montreal team to the Stanley Cup.

ahead of runner-up Chicago (21-18-5) in the league's American Division.

Not only was Boston obtaining scoring from Weiland, Clapper, and Norman "Dutch" Gainor, but Cecil "Tiny" Thompson was rock-solid in goal. Tiny won the Vezina Trophy with a leading goals-against average of 2.23, significantly better than runner-up Charlie Gardiner of Chicago (2.52).

The Bruins' runaway first-place finish in the American Division was not matched on the Canadian side. A three-way battle for first developed between the Montreal Maroons, the Montreal Canadiens, and the Ottawa Senators, each of whom possessed a powerful scorer. Ottawa's sharpshooter, Hec Kilrea, finished the season fifth in scoring (58 points on 36 goals). The Maroons' Nels Stewart was one notch behind (55 points on 39 goals), followed by Canadiens hero Howie Morenz (50 points, 40 goals). Like Kilrea, Stewart and Morenz played in all 44 games.

Boston was the favorite to win a second straight Stanley Cup and it moved right ahead, eliminating the Maroons three games to one in the opening round. Thompson allowed only five goals in four games.

In reaching the finals, the Canadiens first ousted Chicago three goals to two

A competent left winger, Harold "Baldy" Cotton enjoyed his best year in 1929-30, netting 21 goals for Toronto. Cotton, like many of his Maple Leaf teammates, was known for his pranks as well as his skills. The happy-go-lucky Leafs became known as the "Gashouse Gang" of the NHL.

In 1929-30, Boston forward Dit Clapper scored 41 goals to lift his team to the Stanley Cup finals.

1929-30

Best Record
Boston
(38-5-1)

Stanley Cup Finals
Montreal C. 2
Boston 0

Leading Scorer
Cooney Weiland
(43/30/73)

Hart Trophy
Nels Stewart
(39/16/55)

Vezina Trophy
Tiny Thompson

Lady Byng Trophy
Frank Boucher

CHARLIE CONACHER

Some oldtimers insist that Toronto Maple Leafs star Charlie Conacher was the most exciting player they have ever seen, and his shot was the hardest of its day.

Charlie made his NHL debut on November 14, 1929, at Toronto's Mutual Street Arena. Chicago's Blackhawks, with the redoubtable Charlie Gardiner in goal, were the opponents, and the Toronto fans were frankly skeptical of Conacher's ability to skate and shoot with the pros.

The game was close, but Charlie was never out of place. At one point, Conacher caught a pass on the blade of his stick and in the same motion flung the rubber in Gardiner's direction. Before the Chicago goalie could move, the red light had flashed, and Conacher was a Leaf to stay.

Just before Christmas, 1929, Smythe made a move that would alter hockey history. He put Conacher on a line with center Joe Primeau and right wing Busher Jackson. Hockey's first and most renowned "Kid Line" was born.

Success was as dramatic as a volcanic eruption. Toronto defeated the Blackhawks, the Canadiens, and the Maroons right after Christmas and went undefeated until January 23. Charlie went on to become one of the most dynamic NHL forwards.

Maroons scoring ace Nels Stewart liked to chew a wad of tobacco and, as he shot the puck, spit the juice into the face of the goalie. Stewart spat his way to 39 goals in 1929-30.

in a two-game, total-goals series. The Canadiens then stymied the Rangers, 2-1 and 2-0 in a best-of-three affair. The first game wasn't settled until Gus Rivers scored at 68:52 of extra play, a new overtime record.

When the Cup finals opened at Boston Garden on April 1, 1930, the Bruins were without the injured Gainor. His loss was sorely felt, as the Canadiens shut out Boston 3-0. Surprisingly, the

Habs' scoring was opened by Albert "Battleship" Leduc, who had tallied only six goals all season.

The second game of the best-of-three series was played at the Montreal Forum, and Gainor returned to the Bruins lineup. Boston manager Art Ross was hoping that his crack defense of Eddie Shore and Lionel Hitchman would thwart the Canadiens, while Clapper & Co.

provided the scoring.

It wasn't to be. Inspired by the home crowd, *Les Canadiens* jumped into a 3-0 lead, thanks largely to Morenz and Pit Lepine. Shore ignited a Bruins comeback, and as the clock ticked down with Boston trailing by one, a Boston goal by Weiland was disallowed because he kicked it in. The Habs prevailed 4-3 and swept the series in two games.

Quakers Crumble;
Frenchmen Fly to Cup

1 9 3 0 - 3 1

Appropriately, the two finalists for the 1930 Stanley Cup dominated their respective divisions the following season. In fact, their records were almost identical. The Canadiens paced the Canadian Division with a 26-10-8 mark, while Boston finished 28-10-6.

The Habs not only were defending champions, but had established themselves as the most exciting team in the game and worthy of their nickname, the "Flying Frenchmen." Howie Morenz not only was the NHL's flashiest player and fastest skater, but also the leading scorer. In just 39

games, Morenz tallied 28 goals and 51 points playing on a line that dazzled the enemy with its stickwork. Johnny "Black Cat" Gagnon and Aurel Joliat were the ideal accomplices for Morenz on a team that had dynasty written all over it.

Fans were treated to an abundance of top lines. The Maple Leafs had formed an attractive unit comprised of "Gentleman" Joe Primeau, Harvey "Busher" Jackson, and Charlie Conacher and dubbed it the "Kid Line." Meanwhile, the Cooks and Frank Boucher again ignited the Rangers,

while the Bruins again offered the "Dynamite Line" of Cooney Weiland, Dutch Gainor, and Dit Clapper.

Meanwhile, the Maroons made a major trade that they hoped would put them over the top. The Maroons sent defense ace (and later NHL president) Red Dutton to the New York Americans for Lionel Conacher, who later would be voted Canada's Athlete of the Half-Century.

Perhaps the most shocking deal of all involved the Leafs and Ottawa Senators. Struggling at the gate, Ottawa swapped its best defenseman

The 1930-31 Philadelphia Quakers posted an embarrassing 4-36-4 record. The Quakers, owned by boxing champion Benny Leonard, at least knew how to fight. On Christmas Day, they got into such a scuffle with the Bruins that police were called in to stop the savagery. The Quakers were officially laid to rest after the season.

and best gate attraction, Frank "King" Clancy, to Conn Smythe's Toronto Maple Leafs for Art Smith, Eric "Cowboy" Pettinger, and $35,000. The addition of Clancy lifted Toronto into the upper echelon, while his loss reduced Ottawa to last place in the Canadian Division.

The league was rarely as imbalanced as it was this year. Ottawa barely won ten games while the displaced Pittsburgh sextet, now known as the Philadelphia Quakers, finished 4-36-4. If nothing else, the Quakers went down fighting. On Christmas Day, they lost 8-0 to the Bruins at Boston Garden in a game punctuated by so many fights that police had to go on the ice to quell the mayhem. The Quakers showed their gumption by holding the first-place Canadiens to a 4-4 tie in the final game of the campaign—which was also the last game for the Philadelphia franchise.

After several years of mediocrity, Toronto finally made its move in 1930-31, as it posted a 22-13-9 record. One of Toronto's fine young players was Andy Blair, who chipped in 11 goals. The up-and-coming Leafs would become a dominant force during the 1930s.

The Habs' top position caused some concern in Montreal. After all, their opposition in the first round of the playoffs would be Boston. And when Weiland's overtime goal gave the Bruins a 5-4 win in the opener, Boston looked primed to steal the Cup from the Canadiens. However, Montreal prevailed in the best-of-five series, winning the finale on Wildor Larochelle's overtime goal for a 3-2 triumph.

In other playoff action, Chicago eliminated Toronto in a two-game, total-goals series, despite Clancy's heroics. And the Rangers overran the Maroons eight goals to one in the other total-goals affair. Chicago then eliminated New York in two straight and met the Habs in the finals.

Montreal prevailed, winning the decisive fifth game 2-0 on the strength of a brilliant Morenz maneuver. The Habs skated off with their second Cup in a row.

EDDIE SHORE

Some critics say Boston Bruins star Eddie Shore was the greatest defenseman of all time. Ironically, when Eddie reported to training camp in the autumn of 1926, Bruins manager Art Ross wasn't convinced that Shore belonged on the team. This was surprising because Shore, at 24, had already created a Bunyanesque aura about himself in western Canada.

In no time at all, Shore established himself as a hard hitter, brilliant skater, and expert puck-carrier. Besides, he was brash beyond belief and loved to mix it up. In his second NHL season, Shore earned 165 penalty minutes—then a league record. Eddie's boisterous play was immediately translated to the Boston crowd, until it was impossible to determine who was the catalyst for mania—Shore himself or the frenetic Bruins audience.

Shore single-handedly "made" the Boston franchise and starred for the Bruins throughout the 1930s. At one point, he nearly killed Toronto forward Ace Bailey with a check from behind.

In 1939, Ross realized that Shore had only a couple of years left and, despite what Eddie had done for the Boston franchise, Ross was prepared to trade him to any high bidder. Shore ended up with the New York Americans and retired after 1940.

Ralph "Cooney" Weiland centered Boston's Dynamite Line with Dit Clapper and Dutch Gainor. After scoring a whopping 43 goals in 1929-30, Weiland added 25 more in 1930-31. He later coached Boston to the Stanley Cup in 1940-41.

1930-31

Best Record
Montreal C.
(26-10-8)

Stanley Cup Finals
Montreal C. 3
Chicago 2

Leading Scorer
Howie Morenz
(28/23/51)

Hart Trophy
Howie Morenz

Vezina Trophy
Roy Worters

Lady Byng Trophy
Frank Boucher

Toronto Pranksters
Live It Up in the Garden

1931 - 32

Survival of the fittest was the theme during the off-season. Both Philadelphia and Ottawa, each burdened with small rinks, folded. And the NHL became an eight-team league, though still with two divisions.

On the bright side was the opening of the glittering Maple Leaf Gardens in Toronto on November 12, 1932. The pride and joy of Leaf boss Conn Smythe, the new arena opened in time for the new season despite an extraordinarily tight construction schedule. The arena immediately became to hockey what Yankee Stadium was to baseball.

Fittingly, the rink at Carlton and Church Streets was blessed with a magnetic hockey club. Smythe's Leafs were nicknamed the "Gashouse Gang" of the NHL, and for good reason. The rollicking antics of King Clancy, Busher Jackson, Hap Day, and Charlie Conacher, among others, were the talk of the league.

But along with the endless practical jokes was a seriousness on the ice. And although Toronto finished second to the Canadiens in the Canadian Division, it was obvious that Smythe's troops would be a serious force in the playoffs.

Toronto's Kid Line dominated the

league's scoring charts, with Jackson finishing on top with 53 points (on 28 goals), and playmaker Joe Primeau right behind at 50 points (on a league-high 37 assists). Third place went to Howie Morenz of the Canadiens (49 points, 24 goals), but Charlie Conacher was right behind (48 points, 34 goals). Conacher's 34 tallies tied him for the league lead with Bill Cook of the Rangers.

The biggest shock of 1931-32 was the fall of the Bruins powerhouse. Boston not only fell below .500 (15-21-12), but plummeted to last place in the American Division, 12 points behind the league-leading Rangers.

Maple Leaf Gardens opened on November 12, 1931, and by the spring of 1932, it boasted its first Stanley Cup champion. The arena is located at the corner of Carlton and Church Streets in downtown Toronto and has long been considered the queen of hockey rinks.

Under Lester Patrick's direction, the "Broadway Blueshirts" were still formidable. The Rangers were led by the Cook brothers and Frank Boucher, excellent goaltending from John Ross Roach, and a defense led by the bald-headed Ivan "Ching" Johnson, one of the NHL's most fearsome bodycheckers. Patrick added young Ott Heller to his lineup, and the Rangers looked good enough to bring a second Stanley Cup to New York.

Interestingly, the American Hockey League challenged the NHL for the Stanley Cup, asserting that its winners should be eligible. But the challenge was dismissed and the Canadiens took aim at an unprecedented third straight championship.

However, the Habs never really had a chance to get started. After winning the opener 4-3 against the Rangers, Montreal lost the next three games—4-3, 1-0, and 5-2. Although he was a defenseman, Heller proved the hero with two goals in the finale.

Toronto and Chicago met in a two-game, total-goals series, which opened in the Windy City. Behind Charlie Gardiner's air-tight goaltending, the Blackhawks stunned the Leafs 1-0 in Game One. In the second game, however, Toronto blew out Chicago 6-1 and advanced to the semifinals. The Maroons also advanced to the semis by edging Detroit, three goals to one, in their total goals-series.

Against the Maroons, the Leafs were again in trouble. They trailed the Maroons three goals to two before Day tied the score late in the third. The Leafs' Bob Gracie then won the match in overtime, putting Toronto in the finals against the Rangers.

The Leafs' Kid Line dominated New York, sweeping the match in three sets ... er, games: 6-4, 6-2, 6-4. Lorne Chabot starred in goal for the winners.

DIT CLAPPER

D it Clapper, a tower of strength as both a forward and a defenseman, labored for the Boston Bruins for 20 consecutive seasons. During his long and distinguished career with the powerhouse Bruins, he helped them to nine first-place finishes and three Stanley Cups. Clapper scored 228 goals and was named to the All-Star team six times.

Clapper's most memorable seasons as a forward came when he, Cooney Weiland, and Dutch Gainor combined to form the feared "Dynamite Line." This trio swept the Beantowners to the 1929 Stanley Cup. With Dit's aid, the Bruins lost only five games in the entire 1929-30 season, though they were defeated in the playoffs by the Montreal Canadiens.

In 1938-39, after ten years as one of the premier forwards in the league, Clapper made the switch to defense. Paired with the legendary Eddie Shore, Dit was named a first-team All-Star and the Bruins again won the Stanley Cup.

Clapper saw double duty as a player/coach during his last three years with the Bruins, until his retirement as a player in 1946-47. He continued as Boston's coach for a few more years and was elected to the Hall of Fame.

1931-32

Best Record
Montreal C.
(25-16-7)

Stanley Cup Finals
Toronto 3
New York R. 0

Leading Scorer
Harvey Jackson
(28/25/53)

Hart Trophy
Howie Morenz
(24/25/49)

Vezina Trophy
Charlie Gardiner

Lady Byng Trophy
Joe Primeau

A tribute to the Rangers' splendid goalie, John Ross Roach.

Joe Primeau, Toronto's stylish center, receives the 1931-32 Lady Byng Trophy during a center-ice ceremony at Maple Leaf Gardens. On the year, Primeau was second in the league in scoring (50 points) and helped the Leafs to their first Stanley Cup.

Ranger Vets Teach Kid Liners a Lesson

1 9 3 2 - 3 3

Having suffered the loss of Philadelphia and Ottawa, the NHL wondered whether its existing eight teams would survive as the Depression worsened and the dollar became even more dear. Attendance did suffer in some precincts, though the league regained Ottawa for at least a year to become an imbalanced nine-team circuit.

In a remarkable turnabout, the Bruins regained their strength thanks to the purchase of Nels Stewart from the Maroons. Stewart finished second in team scoring (36 points on 18 goals) behind Marty Barry (37 points, 24 goals).

Detroit's entry, known as the Falcons, was led by astute general manager Jack "Jolly Jawn" Adams who had to make ends meet with a very tight budget. One night, Adams allowed a fan into Olympia Stadium in exchange for five bags of potatoes. "If the greatest star was made available to us for $1.98," said Adams, "we couldn't have afforded him."

Still, Adams had talent in the likes of Herbie Lewis, Leighton "Hap" Emms, and Eddie Wiseman, not to mention a budding superstar named Ebenezer Goodfellow. The Falcons finished with an impressive 25-15-8 mark, tying with Boston for first place in the American Division.

On the other side, the Maple Leafs rode the momentum of their Stanley Cup win and won the Canadian Division, finishing four points ahead of the revived Montreal Maroons. Busher Jackson, the left wing on Toronto's Kid Line, reached his peak, notching 27 goals and 17 assists. Ranger veteran Bill Cook topped all NHL scorers with 28 goals and 50 points.

This season, the American Division was clearly the class of the NHL—thanks to the Bruins, Falcons, and Rangers. In fact, third-place New York had as many points as first-place Toronto. By obtaining goalie Andy Aitkenhead and defenseman Babe

Toronto's Kid Line sparked the Leafs to the 1933 Stanley Cup finals, where they bowed to the Rangers. From left to right are Kid Liners Charlie Conacher, Joe Primeau, and Busher Jackson. Of the three, Jackson had the biggest year, as he finished second in the NHL with 44 points.

Siebert, the Rangers had become a powerhouse again.

The end of Prohibition complicated matters for the Americans, since they were owned by notorious New York bootlegger William "Big Bill" Dwyer. His Amerks were losing a fortune, but Dwyer refused to dump the club. As always, the Americans were the underdog in the intra-city rivalry with the Rangers.

Fighting, while not the primary appeal to spectators, still proved an attraction. On January 24, 1933, the Bruins and Canadiens staged a Pier Six brawl involving Eddie Shore and Sylvio Mantha, among others. When referee Cooper Smeaton attempted to stop the fight, he took three punches from Shore and suffered two broken ribs! Another officiating victim was referee Bill Stewart. Stewart was pummeled by Blackhawks manager Tommy Gorman after a disputed call.

Toronto's quest for a second straight Cup began auspiciously in a best-of-five series with Boston. The series went the limit and, in Game Five, was tied 0-0 after regulation time. The teams then engaged in five overtime periods before Toronto's Ken Doraty beat goalie Tiny Thompson at 4:46 of the sixth overtime.

The Rangers ousted the Canadiens and then the Falcons in the playoffs, thus setting up a Maple Leafs-Rangers Stanley Cup final series. With the Cooks-Boucher line still in mint condition, the Blueshirts beat Toronto 5-1 and 3-1 for a two-game lead. The Leafs rebounded for a 3-2 win thanks to Doraty's pair of goals.

Game Four, the finale, was a heartbreaker for the Leafs. Tied 0-0 after regulation time, Toronto was hit with successive penalties to Bill Thoms and Alex "Kingfish" Levinsky in the first sudden-death period. With a two-man advantage, Bill Cook took a pass from Butch Keeling and beat Leafs goalie Lorne Chabot. The Rangers won the series three games to one and brought their second Stanley Cup to Broadway.

LIONEL CONACHER

An amazing specimen of a man, Lionel Conacher was chosen Canada's Athlete of the Half-Century for 1900-1950. He was a superstar in hockey, even though it was only his third or fourth best game. He excelled in baseball, football, lacrosse, and soccer, and once held the amateur heavyweight boxing championship of Canada.

Lionel "Big Train" Conacher joined pro hockey in 1925-26 as a defenseman with the Pittsburgh Pirates of the NHL. For the next eight years, Conacher toiled effectively as a defenseman and forward for Pittsburgh, the New York Amerks, and the Montreal Maroons. But it was with Chicago in 1933-34 that Lionel really excelled. Conacher led the Hawks to the 1934 Stanley Cup while being named a first-team All-Star.

Through a complex, three-cornered deal, Big Train found himself back with the Maroons the following season where he was on another Cup-winning squad. Conacher played two more years with the Maroons, making the All-Star team in 1937, his last year as a player.

Later in life, he was elected to a seat in Parliament, where he died of a heart attack during his term in office.

1932-33

Best Record
Boston
(25-15-8)

Stanley Cup Finals
New York R. 3
Toronto 1

Leading Scorer
Bill Cook
(28/22/50)

Hart Trophy
Eddie Shore
(8/27/35)

Vezina Trophy
Tiny Thompson

Calder Trophy
Carl Voss

Lady Byng Trophy
Frank Boucher

In 1932-33, Boston defenseman Eddie Shore notched 35 points and won his first Hart Trophy.

Detroit's George Hay (16) is foiled at the goalmouth by the Rangers' Andy Aitkenhead. Aitkenhead's fine goaltending (2.23 GAA) helped New York to the Stanley Cup.

Hawks Soar to Title
as Gardiner Sparkles in Net

1933-34

Surviving by a hair, Detroit's hockey club was saved when the franchise was bought by James Norris Sr., a grain millionaire with a fervent love of hockey. Norris had played the game for the Montreal Amateur Athletic Association's famous Winged Wheelers, and therefore decided to replace the name Falcons with a new team name—the Red Wings. A no-nonsense type, Norris was even more brash than his manager, Jack Adams. He laid it on the line with Adams: "I'll give you a year on probation," Norris warned, "with no contract."

Adams wasted no time building a first-place team. He bought Syd Howe (no relation to Gordie) from the St. Louis Flyers for $35,000, and Howe was soon playing the brand of hockey that eventually landed him in the Hall of Fame. Hec Kilrea was purchased from Toronto for $17,000, and the Wings were off and flying to the top.

So were the Maple Leafs in the Canadian Division. Charlie Conacher had hit his prime. And armed with the most intimidating shot in the league, Conacher led the NHL in both red lights (32) and points (52). Conacher's dapper centerman, Joe Primeau, was second in the NHL in points with 46. Ranger Frank Boucher, still one of the league's classiest playmakers, was third with 44 points.

Chicago was a club to be reckoned with because of Charlie Gardiner's magnificent goaltending. A star at the start of the 1930s, Gardiner got still better in the next three seasons—although nobody realized he was suffering from a chronic tonsil infection and the disease had begun to cause uremic convulsions. He still managed to play all 48 games and record a stunning 1.73 goals-against average, the best by far of anyone who had played more than 30 matches.

The league unveiled a couple of changes for 1933-34, including the definition of an assist. From here on, an assist would be awarded "to any player taking part in the play leading up to the scoring of the goal provided that no player on the opposing side shall have touched the puck during the course of such a play." In addition, the

 After the untimely end of Ace Bailey's career, a group of NHL All-Stars held a benefit game at Toronto's Maple Leaf Gardens. This was the NHL's first All-Star Game. The league did not hold an official All-Star Game until 1947.

Pictured is a program for a game between the Canadiens and the Maroons. In 1933-34, the Montreal Forum was home to both rival clubs. On the year, the Canadiens finished in second place in the Canadian Division—one point ahead of the Maroons.

league went with a two-referee system instead of a referee and a linesman.

Despite mounting financial losses, Ottawa continued to operate a franchise—but with appalling results. The Senators finished at 13-29-6, worst in the league. It was apparent that the club would soon fold or merge with the Americans.

On December 12, 1933, the league was shaken when Toronto star Ace Bailey was nearly killed after a vicious check from behind by Bruins defenseman Eddie Shore. Bailey suffered a fractured skull and was close to death for two weeks. Although Bailey survived, he never played hockey again. Shore was slapped with a suspension.

An All-Star Game to benefit Bailey was held on February 10, 1934, at Maple Leaf Gardens, with the stars facing the Leafs. Prior to the game, Shore and Bailey shook hands at center ice. Toronto won the game 7-3.

The Leafs finished first in the Canadian Division and led the league with 61 points (26-13-9). Detroit won the American Division with 58 points.

However, neither first-place team would win the Cup.

Detroit beat the Leafs three games to two in the first round, while Chicago, backed by Gardiner, began a relentless move to the finale. First the Hawks beat Montreal four goals to three in a total-goals opening round, and then beat the Maroons six goals to two in the second round.

That put Chicago in the finals against the favored Red Wings. Despite increasing pain from his ailment, Gardiner backstopped the Hawks to a two-games-to-one lead in the best of five series. "All I want is one goal next game," Gardiner told his mates, "and I'll take care of the other guys."

In Game Four, neither team scored in regulation and Gardiner weakened as the contest went through the first overtime and into the second. But the courageous goalie was true to his word. He held Detroit scoreless until Harold "Mush" March scored for Chicago. The Blackhawks hoisted their first Stanley Cup.

ACE BAILEY

Ace Bailey, a superb puck-carrier and penalty-killer, was one of the few skaters who was nearly killed during a hockey game.

On the night of December 12, 1933, Bailey was skating for the Maple Leafs against the Bruins at Boston Garden. As Toronto nursed a lead in the fateful match, the Bruins grew more and more frustrated. Soon, Boston defenseman Eddie Shore was tripped by King Clancy of the Leafs. Many observers claimed Shore mistakenly thought that Bailey had tripped him. They asserted that Shore then pursued Bailey to get even.

In any case, Shore skated fiercely toward Bailey, who had his back to Shore. Shore struck Bailey across the kidneys, sending him head over heels until he landed on his head with terrifying force.

Bailey was badly hurt and was rushed to a hospital, where he was given little hope of surviving. Doctors performed two brain operations to save his life. Eventually, he recovered enough to return to a normal life, although he never played pro hockey again. Weeks later, Bailey minimized Shore's role in the fracas. "We didn't see each other coming," Ace said graciously.

Shore was suspended by the NHL a month later. He later shook hands with Bailey at a special All-Star Game benefit in Ace's behalf.

1933-34

Best Record
Toronto
(26-13-9)

Stanley Cup Finals
Chicago 3
Detroit 1

Leading Scorer
Charlie Conacher
(32/20/52)

Hart Trophy
Aurel Joliat
(22/15/37)

Vezina Trophy
Charlie Gardiner

Calder Trophy
Russ Blinko

Lady Byng Trophy
Frank Boucher

In April 1934, two months before his death, Chicago's Charlie Gardiner helped the Hawks to a Stanley Cup.

Toronto star Ace Bailey was nearly killed on December 12, 1933, when he was hit from behind by Eddie Shore.

Working-Man Maroons Win Their Final Stanley Cup

1 9 3 4 - 3 5

Early in the autumn of 1934, the NHL approved the move of the Ottawa Senators to St. Louis, where fresh financing was available and the club was renamed the Eagles. The club would play at the handsome St. Louis Arena, which drew 12,600 for the opening game on November 8, 1934. Chicago won the game 3-1, but two nights later St. Louis won its first NHL contest, defeating the Rangers 4-2. That was about it for the Eagles. They lost their next eight games and finished last in the Canadian Division (11-31-6).

The big trade of the year featured the Canadiens' Howie Morenz. The Montreal favorite was shipped to the Blackhawks along with Marty Burke and Lorne Chabot. In return, the Habs received Lionel Conacher, Roger Jenkins, and Leroy Goldsworthy.

In a startling move, the Blackhawks refused to rehire manager Tommy Gorman—even though he just brought his team its first Stanley Cup. Gorman moved on to run the Montreal Maroons, and quickly obtained Lionel Conacher in a deal with the Canadiens. Gorman also gave the goaltending job

to Alex Connell, which turned out to be a brilliant move.

Morenz in Chicago was like Babe Ruth playing for the Boston Braves. Howie seemed lost in his new surroundings and didn't score until his tenth game. But the sad news for Hawks fans was that Charlie Gardiner no longer was in goal. Following his Cup heroics, the goalie's illness worsened and he died two months after his championship shutout. He was replaced by the veteran Chabot, who kept the Chicagoans competitive.

Unnoticed except by the real insiders

MONTREAL MAROONS HOCKEY TEAM

⚠ After narrowly defeating both the Blackhawks and the Rangers in the playoffs, the Maroons upset Toronto in the 1935 Stanley Cup finals. One of their best young players was Toe Blake *(top row, far left)*, who later starred for the rival Canadiens.

were Gorman's Maroons. Without a flashy scorer like league-leader Charlie Conacher, the Montrealers got their goals from a spate of plain workers. One of them was Earl Robinson, who led the Maroons in scoring (17 goals, 35 points) but finished 18th overall in the NHL. More importantly, the Maroons were solid on defense, thanks in part to Lionel Conacher, and impregnable in goal because of Connell's sensational puck-stopping.

The Rangers began slipping, but not because of Frank Boucher. He won the Lady Byng Trophy for an unimaginable seventh time in eight seasons. Lady Byng was so impressed that she gave the trophy to Boucher to keep and had another trophy minted for the next season.

Toronto finished with the NHL's best regular-season record (30-14-4), but would not win the Stanley Cup. However, the Leafs did oust Boston

three games to one in the opening round of the playoffs, earning a spot in the finals.

Meanwhile, the Maroons were making their move. They first defeated Chicago 1-0 in a two-game, total-goals series on Laurence "Baldy" Northcott's overtime winner in Game Two. They then edged the Rangers five goals to four in another total-goals series, winning the right to face the Leafs.

Although Toronto finished a full 11 points ahead of the Maroons during the regular season, the Leafs couldn't handle Montreal in the finals. The Maroons won Game One on a sudden-death winner by Dave Trottier, and took Game Two 3-1 behind Connell's super goaltending. They wrapped up the series at The Forum with a 4-1 victory, as Northcott and Cy Wentworth broke a 1-1 tie with second-period goals. It was to be the Maroons' final Stanley Cup victory.

Lynn Patrick

NEPOTISM IN THE NHL?

No hockey player ever faced more pressure in his major-league debut than Lynn Patrick, the eldest son of hockey patriarch Lester Patrick, manager of the New York Rangers. Lester had managed the Blueshirts since the team's inception, but never faced a more difficult decision than during training camp of 1934.

His son Lynn seemed good enough to play left wing in the NHL, but Dad was worried about charges of nepotism. Before making his decision, Lester consulted with two of the Rangers' older players, Bill Cook and Frank Boucher. "We'd watched Lynn," Boucher recalled, "and told Lester his son had a lot to learn, but we believed he'd eventually help us."

Lynn totaled a modest 22 points during his rookie year, but he improved every season thereafter. In 1937-38, Lynn played left wing on a line with center Phil Watson and Bryan Hextall, comprising what was to be one of the best lines in NHL history. Lynn helped the Rangers win the Stanley Cup in 1940, and during the 1941-42 season he was named to the First All-Star Team.

Lynn eventually turned to coaching. In 1949-50, he directed the Rangers to the Stanley Cup finals, losing to the Red Wings in the second sudden-death overtime period of the seventh game.

1934-35

Best Record
Toronto
(30-14-4)

Stanley Cup Finals
Montreal M. 3
Toronto 0

Leading Scorer
Charlie Conacher
(36/21/57)

Hart Trophy
Eddie Shore
(7/26/33)

Vezina Trophy
Lorne Chabot

Calder Trophy
Dave Schriner

Lady Byng Trophy
Frank Boucher

The Maroons acquired goalie Alex Connell prior to 1934-35 and he rewarded them with brilliant play. He was runner-up for the Vezina and was even more sensational during the '35 playoffs.

Bill "Flash" Hollett played both defense and forward for the Leafs in the mid-1930s. In 1934-35, he helped Toronto score 157 goals—28 more than any other club. Nevertheless, the Leafs couldn't solve the Maroons in the finals.

Wings Survive Marathon Game, Skate to Title

1935 - 36

As expected, the St. Louis Eagles became extinct before the 1935-36 season started. The NHL agreed to buy the St. Louis players and hold a draft. The prize catch was Bill Cowley, a center who was purchased by the Boston Bruins for $2,250. On today's market, he would go for about $2 million. In time, Cowley made it to the Hall of Fame. The Red Wings obtained Carl Voss for $4,000, and he eventually wound up as referee-in-chief of the NHL.

Jack Adams had survived his

"probation" as Red Wings manager and had become so friendly with owner James Norris that he referred to him as "Pops." Adams added, "Pops was the bankroll and the boss, and after he took over, Detroit hockey never looked back."

By March 22, 1936, the final day of the season, Detroit was atop the American Division with a record of 24-16-8, best in either division. In Marty Barry, Herb Lewis, and Larry Aurie, the Wings displayed the best offensive unit in the league. Their distinguished efforts were reinforced by the exploits

of Syd Howe, Johnny Sorrell, Hec Kilrea, and Ebbie Goodfellow.

"Goodfellow," said Adams, "was Gordie Howe before Gordie Howe came along."

In the prime of his career, Normie Smith provided Detroit with more than adequate goaltending. He was also fronted by capable defensemen like Bucko McDonald and Doug Young. However, the Red Wings had yet to bring the Stanley Cup to Detroit and this bothered Adams. The defending champion Maroons were having

Boston's starting lineup in 1935-36 was (*left to right*) Dit Clapper, Eddie Shore, Tiny Thompson, Babe Siebert, Cooney Weiland (7), and Red Beattie. All but Beattie are in the Hall of Fame. Despite their talent, the Bruins finished the year at 22-20-6.

another banner year—though lagging significantly at the gate—and Toronto also was strong.

To win the Cup, the Wings had to dispatch the Maroons in the opening playoff round, which began on March 24, 1936, at Montreal's Forum. The opener was a classic—the longest hockey match ever played in the NHL. After regulation, the two teams played 116 minutes and 30 seconds of sudden-death overtime—almost two additional full games. The winning goal was scored by Detroit's Modere "Mud" Bruneteau at 16:30 of the sixth overtime. The victory gave the Wings enormous confidence, and they wiped out Montreal three games to none.

As expected, Toronto was a playoff force, beating Boston eight goals to six in a two-game, total-goals series. This pitted the Leafs against the Americans, whose Dave "Sweeney" Schriner had

led the league in scoring (45 points on 19 goals) on a team that was up for sale by owner Bill Dwyer. But the Leafs edged New York two games to one and moved on to the finals.

In the final round, McDonald, Howe, and Wally Kilrea paced Detroit to a 3-1 opening-game win. In Game Two, the Wings blew out Toronto 9-4, getting goals from a half-dozen players. The Leafs gallantly rallied from a 3-0 deficit in Game Three to tie the score, and won it in overtime on Buzz Boll's goal.

Toronto coach Dick Irvin had broken up his Kid Line, but decided to reunite its members for Game Four. But it was no use. The Wings pulled ahead to stay in the third period with the winner scored by Pete Kelly. The final score was 3-2, and many suggested that it would be the first of many Detroit Stanley Cups before the decade was over.

Mud Bruneteau

LONGEST GAME EVER

On March 24, 1936, the Detroit Red Wings and Montreal Maroons played the longest NHL game ever. The playoff match lasted into a ninth period, by which time the veterans of both teams were fatigued beyond recovery.

It was essential to employ the players with the most stamina left and, naturally, those were the inexperienced younger skaters. One of them was Modere "Mud" Bruneteau, a fresh-faced Red Wing rookie. He was the youngest man in the longest game.

At the 16-minute mark of the ninth period, Bruneteau went to work. He surrounded the puck in the Detroit zone and passed it to Hec Kilrea. They challenged the Montreal defense, Kilrea faking a return pass, then sliding it across the blue line. Bruneteau cut behind the defense and retrieved the puck in front of goalie Lorne Chabot. He banged it in for the winning goal.

"Thank God," Bruneteau said. "Chabot fell down as I drove it in the net. It was the funniest thing. The puck just stuck there in the twine and didn't fall on the ice."

After 116 minutes and 30 seconds of overtime, the Red Wings had defeated the Maroons—thanks to Mud Bruneteau.

Here is a helmet worn by Eddie Shore—one of the few players to wear head gear in the 1930s.

1935-36

Best Record
Detroit
(24-16-8)

Stanley Cup Finals
Detroit 3
Toronto 1

Leading Scorer
Dave Schriner
(19/26/45)

Hart Trophy
Eddie Shore
(3/16/19)

Vezina Trophy
Tiny Thompson

Calder Trophy
Mike Karakas

Lady Byng Trophy
Doc Romnes

Pictured is Maroon Carl Voss, a journeyman who later became referee-in-chief of the NHL.

Detroit beat Toronto in the 1936 finals to win its first-ever Stanley Cup.

Wings Overcome Depression, Disasters, Win Cup

1 9 3 6 - 3 7

At first, defending the Cup appeared to be an easy assignment for Jack Adams and his men. His Red Wings were mighty from the goal to the forward line and the competition, though strong, was lacking a powerful team. The Canadiens, with Howie Morenz back in the lineup, enjoyed a revival, and the Maroons still had the nucleus of their Cup-winning team of 1935. Then there were the Bruins—always a threat with the inimitable Eddie Shore on defense.

But other once-formidable teams were fading. The Rangers' aging Cooks-Boucher line was losing its speed, and Toronto's Kid Line also dissolved with the retirement of Joe Primeau. Neither the Americans nor Blackhawks were threatening.

The biggest problem for all teams was the Depression, which was eating away at each team's finances, not to mention the NHL's. The financial straits of the Americans were so grave that the league took over the franchise. The Maroons stuck it out, hoping that somehow they could lure enough fans to The Forum to survive.

Once the season began, the Wings encountered an unusual spate of disasters. Captain Doug Young suffered a broken leg and was lost for the season. Orville Roulston also broke a leg. When Detroit's leading goal-scorer Larry Aurie broke his ankle early in March 1937, Adams wondered if and when the bad luck would ever end.

The wounded notwithstanding, the Red Wings finished first in the American Division for the second consecutive year, going 25-14-9. Interestingly, Sweeney Schriner of the lowly Americans again led the league in scoring (46 points). He was followed by a former Canadian Olympian named Syl Apps (45 points), who would become one of the nation's all-

Toronto's famed Turk Broda began his eventful career in 1936-37.

In the 1930s, Boston's Tiny Thompson reigned as the NHL's top goalie.

Shown are a pair of skates worn by superstar Nels Stewart.

time sports heroes. Detroit's Marty Barry and Aurie placed third and fourth in scoring, while Red Wing Normie Smith posted a league-leading 2.13 goals-against average.

To win a second straight Cup, the Wings first had to handle the Canadiens, and that proved a difficult obstacle—especially without the injured Aurie. Detroit swept the first two games of the best-of-five series at Olympia 4-0 and 5-1, but the Flying Frenchmen rebounded to win the next two, forcing a fifth game.

For the second time in two years, the Red Wings were involved in a sudden-death playoff classic. This one was a 1-1 tie that extended past midnight. Finally, at 12:45 a.m. (after 51 minutes and 49 seconds of overtime), Detroit's Hec Kilrea lined a blast past goalie Wilf Cude, giving Adams's sextet a 2-1 victory that shot them into the finals.

The Rangers, though given little chance to reach the finals, knocked off Toronto in two straight games and then did likewise with the Maroons. Davey Kerr, a former Maroons goalie, blanked his former mates 1-0 and 4-0.

Encouraged by their success, the Rangers opened the finals with a 5-1 win over the defending champs. To add injury to insult, Red Wings goalie Smith injured himself in Game One and had to be replaced by Earl Robertson in the second tilt. Robertson beat New York 4-2 in the second game and lost 1-0 in the third, as Neil Colville scored the game's only goal. He then shut out the Rangers 1-0 in Game Four (Barry scoring the only goal) to tie the series at two apiece.

Robertson was flawless in Game Five, shutting out New York, while Barry scored twice for Detroit and Johnny Sorrell punched home a third goal. The Wings won both the game and the Stanley Cup, becoming the first team to both finish first and win the Cup in consecutive seasons.

FRANK BRIMSEK

Few American-born players had as much of an impact on the NHL as goalie Frank Brimsek of Eveleth, Minnesota. In November 1938, Brimsek made his Boston Bruins debut by replacing aging ace Tiny Thompson.

Brimsek did nothing to enhance his image. He had an idiosyncrasy of wearing a pair of old, red hockey pants instead of the gold, brown, and white Bruins outfit, and his footwork was less than sparkling. But his glove hand was amazingly fast and his confidence enormous.

Incredibly, in a stretch of three weeks, Brimsek posted six shutouts in seven games and was immediately dubbed "Mister Zero." He went on to win both the Calder Trophy (as rookie of the year) and the Vezina Trophy.

Brimsek was one of the league's best netminders, until he joined the U.S. Coast Guard during World War II. He returned to the NHL after the war, but he never was the same.

1936-37

Best Record
Detroit
(25-14-9)

Stanley Cup Finals
Detroit 3
New York R. 2

Leading Scorer
Dave Schriner
(21/25/46)

Hart Trophy
Babe Siebert
(8/20/28)

Vezina Trophy
Normie Smith

Calder Trophy
Syl Apps

Lady Byng Trophy
Marty Barry

 Babe Pratt was a fun-loving Ranger defenseman from 1935-42.

William Hewitt was one of hockey's most respected executives. He was secretary of the OHA for 58 years and is partially credited with introducing the goal net to hockey.

Hawks Pull Goalie Off the Street, Beat Leafs

1937-38

The plummet of the Red Wings in 1937-38 was catastrophic. They finished in last place. "I stood pat when I should have been dealing," explained manager Jack Adams. "After this flop, I'll never hesitate to bust up championship clubs."

The Canadiens, meanwhile, were trying to rebuild a club that had been stunned by the untimely death of Howie Morenz. The Canadian hero had been injured in the middle of the 1936-37 campaign, was hospitalized, and then, according to authorities, suffered a heart attack that proved fatal.

An All-Star Game to benefit the Morenz family was played at The Forum on November 2, 1937. Prior to the game, some of Howie's equipment was auctioned off and the star's jersey was presented to his son, Howie Jr. The game featured a team of NHL stars against a combined unit of Canadiens and Maroons players. The All-Stars won 6-5.

With Detroit slumping, the race for the Stanley Cup became a toss-up. Even the Americans had a chance. Particularly impressive were the Bruins, who had fashioned a forward line out of three youngsters from Kitchener, Ontario—Bobby Bauer, Milt Schmidt, and Woody Dumart. The unit was dubbed the "Kraut Line" or, occasionally, the "Kitchener Kids." In addition, Boston bragged about another trio—Charlie Sands, Bill Cowley, and Ray Getliffe—which was as threatening as the Krauts.

Not to be outdone, the Rangers had formed a neat young line of their own, featuring another brother act—Neil and Mac Colville—along with Alex Shibicky. They competed against the Americans triumvirate of Sweeney Schriner, Art Chapman, and Lorne Carr.

Obituaries for the reviled Amerks were premature. Red Dutton, who had become manager and coach, signed veteran defensemen Hap Day and

Ching Johnson, who had been released by the Leafs and Rangers, respectively. Dutton also added Earl Robertson in goal. Completely out of character, the Americans turned contenders and actually finished in second place in the Canadian Division. Schriner led the team in goals (21) and scoring (38 points).

"What made me so proud," said Dutton, "was that I signed Sweeney to his first pro contract. I brought him in along with Art Chapman and Lorne Carr and together they made one of the greatest lines in hockey."

In one of the finest intra-city series in any sport, any time, the Americans took on the hated Rangers in the opening round of the playoffs. Dutton's Americans won the first game 2-1 on Johnny Sorrell's double-overtime goal. The Rangers rebounded, winning the second match 4-3. Thus, the stage was set for the climactic finale on March 27, 1938, at Madison Square Garden.

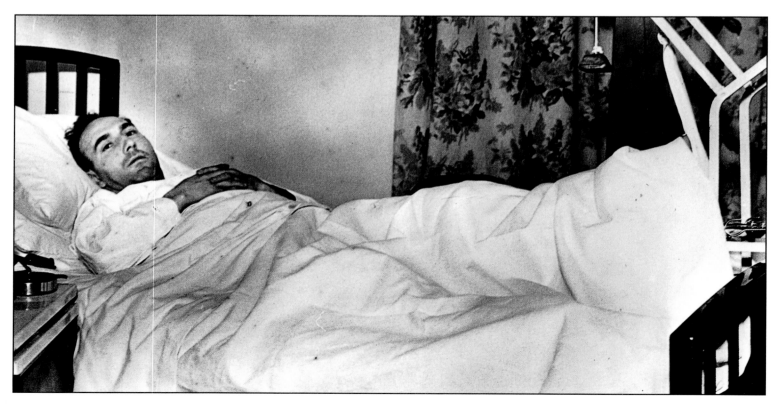

▲ Howie Morenz's comeback in 1936-37 was canceled by a badly broken leg. Inexplicably, he suffered a nervous breakdown and developed heart trouble in a Montreal hospital. He died on March 8, 1937.

The largest crowd of the season, 16,340 fans, jammed the arena and saw a pulsating contest. Paced by Shibicky and Bryan Hextall, the Rangers jumped into a 2-0 lead. But Carr and Nels Stewart tied the game for the Amerks, sending it into overtime. Neither team could break the tie for two sudden-death periods. Finally, Carr scored the winner for Dutton at 0:40 of the third overtime.

"That," said Red, "was the greatest thrill I ever got in hockey. The Rangers had a high-priced team then and beating them was like winning the Stanley Cup for us."

Sad to say, the Americans were knocked out of the playoffs in the next round by Chicago, two games to one. They never achieved such lofty heights again.

Toronto, with league-leading scorer Gordie Drillon (52 points on 26 goals) and league-leading assist man Syl Apps (29), figured to go all the way. This theory was reinforced when the Leafs humbled the mighty Bruins in three straight games—1-0, 2-1, and 3-2.

Chicago, which defeated the Canadiens and the Americans in the playoffs, now faced the Maple Leafs for the Cup. Toronto was a clear-cut favorite over Chicago, which made it to the finals despite a 14-25-9 record in the

regular season. Moreover, Blackhawks goalie Mike Karakas broke a big toe in the previous series and could not dress for the finals.

Chicago coach Bill Stewart requested permission to use Rangers goalie Davey Kerr, but Toronto's Conn Smythe rejected the idea. Desperate for a netminder, the Hawks found a minor-leaguer named Alfie Moore in a Toronto tavern on the afternoon of Game One and signed him to a contract.

Moore beat the Leafs 3-1, but then coach Stewart decided to use minor-leaguer Paul Goodman for Game Two. Bad choice. Toronto won the game 5-1 as Drillon and George Parsons each scored twice for the Leafs. Despite his injury, Karakas suited up for the third game and stopped Toronto 2-1, while Doc Romnes scored the winning goal. The fourth game in the best-of-five series was played at Chicago Stadium and again Karakas rose to the occasion. The Blackhawks won the game 4-1 to take the series three games to one.

The series was a major upset, but it was also notable for another reason: At least half of the Stanley Cup winners were American-born players. Blackhawks owner Frederic McLaughlin, himself an American, couldn't have been more proud.

GORDIE DRILLON

One of the best NHL scorers of the late 1930s was a 6'2", 178-pound right winger for the Maple Leafs named Gordie Drillon. Though he was quite hefty, Drillon had one flaw: He seemed disinclined to fight. And that left Leafs manager Conn Smythe wondering if Gordie could make the grade.

Smythe needn't have feared. In his rookie year of 1936-37, Drillon totaled 16 goals and 17 assists in 41 games. A season later, he established himself as a first-rate forward with 26 goals and 26 assists, leading the league in goals and points.

Nevertheless, Drillon had another rap against him. He had a habit of scoring the kinds of goals that lacked spectator appeal. The public considered Drillon more lucky than skillful and tended to label his efforts "garbage goals."

Those who followed Drillon and studied his craft soon realized that there was a subtle secret to his goal-scoring. Drillon would park himself in front of the net, angle his stick, and allow passes to ricochet off the stick blade and into the cage before the goalie could move. This skill was accomplished after long weeks of practice with Turk Broda, his goaltender.

Drillon was named to the Hockey Hall of Fame in 1975.

Ching Johnson sparked the Americans' revival in 1937-38.

1937-38

Best Record
Boston
(30-11-7)

Stanley Cup Finals
Chicago 3
Toronto 1

Leading Scorer
Gordie Drillon
(26/26/52)

Hart Trophy
Eddie Shore
(3/14/17)

Vezina Trophy
Tiny Thompson

Calder Trophy
Cully Dahlstrom

Lady Byng Trophy
Gordie Drillon

Bobby Bauer (left), Milt Schmidt (center), and Woody Dumart (right) composed Boston's Kraut Line, one of the greatest units of all time. They began their show in 1937-38, helping the Bruins to the best record in the league.

Boston's Hill Wins Three in O.T., Sips Champagne

1 9 3 8 - 3 9

The new season opened on a morose note with the folding of the once-proud Maroons. An attempt was made to transfer the franchise to St. Louis but this ultimately was rejected. Thus, the NHL was reduced to seven teams and one division. All but the last-place team would be eligible for the playoffs.

A number of startling developments took place during the off-season. First off, Boston decided to dispose of goalie Tiny Thompson and replace him with a minor-leaguer named Frank Brimsek. It seemed like a daring move until Brimsek posted so many shutouts that he was dubbed "Mister Zero." Mr. Z led

the Bruins into first place and they never looked back.

Only a trifle less surprising was the fall of the Blackhawks. The Stanley Cup champions plunged right to the league bottom and coach Bill Stewart was replaced by Paul Thompson.

The Canadiens strengthened themselves with the addition of ex-Maroons Herb Cain, Bob Gracie, Jimmy Ward, and Des Smith, among others. In addition, Montreal's Hector "Toe" Blake won the scoring championship, edging the Americans' Sweeney Schriner by three points (47-44).

The Rangers also were impressive

despite the retirement of superstar Frank Boucher, who had played 17 years of major-league hockey at the highest level. Rangers president Lester Patrick had his two sons, Muzz and Lynn, in the lineup and no charges of nepotism could be leveled. Muzz was a bruising defenseman and Lynn a first-rate left winger.

By December 20, 1938, Boston management had become disenchanted with Eddie Shore because of his contract demands and his general demeanor. Young John "Jack" Crawford was imported as a replacement. Crawford was one of the few players

The 1938-39 Bruins won their first Cup in ten years. Depicted above are club president Weston Adams (*left*) and manager Art Ross (*right*).

Reginald "Hooley" Smith enjoyed a fine 17-year NHL career. He was nicknamed "Hooley" after the then-popular cartoon character Happy Hooligan.

to wear a helmet, but not for protection. Jack was completely bald and was embarrassed about displaying his pate during a game.

Boston finished first with a 36-10-2 record, 16 points ahead of New York and 27 points ahead of third-place Toronto. In the first round, Boston would play the Rangers in a seven-game series, and a new hockey hero would emerge.

After Game One went into overtime, Boston manager Art Ross suggested that his top center feed little-known forward Mel Hill. "They're watching Roy Conacher so carefully, it would be better to pass to Hill," said Ross. Sure enough, late in the third sudden-death period, Hill took Bill Cowley's pass and beat goalie Davey Kerr. It was 1:10 a.m. when the light flashed to give Boston a 2-1 win.

The second game also was tied after regulation and once again the Cowley-Hill combination worked. Hill scored

with a 40-foot shot at 8:24 of the first overtime. Boston won Game Three 4-1 and looked forward to a four-game sweep. It wasn't to be. The Rangers tightened up and took the next three— 2-1, 2-1, and 3-1.

The denouement was a dilly. It was tied 1-1 after regulation and eventually entered a third overtime period. At eight minutes of the third sudden-death frame, Cowley dispatched a pass to Hill, who netted yet another overtime goal. From that point on, Mel was known around the league as "Sudden Death" Hill.

Compared to their war with the Rangers, the final round with Toronto was a vacation for the Bruins. Boston eliminated the Maple Leafs in five games to win the Stanley Cup, as Brimsek held Toronto to six goals in the entire series. Ross proclaimed that his Bruins were the best team he had ever seen, and there certainly was substance to his assertion.

Herb Cain

NEAR-FATAL PRACTICE

Herb Cain led the NHL in scoring with Boston in 1943-44, but he almost didn't survive a practice with the Canadiens during the 1938-39 season.

At the time, Montreal manager Tommy Gorman believed too many of his veterans were lugging the puck behind the net before heading for enemy territory. So, prior to a practice session, Gorman blocked off the area behind the net. He attached a rope to the goal and then extended it to each of the sideboards. The players were not to skate behind the goal before starting a rush.

Unfortunately, Herb Cain, who was the first on the ice, had no idea a barricade had been erected. Typical of an enthusiastic skater, Cain leaped on the ice and pursued the puck, which happened to be sitting a few feet behind the rope. Herb was so consumed with the puck that he failed to notice the rope.

Cain was flying at about 20 mph when he struck the rope at neck level, became enmeshed in the twine, and, with the momentum behind him, began whirling upside down like a miniature Ferris wheel. He ultimately landed on his back and was knocked unconscious. Luckily, his injuries were not serious. The rope was never seen again at the Forum.

1938-39

Best Record
Boston
(36-10-2)

Stanley Cup Finals
Boston 4
Toronto 1

Leading Scorer
Toe Blake
(24/23/47)

Hart Trophy
Toe Blake

Vezina Trophy
Frank Brimsek

Calder Trophy
Frank Brimsek

Lady Byng Trophy
Clint Smith

 In 1938-39, Boston rookie Frank Brimsek posted ten shutouts.

It isn't often that a hockey trainer becomes as well-known as the players, but Tim Daley was an exception. Here, the popular Daley shows off Toronto's new 1938-39 jerseys.

CHAPTER 4

THE SOLID SIX

The 1940s unveil Rocket Richard, Gordie Howe, and six hard-nosed hockey teams.

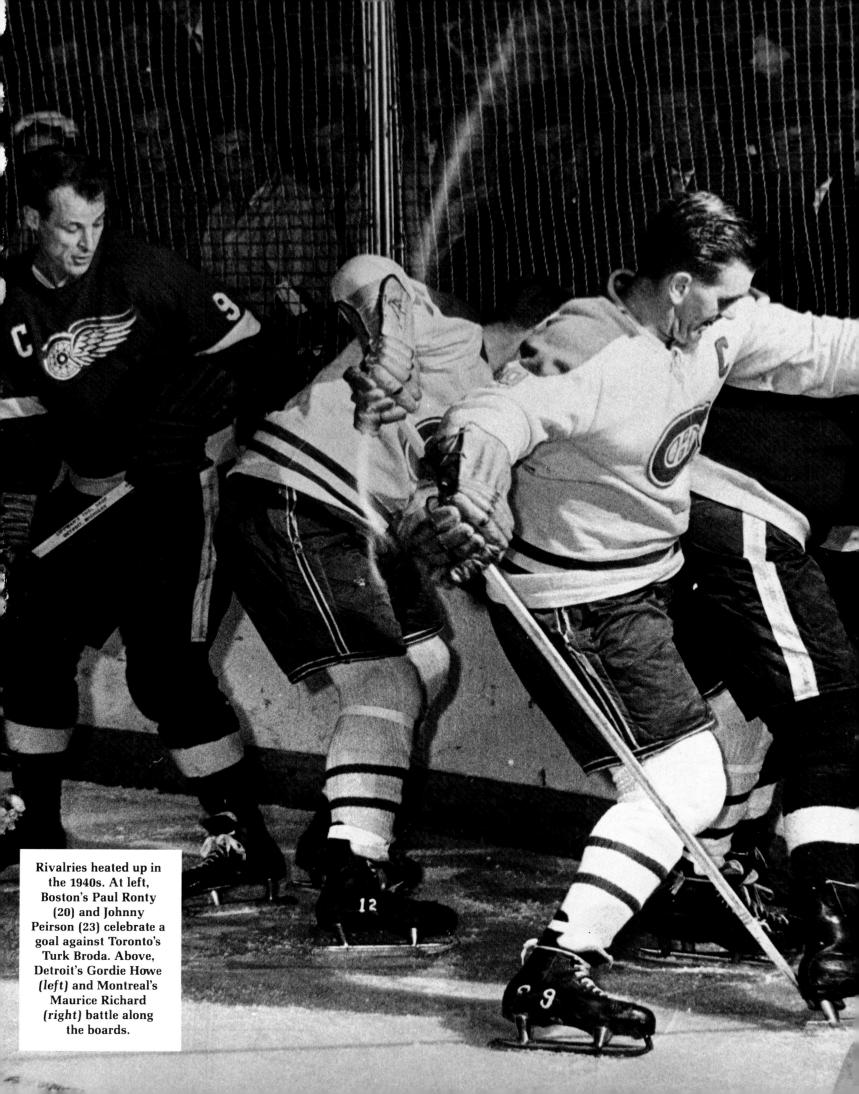

Rivalries heated up in the 1940s. At left, Boston's Paul Ronty (20) and Johnny Peirson (23) celebrate a goal against Toronto's Turk Broda. Above, Detroit's Gordie Howe (left) and Montreal's Maurice Richard (right) battle along the boards.

THE 1940s

The outbreak of World War II in September 1939 would have a profound effect on the NHL. Generally speaking, all rosters gradually became depleted of stars, who had left for war. In time, the NHL owners had to decide whether the league could continue operating for the duration of hostilities. The ultimate decision was to go ahead and play.

At first, the hockey scene was hardly affected by the European conflict, and the dawn of the new decade saw some of the finest action in league history. The Boston Bruins continued to dominate, thanks to the magnificent Kraut Line of Milt Schmidt, Bobby Bauer, and Woody Dumart.

Powerful though they were, the Bruins were nevertheless challenged by both the New York Rangers and the Toronto Maple Leafs. Under the orchestration of the venerable Lester "Silver Fox" Patrick, the Rangers had constructed one of the most productive farm systems hockey had known.

Likewise, Patrick's Toronto counterpart, Conn Smythe, built a contending club around powerful center Syl Apps, goaltender Turk Broda, and defenseman Wilfred "Bucko" McDonald. Toronto would win five Stanley Cups in the 1940s—including a spectacular comeback in the 1942 finals.

The 1941-42 season was also the last year for the New York Americans, who threw in the towel because of manpower problems brought on by the war.

To make hockey more exciting during World War II, Rangers coach Frank Boucher suggested to the rules committee that a center red line be added to the two blue lines. Boucher reasoned that by allowing teams to launch a forward pass all the way to center—instead of only to the near blue line—it would open up the play and prove more appealing to the spectators. The owners agreed, and the addition of the red line turned pro hockey into an even more offense-oriented game.

Another product of wartime hockey was the emergence of the first truly dominating offensive star since the Canadiens' Howie Morenz. The new hero was Maurice "Rocket" Richard, also of the Canadiens. In the 1944-45 season, Richard accomplished an NHL first, as he scored 50 goals in 50 games.

By decade's end, the NHL had fully recovered from the wartime trauma, although the New York Americans never—as originally promised—returned to the fold, leaving the NHL with six teams.

As the 1949-50 season approached, the NHL boasted three strong teams—Detroit, Montreal, and Toronto. Toronto had taken the Cup the three previous seasons.

"The big question going into the final year of the '40s," said Boucher, "was whether any team could stop the Maple Leafs from winning a fourth straight Cup."

Blueshirts Stun the Bruins, Oust the Maple Leafs

1 9 3 9 - 4 0

By the start of the 1939-40 season, war was already underway in Europe and World War II was beginning to affect the NHL. The Canadiens even started recruiting for new talent just as the 1939-40 NHL season began in September 1939.

The major question, though, centered around the Bruins: Could anyone stop Art Ross's juggernaut? Two teams seemed capable of doing it—the Rangers and the Maple Leafs. In fact, the Leafs opened their home season on October 4 by shutting out Boston 5-0. Toronto was strengthened by long-time Americans ace Sweeney Schriner.

But the Bruins soon recouped and made a beeline for first place. And they did it without Ross behind the bench. Ross had retired as coach and brought in former Bruin hero Cooney Weiland as his replacement.

Although the Americans were suffering financially, they did ice an interesting team. Their top name was the legendary Eddie Shore, who was at the end of his playing days, suiting up for only ten games with New York.

The Canadiens suffered through one of their depressing periods, which was aggravated by the death of defensive stalwart Babe Siebert in a preseason drowning accident. As it had in the case of Howie Morenz, the league held a special All-Star Game to raise funds for Siebert's family. The game was held on October 29, 1939, at Montreal's Forum.

The Rangers, who had not won a Stanley Cup since 1933, underwent a startling front-office change—Lester Patrick gave up the coaching reigns to his erstwhile center-ice star, Frank Boucher. Still, the Rangers seemed stronger than ever. Gifted players whom they developed on their farm teams (Philadelphia Ramblers and New York Rovers) had matured into stars, especially forwards Phil Watson, Bryan Hextall (who led the league in goals with 24), and Neil Colville.

But no team in the league could

The 1939-40 Bruins featured the potent line of Eddie Wiseman (7), center Bill Cowley (10), and Roy Conacher (9). This unit, combined with the legendary Kraut Line, helped Boston score 170 goals—34 more than any other club. The team finished with a sterling 31-12-5 record, though it fell in the playoffs.

After claiming the 1940 Stanley Cup, the Rangers were suddenly a hot item. Here, Blueshirts Muzz Patrick (left), Mac Colville (center), and goalie Davey Kerr (right) go through the motions for a Rheingold beer commercial.

match the offensive power of the Bruins' Kraut Line. Center Milt Schmidt led the league in scoring with 52 points, while his wingmen—Woody Dumart and Bobby Bauer—finished second and third, respectively. Not only that, but Bruins center Bill Cowley finished in a tie for fourth in scoring.

The season was not without its silly disputes. Americans manager Red Dutton declared that the Canadian song "God Save the King" would no longer be played with the American national anthem in New York, since Montreal and Toronto ignored playing the "Star Spangled Banner."

Another heated rivalry began between the Bruins and Maple Leafs, particularly among their leaders, Ross and Conn Smythe. When the Leafs played at Boston Garden on December 19, 1939, Smythe took an ad in *The Boston Globe* inviting Bruins fans to come to the arena to see an exciting team, his Leafs. An infuriated Ross protested to the league, but the NHL responded by censuring both.

At the midpoint of the season, a superb race for first had developed; Toronto, Boston, and the Rangers were tied for the top with 33 points apiece. With the creative Boucher behind the bench, the Rangers introduced innovative styles, such as the "box"

defense for penalty-killing. The Rangers also developed a splendid second attacking line featuring Neil and Mac Colville along with Alex Shibicky.

The season was pockmarked with its usual number of fights. But the most unusual fracas involved Toronto's non-belligerent Syl Apps, who slugged big Chicago defenseman Joe Cooper.

Meanwhile, the Leafs faltered in the home stretch, setting up a neck-and-neck race between Boston and the Rangers. The decisive game, played March 12 at Boston Garden—five games before the end of the season—was won by the Beantowners 2-1. The

1939-40

Best Record
Boston
(31-12-5)

Stanley Cup Finals
New York R. 4
Toronto 2

Leading Scorer
Milt Schmidt
(22/30/52)

Hart Trophy
Ebbie Goodfellow
(11/17/28)

Vezina Trophy
Dave Kerr

Calder Trophy
Kilby MacDonald

Lady Byng Trophy
Bobby Bauer

Lester Patrick, the long-time coach and manager of the Rangers, gave the coaching duties to Frank Boucher in 1939-40. Patrick sat back and watched Boucher bring home the 1940 Stanley Cup.

A triumphant Bruins team poses for a rare locker room shot. The aces include Roy Conacher (9), Milt Schmidt (15), Frankie Brimsek (1), Eddie Shore (2), and Flash Hollett (12).

The Maple Leafs acquired forward Sweeney Schriner from the Americans in 1939. Schriner, the 1935 Calder Trophy winner, tallied just 26 points in 1939-40. However, he played a pivotal role in the Leafs' comeback over Detroit in the 1942 Stanley Cup finals.

MILT SCHMIDT

Milt Schmidt is best known as the center for the famed "Kraut Line" of the Boston Bruins in the 1930s. Schmidt played the pivot for Woody Dumart and Bobby Bauer, and was a prime force in the Bruins' Stanley Cup championships of 1939 and 1941. In 1940, Schmidt won the Art Ross Trophy as the NHL's leading scorer, and became the policeman of the Bruins' forward corps.

Although Schmidt's career began with a broken jaw, keeping him out for four weeks in 1937-38, and a painful ankle injury, sidelining him during the 1938-39 season, he recovered to become the foremost forward through the mid-1940s.

Schmidt stayed atop the Bruins organization as general manager from 1966 until 1973. With help from trades that he masterminded, Boston won two Stanley Cups.

Schmidt's greatest trade came prior to the 1967-68 season, when he virtually ripped off the Chicago Blackhawks. Chicago got goalie Jack Norris, defenseman Gilles Marotte, and center Pit Martin, while Boston got forwards Ken Hodge, Fred Stanfield, and Phil Esposito. Hodge, Stanfield, and Esposito formed the backbone of the feared Bruins power play. They led Boston to the Stanley Cup in 1970 and again in 1972.

Bruins finished first with 67 points, with the Blueshirts three points behind.

The Bruins' quest for a second straight Stanley Cup ran into a roadblock in the first playoff round when they encountered the Rangers. The Blueshirts recorded a resounding 4-0 shutout in the opener in Madison Square Garden. Although Boston took the next two games, the Bruins simply could not cope with Ranger goalie Davey Kerr, who shut them out 1-0 in both the fourth and fifth games, and then stopped them in the decisive Game Six 4-1.

Meanwhile, the Leafs disposed of the Blackhawks 3-2 and 2-1 in their first-round series, and then ousted Detroit in two straight in the second round. Thus, the Maple Leafs and Rangers would meet for the championship.

With rookie coach Boucher behind the bench, the Rangers opened with a 2-1 win at home on Alf Pike's sudden-death goal. They also won Game Two 6-2, thanks to Hextall's three-goal hat trick. The move to Maple Leaf Gardens helped Toronto gain a 2-1 win in Game Three, and a 3-0 win in Game Four.

With the series tied at two games apiece, the fifth game went into overtime tied at 1-1. Neither team scored in the first overtime, but at 11:43 of the second sudden-death, low-scoring Ranger defenseman Muzz Patrick took a pass from Neil Colville and beat goalie Turk Broda, putting New York within a win of the championship.

Game Six was no less a thriller, with the Rangers recovering from a 2-0 deficit to tie the score in the third period. Once again overtime was needed, and this time Hextall beat Broda on a pass from Watson at 2:07. It marked the Rangers' third Stanley Cup championship.

Although his team hardly was a threat, Ebbie Goodfellow of the Red Wings won the Hart Trophy, while Kilby MacDonald of the Rangers won the Calder Trophy. MacDonald's teammate, Kerr, took the Vezina Trophy with the best goals-against average (1.60), and the Bruins' Bauer took the Lady Byng Trophy.

Kraut Liners Win the Cup, Join the Air Force

1 9 4 0 - 4 1

Despite the intrusion of World War II and the decline of the Kraut Line, the Bruins were still a formidable outfit. They were led by Bill Cowley, the adroit center who raced away with the scoring title with 62 points. Oddly, five players tied for second in points with 44—Bryan Hextall, Gordie Drillon, Syl Apps, Lynn Patrick, and Syd Howe.

This season had no parity. The Bruins went 27-8-13, while the Americans finished at the bottom of the seven-team league at 8-29-11. Montreal tried to get back into contention by hiring ex-Toronto coach Dick Irvin, but it didn't work; the Canadiens finished in sixth place. The Blackhawks bolstered their attack with the addition of center Max Bentley, who teamed with older brother Doug on the front line. Still, Chicago won just 16 games.

In an attempt to get his Red Wings back into contention, manager Jack Adams dropped veteran goalie Tiny Thompson and replaced him with young Johnny Mowers. The Cup-winning Rangers made only one addition, signing defenseman Bill Juzda, who was a locomotive engineer in the off-season.

The Rangers' defense of their title was conspicuously unimpressive, as they barely played .500 hockey. The Bruins, Red Wings, and Maple Leafs emerged as the class of the league.

Among the more colorful personalities was Toronto defenseman Wally Stanowski, who became the darling of Maple Leaf Gardens thanks to his end-to-end rushes. Toronto's Sweeney Schriner rediscovered his scoring touch, notching 24 goals.

The quality of the game and its intensity was at its peak, and this was reflected in a number of bloody brawls. The most prominent fracas occurred on January 7, 1941, at Madison Square Garden when Chicago beat the Rangers 3-2. Joe Cooper of the Hawks took a pair of five-minute major penalties, the first for toppling Phil Watson with his stick and the second for kayoing the Ranger with his fists.

Boston's Kraut Line included (left to right) Bobby Bauer, Milt Schmidt, and Woody Dumart. In 1940-41, the trio powered Boston to the Cup.

The Americans found it very difficult to win, but they did manage to come up with a pair of dazzling players in rambunctious Pat "Boxcar" Egan and goalie Chuck "Bonnie Prince Charlie" Rayner. In time, Rayner would puck-stop his way to the Hockey Hall of Fame.

Meanwhile, the Bruins ran away with the division following a 23-game undefeated streak. They received phenomenal goaltending from Frankie Brimsek, who finished the season with a 2.12 GAA and a league-leading six shutouts.

As the war in Europe intensified, there were rumors that the NHL would cease operations after the season and remain inactive for the duration of the war. However, the NHL owners were given a mandate to continue operations from both the Canadian and American governments, as long as they were able to ice enough teams. "Somehow," recalled Bruins manager Art Ross, "we were able to find enough players. But it wasn't easy."

Finishing first was simple for Boston. The Bruins' 27-8-13 record gave them a five-point cushion over the Maple Leafs. Solace for Toronto was that Turk Broda won the Vezina Trophy with a 2.06 goals-against average.

Any hopes the Rangers had for repeating as Cup champs were dashed in the opening round of the playoffs— the Red Wings eliminated them in three games. In other playoffs, Chicago edged the Canadiens in three games, whereupon the Red Wings took the Hawks in two straight.

The big series, though, was brewing in Beantown. The Bruins had their hands full with the Leafs, who took a three-games-to-two lead. But the Bruins were undaunted and won Game Six at Maple Leaf Gardens, 2-1, on Herb Cain's winning goal in the final minutes. The decisive seventh game was no less exciting. Toronto took a 1-0 lead on defenseman Bucko McDonald's goal, but Bruin backliner Flash Hollett tied it. The winning goal in the 2-1 contest came from Boston

JACK CRAWFORD

A defenseman's defenseman, Jack Crawford was a Boston Bruins mainstay from 1938-39 until his retirement at the conclusion of the 1949-50 season. Crawford played for both the 1939 and 1941 Stanley Cup winners as well as the Prince of Wales Trophy winners in 1938, 1939, 1940, and 1941. Despite his emphasis on defense, he netted 19 assists in just 40 games in 1944-45.

For a decade, Crawford was unique among NHL regulars as being the only skater to wear a helmet. Curiously, Crawford's helmet was worn not so much for health reasons, but rather for cosmetic purposes. Jack was very, very bald. The helmet did a very, very good job of concealing his pate.

Interestingly, no other player followed Crawford's lead as a helmet-wearer. Now, long after Jack's retirement, nearly all players are required to wear headgear. Only a handful of players protected under a "grandfather clause" are exempt.

1940-41

Best Record
Boston
(27-8-13)

Stanley Cup Finals
Boston 4
Detroit 0

Leading Scorer
Bill Cowley
(17/45/62)

Hart Trophy
Bill Cowley

Vezina Trophy
Turk Broda

Calder Trophy
Johnny Quilty

Lady Byng Trophy
Bobby Bauer

In 1940-41, Toronto's Turk Broda won the Vezina with a 2.06 GAA.

Bruins Jack Crawford (left), Dit Clapper (center), and Bill Cowley return to Boston after beating Detroit for the Stanley Cup.

Long before Gordie Howe starred for Detroit, another Howe led the Red Wings. Syd Howe (pictured) was Detroit's most productive scorer in 1940-41, leading the team with 44 points.

SUGAR JIM HENRY

When goaltender Davey Kerr retired in 1941 after helping the Rangers to the Stanley Cup in 1940, manager Frank Boucher replaced him with Samuel James "Sugar" Jim Henry, who had starred for the Regina (Saskatchewan) Rangers, a senior team.

Henry was an instant hit, orchestrating the New Yorkers to first place in 1941-42. His 2.98 goals-against average that season suggested Vezina Trophies to come. However, Henry immediately enlisted in the Canadian Armed Forces and didn't return until 1945-46, by which time he was a bit rusty. In addition, the Rangers now had Chuck Rayner (formerly with the Americans) in the nets.

Henry and Chuck split the Rangers' goaltending until Sugar Jim was dealt to Chicago in 1948-49, where he played well for a lousy team. Henry did even better for the Bruins, whom he joined in 1951-52. In a three-year stretch with Boston, he allowed about two-and-a-half goals per game. The 1954-55 season was his last in the NHL.

playoff hero of yesteryear Mel "Sudden Death" Hill.

The championship round, most felt, would be close only if Mowers played exceptional goal for Detroit, since the Red Wings finished a full 14 points behind Boston. But the Bruin firepower was just too much. When the Kraut Liners were not dominating, the Bruins got big games from Eddie Wiseman, Hollett, Roy Conacher, and Terry Reardon, as well as Brimsek in goal. The Detroiters were game but lacked fire-power up front.

In the opener at Boston Garden, the Bruins built a 3-0 lead and held off a late Red Wings rally for a 3-2 win. Again, the Motor City sextet made a game of it in the second contest, taking

a 1-0 lead in the third period and holding onto it with less than seven minutes left. But Reardon and Conacher each beat Mowers, and the game ended 2-1 for the Bruins.

Home ice was no advantage for Detroit in Game Three, although Detroit got the first and third goals of the game. The Kraut Line combined for the tying goal by Milt Schmidt, and then Schmidt put Boston ahead to stay in the second period. The final score was 4-2 for the Bruins. The Red Wings last gasp came in the first period of Game Four. They led 1-0 on Carl Liscombe's first-period goal, but saw the lead evaporate when Boston counter-attacked with three goals in the second period to win 3-1.

Cowley was named the league's most valuable player, while Canadien Johnny Quilty was the rookie of the year. For the second year in a row, Bobby Bauer took the Lady Byng Trophy.

As the teams dispersed at season's end, players wondered whether they'd see each other before the end of the war. Muzz Patrick of the Rangers already had made it clear that he was enlisting, as had Kilby MacDonald. In addition, the Kraut Liners indicated that they would enlist in the Royal Canadian Air Force—if not in the off-season, then certainly after 1941-42. Nobody was quite sure that the New York Americans would return, since they were swimming in a deep sea of red ink.

Leafs Shock Wings with Greatest Comeback Ever

1941 - 42

Miraculously, the Americans survived into another season, but so desperate was Red Dutton's club that it changed its name to the Brooklyn Americans, hoping the new title would spur interest in the dying club. (It apparently didn't matter that the team continued to play its home games in *Manhattan's* Madison Square Garden.) Meanwhile, Dutton continued unloading players for cash, the latest being scoring whiz Lorne Carr who was sold to the Toronto Maple Leafs.

By contrast, the Rangers looked stronger than ever with the addition of rookies "Sugar" Jim Henry in goal and Grant "Knobby" Warwick up front. They complemented the Blueshirts' strong forwards and still-solid defense.

The Cup champion Bruins became the first big victims of World War II when the entire Kraut Line enlisted in the RCAF. Their place as the dominant NHL line was taken by the Rangers trio of Bryan Hextall, Phil Watson, and Lynn Patrick. Hextall and Patrick finished one-two in scoring with 56 and 54 points, respectively. Watson finished in fourth place with 52 points.

The only area where the Rangers were topped was on defense. Boston, led by goalie Frank Brimsek, had a league-leading 2.44 goals-against average. Toronto, with Turk Broda, was second at 2.83.

At midpoint in the season, a three-team race for first had developed between Boston (35 points), the Rangers (33), and Toronto (31). But the Bruins began sliding after the Kraut Liners departed, and Bill Cowley was badly hurt. By February 6, the Rangers had moved into first. New York clinched the top spot on March 15 after routing the Blackhawks 5-1.

Toronto won the 1942 Cup with tight defense in the clutch. Goalie Turk Broda *(left)* allowed Detroit just one goal in the last two games.

Ironically, none of the Rangers won the Hart Trophy. That honor went to Tom "Cowboy" Anderson, who notched 41 points for the cellar-dwelling Americans. Toronto captain Syl Apps annexed the Lady Byng Trophy, and New York's Warwick took the Calder prize.

The Rangers were rapidly dethroned in the opening playoff round, losing in six games to Toronto. Meanwhile, the Red Wings advanced to the finals by first beating the Canadiens in three games and then Boston in two straight. That set the stage for a Toronto-Detroit finale and the most extraordinary Stanley Cup finals of all time.

Even though Toronto was a heavy favorite to win the Stanley Cup, the Red Wings went to Maple Leaf Gardens and won the first two games, 3-2 and 4-2, respectively; Don Grosso scored the winning goals in both games. Then, incredibly, the Wings beat the Leafs in Game Three, 5-2 at Olympia Stadium.

Now, behind three games to none and well-aware that no hockey team had ever recovered to win four straight Stanley Cup games, Leafs coach Hap Day was crucified by the Toronto fans and press wherever he turned.

At that time, Day made the decision that was to launch the most amazing comeback in hockey annals. He benched veterans Gordie Drillon and Bucko McDonald, replacing them with rookies. The move, if anything, fired up the Maple Leafs as they averted a sweep by winning Game Four 4-3. Detroit manager Jack Adams climaxed the affair by rushing onto the ice at the final bell and starting a fight with referee Mel Harwood—Adams was incensed at penalties the Wings had

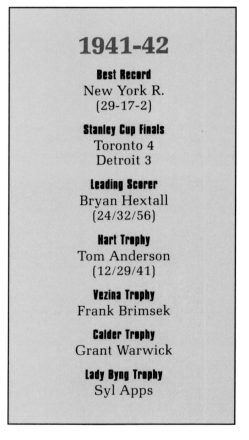

1941-42

Best Record
New York R.
(29-17-2)

Stanley Cup Finals
Toronto 4
Detroit 3

Leading Scorer
Bryan Hextall
(24/32/56)

Hart Trophy
Tom Anderson
(12/29/41)

Vezina Trophy
Frank Brimsek

Calder Trophy
Grant Warwick

Lady Byng Trophy
Syl Apps

Jack Adams was one of the most vitriolic coaches in hockey. Adams assaulted referee Mel Harwood after the fourth game of the 1942 finals, causing his suspension for the rest of the series.

Phil Watson starred at center for the Rangers in 1941-42. Watson compiled 37 assists, the second most in history at the time. He finished fourth in the league in scoring with 52 points.

received during the game. President Frank Calder suspended Adams indefinitely for his actions.

Toronto was unstoppable in Game Five, as it built a 7-0 lead and routed the Wings 9-3. Maple Leaf rookie replacement Don Metz scored a three-goal hat trick and added two assists. The Maple Leafs shut out the Red Wings 3-0 in Game Six at Olympia Stadium, setting up the deciding seventh game at Maple Leaf Gardens.

In Game Seven, Detroit opened the scoring early in the second period on a goal by Syd Howe. Sensing victory, the Wings tightened their defense and preserved the lead through the second period and into the early minutes of the third. But their carefully laid defensive plans were disrupted by a two-minute tripping penalty in the fifth minute of the final period. Maple Leaf Sweeney Schriner converted on the power play to tie the score 1-1. Toronto took advantage of its momentum, scoring less than two minutes later on a goal by Pete Langelle.

Frantic now that they were behind, the Wings plunged headlong into the Maple Leaf zone with little concern for defense. But Toronto capitalized on Detroit's offensive obsession and surged ahead, as Billy "The Kid" Taylor took a pass from Carr and relayed the puck to Schriner, who netted the Leafs' third goal. Interestingly, it was the same Taylor who, after Toronto was down three games to none, had vowed that his club would win the next four games.

Meanwhile, the overhead clock ticked away the remaining seconds. When the bell sounded in Maple Leaf Gardens, Toronto won 3-1, signaling the greatest comeback in hockey history.

SYL APPS

Syl Apps was the Wayne Gretzky of the pre-World War II era, and for some time beyond. The original "All-Canadian boy," Apps was born in the tiny town of Paris, Ontario. His father believed he should become well educated and proficient in both the classroom and on the athletic field.

Syl made it clear that before he considered the NHL he wanted to complete his college education. He also wanted to compete in the 1936 Olympic Games, as a member of Canada's track and field team, to which he had been invited. He wound up fulfilling both of his goals.

Eventually, he signed with the Toronto Maple Leafs. He broke into the NHL as the 1936-37 rookie of the year, and he led the Leafs to Stanley Cup wins in 1942, 1947, and 1948. During the 1947-48 season, Apps also led the Maple Leafs to first place. He retired from pro hockey that year and went on to become a member of the Ontario Legislature for Kingston and a member of the Cabinet.

In 1941, Boston's entire Kraut Line enlisted in the air force, causing the Bruins to drop to third in the standings. Kraut Liner Bobby Bauer is shown here at an RCAF base in Ottawa.

War Depletes Rosters, Wipes Out the Americans

1 9 4 2 - 4 3

World War II sent the NHL into a state of turmoil. As a matter of policy, the league encouraged able-bodied players to enlist—and they did so by the dozens. By far the most seriously decimated squad was the first-place finishers in March 1942, the Rangers.

Gone to the colors were goalie Sugar Jim Henry, the superior line of Mac and Neil Colville and Alex Shibicky, defenseman and team captain Art Coulter, and his sidekicks Muzz Patrick and Bill Juzda. When training camp opened in Winnipeg, the Rangers didn't have a single goaltender. Manager Lester Patrick sent an SOS to scouts all over Canada: "Find me a goalie! Any goalie!"

Finally, one was found playing for an intermediate team in Swift Current, Saskatchewan. His name was Steve Buzinski and he would eventually earn a very dubious nickname: Steve Buzinski, "The Puck Goesinski."

Despite the fact that his goals-against average was abominable (6.11), Buzinski had a delightful way about him and even fancied himself a pretty fair goalie. Asked how it felt to stop big-league shots after jumping straight from the Swift Current Intermediates, Buzinski replied, "Same as back home. It's easy as pickin' cherries off a tree."

Shortly after that deathless remark, Steve stopped a backhander and nonchalantly tossed the puck to the side of the net. Unfortunately, it was the wrong side, the red light pointing out his error to thousands of exasperated fans. Not surprisingly, Buzinski only played nine games for the Rangers.

Because of player enlistments and huge debts, Americans head man Red Dutton was forced to fold the club just when he was starting to pull out from under the debris of the Bill Dwyer days. "We had begun to pay off a lot of Bill's debts," said Dutton, "and it looked as though we were going to come out all right. A couple more years and we would have run the Rangers right out of the rink." Although Dutton was disconsolate at the demise of the Amerks, he was to be back in hockey much faster than he expected.

On his way to a meeting of the

Ⓐ **Among the stars of the 1943 champion Wings were forwards Don "Count" Grosso (*bottom row, second from right*) and Carl Liscombe (*second row, far left*). Detroit was also known for its airtight defense. The Wings yielded a minuscule 124 goals in 50 games.**

league's Board of Governors in Toronto in January, President Frank Calder suffered a heart attack. Two weeks later, the man who had been at the head of the league since its inception in 1917 was dead. The owners chose Dutton as president pro tem with the understanding that Clarence Campbell, the man Calder had chosen as his successor, would eventually take over.

Despite the war-depleted lineups, fans supported the NHL in large numbers. They were treated to some attractive new faces, including Toronto freshman Gaye Stewart who became an early favorite for the rookie-of-the-year award.

Stewart's aggressive play aroused the ire of Red Wings bad man Jimmy Orlando on November 7, 1942, at Maple Leaf Gardens. The fracas began as a fistfight and escalated into a vicious stick-swinging duel that left Orlando's face a bloody pulp. A trio of officials had to restrain Orlando, who eventually was fined $100 and suspended from playing in Toronto. Stewart received a similar fine and was suspended from playing in Detroit.

No less talented, or belligerent, a rookie than Stewart was a steely-eyed French Canadian named Maurice Richard—a right wing with an exceptional backhand shot. At first, Richard was considered too brittle for the big leagues and had a much more modest debut than Stewart.

As the season progressed, the league had to endure more wartime restrictions. Railroad schedules were now dominated by the military, and trains no longer could be held for teams playing overtime periods. Thus, the league discontinued overtime on November 21, 1942.

The Blackhawks sparked some interest by adding Reg Bentley to their roster. That gave Chicago the league's only all-brother unit—Max, Doug, and Reg Bentley. Unfortunately, the latter lacked big-league quality and soon was back in the minors.

The defending Cup champion Maple Leafs were tied for first with Boston at midseason, while Detroit was four points back in third place. Although

BILL CHADWICK

Bill Chadwick spent 16 years refereeing in the NHL, and throughout that time he was blind in his right eye. "During my refereeing career, I didn't think it would be smart to think about it, because I might not have been as effective," said Chadwick.

A native New Yorker, Chadwick was a New York Rangers prospect when he suffered the hockey mishap that changed his career. It was March 1935 and he was going to play in an all-star game at Madison Square Garden. As Chadwick stepped on the ice to start the game, he was hit in the eye by a puck accidentally fired by an opponent. After hospitalization, Chadwick was informed he now had only one good eye.

Amazingly, he returned to play the following season with the Rangers farm club, the New York Rovers, and this time was hit in the good eye. He quit playing at that point, although he recovered full vision in his left eye.

A few weeks later, he was pressed into emergency service as an Eastern League referee when the regular official was snowbound. He soon became a regular arbiter, then an NHL linesman, and finally an NHL referee.

1942-43

Best Record
Detroit
(25-14-11)

Stanley Cup Finals
Detroit 4
Boston 0

Leading Scorer
Doug Bentley
(33/40/73)

Hart Trophy
Bill Cowley
(27/45/72)

Vezina Trophy
Johnny Mowers

Calder Trophy
Gaye Stewart

Lady Byng Trophy
Max Bentley

A salute to the 1943 Cup champion Red Wings. Jack Adams coached and managed the team to the title.

Many NHL players skated for service teams during World War II. Pictured is an RCAF Flyers jersey.

the Red Wings' leading scorer, Syd Howe, would finish just 12th in scoring, Detroit had good balance and super goaltending from Johnny Mowers. Mowers would win the Vezina Trophy with a 2.47 goals-against average.

The Canadiens, mired in last place at midseason, made a remarkable recovery in the homestretch. In fact, on the final day of the season, they nosed out Chicago to clinch the last playoff berth.

Chicago's only consolation was that Doug Bentley led the league in scoring with 73 points. Max Bentley won the Lady Byng Trophy, while

Toronto's Stewart was rookie of the year.

With the league down to six teams in 1942-43, only four teams made the playoffs. The Red Wings got revenge for their 1942 playoff disaster by taking Toronto in a six-game semifinal series, while the Bruins took Montreal in five. Detroit met Boston in the finals.

The Bruins entered the final round fueled with high hopes. Although they had lost the Kraut Line to the armed forces, they still had some scoring power in Herb Cain and Don Gallinger.

But once the finals began, the Bruins disintegrated in every area. Goalie Frank Brimsek failed them in Game

One in Detroit, as Mud Bruneteau scored a three-goal hat trick en route to a 6-2 Red Wing win. The Bruins made a game of it in the second contest, pulling ahead on goals from Jack Crawford and Art Jackson in the second period. But the Red Wings rallied with four straight goals to pull off a 4-3 win.

From that point on, Mowers was invincible in Detroit goal. In Game Three, he embarrassed the Bruins 4-0. Don Grosso got a three-goal hat trick for the Detroiters.

Detroit broomed the Bruins in Game Four. Goals by Joe Carveth and Carl Liscombe were all the Wings needed in the 2-0 clincher.

▲ Art Coulter captained the Rangers' first-place team in 1941-42. The defenseman then enlisted in the U.S. Coast Guard and played for the famed Coast Guard Cutters. He never returned to the NHL.

GUS BODNAR

When Gus Bodnar was promoted to the Toronto Maple Leafs in the fall of 1943 at age 18, coach Hap Day quipped: "It appears that we have reached the Children's Hour in the NHL."

But Bodnar, a slick center, immediately proved he was a winner. In his first NHL game, October 30, 1943, against the Rangers, Bodnar scored 15 seconds after the opening face-off. Gus thus set a record for the fastest goal scored by a rookie in his first NHL game.

He finished his first season with 22 goals and 62 points. His points total set an NHL record for rookies and he was named the outstanding freshman in the league. Surprisingly, his play never again quite reached that standard, although he played on Stanley Cup winners in 1945 and 1947 with the Leafs.

A native of Fort William, Ontario, Gus played for a while with Bud Poile and Gaye Stewart, also from the same city. Their unit, the "Flying Forts," was traded en masse (along with Ernie Dickens and Bob Goldham) to Chicago for Max Bentley in November 1947.

Bodnar played capably for Chicago and assisted Bill Mosienko when Bill broke a scoring record with three goals in 21 seconds on March 23, 1952.

Canadiens Go 38-5-7; Top Stars Play in Service

1943-44

It may seem strange to suggest that a hockey powerhouse emerged in the midst of World War II. But this unlikely development took place during the 1943-44 season, which saw the Montreal Canadiens dominate the league as few teams have before or since. The club saw the emergence of several unlikely stars, most important of which was goalie Bill Durnan. Durnan had been considered over-age by the other teams and was never given a chance in the NHL. But in 1943-44, in his first season with the Habs, Durnan posted a league-leading 2.18 goals-against average and was hailed as one of the great goalies of all-time.

Montreal also benefited from the ascent of Maurice "Rocket" Richard, as well as the development of one of the

game's greatest offensive units—the "Punch Line." The line included Richard on right wing, Elmer Lach at center, and Toe Blake on the left. In addition, the Habs acquired Phil Watson from the Rangers on loan.

The Canadiens jumped to so quick a lead that by midseason their record was 20-2-3 and they were a full 13 points ahead of second-place Toronto. At the halfway point, the Stanley Cup champion Red Wings were 21 points behind the Habs.

But the Canadiens did not boast all the stars. Boston's Herb Cain would lead the league in scoring (82 points on 36 goals) while Chicago's Doug Bentley was runner-up with 77 points (and a league-leading 38 goals).

Interestingly, some of the best

players were no longer in the NHL but playing for Armed Forces teams in Canada and overseas. The most powerful of them all was based at Curtis Bay, Maryland, where the U.S. Coast Guard entered a team in the Eastern League. The Cutters, as they were known, featured a number of NHLers, including former Bruins goalie Frankie Brimsek.

The Coast Guard defense bustled with ex-Rangers captain Art Coulter and former Red Wing Alex Motter. They also had the terrifying tandem of Johnny Mariucci, a Chicago Blackhawks bruiser, and Manny Cotlow, a Jewish defenseman who would just as soon eat railroad spikes as T-bone steaks.

For diversion, the Cutters played

⊿ **Four of Toronto's best players line up in their service uniforms while on leave to see a game. They are (left to right) Billy Taylor, Gaye Stewart, Syl Apps, and Norman "Bud" Poile. Without these four stalwarts, the Leafs were a mere .500 team in 1943-44.**

exhibition games against strong Canadian service teams, who were liberally sprinkled with pros, and invariably beat them. In a contest against the powerful Ottawa Commandos, led by ex-Rangers stars Neil Colville and Alex Shibicky, the Cutters triumphed 5-2.

The only downer was a game against the 1943 Stanley Cup champion Red Wings on January 6, 1944, before a capacity crowd in Baltimore. With Brimsek in goal, the Cutters hung tough until well into the third period—they trailed 4-3—but were ultimately

shellacked 8-3. "They didn't intimidate us," assured Cotlow, "but they were a little smarter."

Back in the NHL, scoring was up all over. On November 21, 1943, Montreal trounced Boston 13-4. Later in the season (March 18), the Habs walloped the Rangers 11-3. But the most one-sided contest in league history took place on January 23 at Olympia Stadium, where the Red Wings fired 15 goals past Ranger goalie Ken "Tubby" McAuley. So bad were the Rangers that manager Lester Patrick considered dropping his team for the duration of

the war; they finished with a record of 6-39-5.

It was considered virtually impossible to beat the Canadiens, who ended the season at 38-5-7. However, Toronto stunned Montreal in the opening round of the Stanley Cup finals by beating them 3-1 in Game One. That was it for Toronto, though. In Game Two, it was all Montreal—specifically Richard. The Rocket powered all five Montreal goals in the 5-1 route. In Game Three, the Leafs closely guarded Richard, but Glen Harmon and Ray Getliffe knocked

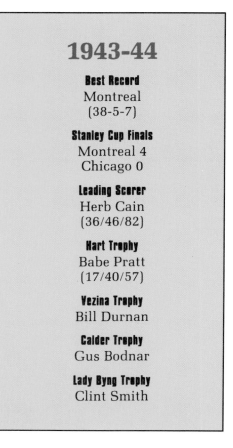

1943-44

Best Record
Montreal
(38-5-7)

Stanley Cup Finals
Montreal 4
Chicago 0

Leading Scorer
Herb Cain
(36/46/82)

Hart Trophy
Babe Pratt
(17/40/57)

Vezina Trophy
Bill Durnan

Calder Trophy
Gus Bodnar

Lady Byng Trophy
Clint Smith

In 1943-44, Montreal rookie Bill Durnan won the Vezina—his first of six such honors.

After being traded from the Rangers to the Maple Leafs in 1942, Babe Pratt shined like never before. In 1943-44, he was Toronto's third leading scorer and was voted the Hart Trophy. Pratt amassed 17 goals and 40 assists on the year.

The tenacious Ted Kennedy broke into the Toronto lineup in 1943-44. Kennedy would help Toronto win five Stanley Cups in the next eight years.

BILL DURNAN

Like legend Georges Vezina, goaltender Bill Durnan played without a pair of skates until his teens. Finally, a friend "borrowed" his father's unused blades and urged Bill to wear them. Durnan protested that it made little sense wearing the blades because he really couldn't skate. In time, he made it to Montreal.

"We weren't impressed with Durnan at first," said Canadiens manager Tommy Gorman, "but he seemed to get better with every game. As goaltenders go, he was big and hefty, but nimble as a cat and a great holler guy."

Prior to the 1943-44 season, Gorman invited Bill to the Canadiens' training camp at Ste. Hyacinthe, Quebec. The 28-year-old rookie quickly impressed Irvin with his ability to glove shots.

"Sign him up," Irvin urged, "and we'll open the season with Durnan in the nets." They did, and *Les Habitants* were off and running to one of the most extraordinary seasons that any NHL team ever enjoyed (38-5-7). Durnan, in turn, developed into one of the NHL's finest goaltenders and the only one in league history to be ambidextrous. He paced Montreal to Stanley Cup wins in 1944 and 1946. Durnan retired in 1950.

home goals in the 2-1 Montreal win.

From that point on, the Canadiens juggernaut was unstoppable. Montreal won 4-1 in Game Four at Maple Leaf Gardens and then wrapped up the series with a devastating 11-0 romp. The Canadiens moved on to the Stanley Cup finals to play Chicago, which dispatched Detroit in five semifinal games.

Montreal jumped all over the Hawks, beating them 5-1 in the first game. Richard scored three goals in Game Two as Montreal built a two-game lead. Back in Chicago for Game Three, the Hawks moved to a 2-1 lead

in the third period. However, Mike McMahon and Watson scored for Montreal to fashion a 3-2 victory and an insurmountable lead in the series.

Chicago played valiantly in Game Four, taking a 4-1 lead after two periods thanks to two goals by defender George Allen. But the powerful Canadiens would not be denied, as they scored three times in the third period to knot the score at 4-4. Toe Blake, the playmaker who set up the three third-period goals, capped his phenomenal performance with a goal at 9:12 of overtime, giving Montreal the Stanley Cup.

The Leafs came out of it with two trophy winners. Babe Pratt, a defenseman who notched 57 points, won the Hart Trophy and Gus Bodnar took the Calder. The Blackhawks' Clint Smith captured the Lady Byng prize.

Other noteworthy accomplishments were turned in by Bodnar and the Red Wings' Syd Howe. Bodnar scored the fastest goal by a rookie in his first NHL game by netting a puck 15 seconds into a contest against the Rangers on October 30, 1943. Meanwhile, Howe scored six goals against the Broadway Blues in Detroit's 12-2 route on February 3, 1944.

Ulcers One-Ups Apple
Cheeks as Leafs Edge Wings

1 9 4 4 - 4 5

As the allied armies marched across France, following the invasion of Normandy, the NHL was hard-pressed to find players to fill rosters. It was even difficult to retain its president, Red Dutton, who asked to be replaced so that he could tend to his family's successful construction business in Western Canada. Dutton eventually decided to stick as president.

With veteran goalie Turk Broda off to the wars, the Maple Leafs were so desperate for a netminder that they settled for Frank McCool. McCool's surname was ironic. He had such a bad

case of ulcers that he frequently had to head for the bench to gulp down milk to settle his churning stomach.

Some teams had the good fortune of having players released from the service. One of them was Toronto's outstanding rushing defenseman, Wally Stanowski. Meanwhile, a number of young stars had arrived, not the least of whom were Red Wings kid goalie Harry "Apple Cheeks" Lumley and Detroit left wing "Terrible" Ted Lindsay.

The 1944-45 season witnessed the ascendancy of Maurice Richard as the most awesome sharpshooter in league

history. By the 19th game of the season, Richard had 19 goals and was taking aim on a hitherto unreachable target—50 goals in 50 games.

The Stanley Cup champion Canadiens looked even better than in the previous season. They fielded a strange defense that featured young Emile "Butch" Bouchard, as well as the goaltending of Bill Durnan, who would win the Vezina Trophy for the second straight year. More importantly, the Habs featured the Punch Line. By season's end, Punch Liners Elmer Lach, Richard, and Toe Blake would finish

▼ Ambidextrous goalie Bill Durnan wore an unusual pair of gloves, which allowed him to snare the puck with either hand. In 1944-45, the Montreal netminder won his second straight Vezina Trophy.

▲ When Toronto won the Cup in 1945, its roster included two of the game's greatest penalty-killers: brothers Nick Metz (*left*) and Don Metz (*right*). Defenseman Wally Stanowski stands between them.

one-two-three in the scoring race.

On February 10, the Canadiens defeated Detroit 5-2 and Richard scored twice to reach the 43-goal mark, one short of the all-time record of 44 held by Joe Malone. On February 25, Richard broke the record in a 5-2 win over the Leafs.

The big question remained: Would Richard make it 50 in 50? On the final night of the season, he had 49. The Habs met the Bruins at Boston Garden that evening and, sure enough, Richard got his 50th in a 4-2 win over the Bruins. The win also gave the Canadiens a final record of 38-8-4.

Despite his feat, Richard did not win the MVP. That went to teammate Lach, who led the NHL with 80 points. Chicago's Bill Mosienko won the Lady Byng Trophy and goalie "Ulcers" McCool was named rookie of the year.

The Canadiens faced McCool and the Maple Leafs in the opening round

of the playoffs, and McCool showed why he had won the Calder Trophy. He blanked Montreal 1-0 in the opening game at the Forum, with young Ted Kennedy scoring the lone goal for Toronto. Incredibly, the Leafs won the second game on Montreal ice, and again Kennedy came through in the 3-2 win. Richard was held scoreless in both games, thanks to the tenacious checking of Bob Davidson.

The Canadiens were not out by any means and rallied for a 4-1 win at Maple Leaf Gardens, although Richard still couldn't get a goal. The Leafs took a three-games-to-one lead on Gus Bodnar's sudden-death goal. But once again, the Canadiens displayed their form, shelling McCool 10-3 back at the Forum. However, the Habs ran out of gas in Game Six; McCool was magnificent as the Leafs won 3-2.

The other semifinal was no less exciting. Boston and Detroit went the

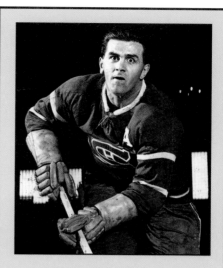

ROCKET RICHARD

Not only will he be a star," Montreal coach Dick Irvin predicted at the start of the 1943-44 season about Maurice "Rocket" Richard, "but he'll be the biggest star in hockey!"

Irvin believed Elmer Lach would be the ideal center for Richard. Soon after, he decided to put Toe Blake alongside Lach. And in no time, the line was made. The trio, soon to be named the "Punch Line," finished one-two-three (Lach, Blake, Richard) in scoring on the team in 1943-44, with Richard collecting 32 goals and 22 assists in 46 games.

Oddly enough, the reaction to Richard's accomplishments was not totally enthusiastic. Some critics said, "Let's see what he'll do next year." Well, next year came and Richard scored 50 goals in 50 games, becoming the first NHL player to ever do so.

Richard's scoring became so prolific that opposing coaches began mapping specific strategies to stop Maurice alone. One of their favorite ways was simply to goad him into a fight.

A coach would select one of his less-effective hatchet men to pester Maurice with an assortment of words, elbows, high sticks, and butt ends until Richard retaliated. Both players would then likely be penalized, but at least Richard would be off the ice.

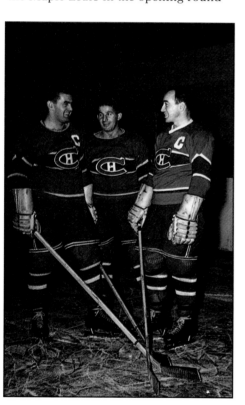

1944-45

Best Record
Montreal
(38-8-4)

Stanley Cup Finals
Toronto 4
Detroit 3

Leading Scorer
Elmer Lach
(26/54/80)

Hart Trophy
Elmer Lach

Vezina Trophy
Bill Durnan

Calder Trophy
Frank McCool

Lady Byng Trophy
Bill Mosienko

Maurice Richard (left), Elmer Lach (center), and Toe Blake (right) formed Montreal's explosive Punch Line. Lach, Richard, and Blake finished one-two-three in NHL scoring in 1944-45. Lach tallied 80 points, Richard 73, and Blake 67. Richard set an NHL record with 50 goals.

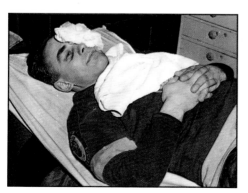

Red Wings defenseman Flash Hollett reclines in the trainer's room after suffering an injury. Though in the twilight of his career, Hollett netted a career-best 20 goals in 1944-45. He also chipped in three more tallies during the playoffs.

full seven games before the Red Wings won Game Seven 5-3. Carl Liscombe was the difference, scoring four goals. Thus, the finals featured Detroit and Toronto in a rematch of the 1941-42 championship round.

The Leafs stormed into Olympia Stadium and beat the Red Wings, 1-0 and 2-0, and then returned to Maple Leaf Gardens. On his home ice, McCool shut out the Detroiters for the third consecutive game, 1-0. He thus became the first goaltender in NHL history to produce three straight shutouts in Stanley Cup play. "It doesn't look like the puck is ever going to go in for us," snapped Red Wings coach Jack Adams.

However, Detroit rallied for a 5-3 victory in Game Four. Then, back home at Olympia Stadium, Detroit's Lumley posted a shutout himself, blanking the Leafs 2-0. Game Six, a scoreless thriller at Maple Leaf Gardens, was decided in overtime. Detroit's Eddie Bruneteau pushed a puck past McCool at 14:16 of the extra period to even up the series at 3-3.

Toronto was on the brink of blowing a three-game lead, just as the Wings had done in 1942. But the Leafs hung tough, McCool shined in goal, and the Leafs won Game Seven at Detroit by a score of 2-1. Mel Hill and Babe Pratt tallied for Toronto, which won its fourth Cup in franchise history.

In 1944-45, future star Ted Lindsay (*right*) was just a 19-year-old rookie. Notice the "V" on his sleeve, which indicated "victory" in the war.

Splitting the defense has always been dangerous. An airborne Red Wing learns that lesson after being sandwiched by a pair of Toronto backliners.

BUTCH BOUCHARD

One of French Canada's most popular hockey players of all time was Emile "Butch" Bouchard, who learned the game on the sidewalks of Montreal not far from the Forum during the early 1930s. At first, Bouchard was considered too awkward to be an effective hockey player. His long arms and legs suggested an octopus trying to maneuver on the ice. And when young Butch tried out for the team at Academic Roussin, he literally fell on his face.

In time, Bouchard was signed to play for the Verdun Maple Leafs, along with another promising young man named Joseph Henri Maurice Richard. From the Maple Leafs, Butch graduated to senior hockey, where Canadiens coach Dick Irvin spotted him and assigned him to Providence of the American Hockey League.

After a season at Providence, Bouchard was signed to a Canadiens contract, although some members of the Montreal front office weren't as enthusiastic about the gangly defenseman as their coach. At least one official of the Canadian Arena Company urged Irvin to demote Bouchard, but he replied succinctly: "That kid will be with the Canadiens as long as I am." Which is precisely what happened.

Not only did Bouchard become a mainstay of the Canadiens, he ultimately achieved Hall of Fame status.

Stars Return from War But Fall Flat on the Ice

1 9 4 5 - 4 6

The first post-war NHL season opened on October 24, 1945. Many hockey stars returned from the war, although some had obviously lost their touch. No team was more disappointed than the Rangers, who welcomed back the line of Alex Shibicky and Mac and Neil Colville. Both Alex and Mac were clearly not their old selves. Neil, a forward, was so slow that he was moved back to defense.

So desperate were the Rangers that they elevated an entire line from their New York Rovers farm club in the Eastern League. Cal Gardner, Church Russell, and Rene Trudell were hailed with great fanfare as the "Atomic Line," but they never really exploded and the Rangers again plummeted to the cellar.

War's end had led some to believe that at least one, if not two, teams would be added to the six-club circuit. Red Dutton had been promised that his Americans would be revived and allowed to play at a new rink in Brooklyn. But the Rangers scuttled that bid, preferring to keep the New York territory for its own interests.

Meanwhile, an attempt was made to revive the old Montreal Maroons franchise and move the club to Philadelphia, but the plan was never realized. Owners obviously preferred the cozy six-team status quo.

In the front office, the most notable change involved the Bruins. Venerable 60-year-old leader Art Ross retired as coach and turned over the job to former star Dit Clapper. It was a job Clapper couldn't refuse, especially since Boston's Kraut Line was

When their veterans returned from the war slow and out of sync, the Rangers turned to their New York City farm team, the Rovers, for help. Two of the better Rovers were Whitey Rimstead (*second from left*) and Lloyd Ailsby (*second from right*). Nevertheless, the elevated Rovers couldn't keep the Rangers out of the basement.

Goalie Glenn Hall once said that when Rocket Richard skated at you, his eyes looked like light beams on a locomotive. In 1945-46, Richard (pictured) helped the Canadiens to a Stanley Cup.

Goaltender Frank Brimsek played for the famed U.S. Coast Guard Cutters during World War II. Brimsek returned to the Bruins after the war but, like many returnees, never regained the old touch.

returning from the RCAF and goalie Frankie Brimsek was back from the U.S. Coast Guard.

The Blackhawks, who had finished fifth the previous year, were bolstered by the resurgence of the "Pony Line," comprised of the brothers Doug and Max Bentley and Bill Mosienko. Max, known as "The Dipsy Doodle Dandy from Delisle" (Saskatchewan), would lead the league in scoring with 61 points and win the Hart Trophy.

A year after winning the Stanley Cup, the Leafs appeared even stronger, as Syl Apps, Billy Taylor, Don Metz, and Gaye Stewart returned from military duty. Strangely, the Leafs skidded and Frank McCool proved disappointing in goal the second time around.

Montreal had no trouble retaining first place. Not only were the Punch Line and Bill Durnan in mint condition, but the Habs added former servicemen Billy Reay, Jim Peters, and Ken Reardon. Their 8-4 opening-game win over Chicago was a portent of things to come. The Hawks could score, but were woefully deficient in goal despite

several changes.

Under Johnny Gottselig's coaching, Chicago managed to score enough to keep pace with the Canadiens. At midseason, the Habs and Blackhawks were tied for first, each with 14-8-3 records, but Detroit and Boston were not far behind.

Toronto was shocked when Babe Pratt admitted to wagering on hockey games. After promising not to bet again, Pratt was allowed to play, following a nine-game ban. His return was no help. The champs faltered in

The NHL may have iced only six teams during the 1940s, but that didn't mean the game wasn't prevalent elsewhere. This is action of a minor-league game in Seattle during the late 1940s. Hockey had been a popular sport in Seattle since the early part of the century.

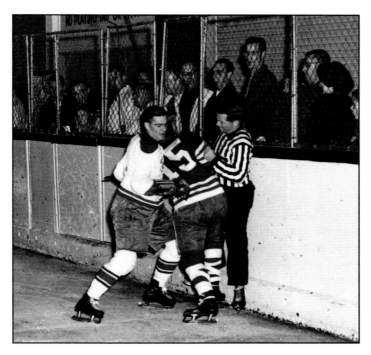

SID ABEL

There may have been better centers in the National Hockey League than Sid Abel (alias "Ole Bootnose" because of his prominent proboscis), but few were more productive in all the vital areas. He was a dogged and creative playmaker, the balance wheel between Gordie Howe and Ted Lindsay on Detroit's "Production Line." He could score (34 goals in 1949-50) as well as develop goal-making plays for others.

Reared in the wheat fields of Melville, Saskatchewan, Abel became a member of the Red Wings in 1938-39, remaining in the Motor City until 1952. At that point, he was released to become player/coach of the Chicago Blackhawks in 1952-53.

Curiously, that season has been overlooked by hockey historians, although it underlined Abel's insatiable drive. Sid inherited one of the worst collections of ragtag major-leaguers in NHL history, a team that had finished last in five out of the previous six seasons, and somehow he made them a winner.

However, Abel is best remembered for his exploits in Detroit. "Sid," said hockey historian Ed Fitkin, "will go down in the Red Wings' history as the greatest competitor and inspirational force the Red Wings ever had."

Like many war returnees, Ranger Chuck Rayner was rusty in 1945-46, as his 3.75 GAA attests.

1945-46

Best Record
Montreal
(28-17-5)

Stanley Cup Finals
Montreal 4
Boston 1

Leading Scorer
Max Bentley
(31/30/61)

Hart Trophy
Max Bentley

Vezina Trophy
Bill Durnan

Calder Trophy
Edgar Laprade

Lady Byng Trophy
Toe Blake

the stretch and—even with the announcement that aging stars Sweeney Schriner and Lorne Carr would retire at season's end—could not inspire themselves to a playoff berth. The Leafs finished a dismal fifth, ahead of only the pathetic Rangers who managed only 13 wins. Once again Montreal was on top, and the Canadiens were determined to regain the Stanley Cup.

The Habs' Toe Blake won the Lady Byng Trophy while their goalie, Bill Durnan, captured the Vezina with a 2.60

goals-against average. In the opening round, the Canadiens would have to stop the Blackhawks and league-leading scorer Max Bentley. Paced by the Punch Line, the powerful Habs swept the Blackhawks by scores of 6-2, 5-1, 8-2, and 7-2. Rocket Richard & Co. were ready for their meeting in the Stanley Cup finals with the hated Bruins.

The first two games, played at Montreal's Forum, were decided in overtime. The Canadiens' Rocket Richard was the hero in Game One, while teammate Peters netted the

winner in Game Two. Montreal won Game Three 4-2 in Boston and looked to sweep the Bruins in Game Four.

However, ex-Canadien Terry Reardon helped Boston avert the Hab sweep by scoring an overtime goal to send the series back to Montreal. It was there that Blake, despite an ailing back, broke a 3-3 tie late in the third period, as he drove in the winning goal. *Les Habs* added two more goals, and the Canadiens had won the Stanley Cup for the second time in three years.

Smythe Inks War Vet and Wheat Farmer, Wins Cup

1946 - 47

In hockey terms, a "dynasty" is defined as any team that wins three or more Stanley Cups in succession. Until the late 1940s, no NHL club in the league's three decades could pull off that trick. But starting in the fall of 1946, an extraordinary foundation for just such a dynasty was set in place by Toronto manager Conn Smythe.

"I should have figured it out years ago," Smythe said. "Youth is the answer in this game. Only the kids have the drive, the fire, and the ambition. Put the kids in with a few old guys who still like to win, and the

combination is unbeatable."

Having regained his energy and recuperated from his war wounds, Smythe was determined to make up for time lost in the army. He dispatched his scouts to all points in Canada, searching for new talent. Smythe himself went on innumerable expeditions and talked with friends in all walks of hockey. Many of them supplied him with worthwhile tips.

Rabbit McVeigh, a star with the old New York Americans, tipped Conn to Vic Lynn, a burly left wing skating for Buffalo in the American League. When

a Montreal sportscaster suggested that Garth Boesch was the best defense prospect in Western Canada, Smythe checked the tip and wound up signing the Saskatchewan wheat farmer.

Then there was Howie Meeker, from New Hamburg, Ontario, who had survived a grenade blast at his feet during the war and showed the kind of right wing speed Smythe liked. Smythe also inked a 19-year-old defenseman from Winnipeg named Jim Thomson, as well as a defenseman from Kirkland Lake, Ontario, named Gus Mortson. Together, Thomson and

▶ **Ten players pursue the puck during a tenacious Rangers-Leafs game.**

▼ **The Art Ross Trophy, for the NHL's leading scorer, debuted in 1946-47.**

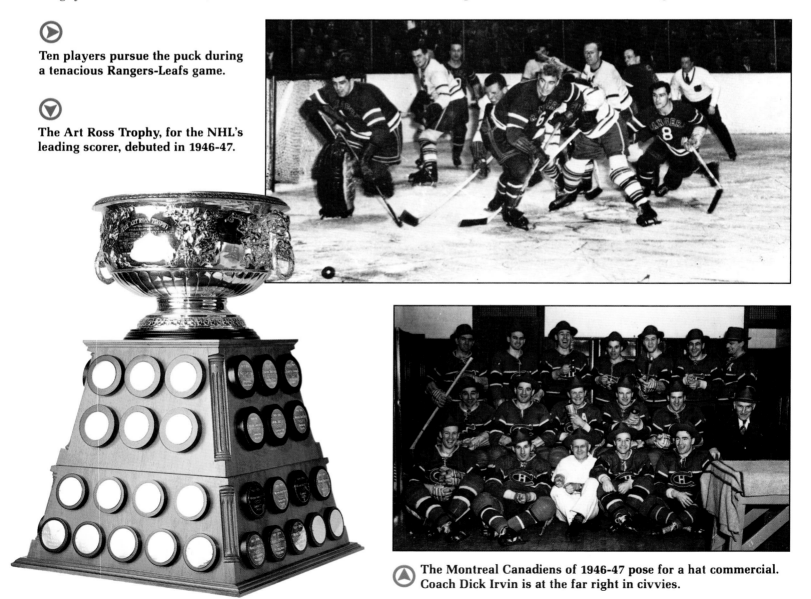

◀ **The Montreal Canadiens of 1946-47 pose for a hat commercial. Coach Dick Irvin is at the far right in civvies.**

Mortson would quickly be known as the "Gold Dust Twins." Also, Joe Klukay, the "Duke of Paducah," had been spotted earlier, and he was signed to the team for keeps.

Already in the Toronto cast were captain Syl Apps, Teeder Kennedy, Harry Watson, the Metz brothers, Gaye Stewart, Bud Poile, Gus Bodnar, Bill Ezinicki, Bob Goldham, Wally Stanowski, and Turk Broda. "We want a hard, aggressive team," said Smythe, "with no Lady Byngers."

Indeed, Lady Byng would have been appalled at this Toronto outfit. "They are the worst team in the league for holding, tripping, and interfering," snapped New York coach Frank Boucher.

Sometimes Smythe showed his players what he meant. For example, one night a Detroit fan hurled a chair at one of Smythe's defensemen, Mortson. Smythe leaped up, hobbled

down the aisle, and tossed a left and a right and another left at the fan, and that was that. The Toronto Maple Leafs followed Smythe's lead, fighting and winning in a way few hockey teams ever have.

Aside from the young Leafs, other new faces in the NHL included Clarence Sutherland Campbell, a Rhodes scholar who served on the legal staff at the Nuremberg (Nazi) War trials. Campbell was named NHL president, succeeding Red Dutton. Another major shift involved the Canadiens, whose manager, Tommy Gorman, retired. Frank Selke Sr., a longtime aide of Smythe's, left Toronto following a dispute and became general manager of the Canadiens.

Then there was a rambunctious youngster out of Floral, Saskatchewan, making his debut on right wing with the Red Wings. He was a man who, in time, would become the game's greatest

MAX BENTLEY

The original "Dipsy Doodle Dandy from Delisle," Max Bentley is regarded by some purists as the most exciting—if not the best—center who ever lived.

Kid brother of Doug Bentley, Max originally starred on the "Pony Line" with Doug and Bill Mosienko at Chicago. All lightweights, the pony boys were extraordinary stick-handlers and playmakers who could only be thwarted by rough play. Max won the NHL scoring championship in 1946 and 1947. He was then dealt to Toronto for five players in one of the NHL's biggest trades.

With Max in the lineup, the Leafs became the supreme NHL power. They finished first in 1948 and then went on to win their second consecutive Stanley Cup. Never before had a team won three straight world championships, but Max led the Leafs to the third Cup in a row in April 1949, and a fourth in five years in April 1951.

After that, age began to erode Max's talents, and the Leafs began losing more and more frequently. In the 1952 Cup semifinals against Detroit, Toronto was routed in four straight games. Rangers general manager Frank Boucher had his eye on Max, and in the summer of 1953 he persuaded him to make a comeback. Bentley retired after the 1953-54 campaign.

1946-47

Best Record
Montreal
(34-16-10)

Stanley Cup Finals
Toronto 4
Montreal 2

Leading Scorer
Max Bentley
(29/43/72)

Hart Trophy
Maurice Richard
(45/26/71)

Vezina Trophy
Bill Durnan

Calder Trophy
Howie Meeker

Lady Byng Trophy
Bobby Bauer

Toronto's Nick Metz (*left*), Vic Lynn (*center*), and Howie Meeker soak up a Maple Leaf victory. Lynn and Meeker comprised two-thirds of Toronto's "Kid Line," along with center Ted Kennedy.

Red Dutton resigned as NHL president in 1946 and was succeeded by Clarence Campbell (pictured). Campbell, a former Rhodes Scholar, would remain president until 1977. Ironically, his biggest problems would center around the league's most dynamic player—Rocket Richard.

player. His name was Gordie Howe.

Buoyed by capacity crowds a year earlier, the league increased its schedule from 50 to 60 games and added new bonuses—$1,000 each—for trophy winners and All-Star selections.

The battle for first place was fought between the defending champion Canadiens and the effervescent Leafs. Meanwhile, two men duked it out for the scoring title—Montreal's Maurice Richard and Chicago's Max Bentley. The scoring race was a neck-and-neck struggle that would go right down to the wire.

Under Dick Irvin's guidance, *Les Canadiens* possessed a combination of accurate shooting, hard skating, and the kind of roughhousing one would expect in a Pier Six brawl. The leading advocate of belligerency was Kenny Reardon, who had found a favorite foe in Toronto's "Wild" Bill Ezinicki. Reardon took the opening decision in an early game at Maple Leaf Gardens.

Tough in their own right, the Leafs didn't accept the punishment without retaliation. Early in February 1947, the Canadiens and Leafs erupted in one of the most acrimonious feuds in their long history. It started when Toronto forward Don Metz collided with Elmer Lach and sent the Montreal center sprawling to the ice. Lach suffered a fractured skull and would be lost to the team for the rest of the season. Metz only received a minor penalty, infuriating the Canadiens. Not surprisingly, the next Montreal-Toronto game was filled with brawls.

Toronto may have possessed the better fighters, but the Canadiens proved to be the better team. They went on to beat the Leafs in the standings by six points.

By the season's final weekend, all eyes were focused on the scoring race between Richard and Max Bentley. Bentley scored a goal and added an assist in New York to edge Richard by a single point, 72-71. However, the

A mainstay of the Toronto defense in 1946-47 was hard-hitting Jim Thomson (pictured), who teamed with Gus Mortson. Thomson was just 19 years old during the season; Mortson was only 21. The pair became known as the "Gold Dust Twins."

Following his stint in World War II, Conn Smythe built a new Maple Leafs dynasty in the late 1940s. Smythe went with the youngsters—like Vic Lynn, Garth Boesch, and Howie Meeker— and they responded with a mantel-full of Stanley Cups.

Toronto forward Gaye Stewart and Montreal goalie Bill Durnan follow the puck behind the net during the 1947 finals. Toronto won the series in six.

BUDDY O'CONNOR

Buddy O'Connor, a 5'7", wisp-like centerman, broke into pro hockey with the 1941-42 Montreal Canadiens, pivoting a line of mighty mites known as the "Razzle-Dazzle Line." This fulfilled a boyhood ambition of Buddy's that began on the frozen ponds of his suburban Montreal home.

But it was easy for the little forward to get lost in the shuffle on the mighty Canadiens. So after six successful but anonymous seasons in Montreal, Buddy was peddled to the New York Rangers in 1947 for the paltry sum of $6,500.

O'Connor was welcomed in New York with open arms, and it was there that he truly began to find himself. He finished out the 1947-48 campaign in grand style, missing out on the NHL scoring crown by a single point, but copping both the Hart Trophy and the Lady Byng.

An automobile accident forced Buddy to miss much of the following season—a mishap that cost the Rangers a spot in the playoffs, according to Ranger manager Frank Boucher. Buddy played two more seasons with the Rangers before finally retiring as a player at the end of the 1950-51 campaign.

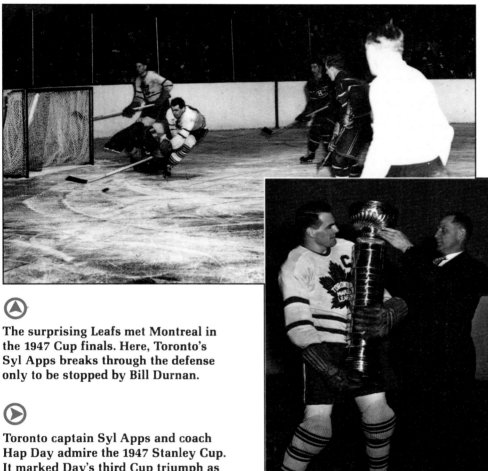

The surprising Leafs met Montreal in the 1947 Cup finals. Here, Toronto's Syl Apps breaks through the defense only to be stopped by Bill Durnan.

Toronto captain Syl Apps and coach Hap Day admire the 1947 Stanley Cup. It marked Day's third Cup triumph as a coach.

Rocket finished the season with a league-leading 45 goals.

In the opening rounds of the playoffs, Richard powered his Canadiens to a 4-1 series win over the Bruins, while the Maple Leafs eliminated the Red Wings in five games. Even before the finals began, the rival coaches were at each other's throats with Irvin verbalizing like never before.

The Canadiens thoroughly wasted the Leafs in Game One, 6-0, commanding play in every period. However, Richard was banished in Game Two by referee Bill Chadwick for two violent slashing penalties, and

the Canadiens disintegrated before the angry Leafs, dropping the game 4-0. NHL President Clarence Campbell reviewed the episode and levied a one-game suspension against the Rocket, as well as a $250 fine.

Toronto smacked four pucks past Montreal goaltender Bill Durnan in Game Three to win 4-2. And though Richard returned to the lineup for Game Four, the Leafs won again on an overtime goal by Syl Apps. Montreal finally came back in Game Five. Led by the Rocket, who scored twice, *Les Canadiens* defeated Toronto 3-1 to pull within a game of tying the series.

Game Six, at Maple Leaf Gardens, looked to be a rout, as the Canadiens' Buddy O'Connor scored just 25 seconds into the match. But the young Leafs battled Montreal on even terms until Lynn scored for Toronto at 5:34 of the second period. The score remained tied well into the third period when Toronto's Kennedy fired a long, low shot past Bill Durnan. The Canadiens fought gamely for the equalizer, but the Leaf defense was virtually impenetrable and Toronto won the game 2-1. The Leafs had captured the Stanley Cup in shocking fashion, four games to two.

Toronto Gambles on Bentley, Hits the Jackpot

1947-48

By now, the NHL had fully recovered from the aftershock of World War II and attendance remained high, as did the quality of play. What puzzled many experts was whether Toronto's 1947 Cup win was real or a fluke. Apart from captain Syl Apps and future Hall of Famer Teeder Kennedy, there were no stars on the team. Manager Conn Smythe knew that this vital factor could make the difference between a good Leafs team and a great one. His belief was solidified when the Leafs stumbled through the opening month.

Smythe knew which man he wanted, but getting him was something else. Max Bentley was the man, a wiry center who skated like a dream, shot like a bazooka, and had led the NHL in scoring the past two years. Smythe already had two fine centers in Apps and the tenacious Kennedy, but he felt he needed Bentley if he was going to create the super team of his visions.

Bentley's club, the Blackhawks, was in last place and seemed ripe for a proposition, but Chicago manager Bill Tobin was a hard bargainer. Smythe finally had to offer five players before Tobin gave in. It was an astonishing deal, described then as "the greatest mass trade in professional hockey history." Included in the package was Toronto's entire "Flying Forts" line of Gus Bodnar, Bud Poile, and Gaye Stewart. These three players, plus

Brothers Doug (left) and Max Bentley were teammates in Chicago until Max was traded to Toronto in November 1947. The Leafs dealt five players for Max in one of the biggest hockey trades ever. It paid off for Toronto. Max helped the Leafs to the 1948 Stanley Cup.

defenseman Bob Goldham, were extremely popular, and Smythe had a lot of explaining to do.

Adding to the gamble was the delicate psyche of Bentley, who had a reputation of being both hypersensitive and a hypochondriac. As expected, Max was nearly heartbroken at the news of the trade, for it meant splitting up with his brother Doug. "It makes me feel," said Max, "like I lost my right arm."

It took a while for Max to adjust to his new surroundings. He went ten straight games without a goal, but once he got going there was no stopping him. He finished with 26 goals, including 23 for the Leafs.

Another remarkable Leaf was right wing Wild Bill Ezinicki. Once Wild Bill had four teeth knocked out in a key homestretch game, but despite pain and nervous shock, he returned to score the winning goal. Ezinicki would collide with opponents—usually bigger opponents—from any direction. Sometimes he would wait for an opponent to speed in his path and then bend forward, swing his hips, and send his foe flying over him.

The NHL was bulging with stars, and they were out in force for the first official All-Star Game at Maple Leaf Gardens. The All-Stars defeated the Cup champion Leafs 4-3 and contributed $25,865 to the players' pension fund. Sadly for the Blackhawks, their ace forward, Bill Mosienko, suffered a broken ankle in the game, and that ensured last place for Chicago.

A major surprise was the resurgence of the Rangers, who had not made the

WILD BILL EZINICKI

Wild" Bill Ezinicki had sinewy arms and a body that bulged from daily weight lifting. A right winger for Toronto in the late 1940s, Ezinicki had a passion for body-checking. He also had a passion for tape, winding reams of it around his legs until they bulged grotesquely.

Ezinicki loved to knock opposing forwards on their butts. If an opponent tried to speed by him, Ezzie would bend forward, swing his hips, and send his foe flying over him. If Ezinicki got the worst of the fracas—which did not happen often—he still got consolation from his insurance policy; the policy paid him $5 for every stitch resulting from a hockey injury. "It's just like double indemnity," he said.

Ezinicki seemed to thrive on pain. Once he had four teeth knocked out in a key homestretch game, but despite pain and nervous shock, he returned to score the winning goal.

Ezzie was adored in Toronto and despised everywhere else. According to legend, a woman in a front-row seat at Madison Square Garden jammed a long hat pin in his derriere as he bent over to take a face-off.

Ezinicki played on Toronto Cup winners in 1947, 1948, and 1949. He later was traded to Boston. After retiring from hockey, he became a successful golf pro in Massachusetts.

The resurgent Rangers were led by veterans Phil Watson (left), Neil Colville (center), and Chuck Rayner.

After an outstanding career, Charlie Conacher (far left) became coach of Chicago. There, his luck ran out. The 1947-48 Hawks finished in the cellar.

playoffs for six years. Thanks to Charlie Rayner's goaltending and Buddy O'Connor's playmaking, the Blueshirts squeaked into fourth place.

No less surprising was news that Billy "The Kid" Taylor of the Rangers and Don Gallinger of Boston were involved in betting on games. NHL President Clarence Campbell suspended both players for life. It was a traumatic event at a time when the league was otherwise flourishing. Detroit now had a magnificent unit of center Sid Abel and wings Gordie Howe and Ted Lindsay. They dubbed it the "Production Line."

Meanwhile, Bruins fans still were cheering the Kraut Line, although the trio had slowed considerably. "We never recaptured the magic," said Milt Schmidt, who was a three-time All-Star and an MVP during his 16 seasons with Boston. "To this day, I think that if the war years hadn't arrived when they did, we could have built a dynasty. We could have won six Cups."

The Red Wings gave Toronto the toughest run for first place. Going into a final weekend home-and-home series with Detroit, the Leafs held a one-point lead. That weekend may have been the most glorious 48 hours of the entire season for the Leafs. Not only did they win both games (5-3 and 5-2), but some individual kudos were achieved too.

Toronto's Turk Broda beat out Detroit's Harry Lumley for lowest goals-against average (2.38) and won his second Vezina Trophy. Even more

The Maple Leafs blew out the Red Wings in four straight in the 1948 Stanley Cup finals. The triumph was followed by a tumultuous victory motorcade through the streets of downtown Toronto.

Toronto forward Howie Meeker (left) is foiled by Red Wings netminder Harry Lumley during the 1948 Stanley Cup finals. Detroit's Red Kelly (upper right) and the Leafs' Ted Kennedy (lower right) follow the puck.

1947-48

Best Record
Toronto
(32-15-13)

Stanley Cup Finals
Toronto 4
Detroit 0

Art Ross Trophy
Elmer Lach
(30/31/61)

Hart Trophy
Buddy O'Connor
(24/36/60)

Vezina Trophy
Turk Broda

Calder Trophy
Jim McFadden

Lady Byng Trophy
Buddy O'Connor

heartwarming was Apps's performance in the two games. He needed three goals to reach 200 for his career, and it was a big order to fill in two high-pressure games. But Apps got goal No. 198 in the first game and he scored a three-goal hat trick the following night.

Montreal's Elmer Lach captured the Ross Trophy for scoring (61 points on 30 goals), while New York's Buddy O'Connor (60 points) won both the Hart Trophy and the Lady Byng prize.

Jim McFadden of the Red Wings was named rookie of the year.

As the league champions, the Leafs should have been big favorites to retain their Stanley Cup. But New York coach Frank Boucher predicted they wouldn't even get past the third-place Boston Bruins in the opening round. He was wrong. The Leafs discarded the Beantowners in five games and were set for a finals matchup with the Red Wings, who had eliminated the Rangers in six games.

"We get paid to play the other teams," said Detroit's Sid Abel. "The Leafs? We'd play them for nothing."

Entering the finals, Leafs coach Hap Day tried to get his players to ignore the odds, which favored them 2-1. His players ignored the odds for four straight games, as that was how long it took them to defeat the Red Wings. Toronto's well-balanced attack outscored Detroit 18-7 in the series. The sweep by the Maple Leafs earned them their second straight Stanley Cup.

Detroit's Ted Lindsay (7) is thwarted by Toronto backliner Wally Stanowski during the 1948 finals. Detroit scored just seven goals in the series.

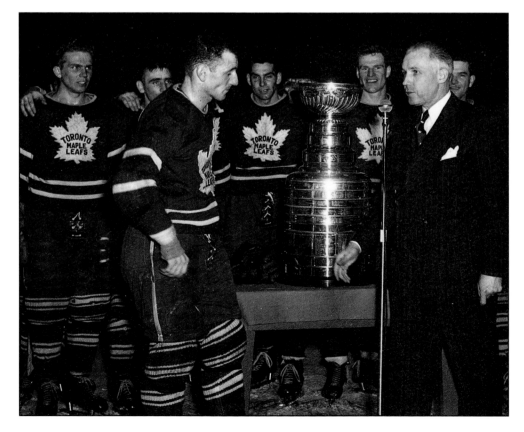

Gordie Howe

THE PRODUCTION LINE

It was 1946 when a muscular youngster with a Saskatchewan drawl arrived in Detroit. His name was Gordie Howe. He was accompanied by another young player, Ted Lindsay, who had joined the Red Wings two years before. After juggling combinations of players, coach Jack Adams eventually placed captain Sid Abel, the center, on a line with Howe on right wing and the truculent Lindsay on left.

No three forwards ever jelled more firmly. And as they began to pump goal after goal into the enemy nets, it was rather appropriate that the city that developed the motor production line should name the Lindsay, Abel, and Howe trio the "Production Line." In 1949-50, Lindsay, Abel, and Howe finished first, second, and third in the NHL in scoring.

The unit remained intact until Abel's retirement, but a new, revised Production Line was formed when sharpshooting center Alex Delvecchio supplanted Abel and proved just as good, if not better. Starting in 1948-49, Detroit finished first seven straight seasons.

A nonchalant Ted Kennedy greets NHL President Clarence Campbell in a Stanley Cup ceremony. At the time, Kennedy was an alternate captain, but he wore the "C" in 1948-49 after captain Syl Apps retired.

Leafs Embarrass the Wings, Broom Them Again

1948 - 49

Toronto was on the threshold of having hockey's first dynasty until two of the best players the Leafs ever had—captain Syl Apps and utility forward Nick Metz—retired. Replacing Apps was impossible, but Conn Smythe did the best he could by trading for Cal "Ginger" Gardner, a tough center with the Rangers.

Gardner showed just how tough he was on January 1, 1949, when he engaged in a vicious brawl with Montreal defenseman Ken Reardon. It began when referee Bill Chadwick sentenced the two with minor penalties for slashing after a brief but violent clash. As Reardon turned toward the penalty box, he overheard a remark from Gardner that displeased him. What's more, Gardner's stick was raised. Reardon wheeled and headed directly for Gardner.

"Then they flailed each other vigorously about the heads and shoulders," wrote a reporter for The (Toronto) Globe and Mail. At this point, burly linesman George Hayes attempted to intervene, and referee Chadwick stood a few yards to the side screaming at the players to cease and desist. His peacemaking efforts fell on deaf ears. Both players dropped their sticks and swung fists in what one observer described as "a life-and-death grapple." Finally, they were pried apart by the officials.

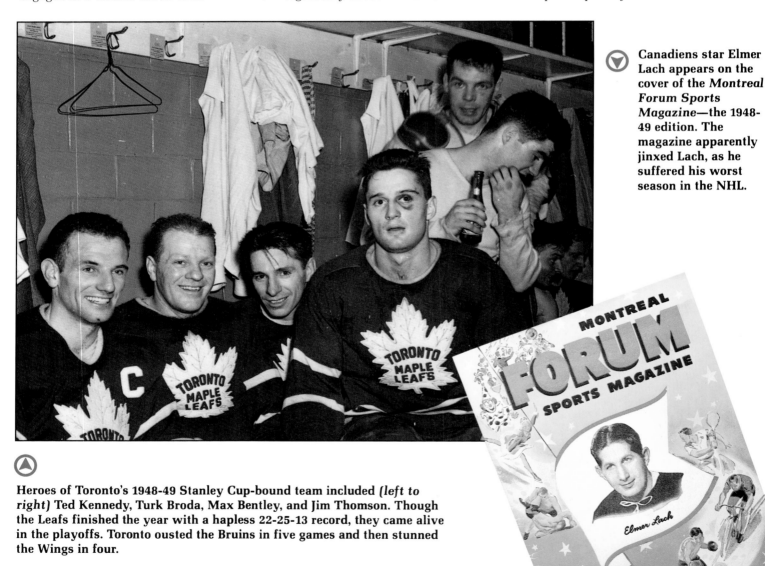

Canadiens star Elmer Lach appears on the cover of the *Montreal Forum Sports Magazine*—the 1948-49 edition. The magazine apparently jinxed Lach, as he suffered his worst season in the NHL.

Heroes of Toronto's 1948-49 Stanley Cup-bound team included *(left to right)* Ted Kennedy, Turk Broda, Max Bentley, and Jim Thomson. Though the Leafs finished the year with a hapless 22-25-13 record, they came alive in the playoffs. Toronto ousted the Bruins in five games and then stunned the Wings in four.

NHL President Clarence Campbell fined Gardner $250 and Reardon $200 and suspended both players for the next meeting of their respective teams. Campbell's mild punishment had no effect. Gardner and Reardon would later engage in an even more gruesome battle.

In addition to fighting, the Canadiens were winning some hockey games in 1948-49. But the big story of the season was an offer made to Montreal's Frank Selke by the Toronto Maple Leafs. Smythe sent coach Hap Day to Montreal with instructions to obtain Maurice Richard's contract.

"Maple Leaf Gardens has never been close with a buck," said Day, "and I have explicit instructions to meet any price mentioned for Richard's services. We consider Richard the greatest right wing in the major league, if not the greatest player."

The Globe and Mail followed suit by printing an arresting photograph of Richard wearing a Maple Leaf jersey, adding a caption, "Wouldn't he look good in a sweater like this?"

Officials of the Canadiens found the proposition ludicrous. "All the money in Toronto wouldn't buy him," carped Selke. Montreal Coach Dick Irvin then underlined the point: "It's propaganda. All this is merely an attempt to upset my boys on the eve of a game."

Richard stayed in Montreal, though Habs All-Star goalie Bill Durnan was threatening to retire. Selke persuaded him to stick it out, though, and the decision proved fruitful. The big goalie was better than ever in 1948-49, and on March 7 he scored his fourth straight shutout, defeating Boston 1-0. The lone goal in the game was scored by Rocket Richard.

TONY LESWICK

The New York Rangers couldn't climb out of their doldrums during the late 1940s, but forward Tony Leswick kept things exciting. He not only led the Rangers in scoring in 1946-47, but was also the club's supreme needler of the opposition and "shadow" of its leading scorers, until traded to Detroit in 1951-52.

More than anyone else, Montreal's Rocket Richard was perpetually pestered by Leswick. Once, at the Montreal Forum, Leswick needled the Rocket, and Richard swung his stick at Leswick. The referee sent Richard to the penalty box with a two-minute minor. Leswick didn't stop there and pestered the Rocket throughout the game. With just a minute remaining, Richard blew up again, and again the ref sent him to the box.

At game's end, Richard bolted from the penalty box and charged Leswick, whereupon the two brawled for several minutes. The Richard-Leswick feud continued for several years.

Of course, Richard wasn't Leswick's only target. Once, in a playoff game against Detroit, he was given a two-minute penalty. The timekeeper, whose duty it was to wave inmates back onto the ice when their penalty time had expired, became Leswick's target.

"Tony chattered and argued about the time he was to return to the ice," said Rangers publicist Stan Saplin, "and so confused the timekeeper that he was allowed back in the game long before his penalty time was up."

The top center on the Red Wings in the late 1940s was Sid Abel, who was known for his high scoring and hard-nosed checking. In 1948-49, Abel scored 28 goals and captured the Hart Trophy.

Durnan won his fifth Vezina Trophy in 1948-49. Red Wings defenseman Bill Quackenbush copped the Lady Byng Trophy while Detroit captain Sid Abel took the Hart. Finnish-born Pentti Lund of the Rangers was named rookie of the year.

Although Toe Blake had retired to become coach of the Valleyfield Braves of the strong Quebec Senior League, Montreal's Punch Line still boasted the Rocket and Elmer Lach. The pair helped Montreal to a third-place finish and the right to face league-leading Detroit in the first round of the playoffs.

Thanks to Abel, Ted Lindsay, a young Gordie Howe, and a well-rounded bench, the Red Wings had become the new class team of the NHL. They were also rough and they proved it in the opening game. Lach left the contest with a broken jaw after colliding with Detroit defenseman Black Jack Stewart. Once again, poor Elmer had become the center of an acrimonious controversy. On the one side, the Canadiens claimed Stewart had deliberately maimed Lach, much in the manner that Don Metz of Toronto had done in the 1946-47 season. On the other side, the Red Wings piously denied any foul play.

"Elmer doesn't carry the puck in his

Canadiens coach Dick Irvin was usually intense, but here he loosens up a little. Irvin's team finished a distant third in 1948-49 but featured the NHL's stingiest defense.

After captain Syl Apps retired prior to 1948-49, Conn Smythe replaced him with Cal Gardner (pictured), a tough center from the Rangers. Gardner's season was marred by a vicious brawl.

Red Wings goalie Harry Lumley follows the puck as Toronto's Max Bentley (7) prepares a backhander during the 1949 finals. Red Wings defenseman Jack Stewart (2) attempts to intercept.

 Detroit goalie Harry Lumley makes a kick-save in the 1949 finals. Toronto scored exactly three goals in each game of its four-game sweep.

GARTH BOESCH

Only two players wore moustaches in the NHL during the 1940s—Don "Bones" Raleigh of the Rangers and Garth Boesch of the Maple Leafs. Raleigh's was only a temporary fixture; Boesch's remained permanent and complimented his cool defensive style.

A Saskatchewan wheat farmer, Boesch was a cog in the Toronto dynasty launched by Conn Smythe in 1946. From the 1947 playoffs through April 1949, the Leafs won three Stanley Cups in three tries, aided by the superb play of Boesch.

His defense partner was Bill Barilko, and together they perfected the "Maginot Line" knee drop, in which they would simultaneously fall to their knees to block enemy shots, as if they were connected by invisible rods.

During the 1949-50 season, when Smythe conducted his notorious fight against fat on his team, Boesch was one of the few Leafs to check in under his established weight. As defensemen go, Boesch was one of the most underrated quality backliners ever to play in the majors.

Maple Leaf captain Ted Kennedy poses with league president Clarence Campbell after Toronto's 1949 Stanley Cup win. The Leafs swept the Red Wings in the finals for the second consecutive year.

teeth," Irvin pointed out, "but that's where they've been checking him." Both Selke and a Montreal columnist tossed in their bits of fuel, charging that Stewart had deliberately injured Lach. As for Elmer himself, he declared that he had had it and would quit hockey. "I'll miss the game," he said, "and I'll have a lot of memories, both good and bad."

Even without Lach, *Les Canadiens*

extended the Red Wings to seven games before bowing out of the Cup round. Meanwhile, the Leafs, who had finished in fourth place, upset Boston in the other playoff round, dusting off the Bruins in five games. Thus, the finals again pitted Detroit and Toronto.

During the regular season, the Wings finished a full 18 points ahead of the Leafs. But when the Wings faced Toronto, they again disintegrated. The

Leafs swept Detroit in the finals for the second year in succession. They won Game One on an overtime goal by Joe Klukay, took Game Two on a hat trick by Sid Smith, and completed the sweep with a pair of 3-1 victories. The Leafs hoisted the Stanley Cup for the third year in a row.

Never before had a club won three straight Cups, and now there was talk of even a fourth.

CHAPTER 5

A DYNASTY IN MONTREAL

The Canadiens soar through the 1950s, reaching the Stanley Cup finals nine times.

Montreal's Flying Frenchmen included *(left to right)* Marcel Bonin, Bernie Geoffrion, Phil Goyette, Henri Richard, Dickie Moore, and Jean Beliveau. Rocket Richard retired late in the 1950s, but he passed the torch to his brother Henri *(above)*. Henri was known as the "Pocket Rocket."

THE 1950s

If, as many critics believe, a hockey dynasty is defined by a team winning three or more Stanley Cups in succession, then the Toronto Maple Leafs circa 1947-51 were the first dynasty in NHL history. Coached by Hap Day, the Leafs won four Cups in five years—and nearly won a fifth.

Managed by Jack Adams, the Red Wings appeared on the verge of their own dynasty. In addition to the feared Production Line, Adams's well-rounded squad featured Leonard "Red" Kelly, one of the most underrated virtuosos the game has known.

The early 1950s were marred by plunging attendance. The advent of television did not help the ice game. Thousands upon thousands of fans preferred to stay home and watch Milton Berle rather than go to an NHL game. The teams most severely hurt by the TV craze were the Bruins and Blackhawks. At one point, many feared that one or both would fold.

Despite these problems, hockey interest grew across the continent, and there was even an attempt to expand the NHL from six to seven teams. The proposed new squad was the Cleveland Barons, an eminently successful team in the American League. Barons owner Jim Hendy even received a tentative NHL approval. But at the 11th hour, a majority of owners led by Toronto boss Conn Smythe voted against Hendy's bid and Cleveland was rejected.

During the 1950s, the Montreal Canadiens amassed an amazing concentration of talent. They were so mighty that the NHL actually was forced to write a new rule to limit their power. Until the mid-1950s, teams could score as many goals as possible during a two-minute power play.

"There were times," said Ranger penalty-killer Aldo Guidolin, "when Montreal would get two or three goals on one power play and end the game then and there."

The NHL changed the power-play rule, stipulating that if a goal were scored on a power play, the offending player would be immediately released from the penalty box.

The antithesis of the mighty Canadiens were the impotent Blackhawks. The Hawks' malaise so worried league owners that they organized a "Help the Poor" campaign. Montreal sold top-flight forward Ed Litzenberger to Chicago, while Detroit allowed Tommy Ivan to move to the Blackhawks as general manager.

Ivan promptly reorganized the Blackhawks' farm system, and by the late 1950s it began sending young talent to the NHL—including Bobby Hull and Stan Mikita.

Meanwhile, no team could stop Montreal. The Toe Blake-led Canadiens won five straight Cups, from 1956-60. The question on everyone's lips at the start of the 1960s was quite simple: Could anyone beat the Canadiens?

Wings Tame the Turkey, Nip the Blueshirts

1949 - 50

Toronto's dynastic Maple Leafs knew they faced a challenge from the mighty Red Wings. Still, many believed that with a patch here and a patch there the Leafs would be able to win an unprecedented fourth straight Stanley Cup. There would be problems, to be sure, and the biggest was Turk Broda.

The corpulent goaltender celebrated his 35th birthday before the season, and many doubted that he still had the reflexes to handle the fast-paced brand of hockey of the 1950s.

At first, Broda allayed everyone's fears, and the Leafs marched into first place on November 1, 1949. But then a series of injuries decimated the lineup, and by November 30 the Leafs had gone six games without a win, tying only one match. It was then that manager Conn Smythe declared his classic "Battle of the Bulge."

"It's condition that's needed," said Smythe. "Nothing but condition. If it isn't Turk's fault, we'll find out whose it is."

Smythe demanded that his players

reduce their weight to specified limits. Broda, who weighed 197 pounds, was ordered to lop off seven pounds. To underline the seriousness of his offensive, Smythe promptly called up reserve goalie Gil Mayer from his Pittsburgh farm team. "We're starting Mayer in our next game," Smythe asserted, "and he'll stay in there even if the score is 500-1 against the Leafs— and I don't think it will be."

The calorie crusade's climactic moment came when, one by one, the penitent Leafs stepped on the scales

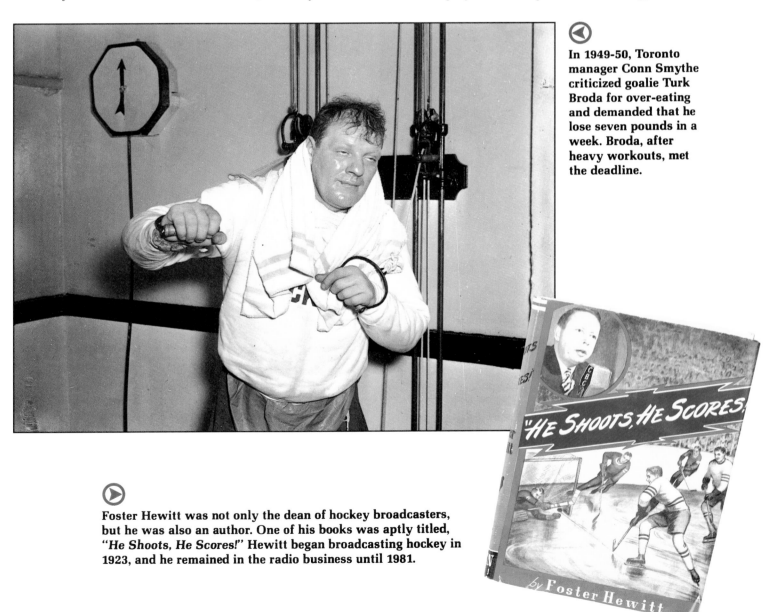

◀ In 1949-50, Toronto manager Conn Smythe criticized goalie Turk Broda for over-eating and demanded that he lose seven pounds in a week. Broda, after heavy workouts, met the deadline.

▶ Foster Hewitt was not only the dean of hockey broadcasters, but he was also an author. One of his books was aptly titled, "He Shoots, He Scores!" Hewitt began broadcasting hockey in 1923, and he remained in the radio business until 1981.

under Smythe's watchful eye. Harry Watson, Garth Boesch, Vic Lynn, Sid Smith, and Howie Meeker all weighed in under the limit. Finally, it was Broda's turn.

Turk moved forward and gingerly placed his feet on the platform. The numbers finally settled—just under 190 pounds. He made it! Turk was delighted, and Smythe was doubly enthusiastic because he regarded his goaltender with paternal affection. "There may be better goalies around somewhere," said the manager, "but there's no greater

sportsman than the Turkey. If the Rangers score on him tonight, I should walk out and hand him a malted milk, just to show I'm not trying to starve him to death." Broda responded with a 2-0 shutout over the Rangers.

The season also marked the fall-off of the Canadiens. First of all, stellar goalie Bill Durnan retired at age 35. Durnan's decision was reinforced by the Canadiens' dismal effort in the first round of the playoffs against New York's fourth-place Rangers. Durnan faltered behind a weakened defense, and

Rocket Richard was overshadowed by Pentti Lund of the Rangers.

The New Yorkers swept the first three games before Elmer Lach scored an overtime goal to temporarily save Montreal in the fourth match. In that same contest, Durnan was replaced by Gerry McNeil, who played well.

Irvin decided to go with McNeil again in the fifth game, which was scoreless until the fourth minute of the third period. Then the Rangers opened the floodgates and poured three goals past McNeil, winning the game 3-0.

One of the most popular defensemen in Toronto history was "Bashin'" Bill Barilko (center, white jersey). Barilko was notorious for his "snake hips" bodychecks. As for the Bruins, they finished below .500 in 1949-50 and wouldn't become a factor until the Bobby Orr era.

Gordie Howe's career almost ended in 1949-50 when he suffered a fractured skull in a playoff game against Toronto. Undaunted, Howe bounced back in 1950-51 to win the Hart Trophy. He would play another 30 years of pro hockey.

Referee Red Storey argues with Leaf defenseman Bill Juzda (white jersey) and Red Wing left wing Ted Lindsay. Lindsay spent 141 minutes in the box in 1949-50—a very high figure at that time.

Though he posted a less-than-spectacular 2.62 GAA in 1949-50, New York netminder Chuck Rayner took home the Hart Trophy. Rayner helped the Rangers to an upset win over Montreal in the opening round of the playoffs.

When it was over, Durnan sat on his dressing room bench, his eyes welled with tears. "Rangers," he kept repeating, "couldn't do anything wrong...couldn't do anything wrong."

The Leafs-Red Wings semifinals proved to be one of the bloodiest ever. Since Toronto's leading scorer, Smith, ranked only 15th in the league, it was remarkable that Toronto finished third in the regular-season race. Detroit, meanwhile, was powered by its eminent Production Line, which finished one-two-three in scoring. Ted Lindsay led the way (78 points, 23 goals), and he was followed by Sid Abel (69 points, 34 goals) and Gordie Howe (68 points, 35 goals).

The Detroit-Toronto rivalry, which was kindled in the mid-1930s by Jack Adams and Smythe, had since multiplied in its intensity. The vicious stick fight between Detroit's Jimmy Orlando and Toronto's Gaye Stewart, the 1942 and 1945 seven-game Cup finals, and, most recently, Toronto's 11 straight playoff wins over Detroit had fueled the burning resentment between the two clubs. On the opening game of their series, an atmosphere of imminent warfare hung over the ice at Olympia Stadium.

Game One saw Toronto compile a 4-0 lead midway through the third period. The fans assumed that the Wings had given up on this game and

TOMMY IVAN

Few non-players ever become incredibly successful NHL coaches and general managers, but Tommy Ivan was an exception. In 1947-48, Ivan made his NHL debut as a coach with the Detroit Red Wings, when Jack Adams relinquished the position to become the Wings' general manager. There, his teams won six straight NHL championships and three Stanley Cups (1950, 1952, 1954) in six years.

In 1954-55, Ivan left the winning Detroit team and took the general manager's job with the Chicago Blackhawks. From 1959 on, with Ivan as general manager, the Blackhawks qualified for the playoffs every year but one, and won the Stanley Cup for the first time in 23 years in 1960-61.

In 1966-67, the Hawks captured their first division title in their 40-year history, added another one three years later, and then won three successive division championships when they moved over to the West Division in 1970-71.

Retiring in 1977, Tommy remained with the Blackhawks as assistant to the president, devoting time to amateur hockey in the United States.

would calmly skate out the final minutes, conserving their energies (and their anger) for the second game. Indeed, they seemed to be playing it safe, as Toronto's Teeder Kennedy sidestepped his way across the Leafs blue line on another down-ice sweep.

But zeroing in from the right side was Howe, and it appeared that he would bump Teeder and throw him off balance. But Kennedy side-stepped Howe and Gordie missed him completely. In the process, Howe tumbled face-first into the thick,

wooden sideboards. Seconds later he was lying unconscious on the ice, his face covered with blood. As 13,659 fans sat, horror-struck, Gordie Howe, the young favorite, was carried off the ice on a stretcher and taken to a hospital with a fractured skull.

As far as Detroit's press and public were concerned, Howe had been lethally assaulted and somebody would have to pay for it. Toronto naturally denied responsibility for Howe's mishap, and the argument raged like a forest fire. Sports writers, coaches, and fans from

both sides kept pouring verbal gasoline on it to keep it going.

The Red Wings won Game Two in a fight-marred contest. Game Three at Maple Leaf Gardens was a calmer affair, as both teams played hockey according to the book. Toronto shut out the Wings 2-0. Detroit tied the series with a 2-1 victory in Game Four, but then the Leafs went ahead again, blanking the Wings 2-0 in Game Five. Now, facing elimination, Detroit stormed into Maple Leaf Gardens, still without Howe, and defeated the Leafs

Edgar Laprade was one of the Rangers' most creative centers. In 1949-50, he tallied 22 goals and 22 assists in just 60 games.

Detroit left wing Ted Lindsay led the league in scoring in 1949-50 with 78 points—including an NHL record 55 assists.

Detroit needed seven games to defeat Toronto in the 1950 semifinals. Here, the Detroit defense intercepts a Toronto attack.

Toronto nearly upset Detroit in the 1950 semis, but Ted Lindsay and the Wings captured Game Seven 1-0.

1949-50

Best Record
Detroit
(37-19-14)

Stanley Cup Finals
Detroit 4
New York 3

Art Ross Trophy
Ted Lindsay
(23/55/78)

Hart Trophy
Charlie Rayner
(2.62 GAA)

Vezina Trophy
Bill Durnan

Calder Trophy
Jack Gelineau

Lady Byng Trophy
Edgar Laprade

Fred Shero, the future Philadelphia Flyers coach, was a solid defenseman for the Rangers in 1949-50.

PETE BABANDO

Like Dusty Rhodes of baseball fame, Pete Babando was a journeyman who might never have achieved acclaim except that he came through, as did Rhodes, in a clutch situation.

Babando was a short, chunky skater who had played two seasons with the Bruins (1947-48, 1948-49). However, his shining moment came as a Red Wing at Olympia Stadium in Detroit on April 23, 1950. The Rangers and Wings were tied at three games apiece in the Stanley Cup finals, and the score of the final game was also tied 3-3. In the second overtime, Babando took a face-off pass from George Gee and beat New York goalie Chuck Rayner with a screened shot. Pete thus earned the greatest of all hockey nicknames, "Sudden Death," and became a national hero.

The Wings were not totally appreciative, though. They swapped Babando to the lowly Chicago Blackhawks the following season. He played two seasons in the Windy City before being traded, ironically, to the Rangers during the 1952-53 season, his last in the majors.

4-0. The seventh and decisive game moved to Detroit.

In the final game, the teams battled through three periods of regulation without a goal. Checking remained close through the opening eight minutes of the sudden-death overtime. Then, the Red Wings launched a dangerous rush only to have the play broken up. However, the Leafs couldn't quite get it out of their zone, and the puck bounced back to Wings defenseman Leo Reise Jr., who was standing near the blue line 60 feet from the goal.

Reise's shot went straight to the net, where Broda appeared to have the short side blocked with his skate, pad, and stick. But the puck bounced over Broda's stick and landed in the back of the net. Detroit won 1-0.

The final round between the Red Wings and the New York Rangers might have been anticlimactic, except that it too went into overtime in the seventh game. Detroit won on a sudden-death goal by Pete Babando, and thus copped the Stanley Cup. When the ancient silver mug was pushed out to center ice, to be claimed by the victorious Wings, Howe gingerly stepped onto the ice to the chants, "We want Howe! We want Howe!" He proudly placed his hands on the Stanley Cup, to the delight of the crowd.

Rangers goaltender Chuck Rayner's gallant efforts were rewarded when he won the Hart Trophy. Former collegian Jack Gelineau annexed the Calder Trophy, and Ranger center Edgar Laprade took the Lady Byng prize.

Though a controversial official in his early days, Frank Udvari eventually made the Hall of Fame.

Toronto Ices Habs
in Series of Sudden Deaths

1 9 5 0 - 5 1

In quest of a second straight Stanley Cup, Red Wings GM Jack Adams concluded a massive deal, sending playoff hero Pete Babando, Dan Morrison, defensemen Al Dewsbury and Black Jack Stewart, and goalie Harry Lumley to the Chicago Blackhawks. In exchange, the Wings received defenseman Bob Goldham, forwards Gaye Stewart and Metro Prystai, and goalie Sugar Jim Henry.

Some NHL critics were bothered by the deal, since the Norris family owned not just the Red Wings but also a good chunk of the Blackhawks. *New York Mirror* columnist Dan Parker referred to the NHL as the "Norris House League." The deal did nothing for Chicago, which remained a doormat, but the Red Wings turned Goldham into one of the league's best backliners. Also, Detroit's young Terry Sawchuk, promoted from the minors, emerged as one of the brightest young goalies since Chuck Rayner.

Regrouping from their upsetting playoff loss, the Maple Leafs also made goaltending news by elevating long, lean Al Rollins as understudy to veteran Turk Broda. Rollins was every bit as sensational as Sawchuk, and the Leafs appeared capable of regaining the Cup. Conversely, the Cup finalist Rangers nose-dived again, principally because playoff heroes Rayner and Edgar Laprade performed terribly in the opening month of the new season.

The Red Wings were relieved that sharpshooter Gordie Howe had

🔺 **New York's Frank Eddolls lies flat on the ice in a game against Toronto. The Leafs flattened a lot of opponents in 1950-51, as they went 41-16-13 and stormed to the Stanley Cup.**

recovered from his playoff brush with death and returned more vigorous—and nasty—than ever. Howe moved to the top of the scoring list, flashing 43 red lights and totaling 86 points. Howe's rise set off endless arguments between Detroit and Montreal factions over the question, "Who's better—Howe or Rocket Richard?" It also produced the single most intense player-vs.-player rivalry in league annals.

Richard continued to complain about, what he considered, overly close checking and poor refereeing. On one occasion, he encountered referee Hugh McLean in Manhattan's Picadilly Hotel, attacking the official before cooler heads intervened. NHL president Clarence Campbell fined Richard $500.

A bloodier confrontation involved Terrible Ted Lindsay of Detroit and Boston's Wild Bill Ezinicki. The pair battled in one of the NHL's most bitter slugfests. Ezinicki, cut by Lindsay's stick, needed more than 20 stitches to close the wound. Campbell fined each $300 and suspended them for three games.

Meanwhile, Toronto and Detroit battled for the top spot in the standings. By November 2, 1950, the Maple Leafs sat securely in first place and had gone nine games without a loss. The kids were coming through as manager Conn Smythe had hoped, and there were even a few surprises. The best surprise of all was the acquisition of an Irish forward named Tod Sloan. The Leafs had twice rejected him because of his small size, but he had given up smoking and gained 15 pounds.

Not only could Sloan score, but he was tough as well. One night, he

CHIEF ARMSTRONG

George "Chief" Armstrong, an Indian lad from Skead, Ontario, was chosen by Toronto Maple Leafs owner Conn Smythe to replace pivot man Syl Apps, who retired in April 1948. Tall and awkward, Armstrong earned a two-game trial with the Leafs in 1949-50 and played 20 NHL games with them in 1951-52. He then signed on as a regular.

It was clear, despite Armstrong's relentless improvement, that he'd never be another Apps, Max Bentley, or Ted Kennedy, the best of the NHL centers in the late 1940s, although he most resembled the latter. Like Kennedy, Armstrong was a plodding skater with a bland shot.

However, Armstrong played a persistent two-way game and eventually was named Leafs captain after Kennedy's retirement. When Punch Imlach took over as Toronto coach, Armstrong reached his apex as a player. During his captaincy, the Leafs won four Stanley Cups.

The Chief remained with Toronto throughout his career, ultimately retiring at the conclusion of the 1970-71 season after playing 1,187 games for the Maple Leafs. He then became coach of the Toronto Marlboros of the OHA Junior A League. In June 1975, he was elected to the Hockey Hall of Fame.

Detroit's Gordie Howe (left) and Boston's Johnny Peirson pose in their 1951 All-Star uniforms. On the year, Howe led the NHL in scoring (86 points).

The Leafs' 1951 Cup win was predicated on the play of Ted Kennedy (left) and Max Bentley (right), each of whom finished among the NHL's top six scorers.

crashed headlong into the boards during a game against the Red Wings and appeared to have broken his collarbone. Rink attendants unfolded a stretcher and dashed across the rink to take Sloan to the hospital. Just as they arrived at Tod's side, the young Leaf flipped himself over on his stomach and got to his knees. He shooed away the stretcher-bearers and skated, rubber-legged, toward the bench. When it came time for his line to take its next turn, Sloan was out there, apparently as fresh as a flower.

Though Joe Primeau replaced Hap Day as coach, the Leafs still were the most disliked team in the league. Opponents employed different methods of expressing their hostility to the surging Leafs, and Richard was one of them.

By coincidence one night, the Canadiens and the Leafs were on the same train, heading out of Toronto after Montreal had lost at Maple Leaf Gardens. Richard had been kept from scoring by Sid Smith, an industrious checker and team humorist. The next

morning, Smith and Richard wound up sitting next to each other in the Pullman diner. Richard got up and left long before Smith was finished, prompting a teammate to remark, "Rocket didn't take much notice of you, Smitty, did he?"

Smith laughed. "He didn't, eh? He upset my bowl of cereal as he went by!"

The Red Wings kept pace with the Maple Leafs and, ultimately, beat them out by six points (101-95). As a consolation, Toronto's goaltending combination of Rollins and Broda was

En route to their fourth Stanley Cup in five years, the Maple Leafs outfought the Bruins in the opening round of the 1951 playoffs. Toronto defeated Boston in five games.

After a blood-spilling collision, Boston's Pete Horeck stares at his nemesis, Toronto's Bill Barilko (5).

Former Toronto center Joe Primeau took over as coach of the Leafs in 1950-51 and promptly guided them to the Cup. The Leafs yielded the fewest goals in the league—just 138 in 70 games.

the league's premier tandem, allowing only 138 goals to Detroit's 139.

Rollins was knocked out of the first game of the playoffs against Boston, as he was charged by Bruin forward Pete Horeck. But old reliable Broda needed only two games to regain his old playoff form. After Game Two ended at curfew tied at 1-1, Broda shut out the Bruins 3-0 and beat them in Boston 3-1. Toronto won the series with 4-1 and 6-0 victories. Meanwhile, the Canadiens upset the defending Cup champion Red Wings to qualify for the finals.

On the eve of their opening battle, Smythe's former aide, Frank Selke, remarked: "I hope this series will be as clean and sporting as ours with Detroit, but unfortunately I doubt it."

The first two games were in Toronto and both ended in overtime. The Leafs' Smith was the hero in Game One,

while the Canadiens' Richard netted an overtime goal in Game Two. Incredibly, Games Three and Four in Montreal also went into sudden-death overtime! Toronto scored in O.T. in both games at the Forum to take a commanding three-games-to-one lead in the series.

As the teams prepared for the fifth game of the series at Maple Leaf Gardens, experts wondered if a fifth overtime game could be possible. It was. Toronto's Sloan pushed a rebound shot past Canadien goalie Gerry McNeil with only 0:32 remaining in regulation to send yet another game into sudden-death.

This time, Toronto's Bill Barilko played the hero role, as he slipped a shot past McNeil early in the extra session to clinch yet another Stanley Cup for the Maple Leafs.

BARILKO TRAGEDY

Bill Barilko died at the height of his career in a plane crash. Ironically, the tragedy came just after he had scored the winning goal in sudden-death overtime to clinch the Stanley Cup for the Toronto Maple Leafs in April 1951.

Although Barilko never was an All-Star, he had gained total respect around the National Hockey League for his fearsome "snake-hip" bodychecks. He was also known for his ability to block dangerous enemy shots on goal along with his partner Garth Boesch.

Barilko became a Maple Leaf during the 1946-47 season, elevated from the Hollywood Wolves of the Pacific Coast League. It was no coincidence that he played on four Stanley Cup championship teams in his five years in the NHL. Barilko was a mere 24 years old at the time of his death.

All five of the 1951 Stanley Cup games were decided by one goal. Here, Toronto's Danny Lewicki tries to snap a shot past Montreal goalie Gerry McNeil.

A falling Bill Barilko wins the 1951 Stanley Cup with an overtime goal in Game Five. The puck flies over the shoulder of Montreal goalie Gerry McNeil.

Hypnotist Can't Help Rangers;
Howe's Wings Win Cup

1 9 5 1 - 5 2

By this time, a pair of patterns had been established, one at each end of the standings. Detroit had established a vigorous machine that reached the 100-point mark for the second year in a row. On the other end, the Rangers and Blackhawks again missed the playoffs.

The Chicago situation was critical because attendance was slipping throughout the league, especially in Boston and the Windy City. As for the Rangers, their following was still big

but so were the losses. At one point, GM Frank Boucher approved the hiring of a hypnotist, Dr. David Tracy, to help his players. Another time, the Blueshirts tried a "magic elixir" prepared by restaurateur Gene Leone, but the Rangers still faltered.

While the Maple Leafs managed to stay above .500 (29-25-16), they were not nearly as effective without defenseman Bill Barilko, who perished in a Northern Ontario plane crash

during the summer. Barilko's replacement, Hugh Bolton, lacked the vitality of "Bashin' Bill" and it carried through the team.

The question, "Who's better—Richard or Howe?" was temporarily shelved, as an injured Rocket scored 44 points in only 48 games. Howe, on the other hand, ran away with the scoring race. He finished with 86 points (including 47 goals), exactly as he had a year earlier.

In a publicity stunt, hypnotist David Tracy tries to persuade the lowly Rangers that they can beat the Bruins. Dr. Tracy works on *(left to right)* Tony Leswick, Ed Slowinski, Chuck Rayner, and Edgar Laprade.

Few thought it possible for Detroit's Terry Sawchuk to improve on his outstanding goaltending, but the crouching, crew-cutted netminder lowered his goals-against average from 1.99 to 1.90. He also posted 12 shutouts, one better than the previous year. Howe and Sawchuk powered Detroit to a 44-14-12 record—22 points better than second-place Montreal.

Despite Richard's prolonged absence, the Canadiens were enjoying the fruits of Frank Selke Sr.'s rebuilt farm system. Among the outstanding new recruits was right wing Bernie Geoffrion, whose shot was so hard he was nicknamed "Boom Boom." Then there was another Montreal product, Dickie Moore, a precocious left wing who could hit as well as score.

Montreal faced off against Boston in the opening playoff round, which went a full seven games. In the last match, Richard scored one of the most spectacular goals in playoff history. Ironically, Richard was knocked nearly unconscious early in the final game, but he somehow managed to skate onto the ice in the third period.

Only four minutes remained in the 1-1 contest when Bruin veteran Woody Dumart carried the puck toward the Canadiens zone. Montreal's Butch Bouchard thrust out his stick, jabbing the puck away from Dumart. The puck was then captured by Richard. The Rocket wheeled around Dumart like a speeding car skirting a disabled auto on the highway. First he reeled to center and then cut sharply to the right, jabbing the puck ahead of him with short pokes.

BILL MOSIENKO

Bill Mosienko was an integral part of Chicago's renowned "Pony Line" with Max and Doug Bentley. A speedy winger, Mosienko carved his niche in the record books on March 23, 1952, when he scored three goals in 21 seconds against the New York Rangers at Madison Square Garden.

Actually, Mosienko's lightning-like moves were evident before and after that memorable game. He came to the Blackhawks at training camp for the 1940-41 season, a frail but promising 19-year-old. At first, Mosienko was farmed out to Providence and then Kansas City, but eventually he was recalled and put on a line with the Bentleys. Dubbed the Pony Line because of the small, coltish moves of the three skaters, the unit ultimately became one of the most exciting in Chicago's history.

Mosienko remained a Blackhawk from 1941-42 until his retirement following the 1954-55 season. He never played on a Stanley Cup winner nor a first-place team, but he collected a creditable 258 goals and 540 points in 711 NHL games. It is likely his three goals in 21 seconds will never be equaled in the NHL.

The 1951-52 Red Wings won all eight of their playoff games. Gordie Howe *(top row, sixth from right)* won the Hart and Art Ross Trophies, while Terry Sawchuk *(front row, far left)* took the Vezina.

After winning the Cup in his debut season, Toronto coach Joe Primeau *(standing)* fell to 29-25-16 in 1951-52. The off-season death of star defenseman Bill Barilko severely hurt the team.

On March 23, 1952, Chicago's Bill Mosienko scored three goals in 21 seconds. The three pucks are pictured below.

Bill Quackenbush, one of the most experienced and intelligent defensemen in the NHL, skated backward on the Bruin defense, prepared to meet the ominous challenge. Richard was now in full flight, his eyes blazing madly, his destination known to all. Quackenbush was traveling at about ten miles per hour in reverse when Richard bore down on him at more than twice that speed. Quackenbush hurled his black-shirted body at Richard, but it was as if he were checking a phantom.

Still, Quackenbush seemed to have done his job quite well, for he had forced Richard to take so circuitous a route along the right side that the Rocket appeared to have taken himself right out of the play.

A right-handed shooter playing right wing would have been cradling the puck too far to his right to release a threatening drive, but Richard, the anomaly, was a left-handed shot. Thus, the puck was on his left side, closer to the net, as he barreled past the flailing Quackenbush. Goalie Sugar Jim Henry, both eyes blackened from previous injuries and barely recovered from a broken nose, guarded the right corner of the net, allowing Richard nothing but the "impossible-angle" shot to the far left corner.

Almost atop Henry's bulky goal pads, Richard finally released his drive. It was low and hard and Henry never managed to touch, let alone see, the puck. "One minute I was facing him, waiting for the shot," said the Boston goalie, "the next he had whizzed by and the puck was in the net."

Art Chapman, manager of the Buffalo hockey club, was watching from the press box and simply stood mouth agape after the red light flashed. "Only Richard could score like that," he said later. The miraculous shot provided *Les Canadiens* with the winning goal, and Montreal marched onto the finals.

Up until the Stanley Cup playoffs of 1952, no team in NHL history had ever swept through the semifinal and final series without losing a game. But the 1951-52 Detroit Red Wings were something very special. If any team appeared capable of accomplishing the impossible, it was this year's Motor City sextet.

Montreal's Doug Harvey (right) emerged as a standout defenseman in 1951-52. Here, he prepares a counter-attack after a Toronto drive at goalie Gerry McNeil.

Boston's Jim Henry fends off Toronto's Max Bentley (left) and Danny Lewicki (21). Henry posted seven shutouts in 1951-52.

An injury curtailed Maurice Richard in 1951-52, but he came back strong in the playoffs. Richard netted an unforgettable goal to beat Boston in Round One.

 In 1951-52, Toronto's Al Rollins won the starting goalie spot and was runner-up for the Vezina. Nevertheless, Rollins platooned in the playoffs with Turk Broda.

 Veteran Woody Dumart (right) chats with a young Boston teammate. Dumart helped the Bruins to the 1952 playoffs, but they fell in the first round to Montreal and the heroics of Rocket Richard.

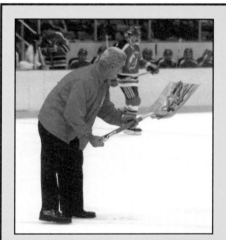

Toronto seemed to have the best chance at taming the Detroiters. During the regular season, the Leafs enjoyed more success against the Wings than any other club, winning four and tying four in 14 games. However, Detroit blanked Toronto 3-0 in the opening game, in which 102 penalty minutes were called. The Leafs were carrying two goaltenders at the time. When Al Rollins lost the first game, the Leafs decided to try veteran Turk Broda in Game Two at Detroit.

Broda had long been regarded as the finest clutch playoff goalie in NHL history, and the one man capable of thwarting the Red Wings. The 37-year-old Turk turned away all but one of the Wings' shots. However, Toronto wasn't able to find the answer to Sawchuk and lost the game 1-0.

The Leafs' hopes were falsely buoyed by the close contest, and they returned to friendly Maple Leaf Gardens for the third and fourth games of the series. Broda was in the nets again, but this time the Red Wings so outclassed Toronto that they left 12-year-old Barbara Broda weeping in the stands, as six goals poured past her beleaguered father.

Rollins replaced Broda in the fourth game, and the Leafs fought as hard as they could. Nevertheless, the Red Wing juggernaut was just too strong and Detroit won the game 3-1, sweeping the series in four straight games.

Montreal was ready for the Red Wing challenge. "We will have the Cup

1951-52

Best Record
Detroit
(44-14-12)

Stanley Cup Finals
Detroit 4
Montreal 0

Art Ross Trophy
Gordie Howe
(47/39/86)

Hart Trophy
Gordie Howe

Vezina Trophy
Terry Sawchuk

Calder Trophy
Bernie Geoffrion

Lady Byng Trophy
Sid Smith

by the 19th of April," predicted Montreal coach Dick Irvin. "Remember that, boys." Instead, Irvin's Canadiens lost four straight games, scoring only two goals in the series and suffering two shutouts at the hands of Sawchuk. The Red Wings had captured the Stanley Cup in an incredible eight-game sweep, the first NHL team to ever accomplish that feat.

OCTOPUS ON ICE

Pete Cusimano and his brother Jerry were diehard Detroit Red Wing fans. During the 1952 playoffs, the Wings were hot—they had already won seven consecutive contests—and the two brothers felt that some symbolic sacrifice was in order.

"My dad was in the fish and poultry business," Pete explained. "Anyway, before the eighth game in '52, my brother suggested, 'Why don't we throw an octopus on the ice for good luck? It's got eight legs and that might be a good omen for eight straight wins.'" It was a stroke of pure genius.

April 15, 1952 marked the first time Pete Cusimano heaved a half-boiled denizen of the deep over the protective glass and onto the ice of Olympia Stadium. With one loud splat, the fate of the Wings' opponents was sealed. Yes, hockey fans, Detroit won the Cup in 1952 and Cusimano, knowing a good thing when he saw one, continued to sling the slimy creatures in every Detroit playoff series for the next 15 years.

"You ever smelt a half-boiled octopus?" asked Pete. "It ain't exactly Chanel No. 5, ya know." And with a maniacal gleam in his eye, he added, "You should see how the refs jumped!"

Boom Boom's Slapshot, Jacques the Roamer Spark Habs

1 9 5 2 - 5 3

It seemed the powerful Red Wings would be a lock for first place in 1952-53. After all, Gordie Howe was still improving and, at last, would take aim at Rocket Richard's hitherto unreachable 50 goal mark. Detroit's only setback was the departure of captain Sid Abel to become player/coach of the Blackhawks. But Abel's replacement on the Production Line, Alex Delvecchio, fit in naturally between Howe and Ted Lindsay.

By far the most remarkable achievement was Abel's, since he inherited an enfeebled Chicago sextet and managed to lead the Blackhawks to a third-place tie. Abel's trump card was goalie Al Rollins, who performed brilliantly. Rollins would win the Hart Trophy a year later.

The desperate Rangers watched former All-Star goalie Chuck Rayner physically disintegrate, and finally elevated young Lorne "Gump" Worsley as his replacement. The Gump played well enough to win the Calder Trophy with a 3.06 goals-against average.

A major development in the 1952-53 season was Bernie Geoffrion's perfection of the slapshot. Previously,

The 1952-53 Blackhawks surprised everyone by making the playoffs. Credit belonged to goalie Al Rollins (*left*) and new player/coach Sid Abel (*right*).

By the 1950s, Clarence Campbell had become well established as NHL president and well liked enough to inspire this cartoon.

In 1952-53, Bernie Geoffrion (*center*) perfected the slapshot. Geoffrion's shot was so ferociously loud that he was given the nickname "Boom Boom."

the puck was propelled in two basic maneuvers—the wrist shot and the backhand shot. In delivering the wrist shot, the attacker cradled the puck at the stick blade and then snapped his wrists, sending the rubber goalward. The backhand shot was fired from the shooter's opposite side and projected from the heel of the blade.

Geoffrion took a leaf from the golfing book. Instead of nursing the puck at the edge of his stick, Boom Boom drew his stick back, as a golfer would, and then blasted away. For want of a better name, hockey writers called it the "slapshot."

What it lacked in accuracy, the slapshot made up for in velocity and intimidation. More importantly, Geoffrion emerged as one of the game's best scorers and, as a result, others began copying him. Andy Bathgate of the Rangers and Bobby Hull of the Blackhawks were among the more successful slapshot adapters, although their impact would not be felt until the 1960s.

Montreal's kids continued to mature, but veterans like Richard and Elmer Lach still generated a number of wins. Although Elmer had vowed to retire a few seasons earlier, he appeared at the 1952-53 training camp with the same vim and vigor he had displayed as a rookie, and he continued to excel as the campaign got under way.

DICKIE MOORE

When the Montreal Canadiens were building one of the best hockey clubs of all time during the early 1950s, Richard Winston "Dickie" Moore was among the most gifted young players signed by the Montreal brass.

Brash to a fault, Moore was at first considered uncontrollable. But the combination of tough coach Dick Irvin and veterans such as Maurice Richard and Doug Harvey settled Dickie into a calmer, more manageable player. The results were sensational.

Dickie was placed on a line with young Henri Richard at center and Maurice Richard on right wing, and it became one of the best the NHL has known. Moore won the scoring championship in 1958 and 1959. He was lionized for playing the second half of the 1958-59 season while wearing a cast on a broken hand, yet he still managed to capture the scoring title.

In 1967-68, Moore signed with the brand-new St. Louis Blues. He played in only 27 regular-season games alongside his old Canadien crony, Doug Harvey, and helped steer the Blues into the playoffs. Moore was absolutely stupendous in the playoffs, old legs and all. He totaled seven goals and seven assists in 18 games, leading the expansion Blues to the Stanley Cup finals. In June 1974, Dickie Moore was inducted into the Hockey Hall of Fame.

The 1952-53 Rangers featured goalie Lorne "Gump" Worsley, who won the Calder. Worsley resembled comic strip character Andy Gump.

On Saturday night, November 8, 1952, the Blackhawks were playing the Canadiens at the Forum when Lach scored his 200th NHL goal. Not surprisingly, it was the Rocket who had fed him the lead pass and it was Richard who was the first to congratulate his old buddy. "Keep piling up the points," kidded Maurice, "but keep away from those fractures."

The partisan crowd lustily cheered the pair, but they were more anxious to see the Rocket score. After all, his next goal would be No. 325 and would break the NHL record held by Nels Stewart. Only 30 seconds after Lach's historic score, the Rocket throttled past the Blackhawk defense and

reached his newest plateau. This time, it was Lach who did the congratulating and the needling. "Nice going, Rocket," he laughed, "and no more broken bones, please!"

Canadiens goalie Gerry McNeil had proven an adequate replacement for Bill Durnan, but coach Dick Irvin was not persuaded that McNeil was the answer. His doubts remained until the playoffs when he made a significant—call it a landmark—change in goal. In the first playoff round, Montreal faced Chicago and fell behind three games to two with McNeil in net. Irvin decided to dump McNeil and put young Jacques Plante in goal.

Plante, a cocky youngster, fashioned

a bizarre goaltending style that would soon be copied by other netminders around the league. Plante often roamed out of his cage to retrieve pucks that had caromed off the boards and skidded behind the net. By so doing, Plante was able to control the puck and pass it to a teammate, while scrambling back to his goal crease before any shots were taken. Though effective, Plante's approach had been considered taboo.

For Plante to experiment with the Canadiens in the playoffs was something else! But Irvin had made a commitment, and Plante was his goalie. "Jacques the Roamer" immediately went into the cage and

Boston's Sugar Jim Henry doesn't blink as a Toronto shot ricochets off his chest. It would be another seven years before NHL goalies started wearing masks.

 One of Toronto's most productive scorers in the 1950s was forward Sid Smith (right). In the first six years of the '50s, Smith was good for a minimum of 20 goals and a maximum of 33.

1952-53

Best Record
Detroit
(36-16-18)

Stanley Cup Finals
Montreal 4
Boston 1

Art Ross Trophy
Gordie Howe
(49/46/95)

Hart Trophy
Gordie Howe

Vezina Trophy
Terry Sawchuk

Calder Trophy
Lorne Worsley

Lady Byng Trophy
Red Kelly

stopped the Blackhawks cold. He foiled a breakaway early in the fifth game, sparking the Canadiens to two straight wins and a spot in the finals.

The Red Wings had little trouble finishing first again, as their 90 points were 15 better than runner-up Montreal's. Howe totaled 49 goals and had 46 assists for a league-leading 95 points in 70 games. Richard finished with 28 goals and 61 points in 70 games. Howe won his third straight scoring title—an NHL first. Likewise, Detroit's fifth straight first-place finish also set a league mark.

Adding to Detroit's laurels, Howe won the Hart Trophy for the second straight year, while defenseman Red Kelly took the Lady Byng. Howe and

Lindsay also made the First All-Star Team for the third straight year. With all those kudos, it was expected that Detroit easily would take the Stanley Cup again.

However, the Red Wings were stunned by the Bruins in a four-games-to-two upset in the semifinal round. Boston had thus qualified to meet Montreal for the Stanley Cup. After building up a 3-1 lead in games, *Les Canadiens* clinched the Cup in overtime of Game Five. The Rocket passed the puck to Lach with the score tied 0-0, and Elmer converted the pass for a goal. The Canadiens were Stanley Cup champions for the first time in seven years.

HARRY LUMLEY

Harry Lumley, an outstanding goalkeeper who labored for 16 years in the NHL as one of the stingiest netminders around, had an inauspicious NHL debut. In a two-game trial with the Detroit Red Wings, Lumley allowed 13 pucks to elude his flailing limbs.

Looking back on that embarrassing goal splurge, one can forgive Lumley if he was a bit awed by it all, since the netminder was only 17 years old at the time.

Harry matured, though, into one of the NHL's most proficient puck-stoppers. He remained with the Wings for six more seasons, guiding them into the playoffs each year and sipping Stanley Cup champagne in 1949-50, his last campaign with the Wings.

However, it was in Toronto that Lumley enjoyed his best years as a pro, leading the NHL in shutouts for two consecutive seasons. Lumley copped the Vezina Trophy in 1953-54 with an amazing 1.85 goals-against average in 69 games.

▲ **In 1952-53, Gordie Howe set an NHL record with 95 points. Here, though, he fires one right into the chest of Toronto goalie Harry Lumley.**

▼ **Chicago's Al Rollins makes a sprawling save against New York's Wally Hergesheimer (18). The little-known Hergesheimer scored 59 points in 1952-53.**

▼ **Montreal rookie Jacques Plante made his mark in the 1953 playoffs. Plante surprised everyone with his tendency to wander outside the crease.**

Wings Edge Canadiens on Leswick's O.T. Tally

1 9 5 3 - 5 4

One of the strangest NHL turnabouts occurred at the very start of the 1953-54 campaign. The Rangers dropped 1952-53 Calder Trophy winner Lorne "Gump" Worsley to the minors and replaced him with long-time minor-leaguer Johnny Bower. In an equally startling move, Rangers general manager Frank Boucher signed ex-Toronto center Max Bentley and assigned him as point man on the power play.

Still another arresting Boucher move involved the signing of fragile Camille "The Eel" Henry. Like Bentley, Henry was hired as a part-timer, working exclusively on the power play. Still, many warned Boucher that the 135-pound Henry would be terribly battered by his larger foes.

But Boucher's gambles soon paid dividends. Bentley still displayed flashes of greatness, while the crafty and elusive Henry confounded opponents with his slithering moves. As for Bower, his years of experience paid off in the bigs; he proved the equal of Terry Sawchuk and other top NHL goalies, finishing with a remarkable 2.60 goals-against average.

The Rangers were competitive for a change, but they couldn't keep pace with the Red Wings, who rebounded smartly from their playoff humiliation. Gordie Howe remained king among forwards, taking a record fourth straight scoring title with 81 points. He again was abetted by left wing Ted Lindsay and center Alex Delvecchio. For the fourth straight year, Lindsay and Howe made

the First All-Star Team.

Sid Abel was unable to keep the Blackhawks afloat in his second year, although he received extraordinary goaltending from Al Rollins. Normally, a player on a cellar-dwelling team is ignored in postseason balloting, but Rollins was awarded the Hart Trophy at season's end. The Blackhawks were goners early on, but Toronto, Boston, New York, and Montreal maintained a lively battle for a playoff berth. In time, the Canadiens and Leafs moved up, while the Bruins and Rangers battled for fourth.

Boucher tried one last ploy to gain an advantage over Boston. In midseason, he persuaded Doug Bentley, Max's older brother and former partner on the Blackhawks, to try an NHL comeback

after being retired for more than two years. Doug rejoined Max on the night of January 21, 1954, at Madison Square Garden. The Rangers were scheduled to face the fourth-place Bruins, whom they trailed by two points.

Shortly before game time, Boucher decided to place Doug on left wing—his normal position—with Max at center, and Edgar Laprade on right wing. Laprade, who was normally a center, had been one of the smoothest, most adroit centers in Rangers history in his prime. But he too had aged, had even retired, and, at age 35, was persuaded to skate once more by Boucher. Many Ranger fans were skeptical about Laprade's ability to adjust to his right wing position while skating with the unpredictable Bentleys.

But nobody was as uncertain as Doug Bentley. As he sat nervously twitching his legs in the dressing room before the opening face-off, Doug wondered why he had ever permitted Boucher to talk him into this crazy stunt. "I was afraid I'd make a fool of myself," the elder Bentley recalled.

Referee Frank Udvari dropped the puck for the opening face-off. Just as quickly, Doug's doubts disappeared. "It seemed," he reflected years later, "that every time we touched the puck we did the right thing."

Doug scored the first goal at 12:29 of the first period on a pass from defenseman Jack Evans. At 15:44, Max set up Wally Hergesheimer for a power-play goal against Bruins goalie Sugar Jim Henry. Then Doug fed Paul Ronty, who gave New York a 3-0 lead. By this time, the crowd knew that they were seeing a re-creation of the Bentley brothers of yesteryear—only the jerseys were different.

In the third period, the Bentleys continued to tantalize the Garden crowd and the Boston netminder. Max received a pass from Laprade and was moving on a direct line for the right goalpost. Laprade, meanwhile, had burst ahead on a direct line for the left goalpost, ready for a return pass. Goalie Henry expected Max to relay the puck back to Laprade, and so Henry began edging toward Laprade's side of the net. Meanwhile, Max faked and faked and faked the pass, but continued to move

TERRY SAWCHUK

One of the greatest and most tragic players of all time was Terry Sawchuk. Quite possibly, Terry was the game's best goaltender, but he was a moody, brooding figure who was a physical and mental wreck of a man when he met his untimely death in 1970.

Terry broke in with Detroit in 1950, making the First All-Star Team during his maiden season and copping the Calder Trophy. Incredibly, his goals-against average never topped 2.00 during his first five years with Detroit, a stretch that saw him rack up 56 shutouts. He finished his up-and-down career with an NHL record 103 shutouts.

Sawchuk's early years were great ones, but he insisted that his finest moment came with the 1966-67 Toronto Maple Leafs, when he dramatically guided the Leafs to an upset Stanley Cup victory.

It was said of Sawchuk that he wasn't a whole man; rather, he was stitched together—held in place by catgut and surgical tape. He suffered a painful shoulder injury early in his career that forever prevented him from lifting his stick hand higher than chest level.

An enigmatic, bitter man to the end, Terry died as a result of injuries received in a scuffle with teammate Ron Stewart on the lawn of his Long Island home.

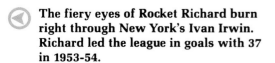

Howie Meeker cuts in on the Chicago goal only to be stopped by Al Rollins. Even though Chicago yielded 62 more goals than any other team in the NHL in 1953-54, Rollins won the Hart Trophy.

The fiery eyes of Rocket Richard burn right through New York's Ivan Irwin. Richard led the league in goals with 37 in 1953-54.

The James Norris Memorial Trophy, awarded to the NHL's top defenseman, debuted in 1953-54.

toward the goal. Without ever shooting the rubber, he calmly skated the puck into the right corner of the net while Henry stood there mesmerized. The audience went wild. "It was like a dream," Doug recalled.

The final score was 8-3 for New York. Max and Doug had combined for a total of eight points between them—Doug tallied one goal and three assists, while Max notched two goals and two assists. It was the brothers' most productive evening since 1942, when they were in their prime with the Blackhawks.

The stirring win appeared to galvanize the Rangers toward a fourth-place finish, but Max and Doug tired in the stretch and neither Bower nor Camille Henry could keep the Rangers afloat. Boston passed New York and finished fourth—six points ahead of the Rangers.

The Toronto Maple Leafs benefited from Harry Lumley's stellar goaltending. The former Red Wing and Blackhawk set an NHL mark with 13 shutouts and won the Vezina Trophy. Defense became more respectable than

ever with the striking of a new piece of silverware. The James Norris Trophy was now awarded to the league's best backliner. Detroit's Red Kelly was the first recipient of the prize. He also annexed the Lady Byng for the third time in four years.

By the time the dust had cleared at regular season's end, Detroit had skated away with an unreal sixth straight first-place finish. Impressive as it was, the title left Motor City hockey fans somewhat skeptical after the previous spring's debacle. Howe & Co. had something to prove, and it would happen in the playoffs to come.

Montreal's hopes for upsetting Detroit rested with veteran Rocket Richard, Boom Boom Geoffrion, Dickie Moore, and a majestic newcomer named Jean Beliveau. Doug Harvey anchored the defense, while Jacques Plante and Gerry McNeil alternated in goal.

Boston's chances were encouraged by the Bruins' 32 wins, the largest number totaled by a Bruins team since 1938-39. The line of Fleming Mackell, Ed Sandford, and John Peirson

spearheaded the Beantown attack, while Jim Henry continued to sparkle in goal.

The Leafs, who finished three points ahead of Boston, were starved for goals, and despite their third-place finish, wound up with the second worst goal total in the league (152). Tod Sloan, with only 11 goals and 43 points, was the Leafs' leading scorer.

Detroit opened the playoffs against the Leafs and, as if the Motor City sextet wasn't strong enough, coach Tommy Ivan added young Earl "Dutch" Reibel. During the season, Reibel notched 15 goals and 33 assists for Detroit. Reibel was so good he frequently spelled Delvecchio on the Production Line.

The Red Wings flexed their muscles in the opening game, whipping Toronto 5-0 at Olympia Stadium. The Leafs rebounded for a 3-1 comeback at Detroit, but lost the next two at Maple Leaf Gardens, 3-1 and 2-1. The Wings wrapped up the series with a 4-3 overtime win at Olympia. Meanwhile, the Canadiens obliterated Boston,

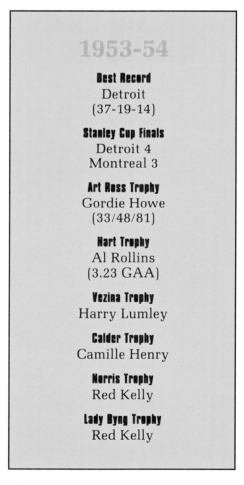

▲ **A surprise Rangers star in 1953-54 was goalie Johnny Bower, who replaced Gump Worsley between the pipes. Bower posted a respectable 2.60 goals-against average despite playing on a weak team.**

◄ **Toronto's Ted Kennedy receives well-wishes from a Leaf rooter. Though only age 29 in 1953-54, Kennedy was an 11-year vet and near the end of his career.**

outscoring the Bruins 16-4, to reach the finals against the hated Detroiters.

The Habs now had the luxury of two accomplished goalies, Plante and McNeil. Coach Dick Irvin decided to go with the younger Plante in the opener of the finals at Olympia. The score was tied 1-1 going into the third period when Reibel beat Plante at 1:52. Detroit skated to a 3-1 victory. Undaunted, the Habs rebounded for a 3-1 win of their own in Game Two, as Richard scored a pair of goals in the first period, including the game-winner at 15:28.

When the series shifted to Montreal's Forum, the Habs defense disintegrated. In Game Three, Detroit ran up a 3-0 lead after two periods and breezed to a 5-2 triumph. When the Red Wings took the fourth game 2-0, Irvin decided to change goalies. He yanked Plante for Game Five at Olympia and started McNeil instead. McNeil responded by blanking the Detroiters after three periods, though Montreal didn't score either. Finally, at 5:45 of the first sudden-death period,

veteran Ken Mosdell beat Sawchuk and the Habs stayed alive.

In Game Six at the Forum, the Canadiens jumped all over Detroit with three goals in the second period—two by Floyd "Busher" Curry—en route to a 4-1 victory. The series went down to a seventh game in Detroit.

As finales go, the decisive match at Detroit was a gem. Curry pushed the Habs into the lead with a goal at 9:17 of the first period. McNeil held the lead until Kelly beat him at 1:17 of the second. Nobody scored in the third period.

The overtime loomed long and intense but, as so often happens in hockey, a mistake won a championship. Early in the first overtime, Red Wing forward "Tough" Tony Leswick looped an easily stoppable shot at McNeil. The Canadiens goalie had the drive lined up for a simple glove save, but at the last moment defenseman Harvey—standing in front of the goalie—attempted to swat the puck harmlessly into the corner.

Unfortunately for the unlucky McNeil (remember the sudden-death goal he blew to Bill Barilko to lose the 1951 Cup to Toronto), Harvey only got a piece of the puck. The rubber deflected off his glove, over McNeil, and into the net at 4:29 of overtime. Detroit won the championship game 2-1.

BOOM BOOM GEOFFRION

Nicknamed "Boom Boom" because of the reverberation of his stick hitting the puck and the puck hitting the endboards (although it often went directly into the net), Montreal's Bernie Geoffrion had many of the incendiary qualities of Maurice "Rocket" Richard.

Geoffrion shined in the first game of his first full season. Boom Boom opened the 1951-52 campaign with two goals against Chicago in a 4-2 Montreal victory. He went on to win the Calder Trophy, and also established himself as the newest Canadiens hero.

During the 1954-55 season, Geoffrion became the center of controversy in the last week of the schedule. It came after teammate Richard was suspended for the remainder of the season by NHL President Clarence Campbell.

Richard was leading the league in scoring at the time and appeared certain to win his first points title. But once the Rocket was suspended, Geoffrion—despite the wishes of Rocket fans—moved ahead of Richard, winning his first scoring championship.

As a result of the triumph, Geoffrion was vilified for several years by his hometown fans. However, he continued to play superbly and won the scoring championship and the Hart Trophy in 1961. In his career, Geoffrion scored 393 goals. On August 24, 1972, he was inducted into the Hockey Hall of Fame.

Chicago's Gus Bodnar (left) and Toronto's Ted Kennedy prepare for a ceremonial face-off at Maple Leaf Gardens. The referee is Bill Chadwick, who officiated with only one good eye.

Montreal's Maurice Richard (center) remained the NHL's most feared shooter in 1953-54. He was particularly successful against the Maple Leafs, whom he hated with a passion.

Rocket's Suspension Triggers Riot in Montreal

1954-55

Stopping the Red Wings juggernaut would not be easy, but the Canadiens had proven they could take the Detroiters, given a break or two here or there. In addition to veterans Maurice Richard, Floyd Curry, Butch Bouchard, and Ken Mosdell, the Montrealers had a mighty nucleus of young stars. Jean Beliveau seemed capable of someday matching Gordie Howe, while Boom Boom Geoffrion and Dickie Moore already had established themselves among the league's most threatening scorers.

Goalie Gerry McNeil retired after the 1953-54 playoff loss, but Jacques Plante appeared ready for full-time duty.

Besides, the Habs had a promising alternate in little Charlie Hodge.

The Red Wings made one significant change—Tommy Ivan relinquished the coaching to Jimmy Skinner. The Red Wings didn't miss a beat and, in fact, improved on their performance of the previous year. Terry Sawchuk was back in goal with Glenn Hall in reserve on the farm. The Production Line was still intact, and Detroit's defense of Red Kelly, Marcel Pronovost, and Benny Woit looked as formidable as ever.

As expected, the Canadiens pursued the Red Wings with zeal, leaving the rest of the pack far behind. The Maple

Leafs, with gregarious King Clancy behind the bench, had more laughs than victories and managed to finish the season at exactly .500 (24-24-22). Sid Smith starred for the Leafs, totaling 33 goals and 54 points. Conn Smythe's toughest enforcer was the turbulent Bob Bailey, a right wing who took particular delight in antagonizing superstars like Richard.

Bailey and Richard battled several times, but one of the most severe clashes caused referee Red Storey to dispatch the Rocket to the dressing room. Before leaving for the showers, the Rocket wheeled in his tracks and accosted Storey with an assortment of epithets.

Montreal captain Butch Bouchard (*left*) wraps his arm around Rocket Richard. Richard nearly won his first scoring title in 1954-55, but a late-season suspension cost him the chance.

For the second straight year, Toronto edged Boston for the final playoff spot. Here, Boston goalie Jim Henry and Toronto's Ron Stewart *(center)* eye the puck.

A tear-gas bomb explodes at the Forum during a Montreal-Detroit game on March 17, 1955. Irate fans were protesting the suspension of Maurice Richard.

RED KELLY

One of the most versatile and talented members of the hockey community was Red Kelly. Kelly broke into the NHL in the late 1940s with the Detroit Red Wings. The big defenseman became an institution in the Motor City, where he was a member of eight regular-season championship squads and four Stanley Cup winners. With Detroit, Kelly was named to eight All-Star teams, won four Lady Byng Trophies, and copped one Norris Trophy.

Kelly was "reborn" in 1960 when he was traded to the Toronto Maple Leafs. At an age when most players consider retirement, Kelly switched to forward, where he helped guide the Leafs to one championship and four Stanley Cup wins.

Kelly finally retired as a player after the Maple Leafs' stunning 1967 Stanley Cup win, and accepted the coaching post for the fledgling Los Angeles Kings. After two seasons with L.A., the redhead served as coach and general manager of the Pittsburgh Penguins.

In 1973, Kelly took over as coach of a young Maple Leaf team and guided it into the playoffs. Crusty Leaf owner Harold Ballard complained at length that Kelly was too nice of a guy, and in 1977 Roger Neilson replaced Red behind the bench.

Police moved in to protect the president, but the mood of the crowd was so surly that it seemed the police would have difficulty preventing an attempt on his life. Just then, someone exploded a tear-gas bomb directly in front of Selke's box. A state of temporary chaos ensued, as spectators made their way to the exits. By next morning, *The New York Times,* which rarely gave much ink to sports, played the "Richard Riot" on page one, as did other distinguished dailies around the world.

In many ways, the playoffs were anticlimatic. Detroit took on Toronto in the opening round and swept the Leafs in four games, outscoring them 14-6 in the process.

Despite the absence of Richard, the Canadiens had little trouble taming the Bruins, who were vanquished in the first two games, 2-0 and 3-1. Boston took Game Three 4-2, but Montreal won the next two—4-3 in overtime and 5-1—to take the series.

By this time, Montreal fans had partially recovered from the Richard Riot, although they were pessimistic about their team's chances against the Red Wings. Detroit came from behind to win Game One, 4-2 at Olympia

Stadium, and then demolishéd the Habs 7-1 in the second game. Once on Forum ice, the Habs were a new team, toppling the Wings 4-2 and 5-3. The series was tied at two.

Clearly this was a homer's series. The Wings regrouped at home and took Game Five 5-1. Back in Montreal, it was the Canadiens' turn, and they handed the Wings a 6-3 shellacking. The game that would decide the Cup was played on April 14, 1955, at Detroit, and remained true to form— the hosts were dominant.

Alex "Fats" Delvecchio was Game Seven's best player, putting Detroit ahead 1-0 in the second period and 3-0 in the third. Curry's tally at 14:35 of the third period proved too little and too late. For the second year in a row, the Red Wings were champions.

Toronto's Smith won the Lady Byng Trophy, and the Calder went to Ed Litzenberger of the Blackhawks. Ted Kennedy of the Leafs took the Hart, while Montreal's Doug Harvey won the Norris. Sawchuk's league-leading 12 shutouts and 1.94 goals-against average earned him the Vezina. Geoffrion passed the Rocket on the final weekend of the season to win the scoring championship.

Toe, Rocket, Pocket
Steer Canadiens to the Cup

1955-56

The turbulence of the previous season inspired many changes. Canadiens managing director Frank Selke Sr. had become fed up with coach Dick Irvin's incendiary tactics that led to the March 17 riot. Convinced that Irvin was a negative influence on Rocket Richard, he released Irvin, allowing him to sign with the Chicago Blackhawks. Richard's former linemate, Toe Blake, took over as coach of the Habs.

In Manhattan, Ranger management decided a change was necessary. They fired GM Frank Boucher and promoted coach Muzz Patrick to the GM position. Patrick, in turn, hired volatile Phil Watson as coach.

But the most startling shake-up of all involved the champion Red Wings. Despite his club's dominance of the league in 1954-55, Jack Adams engineered a major shake-up from goal on out. He traded star goalie Terry Sawchuk, Vic Stasiuk, Marcel Bonin, and Lorne Davis to Boston for Ed Sandford, Real Chevrefils, Norm Corcoran, Gilles Boisvert, and Warren Godfrey.

The monster trade was predicated on Adams's assumption that rookie Glenn Hall was ready for big-league shooting. To a certain extent, he was right. Hall would win the Calder Trophy with a 2.11 goals-against average and a league-leading 12 shutouts.

In 1955-56, Montreal's Jean Beliveau (4) won both the Hart and Art Ross Trophies. Beliveau, who tallied 47 goals and 41 assists, also spent 143 minutes in the penalty box.

In this season of upheaval, there was only one constant. The Blackhawks, despite Irvin's presence, remained the league doormats. Otherwise, the league turned topsy-turvy, with even the Rangers gaining a playoff berth for the first time since 1950. More importantly, there was a change at the top. After leading the league since the 1948-49 season, the Red Wings finally were toppled from the throne—and were they ever dethroned!

The Canadiens, with all elements in place, left the Red Wings in the dust. Blake had precisely the right touch with Richard, as well as the younger players. Jean Beliveau, for instance, led the league in scoring with 47 goals and 88 points. In addition, Blake turned the tenacious Bert Olmstead into one of the league's best left wings. "Dirty

Bertie," as he was known, led the league in assists with 56.

Moreover, Jacques Plante surpassed Sawchuk and Hall as the NHL's best goalie, while the Canadiens' defense—Doug Harvey, Jean-Guy Talbot, Dollard St. Laurent, and Tom Johnson—was unmatched for versatility. So powerful were the Canadiens that it was considered miraculous when Richard's kid brother, Henri, was able to crack the lineup after training camp.

Nicknamed the "Pocket Rocket," Henri was an effortless skater and crafty playmaker who was considerably tougher than his size indicated. Early in the season, the Pocket was challenged by some of the league's heavyweights, who figured young Richard would need his older

FERN FLAMAN

Long before Bobby Orr and the "Big, Bad Bruins" came along in the late 1960s, the Boston hockey club had become notorious as a bashing sextet. From 1954 through 1961, its chief violent basher was Fernie Flaman, a smooth-skating defenseman who broke into pro hockey as a teenager during World War II.

Flaman developed his hard-hitting style with the Eastern League Boston Olympics, playing briefly with the Bruins in 1944-45 and 1945-46. A year later, he became a permanent NHL skater with Boston. In 1950-51, he was traded to the Maple Leafs where his style was less appreciated than in Beantown. He returned to the Bruins at the start of the 1954-55 campaign.

Rare was the night when Flaman lost a fight. He decisioned Rangers bad man Lou Fontinato at Madison Square Garden, and once nearly killed Montreal's Henri Richard with a devastating but legal bodycheck during a game at Boston Garden. Following his playing days, Flaman became a coach, first with the pros, later in the collegiate ranks. He was inducted into the Hockey Hall of Fame in 1990.

Bill Quackenbush starred for the Bruins from 1949-56 after a successful stint with Detroit. Quackenbush was revered for his clean play.

Terry Sawchuk was traded from Detroit to Boston in 1955. In 1955-56, he posted nine shutouts.

brother to protect him. But Henri fought his own battles and demonstrated that he was every inch a big-leaguer.

Montreal finished atop the standings with 100 points—24 more than second-place Detroit. The surprise team, based on past performance, was the Rangers. Watson's needling had a positive effect, but more important was the maturing of younger players. Leading the Ranger attack was hard-shooting right wing Andy Bathgate who, like Boom Boom Geoffrion, had perfected the slapshot. Bathgate led the Rangers in scoring (19 goals, 66 points).

Although nobody used the word "goon" at the time, the 1955-56 season heralded the dawn of the hockey cop, otherwise known as the enforcer, the instigator, the policeman, or, as we now know it, the goon. Whatever the

appellation, his principle role was to intimidate the opposition. The first such enforcer was Ranger defenseman Lou "Leapin' Louie" Fontinato.

Fontinato's favorite prey was Beliveau, who Louie usually singled out for attack before the Canadiens sniper was ready for him. Another Fontinato victim was Rocket Richard. At season's end, Fontinato had accumulated 202 penalty minutes, remarkably high for a rookie.

The Rangers, fortified by less turbulent defensemen Bill Gadsby and Harry Howell, finished third (32-28-10), only two points behind the second-place Red Wings. Gump Worsley, who had replaced Johnny Bower after the 1953-54 season, had established himself as the permanent Ranger goalie. However, the Gump's

2.90 goals-against average was a far cry from Plante's 1.86 or Hall's 2.11.

Many critics believed that the addition of Sawchuk would turn the Bruins into a contender. The temperamental goalie did play well (2.66), but the Bruins were a team in decline and no amount of Sawchuk's acrobatics could save them from fifth place (23-34-13). The Maple Leafs, who finished two points higher, were no bargain either. Captain Ted Kennedy had retired and the brunt of the scoring was shouldered by Tod Sloan, who finished with 37 goals and 29 assists.

Although the Red Wings finished second, many felt they still had enough talent to win a third straight Stanley Cup. They had little trouble with Toronto in Round One of the playoffs, winning the first two games at home,

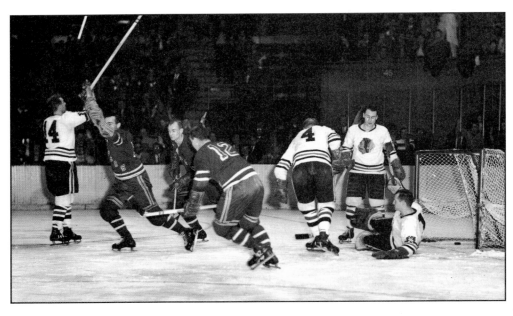

1955-56

Best Record
Montreal
(45-15-10)

Stanley Cup Finals
Montreal 4
Detroit 1

Art Ross Trophy
Jean Beliveau
(47/41/88)

Hart Trophy
Jean Beliveau

Vezina Trophy
Jacques Plante

Calder Trophy
Glenn Hall

Norris Trophy
Doug Harvey

Lady Byng Trophy
Earl Reibel

Ranger Parker MacDonald (*stick raised*) beats Chicago with a rare goal. MacDonald didn't come into his own until the 1960s.

Detroit's Glenn Hall strains to stop an Eric Nesterenko shot. The 1955-56 season was Nesterenko's last in Toronto. He would toil 16 years in Chicago.

With Glenn Hall in goal, the Red Wings defeated Toronto four games to one in the 1956 semifinals. Here, Hall goes to his knees to stop Toronto's Tod Sloan (11).

All eyes are on the official scorer during a Detroit-Toronto playoff game in 1956. Toronto's George Armstrong *(left)*, Detroit's Red Kelly, and referee Red Storey await the verdict.

3-2 and 3-1, and Game Three at Toronto, 5-4 in overtime. Toronto goalie Harry Lumley recorded a shutout in Game Four, but that's as far as the Leafs could go. They exited 3-1 in Game Five.

In the other semifinal round, the Canadiens had to neutralize the aggressive Rangers. Montreal took the opener 7-1, but the Rangers rebounded for a 4-2 win in the second game at the Forum. The aroused Habs took the next three—3-1, 5-3, and 7-0—to qualify for the finals.

With one exception—Game Three at Olympia—Montreal dominated Detroit in the finals. After falling behind 4-2 in the opener at Montreal, the Habs rallied to tie the game 4-4 at 6:20 of the third period. Then quick goals by Beliveau and rookie Claude Provost cemented the win, 6-4.

Game Two was a laugher for the Canadiens. They ran up a 3-0 lead at the end of two periods and closed with a 5-1 decision. Detroit's only solace came in Game Three, when Red Kelly, Ted Lindsay, and Gordie Howe scored in the 3-1 decision. From that point on, there was no question that the torch would be passed.

In Game Four, Plante produced a 3-0 shutout behind Beliveau's pair of goals. In the curtain-closer at Montreal, Beliveau, Rocket Richard, and Geoffrion staked the Habs to a 3-0 lead before Alex Delvecchio got one back for Detroit. It was the Red Wings' last gasp, as they went down to defeat 3-1. A new champion was crowned.

Appropriately, Montreal's Doug Harvey took the Norris Trophy while Beliveau captured the Hart. Jacques annexed the Vezina.

ALEX DELVECCHIO

He's not the brawniest hockey player I ever saw but he is one of the brainiest." Those were the words of long-time teammate and friend Ross "Lefty" Wilson describing Alex Delvecchio, as Lefty presented Alex with the Lester Patrick Award in New York on March 18, 1974.

No one was better qualified to assess Delvecchio than the irrepressible Mr. Wilson, who watched Alex play 22 seasons with the Detroit Red Wings. Lefty saw the forward play in 1,549 games, score 456 goals, and assist on 825 others.

Then, in the 1973-74 season, Lefty watched the likable and well-respected Delvecchio move from Red Wing captain to the team's coach and, then, its general manager. Taking over as coach of the Wings on November 7, 1973, Delvecchio quietly replaced turmoil and uncertainty with harmony and new spirit.

On May 21, 1974, Alex became general manager and coach with full authority in every phase of the club's operations. In 1977, Delvecchio was inducted into the Hockey Hall of Fame.

New York, Boston No Match for Montreal

1956-57

The 1956-57 Canadiens were so explosive on the power play that the NHL had to rewrite the rule book to keep their scoring from getting out of hand. The previous rule stated that the offender must stay in the penalty box regardless of how many times the full-strength team scored. Montreal used this rule to its advantage, often scoring two and three goals while it enjoyed the man advantage.

Coach Toe Blake was so adept at formulating a power-play team that it was almost a given that the Habs would score with a man advantage. With a lineup including Maurice Richard, Jean Beliveau, Boom Boom Geoffrion, Bert Olmstead, and Dickie Moore, the Canadiens possessed the strongest nucleus of all time.

The Red Wings were no less threatening, but in a different way. They had an overall cohesion with particular emphasis on center, where they iced Earl Reibel, Alex Delvecchio, and Norm Ullman, each of whom could have been a first-line center on most of the other teams. Detroit also boasted such productive competitors as Gordie Howe, Ted Lindsay, Johnny "Chief" Bucyk, and Bill Dineen.

The Bruins recovered smartly from their 1955-56 debacle and moved right up into playoff contention. Boston's season, however, would be littered with unhappiness, primarily because of the abject undependability of goalie Terry Sawchuk. When he did play, Sawchuk was nearly flawless and compiled an 18-10-6 record. However, the goalie, who normally weighed well over 200 pounds in his prime, had lost considerable weight following a bout with mononucleosis.

With the great netminder sidelined, Bruins coach Milt Schmidt promoted Norm DeFelice from the American League. DeFelice, who lost five games in eight outings, was not the answer, so the Bruins bought the rights to Don Simmons, a minor-leaguer who played

New York goalie Gump Worsley and referee Red Storey take a breather. The Rangers made the playoffs in 1956-57 despite yielding the most goals in the NHL (227). They lost to Montreal in Round One of the playoffs.

Goalie Terry Sawchuk deflected thousands of shots in his 21 years in the NHL. Shown here are the remains of one of his sticks.

for Springfield. Meanwhile, controversy continued to surround Sawchuk. He was assailed by the Boston media, and in response threatened to sue four Boston papers for their criticism. Adding gasoline to the flames was a charge that Schmidt labeled Sawchuk a quitter, although the coach denied the assertion.

The Rangers, who had played so well the previous year, began rebelling against their autocratic and erratic coach, Phil Watson, who alternately battled with his players and the press.

On the economic side, the NHL showed a remarkable recovery from the doldrums of the early 1950s. It received a boost when one of the three U.S. networks, the Columbia Broadcasting System, began televising league games on Saturday afternoons from four American cities.

The NHL's sad-sacks were the Toronto Maple Leafs and the Chicago Blackhawks, both of whom were in the throes of major long-term

reorganizations that would not bear fruit until the 1960s. The Chicagoans, headed by Chicago tycoon Arthur Wirtz, were committed to a long-term development based on a vast farm system.

The Maple Leafs, who had hired former right wing Howie Meeker as coach to replace King Clancy, suffered through administrative power struggles centering around venerable Leafs boss Conn Smythe. Amid all this confusion, a power struggle developed for control of Maple Leaf Gardens and the hockey club. A group led by Smythe's son Stafford spearheaded the revolution, and soon Conn's "little boy" was running the show.

Stafford Smythe had a rich history in hockey. He had been a coach and manager as an 11-year-old while playing minor hockey, a coach and manager during student days at the University of Toronto, and a manager with the Marlboro Juniors. Stafford alternately lauded and feuded with his father.

ANDY HEBENTON

One of the most durable players of all time, right winger Andy Hebenton played nine consecutive seasons in the NHL without missing a single game. He totaled a record 630 matches without having been sidelined because of injury or incompetence.

In 1956-57, Andy won the Lady Byng Trophy while playing for the Rangers, a club for whom he quietly excelled from 1955-56 through 1962-63. He was then drafted by the Bruins and played in Boston for one season before being dropped to the Western League. There he played superior hockey for several more years.

Hebenton's finest hour as a scorer occurred in a 1957 Stanley Cup playoff in New York. Hebenton scored a sudden-death goal at 13:38 against Montreal's Jacques Bob Plante after eluding defenseman Bob Turner. It was the first overtime playoff game in Madison Square Garden since 1940, and the Rangers won 4-3, although they ultimately lost the series.

Goalie Terry Sawchuk contracted mononucleosis in 1956-57. Despite the illness, he was criticized for missing games and was soon traded.

Former Boston star Milt Schmidt took over as Bruins coach in the mid-1950s. Boston went 34-24-12 in 1956-57 and made it to the Stanley Cup finals.

Stafford Smythe began to take control of the Leafs in 1957. By 1961, he was running the show.

"My dad gave me lots of rope and lots to do," said Stafford. "When I was 30, I was ten years ahead of everybody. And at 40, I was ten years behind everybody." Stafford meant that after his father allowed him to learn so much so soon, Conn continued to regard him as an employee and refused to permit him to make significant decisions—even when he had reached the age of 40. As a result, Stafford decided he had to challenge his father, no matter what the consequences.

"The people my father respects," said Stafford, "are those who stand up to him and fight. After I learned to do this, he respected me . . . but we had plenty of scraps."

In 1957, during the Maple Leafs' depression, Conn Smythe decided to pump new blood into the organization. He appointed Stafford chairman of a new Maple Leafs hockey committee. He fired general manager Meeker. "Meeker," Stafford said, "was too inexperienced."

Stafford Smythe gradually laid the groundwork for a revitalization of the Maple Leafs machine—in much the same way his father had done 30 years earlier. Stafford hired George "Punch"

Imlach, and Conn announced in 1958 that he was preparing to relinquish his control of the Gardens and the Leafs' operation. "Stafford," Conn laughed, "wants to be president of my sand and gravel business, but I want him to be president of Maple Leaf Gardens in three years. It should be quite a battle to see who wins."

The one glimmer of hope for the Leafs was the promotion of 18-year-old left wing Frank "Big M" Mahovlich, a huge forward with long skating strides and superstar potential.

Despite the Canadiens' abundance of talent, they couldn't handle the stretch run and were beaten out by the steadier Red Wings. Detroit finished first with 88 points, six ahead of Montreal. The Bruins were only two points behind the Canadiens, while the Rangers lagged in fourth place with 66 points, nine more than fifth-place Toronto.

All signs pointed to a Detroit-Montreal final-round battle for the Stanley Cup. The Canadiens fulfilled their end of the bargain by disposing of the Rangers in five games—although the Blueshirts caused a stir in Game Two with a 4-3 sudden-death victory. In the following game, Geoffrion

delivered a three-goal hat trick for an 8-3 Canadiens win. They completed the series with 3-1 and 4-3 triumphs.

The Bruins stunned Detroit in Game One of the semis, beating the Wings 3-1 at Olympia Stadium. The Red Wings retaliated with a 7-2 decision in Game Two, but the Bruins were inspired by the goaltending of the young Simmons. In the next three games, Simmons orchestrated successive 4-3, 2-0, and 4-3 wins. Once again, a mighty Red Wings club failed in the clutch. GM Jack Adams blamed goalie Glenn Hall for the defeat and traded him to Chicago prior to the 1957-58 season.

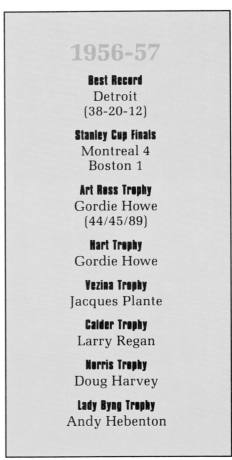

1956-57

Best Record
Detroit
(38-20-12)

Stanley Cup Finals
Montreal 4
Boston 1

Art Ross Trophy
Gordie Howe
(44/45/89)

Hart Trophy
Gordie Howe

Vezina Trophy
Jacques Plante

Calder Trophy
Larry Regan

Norris Trophy
Doug Harvey

Lady Byng Trophy
Andy Hebenton

Boston's young Don McKenney totaled 60 points in 1956-57. McKenney proved to be a 20-plus goal-scorer well into the 1960s.

Rocket Richard's stick fired the most lethal backhand in hockey. Though a 15-year veteran, Richard was still a dangerous threat in 1956-57, scoring 33 goals.

Hilda Chester was the New York Rangers' No. 1 fan. Here, she poses with Ranger coach Phil Watson (*left*) and two other Ranger boosters.

Gump Worsley boots a shot to Bill Gadsby (4) and Lou Fontinato (*center*). In 1956-57, the Rangers beat out Toronto for the final playoff spot.

MARCEL PRONOVOST

If all modern hockey players, Marcel Pronovost probably holds the record for most injuries. Episodes of Marcel's derring-do are legend around NHL rinks.

He broke into big-league hockey with Detroit in the Stanley Cup playoffs of 1950, and was around to play a few games for the Toronto Maple Leafs in the 1969-70 season. In between, he collected hundreds of stitches and innumerable broken bones.

Once, in a game against the Chicago Blackhawks, Marcel sped across the blue line as two husky Chicago defensemen dug their skates into the ice, awaiting his arrival. They dared Pronovost to pass. Pronovost wasn't thinking about getting hurt. He eyed the two-foot space between the Hawks, boldly pushed the puck ahead, and leaped at the opening.

The crouched defensemen slammed the gate, hurling Pronovost headfirst over their shoulders. Marcel swiped at the puck, which was below him, but instead had to settle for a three-point landing on his left eyebrow, nose, and cheek. His nose was broken and his eyebrow required 25 stitches.

Marcel always regarded his misfortunes casually. "To me," he said, "accidents are as common as lacing on the skates."

The Bruins, hoping to score another upset in the finals, stunned the Canadiens with a 1-0 advantage through more than half of the opening game. But the inimitable Rocket Richard could not be contained. The galvanic right wing rallied the Habs with four goals en route to a 5-1 decision.

In Game Two, Simmons and Jacques Plante sparkled in goal, but in the end it was Beliveau's second-period goal that produced the lone score. The Habs' firepower could not be

extinguished. In Game Three, Geoffrion scored twice in the first period and the Canadiens were never headed after that. They won 4-2 and led the series three games to zip.

It was in Game Four that the Bruins would finally redeem themselves. Fleming Mackell scored in the first and third periods, while Simmons was flawless in goal. Boston shut out the Canadiens 2-0.

That did it for the Bostonians. When they returned to Montreal on April 16,

1957, they were blown off the ice by three successive Canadiens goals. By the time Boston got on the board at 13:43 of the third period, the series was over. The Canadiens wrapped it up 5-1 for their second straight Stanley Cup.

Detroit's only consolation was that Howe won both the scoring championship and the Hart Trophy. Slick center Larry Regan of the Bruins captured the Calder Trophy, while Doug Harvey and Plante annexed the Norris and Vezina Trophies, respectively.

Owners Break the Union;
Habs Thump the Bruins

1957 - 58

For a couple of years, NHL owners heard rumblings about the possible formation of a players union. The movement—led by Detroit's Ted Lindsay, Toronto's Jimmy Thomson, and Montreal's Doug Harvey, among others—began to crystalize in the mid-1950s.

Appalled by this move, the owners reacted by trading a number of the organizers. Lindsay and Thomson were dispatched to the Blackhawks at a time when Chicago was viewed as the Siberia of the NHL. The owners succeeded in suppressing the union to a certain extent, but Lindsay and others managed to form an NHL Players Association. They even sued the league for $3 million in an attempt to improve their conditions.

Lindsay's attempt to get the players union off the ground was torpedoed by his former Red Wings teammates, who cut any ties to the Players Association.

The union movement was overshadowed by other arresting events. First of all, pioneer hockey broadcaster Foster Hewitt relinquished play-by-play duties to his son, Bill. Maurice Richard scored his

Toronto's Pete Conacher tries to outflank bespectacled Detroit defenseman Al Arbour and goalie Terry Sawchuk. Sawchuk was back in Detroit after two unhappy years in Boston.

Boston defenseman Larry Hillman eyes Toronto blue-liner Tim Horton, but the two are separated by another heavyweight— linesman George Hayes. Hillman played for eight NHL teams in his long career. Horton played 20 years with the Leafs.

500th goal. And less than a month after the Rocket's milestone tally, he collided with Maple Leafs defenseman Marc Reaume and nearly severed his achilles tendon, which threatened to end his career.

In a portent of things to come, Canadiens goalie Jacques Plante donned a face mask in practice—despite coach Toe Blake's objections. Another milestone was the appearance of the first black player on an NHL team.

The Bruins signed Willie O'Ree, who made his debut for the Bruins against Montreal on January 18, 1958. O'Ree had good speed, but would not hold up against rugged NHL checking. He played only two games for Boston,

though he would come back three years later for a 43-game stint.

One of the most courageous episodes involved Canadiens left wing Dickie Moore, who was challenging for the scoring championship until he suffered a severe wrist injury six weeks before the end of the season. Moore played the final five weeks wearing a cast on his right wrist. Miraculously, Moore continued to score and won the scoring race with 84 points.

The Canadiens received yet another scare when high-scoring right wing Boom Boom Geoffrion collided with teammate Andre Pronovost in practice and suffered a ruptured bowel. So serious was the wound that Geoffrion was given his last rights by a Roman

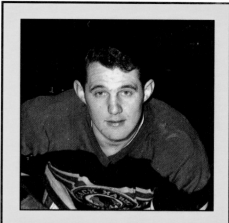

BILL GADSBY

Bill Gadsby broke in with the Blackhawks during the 1946-47 season and remained in the big show until 1965-66, when he retired as a member of the Red Wings. During that span, he was named first-team All-Star three times (1956, 1958, and 1959) and was equally comfortable as a defensive or offensive defenseman.

Gadsby played for Chicago until the 1954-55 season, when he was traded to the Rangers a day before Thanksgiving; he was dealt along with Pete Conacher for Al Stanley and Nick Mickoski. In his very first game as a Ranger, Gadsby dove in front of a Bruins shot, preventing a goal but breaking several bones in the process.

The play symbolized the gutsy style that made Bill a hit on Broadway until 1961-62, when Rangers general manager Muzz Patrick dealt him to the Red Wings where he continued to excel. Curiously, Gadsby never played on a Stanley Cup champion, although he came close in 1963-64 and 1965-66 with Detroit.

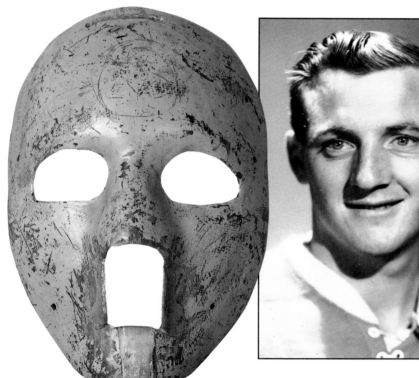

Jacques Plante became the first NHL goalie to wear a mask, as he donned this face guard on November 1, 1959.

Montreal's Dickie Moore led the NHL in both goals (36) and points (84) in 1957-58.

▷

Bruins goalie Don Simmons and teammate Larry Regan (third from right) fight off a Toronto attack.

Catholic priest. The Boomer's life was saved by major stomach surgery.

The major front office change involved the Canadiens. Senator Hartland Molson, of the Canadian brewery family, bought controlling interest in the Canadian Arena Company, which owned and operated the Forum and the hockey club. Molson bought 60 percent of the shares from Senator Donat Raymond.

The Blackhawks, enjoying their first full season under happy-go-lucky coach Rudy Pilous, began showing the fruits of the Wirtz family's youth movement.

Chicago's farm team in St. Catherines, Ontario, already had delivered promising defenseman Elmer "Moose" Vasko, and now produced yet another prospect in 18-year-old Bobby Hull.

Immediately, comparisons were made between the attractive Hull and his dynamic Toronto counterpart, Frank Mahovlich. In their first race for league honors, Mahovlich was the winner, taking the Calder Trophy.

An intense feud developed between Red Wings GM Jack Adams and goalie Glenn Hall—remember, Adams had blamed Hall for the Red Wings' failure

in the previous year's playoffs. Hall was dealt to the Blackhawks with Lindsay for Johnnie Wilson, Forbes Kennedy, Bill Preston, and goalie Hank Bassen. Adams suggested that Hall had become puck shy and would be of little value to the Red Wings. To solve Detroit's goaltending problems, Adams obtained his old favorite, Terry Sawchuk, in a deal with Boston for Johnny Bucyk.

The Red Wings discovered that Sawchuk was not the same goaltender he had been during his prime in the early 1950s. He finished the 1957-58

Toronto defenseman Bob Baun *(left)* collides with Montreal counterpart Jean-Guy Talbot along the boards. Baun's spunky play would help Toronto make the playoffs in 1959.

DOUG HARVEY

Montreal Canadien defenseman Doug Harvey was so laconic in style, so calmly sure of himself, that he executed plays of extreme complication with consummate ease. Lacking the flamboyance of Eddie Shore or other Hall of Fame defensemen, Harvey was slow to receive the acclaim he deserved.

Although Harvey was not known as a dirty player, he was occasionally moved to violence when he was suitably provoked. Once, during a game with the Rangers in New York, Harvey planted the pointed blade of his stick in Red Sullivan's gut, rupturing his spleen.

Honest to a fault, Harvey never denied the attack, but he pointed out that Sullivan had developed a dangerous habit of "kicking skates." When the two went into the corner of the rink, Sullivan would kick Harvey's skates out from under him, making it very easy for Doug to fall on his head. According to Doug, he warned Sullivan about his unfortunate proclivity, and when the warning went unheeded the stick was plunged into Sullivan's stomach.

Harvey helped Montreal to five straight Stanley Cups, starting in 1956. He was the hub of Montreal's smothering power play, associated with Boom Boom Geoffrion, Jean Beliveau, and Rocket Richard. He won seven Norris Trophies in his career.

George Armstrong intercepts Boston defenseman Allan Stanley. Armstrong, a blue-liner himself, reached double digits in goals 17 times in his 20 years with the Leafs.

Alex Delvecchio *(white jersey)* fights a pair of Leafs for the puck. Referee Frank Udvari lifts himself out of the way.

season at 29-29-12 with a mediocre 2.96 goals-against average. In Chicago, Hall went 24-39-7 on an inferior team, but beat Sawchuk with a 2.88 average.

Montreal was clearly the league power, finishing with 96 points, 19 more than the second-place Rangers. While the Broadway sextet did well, vitriolic coach Phil Watson endlessly tilted with his pudgy goaltender, Gump Worsley, who was frequently spelled by the equally rotund Marcel Paille.

The fourth-place Bruins displayed one of the league's best offensive units in the "Uke Line," comprised of Bucyk, Bronco Horvath, and Vic Stasiuk. But there were no better lines than the trios iced by Montreal. Henri Richard centered one unit with brother Maurice on the right side and Dickie Moore on the left. No less adept was the Jean Beliveau-Bernie Geoffrion-Bert Olmstead line.

The Canadiens also had the best checking forward, Claude Provost, who also was one of the finest penalty-killers. And Plante, who won the Vezina Trophy with a 2.11 goals-against average, was no slouch either.

The Canadiens led the league in goal-scoring (250) and fewest goals allowed (158) and finished at 43-17-10. This club has been labeled by some experts as the best hockey team of all time.

The test of the Canadiens' greatness would come in the playoffs, where they pursued a third straight Stanley Cup. Detroit was the first foe and the Habs left absolutely no doubt about their superiority, winning the first two games by an aggregate score of 13-2 (8-1 and 5-1). In Game Three, at Detroit's Olympia Stadium, the Red Wings held the Habs to a 1-1 tie, but lost the match in sudden-death. In Game Four, the Detroiters looked like winners, leading by two goals in the third period. However, Rocket Richard's three-goal hat trick overwhelmed the home club, and the Canadiens departed with a 4-3 triumph, and a ticket to the finals.

The Rangers-Bruins semifinal was intensely bitter, with rival coaches Watson and Milt Schmidt constantly twitting one another. With the series tied at two games apiece, the Bruins broke the series open with 6-1 and 8-2 decisions.

Great as the Canadiens were, the Habs had their hands full with the pesky Bruins in the finals. After dropping the opener 2-1, Boston regrouped and toppled the Habs in Game Two 5-2, with Horvath's pair of goals providing the difference. Plante shut out Boston 3-0 in Game Three, which proved to be a Richard family affair. The Rocket scored twice and the Pocket Rocket once. Game Four saw Don McKenney net two goals in a 3-1 Boston victory to even the series.

The Bruins hung tough in Game Five at the Forum. A late goal by Horvath

tied the score at 2-2, forcing overtime. But the Rocket scored the winner on passes from Henri and Moore at 5:45 of sudden-death.

The series was settled on April 20, 1958, at Boston Garden within the first two minutes of play. Geoffrion took passes from Beliveau and Olmstead and beat Don Simmons at 0:46 of the first period. The Rocket then scored a minute later, at 1:54, to give the Habs a 2-0 advantage. Montreal led 4-1 at the end of the second period and won 5-3. The Canadiens had thus won their third straight Stanley Cup.

BOB PULFORD

Bob Pulford, a classy, two-way centerman, labored for 16 seasons in the National Hockey League with the Toronto Maple Leafs and later the Los Angeles Kings. Never a flamboyant player in the "superstar" category, Pulford quietly and efficiently got the job done, taking a regular shift, skating on the power play, and killing penalties. In his career, Pulford played 1,079 games, totaling 281 goals and 643 points.

Pulford finished his active playing career in 1972, as he retired as the Kings' captain and stepped right into their coaching post. After Bob molded the Beverly Hills squad into one of the finest defensive units in the league and made it a serious contender, Pulford took over as general manager/coach of the Chicago Blackhawks in 1977, but gave up coaching duties two years later. He was promoted to Chicago's vice-president in 1990.

The first black player in the NHL was left wing Willie O'Ree, who played two games for the Bruins in 1957-58. O'Ree again made it to the big show in 1960-61, scoring four goals in 43 games.

152

Toronto's Cinderella Ball Ends in Montreal

1958-59

Slowly but surely, the league's attempt to achieve parity began paying off, mostly through the use of the intra-league draft. This was most evident prior to the 1958-59 season when the Rangers lost several key players, including defenseman Jack "Tex" Evans to the Chicago Blackhawks, Dave Creighton to Montreal, and Guy Gendron to Boston. The loss of these players would have a profound effect on the Rangers' demise later in the season. The Blackhawks,

who had suddenly become a free-spending team, also signed Earl Balfour and Tod Sloan from Toronto, as well as Al Arbour from Detroit.

The Maple Leafs added minor-league executive George "Punch" Imlach to their staff as assistant GM, and Punch immediately raised eyebrows by signing 33-year-old minor-league goaltender Johnny Bower. Bower hadn't played in the NHL since the 1953-54 season. Former Canadien Billy Reay started the season as Toronto coach,

but once Imlach became GM on November 21, 1958, Reay was given his walking papers. Imlach took over as GM and coach.

The Rangers had plenty of firepower in their front line of Andy Bathgate-Dean Prentice-Larry Popein. They also featured a solid defense, anchored by Harry Howell and Bill Gadsby, as well as competent goaltending from Gump Worsley.

No team had ever won four straight Stanley Cups, but it would have been

Camille Henry (foreground) fires a shot at Toronto's Ed Chadwick. "The Eel" tallied 58 points in 1958-59.

Detroit's Gordie Howe was honored with a "night" on March 3, 1959, at Olympia Stadium.

GORDIE HOWE NIGHT
MARCH 3, 1959
OLYMPIA STADIUM · · · DETROIT   25¢

hard to discount the Canadiens, who still outdistanced their five other foes. Montreal was rock-solid at center with Jean Beliveau, Henri Richard, ánd Ralph Backstrom. They carried two other centers—Don Marshall and Phil Goyette—but their lineups were so powerful that these two worthies got precious little ice time.

The Bruins presented a formidable defense with Doug Mohns, Leo Boivin, Fern Flaman, and Bob Armstrong fronting for goalie Don Simmons. With the Uke Line leading the way, Boston finished in second place. Meanwhile, the rejuvenated Blackhawks finally became a playoff contender again, thanks to Glenn Hall's goaltending and the vital play of veterans Ted Lindsay, Sloan, and Arbour.

Nobody could quite figure out the Leafs, who were blending new faces with veterans. Imlach obtained defenseman Allan Stanley from Boston in one of the more brilliant moves of his career, as well as Bert Olmstead from the Canadiens. In addition, he inserted young defensemen Carl Brewer and Bob Baun into the lineup. The defensive duet added considerable spunk to the team. Nevertheless, Toronto did not appear capable of catching the Rangers, who seemed sure of finishing third or fourth.

However, the indomitable Imlach would not permit defeat. He insisted that his boys would eventually catch the Rangers, although they were nine points behind with only two weeks left

Rangers right wing Andy Hebenton (foreground) pivots right for a loose puck after Johnny Bower makes a save. Hebenton scored 33 goals in 1958-59 and finished second in Lady Byng voting. Nevertheless, his Rangers finished one point behind Toronto for the final playoff spot.

Hockey in the post-war West was provided by the Pacific Coast Hockey League and the Western Hockey League. This is WHL action in Seattle. The Seattle Totems (*white jerseys*) were immensely successful.

in the season.

The stage was set for the New Yorkers to deliver their *coup de grace* to Imlach and his Leafs. On Saturday, March 14, coach Phil Watson brought his Rangers to Maple Leaf Gardens for the first of a home-and-home series with Toronto. All New York needed was a single victory on either night in order to finish off the Queen City sextet.

Try as they might, the Rangers could never get themselves untracked on that Saturday night. George Armstrong scored for Toronto at 7:23 of the first period, and Frank Mahovlich got another one for the Leafs at 16:26. Dick Duff scored twice for Toronto in the second period, and Mahovlich collected his second goal of the contest later in the game. Toronto shut out the Rangers 5-0.

The Rangers went home to presumably polish off the Maple Leafs. Toronto was in another must-win situation.

New York defenseman Gadsby delivered the first blow less than four minutes after the game began, putting the Rangers ahead 1-0. But Duff and Armstrong rallied Toronto with a pair of goals, and the game soon took on wild proportions. Bathgate tied the match 2-2 early in the middle period, only to have Mahovlich and Armstrong put Toronto into a 4-2 lead. Then Jimmy Bartlett of the Rangers narrowed it to 4-3 a few minutes before the second period closed.

Imlach nearly crushed his fedora in his palm when big Hank Ciesla tied

Ⓐ **Fern Flaman was one of the hardest hitting defensemen to ever play in the NHL. Flaman played four years in Boston, four in Toronto, and then seven more with the Bruins.**

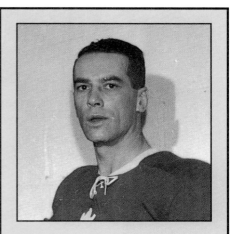

BERT OLMSTEAD

Known around the NHL as "Dirty Bertie," Montreal's Bert Olmstead gained the reputation as one of the best left wingers in the sport. Rarely would he get involved in fistfights, although he started many of them by provoking his opponent.

Olmstead's most famous bouts were with Lou Fontinato of the Rangers. Dirty Bertie had moved on to Toronto by 1959 when the two assailed each other. Bert started it with a high stick, and Fontinato responded by blackening Olmstead's eye with a punch. The two, of course, were banished to the penalty box.

As the pair attempted to leave the box after their time was up, Olmstead jumped in front of Fontinato in an effort to get on the ice first. Lou simply opened the door to the box, knocking Bertie down, then proceeded to beat up on his rival.

The battle continued later in the season before a sellout crowd in Madison Square Garden. Fontinato skated from the face-off circle toward Olmstead and hurled himself, nearly parallel to the ice, at Bertie.

"I don't know how Olmstead got up," related Camille Henry, who was on the ice at the time. "Louie broke his stick on Olmstead's face, put his knee in his ribs, and threw him into the glass. It was the dirtiest check I've ever seen."

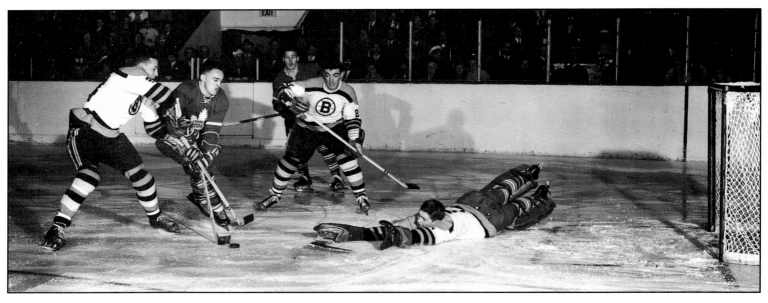

Boston goalie Harry Lumley (still wearing his old Maple Leaf stockings) dives to block a shot by Toronto's Frank Mahovlich in the 1959 playoffs.

Chicago's Danny Lewicki (8) duels with Toronto's Johnny Bower. In 1959, Chicago made the playoffs for the first time in six years.

the contest for New York at 5:37 of the last period. And he almost leaped off the bench when Armstrong put him ahead again at 12:40. But Bower was having an unusually inept night in the Toronto goal, and at 15:21 Red Sullivan scored for the Rangers and the game was tied once more, 5-5.

Imlach hoped for a miracle, and he got one. Allan Stanley moved the puck away from Bower and toward the Rangers' zone. He passed it to Bert Olmstead on the left. Two more strides

and Olmstead detected Bob Pulford in motion at center ice. The pass was true, but Pulford chose not to bisect the Rangers' defense. Instead, he cracked his wrists and sent a rather ordinary long shot at Worsley. The Garden crowd sat thunderstruck, as Pulford's shot breezed past Worsley's arm, glove, and leg pad. Toronto won the game 6-5.

Still, in order to make the playoffs, Toronto needed to beat Detroit on the final night of the season and hope for a

Rangers' loss to the Canadiens. The Rangers lost at Madison Square Garden, 4-2 to the Habs, and looked on horrifyingly at the score that came across the ticker: FINAL—TORONTO 5, DETROIT 4. The Blueshirts were out.

The Leafs' home-stretch rally created an interesting playoff scenario, with Toronto suddenly becoming the Cinderella team of hockey. Imlach's skaters took it on the chin in the first two games of the semifinals against Boston, losing 5-1 and 4-2, but the

Henri Richard tests Toronto goalie Ed Chadwick in the 1959 finals. Montreal breezed by the Leafs for its fourth straight Cup.

Johnny Bower jumps to make a save against Montreal's Dickie Moore *(left)*. Bower's goaltending was not enough to stop the Canadiens in the 1959 finals. *Les Habs* won the series in five.

ANDY BATHGATE

At first, Andy Bathgate appeared too much the pacifist for the NHL jungle. But he put up his dukes when necessary, licking such notorious hockey cops as Howie Young and Vic Stasiuk. By 1954-55, Andy was in the NHL to stay, and soon was favorably compared with the Rangers' greatest right wing, Bill Cook.

While it's never been firmly established who invented the slapshot—Bernie Geoffrion and Bobby Hull often are mentioned—Bathgate was among the earliest practitioners. It was Andy's shot at Madison Square Garden in November 1959 that smashed Montreal goalie Jacques Plante's face and inspired Plante to don a face mask permanently, thus ushering in the era of the goalie mask. Bathgate also was among the first to develop a curved "banana" blade on his stick.

By the end of the 1961-62 season, during which Andy notched 84 points, he had become the Rangers' team captain and their most popular player. He also was prime trade bait, and in February 1964 he was dealt to Toronto in a huge deal. New York traded Bathgate and Don McKenney to the Leafs for Dick Duff, Bob Nevin, Rod Seiling, Arnie Brown, and Bill Collins. As a result of the trade, Toronto won the 1964 Stanley Cup.

Bathgate was inducted into the Hockey Hall of Fame in 1978.

Leafs returned to Maple Leaf Gardens and took two straight overtime games by scores of 3-2 each. Toronto even won Game Five, winning 4-1 at Boston. The seesaw series continued at Toronto, this time with the Bruins rallying for a 5-4 edge. The series went back to Beantown for the last match. Sure enough, Toronto won it, 3-2.

The powerful Canadiens had their hands full with the upstart Blackhawks, winning only two of the first four games. It wasn't until the fifth game that Montreal took over. Montreal pocketed the last two games, 5-2 and 5-4, setting up an all-Canadian finals.

Imlach hoped the Toronto magic would continue in the finals, but the Habs would have none of that. They bested the Leafs 5-3 and 3-1 at Montreal. Toronto took Game Three 3-2 on Duff's sudden-death goal, but dropped Game Four 3-2. The teams returned to the Forum for Game Five. The Montrealers were just too powerful, grabbing a 3-0 first-period

lead and winning 5-3. The Canadiens had thus clinched their fourth straight championship.

Ironically, the Hart Trophy winner was Bathgate of the Rangers, even though his club missed the playoffs. The Norris Trophy went to the Canadiens' Tom Johnson, after teammate Doug Harvey had won it for four straight years. Backstrom was named rookie of the year, and Alex Delvecchio of the last-place Red Wings took the Lady Byng.

CHAPTER 6

TURNING OVER A NEW LEAF

Amidst the revolutionary decade of the 1960s, Toronto emerges with four Stanley Cups.

Jacques Plante *(left)*, hockey's first masked goalie, helped the Canadiens to their first of five Stanley Cups during the 1960s. Frank "Big M" Mahovlich *(right)* sparked his Leafs to four coveted mugs.

THE 1960s

The 1950s were a decade of stability and tradition for the NHL, but that stability ended abruptly in the 1960s. The '60s were an era marked by innumerable innovations. First off, the '60s saw the evolution of the "wandering netminder." The first goalie to leave his goal crease as a matter of strategy was Jacques Plante of Montreal.

Plante often skated behind the net when an opponent shot the puck into the corners. He would trap the rubber and hold it in place for a defenseman. Soon, Plante became more courageous, often skating far out of his crease to deliver passes.

Plante also became the first masked goalie. At first, he remained the only masked netminder, but as the 1960s unfolded and more goalies suffered facial injuries, they eschewed their macho thoughts and began donning Plante-type masks.

The slapshot introduced by Boom Boom Geoffrion in the 1950s grew in popularity in the '60s. Blackhawks sharpshooters Bobby "Golden Jet" Hull and Stan Mikita took the slapshot to a higher level. By inventing the curved banana blade, Hull and Mikita inadvertently found a new way of tormenting goaltenders. The curve in their stick blades caused a knuckleball effect on the puck.

Another characteristic of the 1960s was the rise of the "enforcer." A perfect case in point was John Bowie Ferguson. "My job," he explained, "is to stick up for the more talent-ed players on the team like Jean Beliveau and Henri Richard."

Montreal continued to reign as a league power, as it copped five Stanley Cups during the decade. Meanwhile, the Toronto Maple Leafs regained their 1940s glory, as they went to the finals on five occasions and took home the hardware four times.

The turbulent '60s were also marked by expansion. In the fall of 1967, six new teams--Philadelphia, Pittsburgh, Minnesota, Oakland, Los Angeles, and St. Louis—were admitted into the league, each for a fee of $2 million.

Arriving in the league in 1966 was a young defenseman from Parry Sound, Ontario, named Bobby Orr. Orr's advanced skating and puck-handling skills would revolutionize the role of defense. His end-to-end rushes for the Boston Bruins influenced a new generation of blue-liners.

Another innovation—in equipment—was introduced in the late 1960s. It was triggered by a tragic episode that took place on January 13, 1968, during a game between Minnesota and Oakland. Minnesota forward Bill Masterton attempted to break through the Oakland defense and was dropped to the ice, striking his head. Masterton was knocked unconscious and rushed to a hospital. His death shortly thereafter sent shock waves throughout the NHL, sparking demands that all players wear protective helmets.

A Masked Plante Lifts Habs to Fifth Straight Cup

1 9 5 9 - 6 0

Before the 1959-60 season even opened, the annual bloodletting had begun. Rangers coach Phil Watson declared, "That's the last time my team will play an exhibition game against another NHL club."

Watson was referring to a September exhibition game between the Rangers and the Maple Leafs, played in Peterborough, Ontario. The Rangers'

colorful Eddie Shack was hospitalized with a concussion and a ten-stitch cut, while two other New York stars—Bill Gadsby and Andy Bathgate—were seriously roughed up. Sixty-nine penalty minutes were meted out, including a misconduct and game misconduct to feisty Leaf defenseman Carl Brewer. Less than a week later, the Blackhawks and Leafs staged a

similar donnybrook.

Several prominent players were holdouts during the exhibition season, and Toronto GM/coach Punch Imlach had so many no-shows that he threatened to publish salaries unless his holdouts came into the fold. (It's ironic that Imlach used publishing salaries as a threat. By 1990, the Players Association had realized that

Toronto's Red Kelly (4) amassed 11 points in the 1960 playoffs, but most of his damage came in Round One. Kelly found it tougher going in the finals against Montreal's Jacques Plante. The Canadiens swept Toronto in four games.

publishing salaries gave players better leverage in negotiations!)

At the other extreme, Rocket Richard was the first Canadien to sign his contract, for his 18th NHL season. "I never have any problems with Maurice," said Frank Selke, managing director of the Canadiens. "I tell him what I'm going to give him and he signs."

Another Canadien, goalie Jacques Plante, received the approval of league president Clarence Campbell to wear his revolutionary new goalie mask. However, coach Toe Blake was still nixing the idea.

On November 1, 1959, New York's Bathgate slapped a shot at Plante that left a seven-stitch gash on the goalie's face. When Jacques finally reappeared on the ice after taking sutures in the dressing room, he was wearing the mask so hated by Blake. Luckily for the future of all NHL goalies, Plante held off the Rangers and the Canadiens won the game 3-1 (their eighth straight without a loss, to be followed by ten more matches before losing one).

For the rest of the season, Plante wore a mask; he also captured his fifth consecutive Vezina Trophy. The

Ⓐ After stints with the Rangers, Red Wings, Blackhawks, and Maple Leafs, Harry Lumley completed his career with Boston from 1957-60. Here, he goes up against Toronto captain George Armstrong.

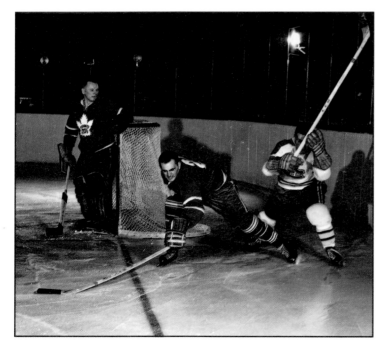

Ⓐ Mighty defense helped rejuvenate Toronto in the 1960s. The defensive work of Bob Baun, shown here stopping a Montreal attacker, was outstanding.

Ⓐ Chicago's Bobby Hull signs autographs for adoring fans. With his speed, strength, and devastating shot, Hull led the NHL in scoring in 1959-60 with 81 points.

JACQUES PLANTE

The most remarkable of the modern goaltenders, Jacques Plante pioneered the use of a goalie mask after a near-fatal injury at Madison Square Garden on November 1, 1959. Plante was struck in the face by a hard shot fired by Ranger Andy Bathgate. Jacques, who had been experimenting with the mask in practice scrimmages, donned the protector and reappeared on the ice.

Nicknamed "Jake the Snake," Plante broke into the NHL with the Canadiens in 1952-53. That same year, he starred for Montreal in a critical semifinal playoff round with Chicago in which the Canadiens triumphed. He soon was hailed as a superb goalie—and an innovative one at that. A superior skater, Plante frequently wandered from his net to field pucks and relay them to teammates.

Plante was extremely gifted, but also troublesome in many ways. He was an excellent tutor and helped refine the style of goalie Bernie Parent when he and Parent played for Toronto. On the other hand, Plante was notorious as a clubhouse lawyer. This may explain why he was traded by Montreal, New York, and St. Louis.

At age 45, Jacques joined the Edmonton Oilers in 1974-75 and appeared to have lost little of his ability. After 31 games, however, Plante decided to call it quits.

"masked marvel" caused endless rounds of debate and discussion during the season. Ranger GM Muzz Patrick had an interesting anti-mask argument.

"Our game," reasoned Patrick, "has a greater percentage of women fans than any team sport I know. And women fans want to see men, not masks. They want to see the blonds, the redheads.... That's why I'm against helmets and masks. They rob the players of their individuality."

Although the Canadiens started a little slower than in years previous, they reached the top of the standings by the season's 11th game. They finished first, 13 points ahead of the second-place Leafs. Chicago finished third, ahead of Detroit, Boston, and the basement-dwelling New York Rangers.

Significantly, an American debuted for the Rangers as the regular season drew to a close. And while this American, goalie Jack McCartan, never lasted long in the NHL, his arrival heralded the future.

First off, McCartan had helped the underdog U.S. Olympic team win a gold medal in the winter of 1960. Already signed by the Rangers,

McCartan then debuted in New York on March 5, 1960 against the Red Wings. He made 33 saves, stopping several rushes from the great Gordie Howe, and the pitiful Rangers took a rare victory.

Why was this debut significant? First, an American team had just beaten the world-renown Russian squad. Secondly, an American playing in the NHL—even briefly—during this era was a real rarity. Finally, McCartan's quick jump from the Olympics to the NHL set a precedent. In later years, many players would immediately leap from the Winter Games to the NHL.

This season, Chicago's Bobby Hull won the first of three Art Ross Trophies (with 81 points on 39 goals), as he edged past Boston's Bronco Horvath for the scoring title. Howe took his fifth (of six) Hart Trophies, and Doug Harvey won his fifth of seven Norris Trophies. Don McKenney of Boston earned the Lady Byng. Chicago rookie Bill Hay won the Calder, while freshman teammate Stan Mikita emerged as the Blackhawk of the future.

Montreal opened the Stanley Cup playoffs against the third-place Hawks, proceeding to wallop them in

Montreal goalie Jacques Plante deflects a drive from Bert Olmstead (left) as Bob Pulford (center) zeroes in for a rebound. Toronto scored just five goals in the 1960 finals.

Toronto's George Armstrong tests Jacques Plante in the 1960 Stanley Cup finals.

FRANK MAHOVLICH

Perhaps the most misunderstood man in pro hockey was Frank Mahovlich, the skating behemoth of the NHL who weathered two nervous breakdowns in his successful quest for superstardom.

As a young, dashing left winger with the Maple Leafs, Frank scored 48 goals in 1960-61, almost matching Maurice Richard's record 50-goal plateau. For Mahovlich, it was too much too soon. The demanding fans expected the huge, gifted skater to surpass his 48 goals the following year. But the new pressure-cooker atmosphere did not suit Frank's psyche. And the more he pressed, the more he worried.

Mahovlich was then dealt to Detroit. Skating on a line with Gordie Howe and Alex Delvecchio, the trio scored a record 118 goals, shattering the old record of 105.

Still, there was a gray cloud hanging over Mahovlich's future in Detroit. His brother Peter, an enormously gifted center, had fallen into disfavor with Red Wings management and was traded to Montreal. In addition, the Red Wings now had a new coach, Ned Harkness, who had new ideas. A trade was inevitable, and on January 13, 1971, Mahovlich was dealt to the Canadiens.

The Canadiens fans immediately took Frank to their collective hearts, and he responded by helping Montreal win the 1971 Stanley Cup. Mahovlich scored 533 goals during his career.

Maurice Richard fondles the 1960 Stanley Cup. Richard, who won eight mugs in his career, retired after the 1960 series.

four straight games. The masked Plante earned shutouts in the last two contests.

In the meantime, Toronto took on Detroit—and Leafs coach Imlach did his best to motivate his troops. Punch actually stacked $1,250 in bills on the team's dressing room floor to remind them of the difference between winning and losing! They got the message. Toronto eliminated the Wings

in six games to face the Canadiens in the finals.

It was basically no contest. Montreal whizzed past Toronto in four straight games, outscoring the Leafs 15-5, to take their astounding fifth straight Stanley Cup. No other team ever had, nor to this day ever has, won five straight Stanley Cups.

The 1959-60 season marked the end of one of the game's greatest careers,

as Maurice Richard decided to hang up his skates after notching only 19 goals and 35 points. Maurice's younger brother, Henri, completed his fifth season with the Canadiens, skating all the while in his older brother's shadow. Henri would play 20 seasons with Montreal and eventually played on 11 Stanley Cup winners. Still, he would be overshadowed by brother Maurice.

Big M, Boom Boom
Take Shots at the Rocket

1 9 6 0 - 6 1

After 18 years and 544 goals, Rocket Richard was gone, but his name remained in the headlines nonetheless. In 1960-61, just months before Roger Maris and Mickey Mantle challenged Babe Ruth's single-season home run record, two NHL players were challenging Richard's goal-scoring record. Toronto's Frank Mahovlich and Montreal's Boom Boom Geoffrion both took aim at Rocket's 50-goal mark.

Amazingly, Mahovlich had 37 goals by midseason and looked a shoo-in to score 50—yet he finished with 48. Meanwhile, Geoffrion missed six games due to an injury and had only 29 goals with a month and a half left in the campaign. It looked as though 21 more goals would be impossible.

But Boom Boom, always a player with hot and cold spells, hit one of his hottest spells ever, scoring 18 times in 13 games and gaining his 50th in the Canadiens' 68th game—which just happened to be against Mahovlich and the Leafs. Geoffrion was unable to squeak past Richard's record in the last two games of the season, though he won the scoring title with 50 goals and 95 points.

▲ Toronto star Frank Mahovlich signs autographs for a group of youngsters. Mahovlich occasionally signed bubble gum cards, which became popular in the 1960s.

Bernie was named right wing on the First All-Star Team with rival Mahovlich on the left side. Jean Beliveau made it at center, Doug Harvey and Marcel Pronovost on defense, and Johnny Bower in goal. Bower also ended Jacques Plante's five-year lock on the Vezina. Boom Boom got the Hart, Harvey won his sixth Norris, and young Dave Keon of Toronto was the Calder winner. Red Kelly, who had been switched from defense to center when he was traded to Toronto from Detroit in 1960, won his fourth Lady Byng award.

The Canadiens finished the regular season atop the league for the fourth consecutive year and were heavily favored to take an amazing sixth straight Cup, as they opened the playoffs against the third-place Chicago Blackhawks. But everyone seemed to have forgotten Mr. Goalie, Glenn Hall. With the combination of some rare body contact from the Chicago players and two shutouts from Hall (in Games Five and Six), the Blackhawks defeated the Cup-defending Canadiens four games to two.

Game Three was the back-breaker for Montreal, as the Hawks won in triple overtime on a goal from Murray Balfour. Canadiens coach Toe Blake was so enraged at what he considered lousy officiating by Dalton McArthur that he charged out on the ice and tried to land a haymaker on the chin of McArthur. Not only did his team lose, but the attempted knockout cost Blake $2,000.

The Toronto Maple Leafs, who finished just two points behind Montreal in the standings, were also upset in the playoffs. Third-place Detroit ousted them in five games in the semis, thus setting up a Detroit-Chicago finals. Again complaints about the officiating occurred. But although Chicago coach Rudy Pilous's and GM Tommy Ivan's remarks cost $500 between them, they had no bearing on the outcome of the series. Chicago bested the Red Wings in six games. The Hawks won the finale 5-1

1960-61

Best Record
Montreal
(41-19-10)

Stanley Cup Finals
Chicago 4
Detroit 2

Art Ross Trophy
Bernie Geoffrion
(50/45/95)

Hart Trophy
Bernie Geoffrion

Vezina Trophy
Johnny Bower

Calder Trophy
Dave Keon

Norris Trophy
Doug Harvey

Lady Byng Trophy
Red Kelly

Coach Randy Pilous (standing)
guided Chicago to a surprise Stanley Cup in 1961. On the year, the Hawks finished a distant third to the Canadiens and Leafs.

Montreal goalie Jacques Plante leaps out of danger as Eddie Shack (left) and Dick Duff (9) barrel into the goalmouth.

JOHNNY BOWER

Goaltending was the Toronto Maple Leafs' big weakness before manager Punch Imlach arrived. When the club finished last in 1957-58, Ed Chadwick, goaltender in all 70 games, finished the season with a 3.23 goals-against average, worst of all the league regulars.

Billy Reay, Imlach's predecessor, scouted the minors for a replacement. Reay's choice was Johnny Bower, a veteran who had bounced around the minors for years and had a brief stint with the New York Rangers (1953-55) before returning to the bushes.

Cynical about past treatment and uncertain about his NHL future, Bower rejected Reay's first offer. Then something changed Bower's mind and he decided to sign with the Leafs. Bower, age 34, was an immediate improvement for the Leafs, posting a 2.74 GAA.

He was a glutton for punishment, especially during practice sessions when he performed as diligently as the rawest of rookies. "I've always had to work hard," Bower explained. "I don't know any other way to play the game."

Bower played 11 seasons with Toronto, hanging up his pads in 1969-70 at age 45.

to take their third, and last, Stanley Cup championship.

The finals between Detroit and Chicago presented a microcosm of the old and the new, of what was best and worst, traditional and radical in hockey at the start of the 1960s. Hall faced the team that had traded him to Chicago in July 1957 because it had re-acquired Terry Sawchuk. Hall represented the last of a dying tradition—the iron-man goalie. Until the modern era, teams had only had one goaltender, period. Then slowly the use of a star goalie and a part-time backup became more and more common.

At this point in hockey history, Hall completed the sixth of seven seasons playing every single moment in goal for his team. Sawchuk, on the other hand, had only played in 37 of 70 regular-season games for the Red Wings. The tandem goalie system was definitely on the way in.

The Wings and Hawks also differed offensively. Detroit's Alex Delvecchio and Gordie Howe were the quintessential traditionalists.

Delvecchio, at center, carried the puck up ice, then invariably passed it off to one of his wingers. And if the pass went to Howe, Gordie would invariably drill a wrist shot or a backhand.

The veteran Wings also handled their own forechecking and "policing." In fact, Howe was known to have one of the meanest set of sneaky elbows in the league and was so tough that he was virtually untouchable. "You could be sure," said former teammate and tough guy Larry Zeidel, "that you didn't get away with anything against them. And

▲ Toronto's George Armstrong watches the puck whiz by Glenn Hall's ear. Hall was runner-up for the Vezina in 1960-61.

▲ Toronto's Dave Keon fires one at Chicago's Glenn Hall. The young Keon was known for his great speed.

▲ Among Toronto's best veterans were defenseman Tim Horton (left) and Johnny Bower (right).

Detroit goalie Terry Sawchuk receives medical attention after being struck by a puck in the 1961 semifinals. Alex Delvecchio (10) and Marcel Pronovost (3) help out.

Red Wing Gordie Howe beats Toronto's Johnny Bower in 1961 playoff action. Detroit ousted Toronto in five games before falling to Chicago.

PUNCH IMLACH

One of the most successful and cantankerous coaches in major-league hockey history is George "Punch" Imlach. Imlach's tough-as-nails approach to the game won him four Stanley Cups with the powerhouse Leaf teams of the 1960s.

Before his days as coach of the Leafs, Punch spent 11 years with the minor-league Quebec Aces as a player, coach, general manager, and, eventually, part-owner. Then Imlach joined the Boston Bruins organization as manager/coach of the AHL's Springfield Indians for one year until he took over the coaching duties for the Leafs.

Imlach was named coach and general manager of the Buffalo Sabres in 1970 and built the team into a powerhouse in two seasons. However, he was forced to step aside from coaching duties following a massive heart attack during the 1971-72 season. He later returned for one more stint as Leafs general manager.

I mean anything. They'd use the stick on you as easily as they'd breathe."

Players were actually frightened of the multi-talented Howe. A member of the Rangers once confided to a reporter that Howe was, by far, the dirtiest player in the game. When the newsman quoted the player by name the next day, the player expressed outrage. "If Gordie reads that," the Ranger worried, "he's liable to kill me!"

Chicago's Bobby Hull and Stan Mikita, on the other hand, were the essence of the "new" hockey. While Mikita could stick-handle the puck down the ice with finesse, he and Hull were perfecting the curved-stick and employing the fly-down-the-ice-and-slap-it brand of hockey that would become prevalent by the mid- to late 1960s.

After the season, the NHL acquired a permanent home for its Hockey Hall of Fame. For many years, people debated whether the Hall should be in Montreal, Ottawa, Toronto, or Kingston. After years of squabbling, the Canadian National Exhibition, the City of Toronto, and the NHL finally agreed to construct the Hockey Hall of Fame on the CNE grounds. The Hall opened on August 26, 1961.

Hall of Fame Opens Doors;
Leafs Sip from Cup

1 9 6 1 - 6 2

When the Hockey Hall of Fame opened in August 1961, it included 89 members, 43 of them still living. Among that year's inductees were Rocket Richard (the Hall waived its tradition of waiting five years after retirement to elect a player) and the first three referees ever included: Mickey Ion, Cooper Smeaton, and Chaucer Elliott.

Toronto's King Clancy recalled his first game in the NHL—Ion was the referee: "He told me to just remember that everyone else in the rink was crazy but him and me."

When it came time for training camp, the Canadiens chose to practice in Victoria, B.C., and hold several exhibition games on the West Coast. Hal Laycoe, then coach of the Portland

team in the World Hockey League, said prophetically, "Major-league hockey on the (West) Coast is as inevitable as night follows day. Los Angeles, San Francisco, Seattle, Portland, Vancouver, Calgary, and Edmonton would make a solid major-league circuit." Little did he know....

The Habs, though, started the season heavily wounded (much as they had

Frank Mahovlich attempts to dislodge the puck from Jacques Plante's grip. Montreal and Toronto again dominated the NHL in 1961-62, with the two teams finishing first and second, respectively.

been in the playoffs against Chicago the previous spring). Dickie Moore was out with a re-injured knee, as was Jean Beliveau. Henri Richard and Donnie Marshall were nursing groin pulls. Phil Goyette couldn't shake a flu, and rookie Bobby Rousseau was out with a sore ankle. Furthermore, they were without the services of defensive star Doug Harvey, who had signed a three-year contract with the New York Rangers as player/coach. The Habs acquired "Leapin' Lou" Fontinato from New York as compensation, but the tough guy was no substitute for Harvey's expertise as a defenseman.

The one major consolation was that goalie Jacques Plante was back in good form after missing half of the previous season with a bad knee. (Plante had surgery after the 1960-61 season.) With nowhere to go but up, the Canadiens did just that, finishing the season at 42-14-14 and on top of the league (for the fifth straight time), 13 points ahead of the Leafs.

In New York, veteran centerman Red Sullivan had a poor training camp and decided to retire, paving the way for a youngster named Jean Ratelle. Though Ratelle would eventually become an NHL star, he scored only 12 points in 1961-62 and wouldn't break the 20-goal mark until the 1965-66 season. Nevertheless, the Rangers finished this season in the playoffs for the first time since 1958, landing in fourth place ahead of Detroit and lowly Boston.

The Bruins started the season with seven rookies on the roster, including a young winger named Ed Westfall and a novice defenseman who would become known as "Terrible" Ted Green. Unfortunately, Green broke a knuckle trying to rearrange Frank Mahovlich's face in the Bruins' first exhibition game and missed the season opener. Boston was abysmal in 1961-62, winning only 15 games and allowing a whopping 306 goals.

The Blackhawks were initially favored to win a second straight Cup, largely because of the continued brilliance of goalie Glenn Hall and the blistering scoring of Bobby Hull. Hull tallied his record-tying 50th goal in the

In 1961-62, Andy Bathgate (pictured) tied Bobby Hull for the NHL lead in points with 84. However, Hull won the Art Ross Trophy by outscoring Bathgate 50-28.

Montreal's Jacques Plante kicks away a Toronto shot while Canadiens forward Gilles Tremblay (21) looks on. Tremblay, just a sophomore in 1961-62, scored 32 goals on the year.

CARL BREWER

Carl Brewer had an unusual hockey career, to say the least. At the age of 26, in the prime of his ice life, Brewer quit the Maple Leafs to study at the University of Toronto. He campaigned successfully to regain his amateur status, then performed with the Canadian National Team. Carl coached in the International Hockey League and also coached the Helsinki IFK sextet in Finland.

"The funny part of it," he said, "is that I didn't have any master plan in mind when I made the changes."

His professional tenure included ten NHL seasons with the Leafs, Red Wings, and Blues, and a year in the WHA with the Toronto Toros. He was a four-time All-Star—and an all-time philosopher. "The game of hockey itself is very easy," he professed. "It's the thinking about it that makes it hard."

Brewer retired in 1974 to do TV color commentary for the Toros.

last game of the regular season.

Bobby tied in points with New York's Andy Bathgate (84), but earned the Art Ross Trophy because he had 22 more goals than Bathgate. Harvey earned his seventh (and final) Norris Trophy, while Plante won both the Vezina (his sixth) and the Hart Trophies. Montreal's Rousseau captured the Calder Trophy, and sophomore Leaf Dave Keon was awarded the Lady Byng.

The 1962 First All-Star Team was composed of Bathgate at right wing, Chicago's Stan Mikita at center, and teammate Hull on the left wing. On defense, Harvey and Montreal's Jean-Guy Talbot were picked. Harvey had thus earned his tenth berth on the First All-Star Team in 11 seasons (making the Second All-Star Team the other year).

Early in the season, Conn Smythe, builder of Maple Leaf Gardens and architect of the Leaf dynasty, stepped down as chairman of the board of the Leafs and passed the baton to his son, Stafford. Stafford joined forces with John Bassett and a wild, flamboyant entrepreneur named Harold Ballard to purchase controlling interest in the Gardens from Conn Smythe. Ballard replaced Stafford Smythe as president of the Leafs' hockey committee.

At the end of the regular season, Red Kelly, who had made the switch from defense in Detroit to playing center in Toronto, announced an even bolder career move. Kelly declared that he would stand for Parliament as the Liberal nominee from Toronto's York West district. Kelly won the election and proceeded to combine politics and hockey successfully for a number of years. One person who definitely would not vote for Kelly was New York's star goalie, Lorne "Gump" Worsley.

Although Toronto was favored to win its semifinal playoff series against the Rangers, New York pushed the Leafs hard, and it took six games for Toronto to eliminate the Broadway

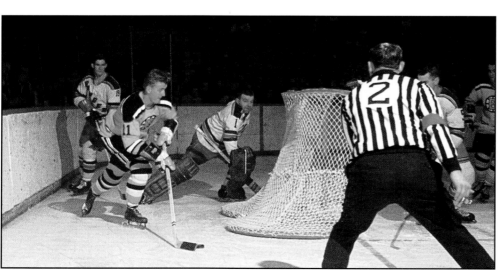

In 1961-62, Harold Ballard (left) and Stafford Smythe (right) bought controlling interest in Maple Leaf Gardens. Ballard would eventually own the Leafs.

Boston's Tom Williams (11) tries a wrap-around play, as Ranger goalie Gump Worsley scrambles to the net.

▲ Toronto's Allan Stanley (26) crushes two Blackhawks and teammate Bob Baun into the boards. In the 1962 finals, Toronto ousted Chicago in six games.

▲ Chicago's Bobby Hull knocks home one of the 58 goals he scored during the 1961-62 season—eight of which came in the playoffs.

GLENN HALL

Glenn Hall, one of the greatest professional netminders of all time, managed to appear in an amazing 502 consecutive games. Yet Hall was so fearful of his hazardous occupation that he would often get violently ill before games.

Over his 18-year, big-league career, Hall labored for three NHL clubs—the Detroit Red Wings, Chicago Blackhawks, and St. Louis Blues. He was named a first-team All-Star goalie seven times, three times having his name inscribed on the Vezina Trophy as the league's top goaltender.

Despite taking scores of painful stitches in his face, Hall did not don a goalie mask until the twilight of his career, claiming it restricted his vision when the puck was at his feet.

One night, during the 1957 Stanley Cup playoffs, a screened shot suddenly flashed out of a tangle of bodies and smashed into Hall's maskless face. The game was delayed for a half-hour while he took 23 stitches in his mouth before returning to finish the game.

Hall was named to the Hockey Hall of Fame in June 1975.

Blueshirts. A prominent thorn in Toronto's side was the goaltending of Worsley, particularly in Game Five of the series. Tied 2-2 after regulation, the game went into its second overtime. It ended when Kelly snagged the puck from under Worsley's splayed body and snapped in the winner. Even though he had saved 56 shots in 84 minutes, Worsley later admitted that Kelly's tally was the most miserable moment in his hockey life.

In the Hawks-Habs semifinal series, Montreal looked like a sure winner, taking the first two games. But Chicago then proceeded to win four straight, shutting out Montreal 2-0 in Game Six. Ironically, when the Hawks were floundering in years previous, the Canadiens sent several players to Chicago to help bolster the franchise. They were now paying for their generosity.

Chicago again dropped the first two games of the finals, losing to Toronto 4-1 and 3-2. But when the Leafs arrived in Chicago for the next two games, they met a transformed Hawks squad. Chicago won the next two contests, 3-0 and 4-1. A Hull shot caused Leaf goalie Johnny Bower to pull his groin in Game Four, and suddenly the favored Leafs were in trouble.

The loss of Bower and insertion of Don Simmons in goal seemed to inspire the Leafs, however, as they romped to an 8-4 Game Five victory over the stunned Hawks. Toronto was powered by three goals from Bob Pulford (who, ironically, would someday become the GM of Chicago).

Game Six in Chicago Stadium was a classic thriller. The game was scoreless until 8:58 of the third period, when Hull netted the first tally. Less than two minutes later, Bob Nevin put Toronto on the scoreboard. And finally, at 14:14 of the third period, Dick Duff scored the winner for Toronto. Duff got an assist from blue-liner Tim Horton, who set a record for defensemen in Stanley Cup play with 12 assists in 13 games. More importantly, the Leafs had their first Stanley Cup in 11 years.

Maple Leafs Prove the Best
of a Mediocre Lot

1 9 6 2 - 6 3

Shortly after the end of the 1961-62 season, a figure who had been on the NHL scene for more than four decades chose to leave. After being coach and GM of the Detroit Red Wings for more than 35 seasons, Jack Adams resigned to become president of the Central Professional Hockey League.

The Hockey Hall of Fame acquired its first father-son combination in June 1962, when James Norris Jr. of the Blackhawks was inducted into the Hall. James Jr. followed his father, James Sr., who had been added to the Builders section some years earlier.

Doug Harvey, father of five youngsters who had remained in Montreal while he coached his first season in New York, yielded his behind-the-bench position in order to spend time with his family. Muzz Patrick took over the Rangers as manager/coach. Patrick finally named Red Sullivan coach, but it was too late in the season to help the team into the playoffs.

New York finished ahead of Boston, which managed to cut down its goals-against to 281 but won only 14 games in the process. While the Rangers and Bruins finished well out of playoff

Detroit's Terry Sawchuk makes a brilliant sliding save against Toronto's Eddie Shack. Toronto defeated Detroit in five games in the 1963 finals, scoring 17 goals against Sawchuk.

contention, the four playoff teams finished neck-and-neck with one another. Toronto won regular-season honors with 82 points, while fourth-place Detroit totaled 77 points.

Toronto turned on the juice in the playoffs. Led by Johnny Bower's goaltending and Dave Keon's clutch scoring, the Maple Leafs powered past the Canadiens in the semifinals, four games to one. Meanwhile, Detroit eliminated the favored second-place Hawks in six games, after dropping the first two.

The final round between Toronto and Detroit was a fast-paced affair that the Leafs won in five games. Toronto overcame the outstanding efforts of Gordie Howe—who led all playoff scorers with seven goals and 16 points—as well as the ineffectiveness of their own Frank Mahovlich, who failed to score a goal in the entire playoffs.

Mahovlich's regular-season production was a different story, however, as he tied for fourth in league scoring (73 points) with Montreal's Henri Richard. This apparently didn't satisfy Toronto coach Punch Imlach. After a midseason scoring spree by Frank (eight goals in eight games), the dour Toronto skipper lashed out at the "Big M" for not playing up to his potential.

Despite such criticism, his lackluster playoff performance, and threats of a trade to Chicago, Mahovlich was selected to the First All-Star Team at left wing. He had the distinction of being the only player to displace Bobby Hull as a first-team All-Star in the decade of the '60s.

The First All-Star Team, in addition to Mahovlich, included Glenn Hall at goalie, Pierre Pilote and Carl Brewer on defense, Stan Mikita at center, and the ageless Howe on right wing. Howe led the league in both goals (38) and points (86) and won the Hart Trophy—the last time he accomplished any of these feats.

Pilote of Chicago earned his first of three Norris Trophies, wresting the award from the clutches of a now-fading Harvey. Keon took his second straight Lady Byng Trophy after only

🔺 **Bobby Hull (left) led the NHL in scoring in 1961-62, but Gordie Howe (right) took the honors in 1962-63, as he amassed 86 points.**

EMILE FRANCIS

Emile "The Cat" Francis, the long-time Ranger coach, started out as an NHL netminder. Francis debuted in 1946-47, appearing in 19 games for the Chicago Blackhawks. The following season, he guarded the cage 54 times. At best, The Cat (nicknamed for his catlike moves in the cage) was a mediocre goalie for a rather poor Chicago outfit.

Emile eventually found his way to New York, where he occasionally tended goal for Frank Boucher's Rangers. Francis ended his playing career at Spokane of the Western League, after having "dislocated both shoulders" in 1960. He immediately began coaching at Guelph, Ontario, a junior team with Rod Gilbert and Jean Ratelle, who both went on to star for Francis with the Rangers.

Francis quickly climbed the Ranger ladder, and by 1964 he was New York's general manager. The next season, he took over as coach. His career was the most successful of any Ranger mentor.

Francis later became general manager of the St. Louis Blues and, finally, the Hartford Whalers.

two minor penalties in two seasons. Hall won his first (and long overdue) Vezina Trophy after leading the league in wins (30) and shutouts (five). And the Calder Trophy went to rookie Kent Douglas, a Toronto defenseman who played only six more seasons in the NHL. Coach Imlach had yielded five players to Eddie Shore, owner of the Springfield Indians of the American Hockey League, to acquire Douglas. Kent was the first defenseman to win the Calder Trophy.

The season's tragic note was struck on March 9, when Montreal defenseman Lou Fontinato was seriously injured after attempting to check Vic Hadfield of the Rangers. Thrown headlong into the boards, Fontinato crushed a cervical vertebra and was, in fact, paralyzed for a short time. Although he recovered from the injury, it was the last NHL appearance for Leapin' Lou. Fontinato's then-league record of 202 penalty minutes was broken that same season by

Detroit's talented but highly unstable defenseman, Howie Young, who spent 273 minutes in the box.

Despite Fontinato's injury and their failure in the playoffs, the Canadiens enjoyed some bright moments in 1962-63. Montreal assembled a young, talented defense tandem of Jacques Laperriere and Terry Harper. Richard displayed his playmaking skills with 50 assists. And in January, Jean Beliveau tallied his 300th goal.

Although Hall achieved his first

1962-63

Best Record
Toronto
(35-23-12)

Stanley Cup Finals
Toronto 4
Detroit 1

Art Ross Trophy
Gordie Howe
(38/48/86)

Hart Trophy
Gordie Howe

Vezina Trophy
Glenn Hall

Calder Trophy
Kent Douglas

Norris Trophy
Pierre Pilote

Lady Byng Trophy
Dave Keon

In 1962-63, Detroit featured the high-scoring line of Alex Delvecchio (left), Gordie Howe (center), and Parker MacDonald. They each surpassed the 60-point barrier on the year.

Toronto center Red Kelly (left) fights off Boston defenseman Ted Green. Red was one of the NHL's first helmeted players. Green, ironically, would suffer a near-fatal head injury in 1969.

Vezina Trophy, he did so after ending his own "iron-man" record. In November, Glenn was forced to leave a game with a strained ligament in his back and was replaced by Denis DeJordy. Since entering the league, Hall had played in 502 consecutive games (553 counting the playoffs) before the injury. It was a record that would most likely never be broken, now that the tandem goalie system had arrived.

The 1962-63 season was again marred by violence and official-baiting. After a 6-3 loss to Toronto, Montreal coach Toe Blake was so unhappy that he implied that referee Eddie Powers had handled the game "as though he had bet on the outcome." Blake's remarks elicited a promise from league prexy Clarence Campbell to investigate the matter. Campbell subsequently slapped Blake with a $200 fine for his remarks, whereupon Powers promptly submitted his resignation. Powers claimed that the fine was inadequate and, further, that Campbell didn't give sufficient support to the league's officials.

Montreal's Gilles Tremblay and Chicago's Reg Fleming engaged in a stick-swinging duel that onlookers agreed was the worst in more than a decade. The episode earned both gladiators a three-game suspension. Then in March, Boom Boom Geoffrion took such offense at referee Vern Buffy that he threw his stick and gloves at the official. This earned Boom Boom a five-game suspension.

YVAN COURNOYER

There was never a Montreal Canadien who flied faster than Yvan Cournoyer, the compact right wing.

As a member of the Junior Canadiens, a regal teenage version of the parent club, Cournoyer impressed coach Claude Ruel. "I could tell right away," said Ruel, "that he had the same scoring knack as the Rocket."

During the 1963-64 season, the Montreal Canadiens called up Yvan for a five-game tryout and he scored in his first game. "He pounced on the puck like a cat," said Jean Beliveau. However, coach Toe Blake was less enthused. He gave Yvan part-time work during his rookie year, 1964-65, and Cournoyer scored only seven goals. "But I never let down," said Yvan, "because when you let down you're finished."

During the 1968 Stanley Cup finals against the St. Louis Blues, Cournoyer put two enemy defensemen out of action with slapshots on the same shift. After both Al Arbour and Barclay Plager were felled by Yvan's bazooka shots, the puck came back to Cournoyer who finally shot it past goalie Glenn Hall.

Yvan captained the Canadiens during their run of four straight Stanley Cups victories (1975-79).

King Clancy *(left)* and Punch Imlach *(right)* were an inseparable pair during Toronto's glory years in the early 1960s. Imlach was the coach and GM while Clancy was his aide-de-camp.

Detroit defenseman Bill Gadsby (4) toiled 20 years in the NHL and never played for a Stanley Cup winner. He had his chance in 1963, but the Wings fell to Toronto in five games.

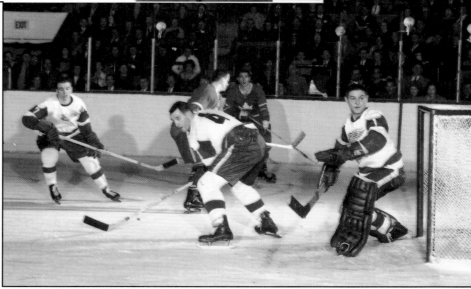

Deja Vu: Toronto Tops
the Wings One More Time

1 9 6 3 - 6 4

On June 5, 1963, the NHL held its first universal amateur draft. According to the league, "all players of qualifying age (17) unaffected by sponsorship of junior teams (are) available to be drafted." In the inaugural draft, the six NHL teams picked 21 young players.

Two days later, the world saw a closing to one of the most tragic chapters in NHL annals, a chapter that began back on April 21, 1951.

Back on that April day, Toronto's Bill Barilko converted a Howie Meeker pass into an overtime goal, which gave the Leafs an unprecedented third straight Stanley Cup. Unbeknownst to the big blond defenseman, it would be his last game in the NHL. Only weeks later, Barilko and a friend were reported missing aboard a small plane flying over the bush country of northern Ontario. The Royal Canadian Air Force searched for weeks without success.

Then, almost 12 years later, on June 7, 1963, the wreckage and their remains were discovered. An ironic catharsis occurred in the subsequent 1963-64 season, as Toronto once again would win a third successive Stanley Cup.

On November 10, 1963, Terry Sawchuk (left) notched his 94th shutout, tying the NHL record, and Gordie Howe (right) scored his 545th goal, breaking the all-time record. In the finals, though, Detroit fell to Toronto in seven games.

The league's top two teams during the season—Montreal and Chicago, respectively—were ousted in the opening rounds of the playoffs. The 1964 Stanley Cup finals were a terrific battle between the Maple Leafs and the Red Wings, featuring several thrilling contests that were decided in the waning moments.

Toronto took the first game 4-3 when Bob Pulford outraced Gordie Howe to a puck, then scored with only two seconds left in regulation time. In Game Two, Toronto's Gerry Ehman tied the game at 3-3 with 43 seconds left, but the Leafs' comeback was thwarted when Detroit's Larry Jeffrey netted an overtime goal. Toronto wasted another comeback in Game

Three, when it erased a three-goal deficit only to allow Alex Delvecchio to score with 17 seconds remaining in the game.

Down three games to two after five, the Leafs got an overtime tally in Game Six by Bobby Baun and knotted the series at three games apiece. Toronto goalie Johnny Bower secured the Cup in the decisive seventh game with his fourth career playoff shutout. Andy Bathgate, acquired with Don McKenney in a midseason trade with the Rangers, netted the Cup-winning goal.

The Bathgate trade was but one of several personnel changes made on Broadway. Garden fans didn't like it when GM Muzz Patrick dealt away the popular Bathgate, and they were

JOHN FERGUSON

John Ferguson earned a fistful of respect after joining Montreal in the 1963-64 season, and not merely for his fighting ability. During the Stanley Cup semifinals against the Rangers in 1967, Fergy clinched the series by scoring the winning goal in sudden-death overtime of the fourth game.

But scoring certainly was not his forte. A lumbering skater, he often suggested a rhinocerous galumphing up and down the rink. His shot was just average at best, and he was not exactly known for his stick-handling ability.

Fergie's intense hatred for the opposition extended beyond the ice, and he was known to snub his rivals even during the off-season. In 1976, Fergy was coaxed back to hockey as general manager/coach of the New York Rangers. His stay was less than successful. Right after the 1978 season, Ferguson was given his walking papers.

But before he left, he was responsible for obtaining the Swedish tandem of Ulf Nilsson and Anders Hedberg from the Winnipeg Jets. Ironically, when Ferguson left New York, he became general manager of the Jets, where he could well have used the services of the flashy Swedish pair. He remained Winnipeg's GM until the 1988-89 season.

In the 1960s, Bob Pulford was Toronto's best two-way player. He was a tenacious checker who scored many timely goals.

This is the stick Gordie Howe used to score his 544th goal, which tied Rocket Richard's NHL record.

soon chanting "Muzz must go!" The chant grew louder and louder during the second half of the season, as Bathgate went on to finish first in assists—something no Ranger has accomplished since.

New York did feature several new faces, including Red Sullivan, who began his first full term as coach. Other Broadway debuts were made by Jacques Plante, Phil Goyette, and Donnie Marshall. They were picked up from Montreal before the season in exchange for Gump Worsley, Dave Balon, and Leon Rochefort. The Rangers also said an unfond farewell to defenseman Doug Harvey, giving

the future Hall of Famer his unconditional release.

Harvey had just finished his second of a three-year deal with the Rangers, in which he had agreed initially to be player/coach. Even though he got the Rangers into the playoffs his first season, Harvey, whose family had remained in Montreal, found the double duty too much. For the 1962-63 season, he resigned as coach, leaving a disgruntled Patrick with double duty instead (until Sullivan was hired). Harvey then spent the entire season commuting between New York and Montreal in order to spend time with his family.

It was during that season that Patrick, the media, and, to some extent, the fans began to get on Harvey's back. Grousing and complaining in print that Harvey was getting "special treatment" because of his furloughs to Montreal, everybody had become disenchanted with the arrangement. Finally, after just two assists in 14 games in 1963-64, Harvey was released. He left hockey as the NHL's then-all-time leading scorer among defensemen. (Harvey would attempt a comeback three years later.)

In Detroit, two significant milestones were achieved on the same night by members of the same team. When the

1963-64

Best Record
Montreal
(36-21-13)

Stanley Cup Finals
Toronto 4
Detroit 3

Art Ross Trophy
Stan Mikita
(39/50/89)

Hart Trophy
Jean Beliveau
(28/50/78)

Vezina Trophy
Charlie Hodge

Calder Trophy
Jacques Laperriere

Norris Trophy
Pierre Pilote

Lady Byng Trophy
Ken Wharram

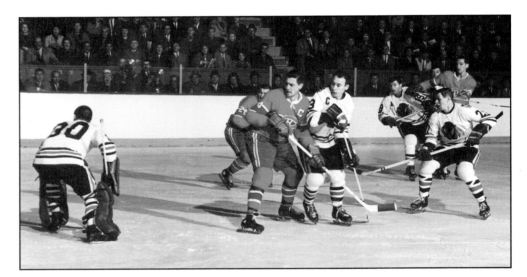

Montreal finished first in 1963-64, one point ahead of Chicago. Here, captains Jean Beliveau (left) and Pierre Pilote jockey for position.

In 1963-64, Rangers GM Muzz Patrick (pictured) traded Andy Bathgate to Toronto in a highly unpopular deal. Patrick resigned after the season.

Red Wings blanked the Canadiens on November 10, it was the 94th career shutout for Terry Sawchuk, equalling George Hainsworth's all-time record. In that same game, Howe added a shorthanded goal, which gave him a career total of 545, one more than Maurice Richard's previous mark of 544.

The 1963-64 season also featured the debut of two promising forwards, both of whom would find their way into the Hall of Fame. One was a burly young centerman for Chicago named Phil Esposito. After three years in the minors, Espo saw action in only 27 NHL games, collecting a paltry five points. His impact was yet to be felt.

The other rookie, Montreal's Yvan Cournoyer, displayed a much different style of play. The "Roadrunner" appeared in just five games, but his exceptional speed and quick moves would make him an integral part of the Habs' offense for the next 15 seasons.

By the end of 1963-64, the Blackhawks accomplished what only one other team in NHL history had done. Like the 1944-45 Canadiens, the 1963-64 Hawks claimed five of the six First All-Star Team berths. Glenn Hall was the goalie; Bobby Hull was the left wing, Ken Wharram the right wing, and Stan Mikita the center; and Pierre Pilote made it on defense. Toronto

defenseman Tim Horton was the lone non-Hawk on the first team. However, Hawk blue-liner Elmer Vasko made it on the Second All-Star Team.

The Canadiens and the Blackhawks were the only clubs whose players captured individual awards. For Montreal, Jean Beliveau won his second of two Hart Trophies, Charlie Hodge took the Vezina with a league-leading eight shutouts, and defenseman Jacques Laperriere took the Calder. In Chicago, Mikita earned the first of his four Art Ross Trophies (89 points), Pilote grabbed his second Norris, and Wharram nabbed the Lady Byng after totaling only 18 minutes in penalties.

🔺 **Montreal defenseman Terry Harper (19) intercepts Toronto's Dave Keon during the 1964 semifinals. The Leafs defeated the Canadiens in seven.**

🔺 **In 1963-64, Toronto traded for Andy Bathgate (9). Bathgate helped the Leafs defeat Montreal in the semis and Detroit in the finals.**

HENRI RICHARD

Brothers Henri and Maurice Richard both starred for Montreal, but their styles were as different as can be. The Rocket was the home run hitter for Montreal, while the younger "Pocket Rocket" was more like the base-stealer and opposite-field hitter.

Within five seasons of big-league hockey, Henri helped Montreal win five Stanley Cups—he even scored the Cup-winning, sudden-death overtime goal in 1966. In those five years, Henri made the All-Star team, led the league in assists, finished second in scoring, and was called the fastest skater of all time.

"The Pocket," said Canadiens coach Toe Blake, "became a better all-around player than Rocket was." The general consensus was that Henri was mechanically better than Maurice but lacked Rocket's killer instinct to be a great scorer.

Henri himself once elaborated on that theme. "My brother's biggest thrills came when he scored many goals," he said. "I am most satisfied when I play in a close game and do not have any goals scored against me."

Depleted Habs
Fight Their Way to the Cup

1 9 6 4 - 6 5

The 1964-65 season saw some major changes throughout the league. The Canadiens, Cupless for four years, lost the services of Frank Selke, who retired as managing director of the team. Replacing Selke was Sammy Pollock, who had worked his way up through the behind-the-scenes ranks in the Canadiens organization. Meanwhile, Canadien Boom Boom Geoffrion retired

to become the coach of the AHL's Quebec Aces. Through 14 seasons with Montreal, Geoffrion had amassed 759 points in 766 games, including his 50-goal campaign in 1960-61.

Although he couldn't compensate for the losses of Selke and Geoffrion, young defenseman Ted Harris slipped into the Montreal lineup, where he would spend six seasons as one of the league's

toughest blue-liners. Another tough youngster, winger John Bowie Ferguson, would become Montreal's policeman, garnering 17 goals, 27 assists, and 156 hard-fought penalty minutes.

In New York, Muzz Patrick resigned as GM to become vice-president of the new Madison Square Garden (which would open during the 1967-68 expansion season). Patrick was replaced

▲ Chicago's Bobby Hull outraces Montreal's Dave Balon (center) and Jacques Laperriere (right). Hull scored eight goals against Detroit in the 1965 semis, but only two vs. Montreal in the finals.

by Emile "The Cat" Francis, a former journeyman goaltender who had been Patrick's assistant in 1962. As coach of the Rangers' Guelph, Ontario, farm team, Francis had nursed the talents of Rod Gilbert and Jean Ratelle. The two would soon become stars for the Broadway Blueshirts.

None of these changes helped the Rangers in 1964-65, however, as they finished the season in fifth place. Almost unnoticed was a four-game stint in New York by a rookie named Ulf Sterner. Sterner didn't score a point and never played another NHL game, but he made history as the first Swede ever to play in the NHL. It would be another decade before the "European invasion" began in the

league, with the arrival of Swedes Borje Salming and Inge Hammarstrom.

Poor Boston graced the league cellar once again. The Bruins were disappointed by the performance of new acquisition Ab McDonald, but somewhat heartened by the 18 goals from another new Bruin, Reg Fleming.

The Red Wings were bolstered by the acquisition of Gary Bergman, Murray Hall, George Gardner, and others, including the return from retirement of Ted Lindsay. Lindsay took up his on-ice career almost exactly where he had left off, re-establishing a feud with Dickie Moore (who also left retirement to sign with the Leafs) and verbally abusing referee Vern Buffy. Lindsay finished the

season, at age 38, with 14 goals, 14 assists, and a wicked 173 penalty minutes—second only to Leafs blue-liner Carl Brewer.

The Red Wings clicked behind the goaltending of young Roger Crozier and the offense of Norm Ullman, Alex Delvecchio, and Gordie Howe. Detroit finished the season at the top of the standings (40-23-7) for the first time since 1957.

Toronto slipped to fourth place despite the spark of newcomers Ron Ellis and Pete Stemkowski, who helped augment the seasoned scoring of Frank Mahovlich, Dave Keon, and Red Kelly. But the prize of the club that year was the goaltending combo of Johnny Bower and Terry Sawchuk.

Chicago's Phil Esposito tries to poke one past goalie Terry Sawchuk while Bob Pulford (20) and Larry Hillman (2) cage him with their sticks.

HARRY HOWELL

Harry Howell spent 22 years in the NHL. Seventeen of those years were spent with the New York Rangers, for whom he played more than 1,000 games—a team record. Howell debuted with the Rangers in 1952. He went on to become one of the game's best defensive defenseman with his subtle—some deprecatingly called it dainty—style of play.

Howell was named to the NHL All-Star squad in 1967. He was the last player to win the Norris Trophy (1966-67) before Bobby Orr virtually took possession of the award.

After leaving the Rangers in 1969, Howell played two years with the Oakland Seals and three with the Los Angeles Kings, then jumped to the San Diego Mariners of the WHA. In 1977, Harry became general manager of the Cleveland Barons, and when they merged with the North Stars in 1978, he was named coach of the team.

But coaching wasn't for Harry. When his health began to suffer shortly after the start of the 1978-79 season, he resigned to become a scout with the North Stars, and more recently the Oilers.

Sawchuk had been snatched for the bargain price of $20,000 when the Red Wings left him unprotected in order to retain their rookie star, Crozier. The Leafs finished with the league's lowest goals-against mark, but Bower and Sawchuk, who had played 34 and 36 games for the Leafs, respectively, refused to accept the trophy unless both of their names were inscribed on it (and unless they each received the same cash award). The league agreed, and the Vezina would thereafter be a trophy emblematic of the new two-goalie system.

On paper, as always, the Chicago Blackhawks looked like a sure winner. But the team managed only a third-place finish, despite the growth of young Phil Esposito who notched 23 goals. The Hawks decided that two Hulls must be better than one, and signed Bobby's brother, Dennis, who managed ten goals in 55 games. Despite their lack of team success, four Hawks reaped individual trophies in 1964-65. Bobby Hull took the Hart and Lady Byng, Stan Mikita earned the Art Ross (87 points on 28 goals), and Pierre Pilote won his third Norris.

Detroit's Crozier won the Calder Trophy, but lost the Vezina by a game to Bower and Sawchuk. On the last night of the regular season, the Leafs shut out Detroit 4-0.

The big award news of the season, though, came when Jean Beliveau was chosen as the first-ever winner of the Conn Smythe Trophy. Presented to the league by Maple Leaf Gardens in honor of their builder, the award was given to the most valuable player of the Stanley Cup playoffs. The award was selected by the Professional Hockey Writers Association after the last game of the finals.

In the semifinal round of the playoffs, Detroit took the first two games of its series against the Chicago Blackhawks, only to drop the next two. Detroit returned to take Game Five, but succumbed in Game Six to the goaltending of Glenn Hall and the scoring of the "Scooter Line" of Doug

1964-65		
Best Record		
Detroit		
(40-23-7)		
Stanley Cup Finals		
Montreal 4		
Chicago 3		
Art Ross Trophy		
Stan Mikita		
(28/59/87)		
Hart Trophy		
Bobby Hull		
(39/32/71)		
Vezina Trophy		
Terry Sawchuk		
Johnny Bower		
Calder Trophy		
Roger Crozier		
Norris Trophy		
Pierre Pilote		
Lady Byng Trophy		
Bobby Hull		

A rare overhead view of Maple Leaf Gardens. Montreal's Bobby Rousseau falls to the ice as Toronto's Tim Horton (7) pursues the puck.

Boston's Dean Prentice (17) battles for position with Toronto blue-liner Bob Baun. In 1964-64, Boston was a miserable 21-43-6.

Mohns, Mikita, and Ken Wharram. Then in Game Seven, Hull simply took over, scoring his eighth goal of the playoffs and leading the Hawks into the finals.

Montreal won Game One of the semis against Toronto, but only after referee Vern Buffy had meted out 75 minutes in penalties. The Habs also took Game Two 3-1, but Toronto battled back in Game Three to win 3-2 in overtime. The Leafs also won Game Four, 4-2, but then lost on a 50-foot slapshot from Bobby Rousseau in Game Five, losing 3-1. Finally in Game Six, Claude Provost's overtime goal shot Montreal into the finals.

The Canadiens ended their Cup drought in the seventh game of the finals, courtesy of Gump Worsley's clutch shutout against Chicago. Worsley, incidentally, was appearing in his first Cup finals after a long and checkered career. Beliveau provided his team's only goal of Game Seven—which came only 14 seconds into the contest.

Crozier's rookie-season brilliance earned him a berth on the First All-Star Team. Other first-teamers included Pilote and Jacques Laperriere on defense, Ullman at center, Hull on left wing, and Claude Provost at right wing. The Cup-winning Canadiens romped over the All-Stars 5-2, with Beliveau copping the game's MVP Award.

JEAN BELIVEAU

Throughout Jean Beliveau's 18-year NHL career, the princely, 6'3", 205-pound center was hobbled by an assortment of physical problems. One of the worst occurred during the 1966-67 season, when the Montrealer was hit in the eye by a wildly swung stick that imperiled his sight.

"The pressure on my nerves bothered me more than the pain," said Beliveau. "But all the time I kept wondering how I would react when I started playing again."

The moment Beliveau rejoined the team, the fear reflex evaporated and he was the Beliveau of old. This was never more evident than during the 1967-68 season, when the Canadiens were lodged in last place in the East Division. Beliveau netted a dramatic midseason goal that lit a fire under the Habs, who went on to win the championship. Beliveau finished the campaign with 68 points in only 59 games.

As a center, Beliveau was majestic, creative, and difficult to dislodge from the puck. He remained a Canadiens hero through their halcyon years of five straight Stanley Cups (1956-60), and captained the team through the successful 1960s. Beliveau even helped the Canadiens win another Stanley Cup in 1971. A Hall of Famer, Beliveau is the Canadiens' senior vice-president.

By the 1965 finals, Chicago's Bobby Hull had established himself as the most exciting player in the NHL. Here, he outflanks Montreal defenseman Jacques Laperriere.

The Montreal defense was brilliant in the 1965 finals, shutting out the Blackhawks three times. Here, Jean-Guy Talbot hauls down Chicago's Ken Hodge (center).

NHL Bulging with Talent, Ready to Expand

1 9 6 5 - 6 6

The most significant announcement of the season came on February 9, 1966, when the NHL awarded conditional franchises to the cities of Los Angeles, San Francisco, St. Louis, Pittsburgh, Philadelphia, and Minneapolis-St. Paul. Vancouver's application was rejected, resulting in much mumbling and complaining in Canada. The new franchises would actually ice teams in the 1967-68 season. The requirements for a new franchise were an entry fee of $2 million and the existence of an arena with at least a 12,500-seat capacity.

The NHL was clearly ready for expansion. First of all, the junior and juvenile hockey programs that the NHL sponsored were producing a flood of youngsters prepared for professional careers. Secondly, hockey ticket sales were at an all-time high, as seemingly every NHL game was filled to capacity. In fact, the cellar-dwelling Bruins even outsold the NBA champion Boston Celtics. Finally, the NHL was close to signing a national TV contract in the United States. The addition of six U.S. franchises would surely help those odds.

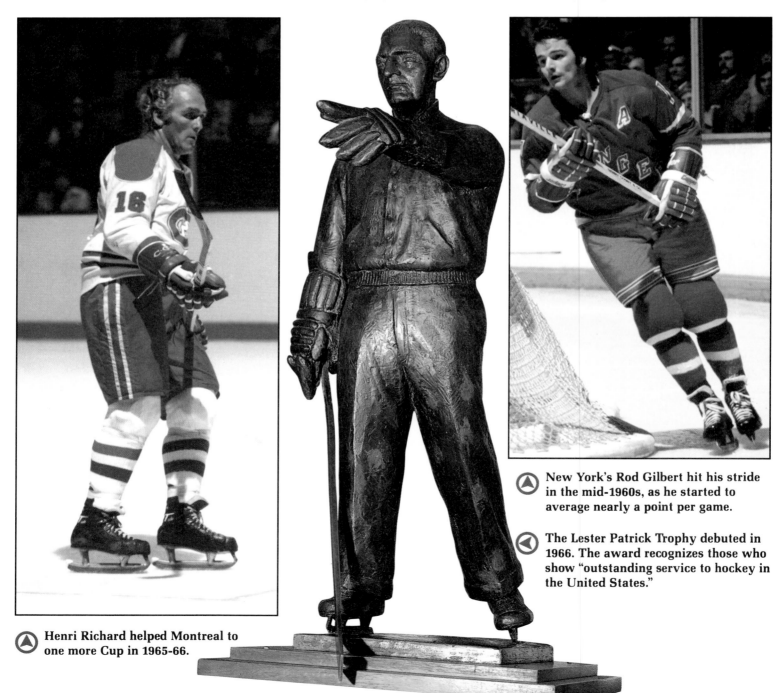

New York's Rod Gilbert hit his stride in the mid-1960s, as he started to average nearly a point per game.

The Lester Patrick Trophy debuted in 1966. The award recognizes those who show "outstanding service to hockey in the United States."

Henri Richard helped Montreal to one more Cup in 1965-66.

The NHL talent pool, then at an all-time high, made expansion possible. The original six teams, so well-stocked, all had capable NHL talent waiting in the minor leagues. To illustrate the league-wide abundance of stars who graced the ice in 1965-66, just look at the number of eventual Hall of Famers on each roster.

Toronto's bench groaned under the weight of eight future Hall of Famers: Frank Mahovlich, Red Kelly, Dave Keon, George "Chief" Armstrong, Tim Horton, Allan Stanley, and goalies Johnny Bower and Terry Sawchuk. Chicago and Detroit came next with five prospective immortals each. Chicago boasted Bobby Hull, Phil Esposito, Stan Mikita, Pierre Pilote,

and Glenn Hall; while Detroit iced Gordie Howe, Alex Delvecchio, Norm Ullman, Andy Bathgate, and Bill Gadsby.

New York and Montreal had four future Hall of Famers apiece. The Canadiens featured Jean Beliveau, Henri Richard, Yvan Cournoyer, and Jacques Laperriere; and the Rangers had Jean Ratelle, Rod Gilbert, Harry Howell, and Ed Giacomin. Even Boston, which had been in the basement five of the last six seasons, had three future Hall of Famers on its roster: John Bucyk, Bernie Parent, and a kid goalie by the name of Gerry "Cheesy" Cheevers.

On the ice, the Canadiens won their 13th Stanley Cup when Richard's

overtime goal eluded Red Wings netminder Roger Crozier in Game Six of the finals. Crozier became the first goalie—and the first recipient from a losing team—to take home the Conn Smythe Trophy. It was a disappointing swan song for Detroit star Gadsby, who was finishing a distinguished 20-year career. (What's worse, Detroit hasn't made the finals since.)

Hull took both the Hart and the Art Ross Trophies by outscoring teammate Mikita. In fact, Hull broke Rocket Richard's 50-goal mark with 54, as well as earning a record 97 points. Chicago boasted four first-team All-Stars: Hall in goal, Pilote on defense, Hull at left wing, and Mikita at center.

Detroit's Delvecchio won the 1966

In the mid-1960s, Montreal boasted superior defensemen. One of the best was tall Jacques Laperriere, shown here checking an attacking Blackhawk.

Gerry Cheevers, a rookie in 1965-66, played in just six games and posted a 6.00 GAA. Boston again yielded the most goals in the NHL.

EDDIE GIACOMIN

Eddie Giacomin played 36 games for the dreadful Ranger team of 1965-66. He was hardly impressive and the Ranger management sent him to the Baltimore Clippers of the AHL. Giacomin, though, was determined to come back.

In 1966, the Ranger brass staked everything they had on Giacomin. General manager and coach Emile Francis stuck Eddie in goal for 66 games, and he finished the season with a 2.61 average and a league-leading nine shutouts. The Rangers made the playoffs and Giacomin was given a berth on the First All-Star Team.

When Giacomin returned to the Rangers training camp the following season, he learned he would be sharing the goaltending chores with Gilles Villemure. Giacomin disapproved of the two-goalie system. He had no choice, however, except to abide by Francis's decision.

The two-goalie system worked, and by the end of the 1970-71 campaign Giacomin had captured the coveted Vezina Trophy by posting a goals-against average of 2.15, the best of his professional career. He finished his career with Detroit and won his way to the Hockey Hall of Fame.

Detroit goalie Roger Crozier watches Gordie Howe prepare a Red Wing counter-attack. Detroit finished fourth in 1965-66 and knocked off Chicago in the playoffs.

Montreal's Claude Provost hones in on Leafs goalie Terry Sawchuk while Toronto's Allan Stanley eyes the puck. Montreal defeated Toronto in four games in the 1966 semifinals.

1965-66

Best Record
Montreal
(41-21-8)

Stanley Cup Finals
Montreal 4
Detroit 2

Art Ross Trophy
Bobby Hull
(54/43/97)

Hart Trophy
Bobby Hull

Vezina Trophy
Lorne Worsley
Charlie Hodge

Calder Trophy
Brit Selby

Norris Trophy
Jacques Laperriere

Lady Byng Trophy
Alex Delvecchio

Lady Byng Trophy, Toronto's Brit Selby copped the Calder, and Montreal's Laperriere won the Norris—which Chicago's Pilote had hogged the previous three seasons. The Canadiens' goaltending duo of Gump Worsley and Charlie Hodge was awarded the Vezina Trophy. A new trophy, donated by the New York Rangers for outstanding services to hockey in the U.S., was struck. It was called the Lester Patrick Award, and the first recipient was Jack Adams.

The All-Star Game marked the last time the contest was held prior to the start of the season. The new midseason format was adopted a year later. Although the All-Stars downed the Montreal Canadiens 5-2, the exhibition almost didn't happen because of the abundance of stars who were without a contract at the time. Wisely, the league allowed the players without contracts to play anyway.

Howe took advantage of his 17th All-Star appearance to score two goals and surpass Rocket Richard's record of seven All-Star goals. Later, during the regular season, Howe added another milestone, beating goalie Worsley at the Montreal Forum for his 600th career goal.

The 1965-66 season was sort of a transitional year. Quite a few changes took place in the sport—even in equipment. Mikita, who carried a curved stick and donned an archaic helmet on his ebon-haired head, presented the perfect preview of modern ice hockey equipment. Ranger coach Red Sullivan, displaying an amusing lack of foresight, blamed his

Detroit's Billy Harris *(left)* and Roger Crozier cut off Chicago's Bobby Hull. In the 1966 semifinals, Detroit defeated the Hawks in six games.

Detroit's Alex Delvecchio pivots on the attack in the 1966 finals, which were won by Montreal in six games. Detroit has not made the finals since.

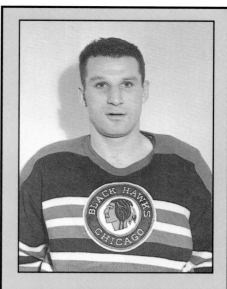

LARRY ZEIDEL

Few sports comebacks have ever had as much flair as Larry Zeidel's, who jumped back into the spotlight in 1967. Zeidel was one of the few Jewish players in professional hockey, and in Yiddish there's a word for what he did—it's called *chutzpah*.

A rugged type, Zeidel played briefly in the NHL for Detroit and Chicago before being demoted to the minors in 1954, where he wallowed for more than a decade. However, when the NHL expanded from six to 12 teams in 1967, Zeidel saw a chance to return to the big show. In the summer of '67, Zeidel, age 39, compiled a flashy resume complete with a letter from a doctor stating that he had the heart of a 22-year-old. He sent the resume to each of the 12 NHL teams.

The Philadelphia Flyers were the only club willing to take a chance. Manager Bud Poile signed Zeidel and started him alongside Joe Watson. The Flyers began winning and Larry appeared to be playing better hockey than he had with the Cup champion Red Wings or the Blackhawks.

The Flyers finished first, winning the Clarence Campbell Bowl, and Zeidel was among the best players on the club.

club's lack of offense on "those curved sticks" that Mikita introduced.

Almost simultaneously, Bruins coach Milt Schmidt opined that all players should wear helmets. His remark came after a Bruins-Leafs game in which Boston's Bob Dillabough suffered a bloody head injury after colliding with Eddie Shack and goalie Parent.

The NHL saw more changes in 1965-66. For the first time in league history, teams were required to dress two goalies for each game. The Rangers, vying continuously with Boston for the

league cellar, changed their goaltending tandem from Plante and Marcel Paille to Giacomin and Cesare Maniago. This move would help New York become a contender within a season.

The NHL's economic strength failed to help Hull's bid to become hockey's first $100,000-a-year player. When Chicago refused Hull's demands, he had to settle instead for $40,000.

But in Toronto, young defensive star Carl Brewer decided to retire when his contract negotiations with Punch Imlach failed. Brewer's actions (and the fact

that he had conducted negotiations with an agent) were the precursor to the creation of the Players Association.

The Bruins, having set an NHL record with five consecutive last-place finishes, were desperate to revive their hapless club. Management seriously considered calling up a young blue-liner from the Oshawa Generals but decided to wait one more year. Thus, a 17-year-old juniors star named Bobby Orr would have to wait another season to see if he would make the enormous splash in the bigs that everyone was predicting.

Mikita Wins Triple Crown, But Leafs Take the Cup

1 9 6 6 - 6 7

In this the 50th anniversary of the NHL, Stan Mikita won his third of four Art Ross Trophies, turning the tables on teammate Bobby Hull, who had edged by him the previous season. It was definitely a career year offensively for "Stosh," who achieved the hockey equivalent of baseball's triple crown. Not only did Mikita win the Ross, but he also took the Hart and Lady Byng Trophies. Mikita tied Hull's NHL record with 97 points and set a new league record with 62 assists. Not surprisingly, Mikita was named center to the First All-Star Team.

The individual feats of Mikita and Hull couldn't help the Blackhawks in Stanley Cup play. However, the team's regular season was a smashing success, as it won the regular-season title for the first time ever and led the NHL in goals scored for a fourth consecutive season. Chicago's 264 goals broke the single-season record of 259 established by Montreal in 1962—although Chicago's record would in turn be eclipsed quickly with the advent of expansion.

Still, the Hawks were always less than the sum of their parts. They

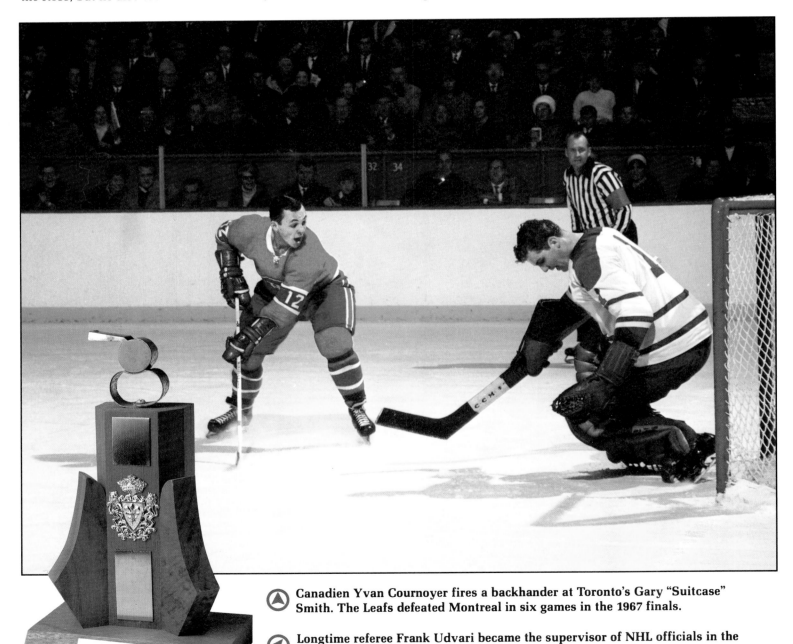

Canadien Yvan Cournoyer fires a backhander at Toronto's Gary "Suitcase" Smith. The Leafs defeated Montreal in six games in the 1967 finals.

Longtime referee Frank Udvari became the supervisor of NHL officials in the mid-1960s. He was honored with this trophy in 1966.

reached the finals in 1961, '62, and '65, but garnered only one Cup (1961). Their roster—which included such notable icemen as Bobby and Dennis Hull, Mikita, Phil Esposito, Glenn Hall, Ken Wharram, Ken Hodge, Pierre Pilote, and Doug Mohns—was mysteriously insufficient.

Many attributed the club's failures to "Muldoon's Curse." On April 2, 1927, after the Hawks lost their first-ever playoff series (against Boston), owner Frederic McLaughlin castigated and then fired his coach, Pete Muldoon. Stunned and enraged, Muldoon allegedly looked his former employer in the eye before storming out and said, "I'm not through with you. I'll 'hoodoo' you! This club will never

finish in first place!"

Strangely enough, even though they went on to win Cups in 1934, 1938, and 1961, the Hawks never finished the regular season in first place. Then, on April 2, 1967, Chicago played their last game of the regular season, finishing in first place exactly 40 years to the day after Muldoon had lowered his hex upon the team!

Team success came much more readily to the Toronto Maple Leafs. In 1966-67, the Leafs won the Stanley Cup—their fourth in six seasons. The Leafs had been blown away in the previous postseason competition, losing four straight to Montreal, but coach Punch Imlach had resisted making major alterations. His patience

paid off, as Jim Pappin led all playoff scorers (15 points) and Dave Keon's two-way play earned him the Conn Smythe Trophy. Toronto ousted Montreal in the Stanley Cup finals in six games. Imlach later described it as his most satisfying championship. Sadly, it also marked the beginning of a long decline for the once-mighty Leafs, a franchise that has floundered since then.

As quickly as the Leafs were descending, the Bruins were ascending, thanks to hitching their wagon to a star named Orr. Bobby Orr, defenseman par excellence, made his NHL debut on October 19, 1966. By season's end, No. 4 was the talk of the league, drawing large crowds at all

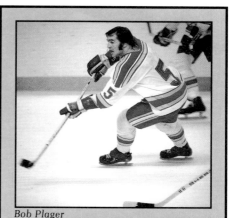

Bob Plager

THE PLAGER BROTHERS

Once the team captain of the St. Louis Blues and the guts of its defense, Barclay Plager was picked to coach the blundering Blues in 1978. Barclay, the eldest of three flamboyant Plager brothers, had been the leading shot-blocker, body-cruncher, and scorer of the St. Louis blue-line corps.

Although Barclay's brother Bob was unable to crack the New Rangers defensive line, his NHL career flowered when he was traded to St. Louis in 1967. He remained a regular with the Blues for six seasons. Bob was injury-prone throughout his big-league career, probably because he was such a tough competitor and mean hitter.

When his playing days were over in 1978, Bob became a scout for the Blues while brother Barclay ruled behind the St. Louis bench. Illness limited Barclay's ability to coach, and he died in 1988.

In 1966-67, Chicago's Stan Mikita tied an NHL record with 97 points and set a record with 62 assists.

arenas. He earned a berth on the Second All-Star Team, won the Calder Trophy, and finished second among defensemen in scoring (41 points, including 13 goals), behind only Pilote. Unfortunately, Orr was plagued by a shoulder injury in the exhibition season and strained knee ligaments in December. They served as an omen. Orr would be stricken with injuries throughout his career.

Although Orr was not the creator of the blue-line rush, he popularized it as no one ever had before him. His style of play—he regularly joined the offense as a fourth forward and completely orchestrated the power play from the point—served as a model for a whole generation of offensive defensemen.

Ranger veteran defenseman Harry Howell won the Norris Trophy in 1967. But after that, Orr would win the next eight straight. In fact, because of Orr's virtual ownership of the Norris, league pundits discussed the idea of another trophy for defensemen. The new award would be granted to the best stay-at-home, defensive defensemen, since it seemed that nobody but the offensive, rushing sort of blue-liner would ever win the coveted Norris again.

While the Bruins were on the upswing, the Red Wings were tumbling down. They finished out of the playoffs for the first time in five years. However, Gordie Howe's enormous talent and drawing power was recognized. He was awarded the Lester Patrick Trophy, along with U.S. hockey architects Charles Adams and James Norris.

The 1966-67 season was definitely not a good one for officiating. Bernie Geoffrion (who had left retirement to play for the Rangers) was suspended

 Dave Keon garnered 52 points for Toronto in 1966-67. Despite a modest 32-27-11 record during the regular season, Toronto skated all the way to the Cup.

Toronto celebrates its 3-1 win in the decisive Game Six of the Cup finals. This proved to be the Leafs' 13th Stanley Cup. It would also be their last.

1966-67

Best Record
Chicago
(41-17-12)

Stanley Cup Finals
Toronto 4
Montreal 2

Art Ross Trophy
Stan Mikita
(35/62/97)

Hart Trophy
Stan Mikita

Vezina Trophy
Glenn Hall
Denis Dejordy

Calder Trophy
Bobby Orr

Norris Trophy
Harry Howell

Lady Byng Trophy
Stan Mikita

Bob Pulford (20) scored with 11:34 left in the second overtime to give Toronto a 3-2 win in Game Three of the Stanley Cup finals.

ALAN EAGLESON

Alan Eagleson, a bespectacled Toronto attorney, has impacted the game of professional hockey as much as Clarence Campbell or Bobby Orr did.

It was through Orr, hockey's version of the Messiah, that Eagleson first burst brashly into the public eye. When Orr was only a teenager, he was a million-dollar commodity in the eyes of the lords of hockey. And Orr's father, a sensible chap, figured that if his son was properly represented, he could swing one whopper of a deal. How right he was.

Under the eagle eye of Eagleson, Orr negotiated an absolutely unheard-of contract for a first-year player—$40,000 per year for two years. It was almost four times the original figure offered by the Boston Bruins.

Eagleson's impact on the NHL was just beginning. In short order, his crusades led to the reinstatement of Carl Brewer's amateur status, the formation of the NHL Players Association, and the classic 1972 Team Canada-USSR series.

Eagleson has also represented scores of skaters and, said Bobby Hull, "he did more for hockey in two years than anybody else did in 20, as head of the NHL Players Association."

for three games after elbowing linesman Walt Atanas. This resulted in a directive from league president Clarence Campbell that officials not be lenient to such gross disrespect. Later, an irate Imlach blamed Toronto's ninth straight loss on referee Bruce Hood, citing it as the worst officiating he had seen since coming to the NHL.

Canadiens policeman John Ferguson was given a misconduct penalty after a collision with Esposito that sent linesman Brent Casselman into the players' bench. Ferguson then struck Casselman as he was getting up. Fergie

confessed to NHL Prexy Campbell and received a three-game suspension.

The anti-referee crusade was not over. Montreal's Bobby Rousseau, angry that referee Art Skov had watched calmly while Orr pulled Rousseau down and didn't penalize the Bruin, proceeded to elbow Skov as he skated by. In addition to a $50 fine and a game misconduct, Rousseau received a two-game suspension.

After a game against Detroit, Montreal's Jean-Guy Talbot was fined a total of $175 for abusing referee John Ashley. New York's Reggie Fleming got

a fine and a game misconduct for shoving linesman Pat Shetler while Reg was attempting to fight Montreal's Claude Larose. Finally, referee Skov threatened to resign after being hit by a flying program. The alleged culprit was none other than league governor Stafford Smythe! Smythe had no comment.

In the first All-Star Game played in midseason, Montreal's Ferguson scored twice and Henri Richard scored once, as Montreal beat the stars 3-0. It was the first—and only—shutout in All-Star history.

The Modern Era Begins as NHL Doubles in Size

1 9 6 7 - 6 8

The 1967-68 season was the start of a new era in hockey, as the NHL doubled in size. The league added six new teams: the Minnesota North Stars, the Pittsburgh Penguins, the Philadelphia Flyers, the Los Angeles Kings, the St. Louis Blues, and the California Seals (who would change their name to the Oakland Seals on December 8, 1967). The NHL also expanded back into two divisions, with the new teams comprising the West Division and the "original six" making up the East Division.

In order to create intra-divisional rivalries, the NHL made teams play their division opponents ten times apiece and the teams in the other division four times apiece. Also, the schedule was upped to 74 games.

On paper, the new teams looked well-thought out and intelligently backed. The man behind San Francisco's bid was Barry van Gerbig, a former goaltender for Princeton University and backup to Jack McCartan in the 1960 Olympics. Van Gerbig and his partners paid $450,000 to the Western Hockey League for the rights to the Bay Area team and the liquidation of its franchise. The owners chose not to ice the NHL team in San Francisco's venerable Cow Palace; they moved the team across the Bay to Oakland's Alameda County Coliseum. Bert Olmstead was hired as coach and GM.

The Minnesota North Stars appeared to be a natural. The Twin Cities area had long been a hotbed of

hockey. The only American player currently in the league, Tommy Williams, was a native of Duluth, Minnesota. And one of the team's owners, Walter Bush Jr., was co-owner of the CHL's Minnesota Bruins. However, there was no appropriate arena. Bush and his co-owners decided to build in nearby Bloomington, equidistant from St. Paul and Minneapolis. Wren Blair, formerly the Bruins' director of personnel and the discoverer of Bobby Orr, was hired to be coach and GM.

Pittsburgh also had a long hockey history. In addition to having been an early NHL entrant, the city's AHL team (the Pittsburgh Hornets) had just won the Calder Cup in April 1967. The new NHL team would play in the Pittsburgh

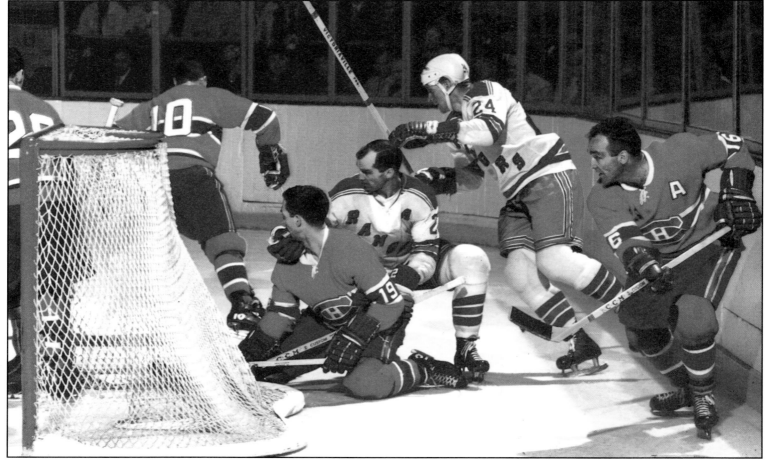

A host of Canadiens and Rangers scramble for the puck. Montreal kicked off the Modern Era with another Stanley Cup.

Civic Arena, nicknamed the "Igloo" because of its white domed roof. The team name, Penguins, came from the arena's nickname, and a live Penguin, Pete, was even obtained as a team mascot. Unfortunately, the poor refugee from the Antarctic died in midseason.

The Steel Town owners hired Jack Riley as GM, tearing him away from a job as president of the AHL. Red Sullivan, chief scout for the Rangers, was hired to coach the Pens.

The Philadelphia Flyers' consortium consisted of financier William R. Putnam, NFL Eagles owner Jerry Wolman, and Eagles VP Ed Snider. Philly was another town without an appropriate rink, however, until the owners bought several acres next to the John F. Kennedy Memorial Stadium (where the annual Army-Navy game was played). Normand "Bud" Poile, a manager from the WHL, was hired as GM. Poile, in turn, hired another WHLer, Keith Allen, to handle the Flyers' bench duties.

Ownership in St. Louis was a father-son combo—Sid Salomon Jr. and Sid III.

While St. Louis did have an arena, it was owned by Blackhawks James S. Norris and Arthur Wirtz. The Salomons purchased the elderly St. Louis Arena for $4 million and then had to refurbish it for an additional $2 million. Delving into the WHL, the Salomons came up with Lynn Patrick, eldest son of Lester, to manage the team. Lynn, before his stint as coach and GM of the Los Angeles Blades, had coached both the Bruins and the Rangers. Patrick hired Scotty Bowman away from the Canadiens to be his assistant.

In Los Angeles, the flamboyant Jack Kent Cooke, a Canadian communications mogul and owner of the L.A. Lakers, outbid L.A. Rams owner Dan Reaves for rights to the L.A. Kings. Cooke decided to build a huge new arena in Inglewood, which would be called The Forum. He hired 1957's Calder Trophy winner, Larry Regan, to manage the club. He then named Red Kelly as coach.

In order to supply quality players for the new clubs, the NHL held an expansion draft on June 6, 1967, in

MASTERTON TRAGEDY

In 1963, Bill Masterton scored 82 points for the Cleveland Barons of the American League. However, he decided to quit pro hockey when none of the NHL teams drafted him. He went to Denver University and obtained a master's degree in finance.

But, when the NHL expanded to 12 teams, the Minnesota North Stars expressed an interest in Masterton. He went to training camp and won a berth on the team.

On January 13, 1968, the North Stars played the Oakland Seals in Bloomington, Minnesota. In the first period, Masterton led a North Star rush into Oakland territory. The Seals defensemen, Larry Cahan and Ron Harris, braced for the attack. Both Cahan and Harris nailed Masterton with a hard but clean check. A split-second after Masterton was hit, he flipped backward, hitting his head on the ice.

Masterton never regained consciousness. For 30 hours, doctors managed to keep him alive by use of a respirator, but the massive internal brain injury was too severe. Early on the morning of January 15, Masterton died.

Following the tragedy, league governors, in cooperation with the National Hockey League Writers Association, created a Bill Masterton Memorial Trophy. It goes to a player who demonstrates the qualities exemplified by the late North Stars center.

In 1967-68, Boston defenseman Bobby Orr captured the Norris Trophy. He was just 19 years old.

Boston's Eddie Shack and the Flyers' Larry Zeidel trade blows during a bloody match in 1968.

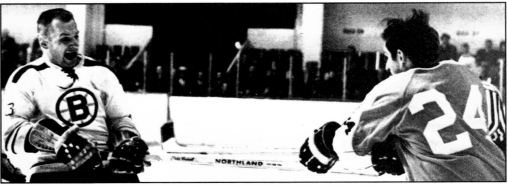

Montreal. The existing six clubs were allowed to protect one goalie and 11 skaters, and the new clubs were allowed to select players from the entire development systems of the old clubs. All junior-age players signed by the original six teams the previous years were exempt from the draft, which meant that Boston did not have to protect Bobby Orr, who was only 19 at the time.

The day before the expansion draft, Cooke announced a shocker: He had bought the entire AHL Springfield Indian franchise from Eddie Shore, thereby making his Kings the only expansion team with a ready-made farm system. The reaction was immediate, as the Flyers hastily bought up the AHL Quebec Aces.

In order to protect top players on their clubs, the established teams made several behind-the-scenes deals with expansion clubs. In these deals, the expansion teams agreed not to draft unprotected talent. A perfect instance involved the Montreal Canadiens and the Minnesota North Stars. As its first pick in the draft, Minnesota surprised everyone by drafting journeyman forward Dave Balon from the Habs, instead of Canadien Claude Larose, considered to be the top unprotected forward in the draft. The surprise was over, however, as soon as the Canadiens announced that they were sending Andre Boudrias, Mike McMahon, and Bob Charlebois to Minnesota for "cash and future considerations."

Since the established teams were only allowed to protect one goaltender, the new clubs snatched up seasoned netminding talent greedily. Terry Sawchuk went from Toronto to the Kings; Bernie Parent went from Boston to Philadelphia; St. Louis risked picking retired Glenn Hall from Chicago; New York lost Cesare Maniago to Minnesota; and Charlie Hodge left Montreal for the California Seals.

Two enormous trades were also made before the start of the momentous 1967-68 season. New Bruins manger Milt Schmidt absolutely robbed the Chicago Blackhawks, trading Gilles Marotte, Pit Martin, and Jack Norris to Chicago for Phil Esposito, Ken Hodge, and Johnny "Pie" McKenzie. Marotte would

1967-68

Best Record
Montreal
(42-22-10)

Stanley Cup Finals
Montreal 4
St. Louis 0

Art Ross Trophy
Stan Mikita
(40/47/87)

Hart Trophy
Stan Mikita

Vezina Trophy
Lorne Worsley
Rogatien Vachon

Calder Trophy
Derek Sanderson

Norris Trophy
Bobby Orr

Lady Byng Trophy
Stan Mikita

Oakland Seals defenseman Larry Cahan thwarts a scoring chance by Toronto's Dave Keon. Cahan was typical of fringe players who gained new life with the arrival of expansion in 1967-68. Cahan couldn't save the Seals, however, as they finished 15-42-17.

RED BERENSON

When Red Berenson was traded by the New York Rangers to the St. Louis Blues in November 1967, the deal was largely ignored. But when Berenson was dealt from St. Louis to the Detroit Red Wings early in February 1971, the news resounded with the impact of a thunderclap.

In less than four years, the anonymous redhead from Regina, Saskatchewan, emerged as the Babe Ruth of St. Louis hockey—the man who put the Blues on the ice map and into the Stanley Cup finals. It was Berenson who scored six goals in a single game against Philadelphia in 1968 and who became the first superstar of the National Hockey League's expansion West Division.

Berenson claimed that the deal that sent him to the Wings was simply a union-busting move on the part of the Blues' front office. "I think the Blues traded me because I was president of the NHL Players Association," said Berenson. "I was shocked and disappointed."

Red would eventually return to the Blues in January 1975, where he played until his retirement following the 1977-78 season.

Serge Savard (18) and Montreal defeated goalie Denis DeJordy and Chicago in the 1968 semis.

A swarm of Canadiens engulf Boston's Phil Esposito in Round One of the 1968 playoffs.

thump around the league for awhile, Norris would disappear, and Martin would be adequate. But Esposito and Hodge—along with Orr, Gerry Cheevers, Fred Stanfield, and Wayne Cashman—would form the nucleus of a sensational Boston Bruins club.

In the other blockbuster trade, Toronto sent the gifted but erratic Frank Mahovlich, Garry Unger, Pete Stemkowski, and the rights to Carl Brewer to Detroit for Norm Ullman, Paul Henderson, and Floyd Smith. While the trade was pretty good for both clubs, it didn't solve the teams' other problems. Neither Toronto nor Detroit would make the playoffs.

The league finally managed to sign its sought-after TV deal in the States. CBS agreed to televise a "Game of the Week,"

as well as the Stanley Cup playoffs. The network's first game, on December 30, 1967, showcased the Flyers and Kings. It was the first hockey game ever played at the L.A. Forum.

The first face-off between the "old" and "new" clubs was on October 11, 1967, between the Montreal Canadiens and the Pittsburgh Penguins. The game featured two significant goals. Montreal's elegant Jean Beliveau notched the 400th goal of his career, while Andy Bathgate scored the Pens' first NHL goal. The Canadiens defeated Pittsburgh 2-1.

In January 1968, the NHL experienced the first death of a player from an injury occurring during a game. Bill Masterton, a journeyman who had come out of retirement to

play for the North Stars, was checked by Oakland defenseman Ron Harris. Masterton banged into the Seals' Larry Cahan and fell backward to the ice, striking his head. Masterton died from a brain injury.

After the tragedy, an outcry began for all players to wear helmets. Shortly thereafter, Stafford Smythe, representing the Leafs at an NHL governors meeting, predicted that helmets would soon be mandatory. He immediately ordered his Toronto Marlboros junior club to begin wearing protective headgear.

Disasters seemed to haunt the 1967-68 season. Violent winds blew the roof off of the brand new Philadelphia Spectrum, forcing the Flyers to play their remaining "home" games in

In 1967-68, Stan Mikita won his second straight "triple crown," taking home the Hart, Art Ross, and Lady Byng.

Toronto and Quebec. The California Seals were so abysmal that Olmstead resigned as coach "to keep my sanity." Gord Fashoway replaced Olmstead. The Seals, even with their name changed to the Oakland Seals in order to attract local fans, finished dead last—financially as well as statistically. Their record was 15-42-17.

The New York Rangers began playing in the new Madison Square Garden after much hoopla and fanfare—only to have famed astrologer Jeanne Dixon predict that the cable-suspended ceiling would collapse on a capacity crowd. While the ceiling remained, the Rangers' playoff hopes collapsed, as they were ousted in the first round.

On the upside, Pittsburgh found a

goalie sensation in 31-year-old rookie Les Binkley, a former trainer and spare netminder for the AHL Cleveland Barons. But Binkley, who was noted for wearing contact lenses, couldn't get the Pens into the playoffs. They finished fifth in the West Division.

Gordie Howe reached the 30-goal plateau for the 12th time in his astounding career, but couldn't help the fortunes of the Red Wings. GM/coach Sid Abel blamed it all on the newly formed Players Association, headed by Canadian lawyer Alan Eagleson. "Players are fat in the pocket book," moaned Abel. "They've got you over a barrel. They know that if they don't play here, they'll play somewhere else now that there are 12 teams in the league." Detroit languished in the East

Division cellar, ten points behind fifth-place Toronto.

Montreal finished the season atop the East Division, while Philadelphia surprised many by finishing first in the West—despite a roofless Spectrum.

In the first round of the East playoffs, the Canadiens swept Boston in four games while Chicago eliminated the Rangers in six. In the West playoffs, the St. Louis Blues upset Philadelphia in seven behind the aged legs of Doug Harvey and Dickie Moore and the superb goaltending of Hall. In the division's other round, the North Stars defeated the Kings in seven.

In the semifinals, Montreal took only five games to oust the Chicago Blackhawks. Meanwhile, St. Louis charged past Minnesota in seven games. After trailing 3-0 in Game Seven, St. Louis netted four straight goals to win the game 4-3. In the finals, the discrepancies between East and West were painfully apparent, as the Canadiens trounced the St. Louis Blues in four straight games to win their 14th Stanley Cup.

Stan Mikita achieved another hockey "triple crown" by winning the Art Ross, Hart, and Lady Byng Trophies for the second year in a row. Montreal's Gump Worsley and Rogatien Vachon gained the Vezina; a flashy Bruins forward, Derek Sanderson, took the Calder; and Orr won his first of an astounding eight Norris Trophies.

Hall was awarded the Conn Smythe for his Herculean efforts in the Blues'

playoff loss to Montreal. It was also the first award of an established trophy to a player on an expansion team.

In memory of the dedication, hard work, and perseverance exhibited by the late Masterton, the NHL Writers Association donated the Bill Masterton Memorial Trophy to the league. It was awarded in 1968 to Claude Provost of the Montreal Canadiens.

By finishing first in the East, the Canadiens also won the Prince of Wales Trophy. This trophy was once awarded to the winner of the American Division of the NHL (from 1927 through 1938). The Prince of Wales then went to the top club in the six-team league. Now, in the year of expansion, the trophy was awarded to the regular-season leader of the East Division.

The winner of the West Division also got a trophy—the Clarence S. Campbell Bowl. While this was a new award, the bowl itself was an antique. It was crafted by a British silversmith in 1878. The Philadelphia Flyers became the first team to have its name engraved upon the trophy.

Worsley gained his first—and only— First All-Star Team slot, along with Orr and Tim Horton on defense and Mikita, Hull, and Howe in the forward positions.

It was quite an eventful year, to say the least. But according to league president Clarence Campbell, the good moments outweighed the bad. "Expansion," explained Campbell, "was successful beyond our fondest hopes."

ROD GILBERT

Rod Gilbert's NHL career almost ended before it started. Playing for the Guelph Royals in the Ontario Hockey Association, he skidded on an ice cream container top thrown to the ice by a fan and injured his back. A few days later, an opponent leveled him with a strong check; Gilbert fell to the ice, his back broken.

The first operation on his back was a near disaster—his left leg began to hemorrhage and amputation was seriously considered. During the summer of 1965, the bone grafts in his back weakened and another operation was needed.

Rod's career was in jeopardy. He played 34 games in a restrictive brace and then submitted to another operation. Happily, Rod's story brightened after that. On February 24, 1968, at the Montreal Forum, Gilbert scored four goals for the Rangers and also established an NHL record—16 shots on goal.

In 1971-72, Gilbert hit for 43 goals, finished fifth in the NHL scoring race, and was named to his sixth All-Star team. In 1974, he passed Andy Bathgate as the Rangers' all-time leading scorer. His milestone goal was celebrated by a five-minute, deafening ovation. After his retirement, Gilbert was inducted into the Hockey Hall of Fame.

In 1967-68, Phil Esposito emerged as a major offensive force, amassing 84 points on the year.

Boston acquired Ken Hodge in 1967 and he blossomed into a big-time scorer, netting 45 goals in 1968-69.

Espo, Hull, Howe All Reach the Century Mark

1 9 6 8 - 6 9

Expansion of a different sort marked the 1968-69 season, as scoring records were shattered all over. At the remarkable age of 40, Gordie Howe broke his own personal scoring record, breaking the century mark with 103 points. However, that was only good enough for third in the race for the Art Ross Trophy, as Bobby Hull (despite a fractured jaw) totaled 58 goals and 107 points.

But Hull's mark wasn't good enough either, as Boston's Phil Esposito, poised continuously in front of his enemies' nets, collected an incredible 126 points— 29 more than the previous record of 97 points shared by Hull and Stan Mikita. Esposito notched 49 goals and recorded an unheard-of 77 assists. Bobby Orr broke a pair of records for defensemen with his 21 goals and 64 points, while Chicago defenseman Pat Stapleton's 50

assists set another record.

Playing for the St. Louis Blues, a Ranger and Canadien castoff named Red Berenson broke loose for six goals in a single game, tying the mark last set by Syd Howe in 1944. Finally, Leaf rookie defenseman Jim Dorey set two negative single-game records in his second NHL game on October 16, when he amassed eight penalties and 38 penalty minutes before being ejected

In 1968-69, Bobby Hull set an NHL record for goals with 58, breaking his own record of 54 which he set three years earlier. Nevertheless, Hull's Hawks finished in the basement in the East Division.

by referee Art Skov. The record list is almost endless, as the season ended with 40 marks being tied or broken.

The league's coaching ranks were just as unstable. Most notably, Montreal coach Toe Blake retired and was replaced by 29-year-old Claude Ruel. In other moves, Bill Gadsby was hired to replace Detroit's Sid Abel, Bernie Geoffrion took over the Rangers' bench, Fred Glover took over as coach of the Seals, and John Muckler was brought up from the minors to coach the Minnesota North Stars. Even the new coaches didn't last. Geoffrion was later replaced by Emile Francis, and Wren Blair fired Muckler after Minnesota went through 14 winless games.

In the West, St. Louis, fired up by the Vezina Trophy-winning combo of Glenn Hall and Jacques Plante (who had been coaxed out of retirement), finished the season atop its division— 19 points ahead of second-place Oakland. The third-place Flyers had the dubious distinction of playing to a record number of ties—21!

Montreal and Boston battled for first place in the East, until Montreal clinched the title on the last weekend of the regular season. In consolation, the Bruins broke two major records. They scored a league record 303 goals and accrued a record 1,297 penalty minutes—that's nearly a full day in the penalty box. Boston's rough style of play earned them the moniker "Big, Bad Bruins."

Esposito copped the Hart Trophy as

BOBBY ORR

Bobby Orr was an effortless skater (when the knees were right) and an intuitively brilliant tactician. Orr was so idolized by friend and foe alike that he rarely was challenged by the NHL's woodchoppers.

In his prime, Orr was evaluated as the "perfect hockey player." He played defense well enough to win the Norris Trophy for eight straight seasons (1968-75). Offensively, Orr was no less awesome. Although he was listed as a backliner, he led the league in scoring in 1970 (120) and 1975 (135).

Before joining the league, Orr sent shock waves through the NHL's establishments. Bobby was the first star to have an agent—attorney Alan Eagleson. Eagleson stunned Bruins manager Hap Emms by declaring that Orr would only sign if the money was right.

The result was a two-year, $150,000 contract that caused reverberations throughout the league. Although nobody knew it at the time, Orr was helping to organize and perpetuate an NHL Players Association with Eagleson at the helm.

In a sense, the NHL became too dependent on Orr. When his knees began crumbling in the late 1970s, so too did the NHL. It lost a network television contract and suffered at the gate. There simply was no successor to the golden boy.

In 1968-69, Boston's Phil Esposito set NHL records for points (126) and assists (77), while his 49 goals fell five short of the league record. Espo helped the Bruins become the first team in NHL history to score 300 goals. They netted 303.

well as the Art Ross; his teammate, Orr, earned his second Norris; Alex Delvecchio copped the Lady Byng; and Montreal defenseman Serge Savard was awarded the Conn Smythe. Two West Division players also had their names engraved in silver, as Oakland's Ted Hampson won the Masterton and Minnesota's Danny Grant won the Calder. Hull was given the Lester Patrick Trophy along with U.S.

collegiate coach Ed Jeremiah.

No one was surprised when Esposito made the First All-Star Team. Also on the squad were defenseman Tim Horton and four guys whose names tend to blend together: Gordie Howe, Glenn Hall, Bobby Hull, and Bobby Orr.

In the East playoffs, Montreal and Boston breezed past New York and Toronto, respectively, in the minimum four games. The opening game of the

Toronto-Boston series should be noted, however, since several more records were set. Esposito equaled Dickie Moore's playoff record with four goals and six assists, while Toronto's Forbes Kennedy managed to establish several NHL playoff penalty records. He set marks for most penalties in one game (eight) and one period (six), as well as most penalty minutes in a game (38) and in one period (34).

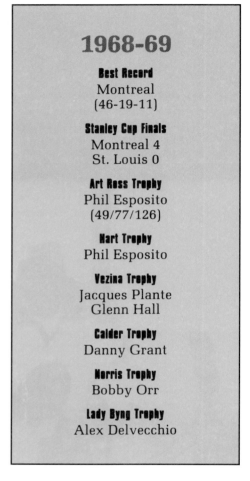

1968-69

Best Record
Montreal
(46-19-11)

Stanley Cup Finals
Montreal 4
St. Louis 0

Art Ross Trophy
Phil Esposito
(49/77/126)

Hart Trophy
Phil Esposito

Vezina Trophy
Jacques Plante
Glenn Hall

Calder Trophy
Danny Grant

Norris Trophy
Bobby Orr

Lady Byng Trophy
Alex Delvecchio

Bruins goalie Gerry Cheevers attempts a save during the 1969 semifinals, which were won by Montreal in six games. Between 1946 and 1987, Montreal and Boston met in the playoffs 18 times; the Habs won all 18 series.

The classy Jean Beliveau, still going strong in his 16th season with Montreal, helped the Canadiens eliminate the Bruins in the 1969 semifinals. Three of the games went into overtime.

In the West, St. Louis dusted off Philadelphia in four contests, while Los Angeles took the full seven games to edge past Oakland. The semifinals between Montreal and Boston took six games, three of which were decided in overtime, as the Canadiens gained a spot in the finals. St. Louis swept the Kings in four straight to earn its place in the final series.

Again, the inspired goaltending of St. Louis was no match for Montreal's talent. The Habs swept the Blues for their 15th Stanley Cup.

"This may be the last dynasty in professional sport," said Minnesota's Blair of the Canadiens. "It's going to be harder to pull down the Canadiens than the New York Yankees or the Green Bay Packers."

Esposito, Orr, and the Big, Bad Bruins would prove Blair's words false.

HARRY SINDEN

Harry Sinden was the right man in the right place at the right time when the Boston Bruins handed him their coaching reins at the start of the 1966-67 campaign. The Bruins had finished dead last five times in the previous six seasons and the city was hungry for a winner.

It didn't happen immediately. The Bruins finished sixth in Harry's first year on the job, but a hotshot rookie named Bobby Orr provided plenty of consolation. The following season, the Bruins made the playoffs for the first time in nine seasons. And then, in the 1969-70 season, Boston won its first Stanley Cup in 29 years.

The whole town was just wild about Harry. However, in the midst of that grand celebration, Sinden abruptly quit the Bruins—publicly charging the brass with underpaying him—and began a new career in the modular home industry.

When a new owner bought the Bruins, the first move was to bring Sinden back, this time as general manager. In November 1975, Sinden made one of hockey's most controversial trades, sending Boston's beloved Phil Esposito to the New York Rangers for Brad Park (a hated man in Boston).

The 1990-91 campaign marked the 19th season Sinden has spent as general manager of the Bruins.

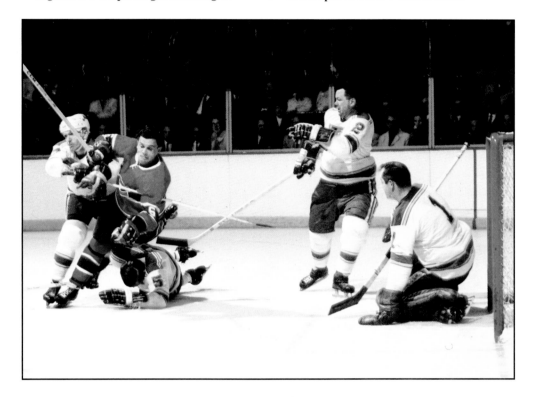

Montreal's Ralph Backstrom trips over Bob Plager (5) and collides with Red Berenson. For the second straight year, the Canadiens swept St. Louis in the Stanley Cup finals.

Henri Richard chases the puck while Barclay Plager (left), Doug Harvey (2), and goalie Glenn Hall look on. Montreal outscored St. Louis 12-3 in the 1969 Stanley Cup finals.

THE NHL
AGAINST
THE WORLD

Throughout the 1970s, the
NHL battles toe to toe with
the WHA and the USSR.

Hockey fans found new teams to root for in the 1970s. At left, the WHA's New York Raiders (*white jerseys*) face the Minnesota Fighting Saints. Above, Team Canada's Bobby Clarke fires one at the Soviet goal in the classic 1972 series.

THE 1970s

As the 1970s unfolded, most everybody was pleased with the NHL's expansion (except for those poor souls in Oakland). Expansion was so successful that the league added two more teams in 1970—the Buffalo Sabres and the Vancouver Canucks. However, the NHL was becoming victimized by its own success.

Hockey was suddenly becoming a glamour investment sport, as millionaires across the continent wanted into the NHL. But when it became apparent that the league was taking its sweet time admitting more teams, a group of Californians (led by Gary Davidson and Dennis Murphy) organized the first major rival to the NHL. It was called the World Hockey Association.

The WHA made its mark when it persuaded Chicago ace Bobby Hull to leave the Blackhawks and sign with the Winnipeg Jets. Almost immediately, other NHLers signed big contracts with the new league. The WHA opened its first season in October 1972.

To counter the move, the NHL accepted two new franchises for the 1972-73 season—the New York Islanders and the Atlanta Flames. But while many NHL moguls waited for the new league to go under, it managed to survive, overcoming innumerable crises. Other famous NHL names, led by the immortal Gordie Howe, signed on with the WHA and the war continued through the decade. The chief beneficiaries of the conflict were players and agents, as teams tried to outbid each other for talent.

Another blow to the NHL—at least to its prestige—was the rise of the Soviet Union as a power in international hockey. This was firmly established in 1972, when an All-Star NHL squad played its Russian counterpart in an eight-game series. The Soviets shocked the NHLers, losing the series only in the final minutes of Game Eight. In later series with the NHL, the Soviets would prove victorious.

The '72 series marked a new era in professional play, and soon the NHL and WHA began looking to Europe for talent. The Toronto Maple Leafs blazed a trail when they signed Swedish aces Borje Salming and Inge Hammarstrom. Salming proved so adept that more Swedes were pursued by NHL clubs and, in time, so were Finns and other skilled Europeans.

The 1970s marked the emergence of the first powerful expansion team, as the Philadelphia Flyers won Stanley Cups in 1974 and 1975. The Flyers were such a rough team that they were called the "Broad Street Bullies." They were succeeded by one of hockey's greatest teams, Scotty Bowman's Canadiens, who won four straight Cups from 1976 through 1979. When 1980 began, puck pundits wondered whether the Habs could equal their record of five in a row.

Orr Breaks New Ground, Takes Bruins All the Way

1 9 6 9 - 7 0

Before the 1969-70 season even began, a tone for hockey in the new decade had already been set. A preseason exhibition game between Boston and St. Louis was marred by a vicious fight. Boston defenseman Ted Green, who had been notorious for his rough play, became embroiled with young Wayne Maki. Maki felled Green with a stick-swing to the head that fractured Ted's skull. Green was rushed to the hospital and barely clung to his life. He would be sidelined for the entire season.

Despite the setback, the Bruins were able to ice the most formidable team of the new decade. Young defenseman Bobby Orr had emerged as the best player in hockey. In a matter of one season, he had lifted his point total from 64 (on 43 assists) to a league-leading 120 (on 87 assists!). He was the only player to surpass 100 points in 1969-70. The idea of a defenseman leading the league in scoring had been preposterous until Orr came along.

Blond Bobby developed a superb one-two combination with his center, Phil Esposito. Orr frequently started a rush in his own end, outraced several opponents, dished off to Esposito, and either took a pass in return or watched his pal put one in. Esposito, who had emerged as one of the league's best centers, didn't match his previous season's arithmetic but wound up with a league-leading 43 goals for 99 points. Boston was equally powerful in goal, where Gerry Cheevers and Ed Johnston proved an excellent pair.

Despite the Bruins' power, they were given a mighty run for first place by the Chicago Blackhawks (who had finished last a year earlier). Under Billy Reay's coaching, the Hawks had become more attentive to defense. They received a boost from rookie goalie Tony Esposito, who posted a record-breaking 15 shutouts. His 2.17 goals-against average would win him the Vezina Trophy.

While the Blackhawks lacked a scoring machine like Orr, they nevertheless had plenty of horsepower in Bobby Hull, Stan Mikita, Pit Martin, and crack defenseman Pat Stapleton. By season's end, the Hawks had pulled

 Ranger backliner Arnie Brown tries to stop superstar Bobby Orr. The Bruins defeated New York in the 1971 playoffs.

off two stunning surprises: They caught and then edged the Boston Bruins in the standings, and they helped oust the Montreal Canadiens from a playoff berth for the first time in 22 years.

By finishing on top, the Blackhawks became the first NHL team ever to leap from the cellar to first place in one season. Since Montreal and Toronto finished fifth and sixth, respectively, it marked the first time the Stanley Cup playoffs were held without a Canadian entry.

What made all the events so unreal was that none of the playoff positions were decided until the final day of the season; and, at that, some higher mathematics were involved to settle matters. Both Boston and Chicago completed the season with 99 points,

but the Hawks annexed first because they had five more victories than the Bruins. The Detroit Red Wings, who had not made it to the playoffs in four years, wound up third. Then there were New York and Montreal, who tied for fourth place with identical records. According to league rules, the team with the most goals would earn the playoff spot. The Rangers won this spot, but they needed some last-day heroics to do so.

The Rangers entered the final day of the season trailing Montreal by two points in the standings and five tallies in the goals-scored column. That meant, to make the playoffs, the Blueshirts not only had to win and hope Montreal lost to Chicago, but they also had to score at least five more goals against Detroit than the

Canadiens did against the Blackhawks.

New York blitzed Detroit 9-5 on the final Sunday afternoon, whereupon the Blackhawks trounced Montreal 10-2. Both the Rangers and Canadiens lifted their goalies in the final minutes, ignoring empty net opposition goals in an effort to increase their own scoring totals. As pulsating as the finish was, it was tainted with severe criticism. The NHL office was chastised for using the "goals scored" criteria for determining playoff teams, and many demanded that a playoff be held between the tied teams. This demand was ignored, however.

Meanwhile, the Red Wings, fortified with Carl Brewer on defense and the surprising scoring of young center Garry Unger, remained a contender throughout the season and actually

Boston's Ted Green lies on the ice after St. Louis' Wayne Maki pole-axed him during an exhibition game. Green suffered a severe skull fracture.

Blue-line vet Gary Bergman (right) helped Detroit win 40 games in 1969-70.

TED GREEN

For almost eight years, "Terrible" Ted Green epitomized the style of the Boston Bruins. He bruised, roughhoused, and intimidated opponents every time he stepped out for a shift.

Then came the infamous stick-swinging incident with the late Wayne Maki, then of the St. Louis Blues, on September 21, 1969. As Green was clearing the puck from the Boston zone, Maki hit Ted from behind. Green turned and knocked Maki down, but Maki speared him as he rose from the ice. Green swung his stick at Maki, again knocking him down, and fell off-balance.

Maki then swung his stick and hit Green across the top of his head. Green went down in a heap, his brain embedded with chips from his skull. Two operations were required to save his life. Green's left side was paralyzed. It was a question of whether or not he could live a normal life, much less skate or play hockey.

Green sat out the 1969-70 campaign and watched his team win the Stanley Cup. Then, with his doctor's permission, he made a comeback the following year. He was a key contributor when the Bruins won the Cup again in 1972.

Jacques Laperriere (*left*) runs up against Boston part-timer Jim Lorentz during a regular-season contest. Laperriere could not prevent *Les Habitants* from sinking to fifth place in 1969-70. It was their lowest finish in 22 years.

1969-70

Best Record
Chicago
(45-22-9)

Stanley Cup Finals
Boston 4
St. Louis 0

Art Ross Trophy
Bobby Orr
(33/87/120)

Hart Trophy
Bobby Orr

Vezina Trophy
Tony Esposito

Calder Trophy
Tony Esposito

Norris Trophy
Bobby Orr

Lady Byng Trophy
Phil Goyette

had a chance to finish first up until the last week of the campaign. For Detroit, the most remarkable accomplishment was that of Gordie Howe. Howe led the team in scoring even though he was the oldest player in the league (age 42).

Besides the Green incident, the Bruins were manacled by other problems in the early part of the schedule. High-scoring Ken Hodge was sidelined by an emergency appendectomy; hard-checking Derek Sanderson was bothered by knee and hip ailments; and Ron Murphy, who played on the record-breaking Esposito line, had to retire because of a back ailment.

As the Bruins struggled along, they became enveloped in a fog of dissension. After he returned to the lineup, Hodge rebelled against coach Harry Sinden for benching him before a midseason game. The more

defensive-minded Don Marcotte was elevated from Hershey and suddenly the Bruins caught fire. Sanderson returned, Hodge reformed, and Boston began getting steady goaltending from Johnston and Cheevers. They entered the playoffs hitting on all cylinders.

If the Bruins' failure to finish first was a disappointment, the Canadiens' descent to fifth place was regarded as absolutely calamitous. Only a year earlier, Montreal won both the Prince of Wales Trophy (as the best team in the East Division) and the Stanley Cup. Now they were has-beens and the reasons were plentiful. Captain Jean Beliveau had aged to a point where he lost his old spark. He had been coaxed into playing another season— apparently against his will—and he played as if his heart wasn't in the game. On top of that, the Canadiens

were wrought with team dissension.

Once again, Scotty Bowman's St. Louis Blues ran away with the Clarence Campbell Bowl, emblematic of supremacy in the West. For a change, the Pittsburgh Penguins—who missed the playoffs for two straight years—made it this time under the studious direction of coach Red Kelly. After advancing with relative ease in the opening playoff round, St. Louis and Pittsburgh met in the West finals.

With Kelly behind the bench, many thought the Penguins would beat the Blues. However, St. Louis easily captured the opening two games on home ice, both outscoring and outfighting the smaller Pittsburgh skaters. The series then moved to Pittsburgh, where the Penguins scored two hard-fought, one-goal victories. However, St. Louis took the next two games and entered the Stanley Cup finals for the third year in a row.

In the East semifinal rounds, both Boston and Chicago emerged victorious. The Bruins traveled to Chicago Stadium to start the East Division finals. Boston captured the momentum in Game One, pumping six goals past Esposito for a 6-3 win. Two nights later, the Bruin forwards—and Orr—toyed with the beleaguered Hawks and skated off with a 4-1 victory. The Bruins overwhelmed Chicago in the next two games at Boston and moved into the Stanley Cup finals against the Blues.

For two consecutive years, the Blues had been humiliated in the Cup finals by the Montreal Canadiens, who beat them in eight straight games. This time, however, St. Louis was up against a new foe, and many believed

Bowman's team would do better— especially since the Blues would be at home for the first two games.

But, once again, the East Division representative humbled the Blues. They not only lost in four straight games to Boston, but they were easily manhandled on St. Louis ice. The series proved what most serious hockey observers had suspected all along: The West Division was nothing more than a glorified minor league, and the Blues had no more right to challenge for the Stanley Cup than the Toronto Maple Leafs, who finished last in the East Division.

The only West player to receive a postseason award was Phil Goyette of the Blues, who took the Lady Byng. Orr captured the Hart and Norris Trophies, while Tony Esposito took the Calder and Vezina prizes.

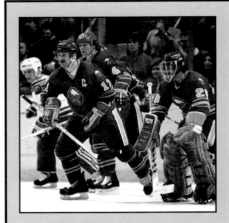

BUFFALO SABRES

For many years a strong minor-league hockey town, Buffalo attempted to enter the NHL with the 1967-68 expansion. They were foiled by the Toronto Maple Leafs' influence; the Leafs had developed a following in Buffalo and they didn't want a new team cutting into their revenue.

Nevertheless, opposition eventually cooled. And by 1970, led by brothers Seymour and Northrop Knox and their backers, Buffalo entered the NHL.

In a brilliant and ironic move, the Knoxes hired former Leafs coach Punch Imlach as general manager/coach. The experts said that hiring Imlach couldn't produce a miracle, but they were wrong. Imlach's ingenuity, along with sensational rookie center Gil Perreault, created a fair starting club.

The following year, Punch struck again, choosing high-scoring left winger Rick Martin in the NHL draft. In 1972, Imlach acquired right winger Rene Robert from Pittsburgh. Robert, along with Perreault and Martin, formed the deadly accurate scoring line known as the "French Connection."

Just three years after their start, the Sabres made the playoffs but lost in the quarterfinals to the Canadiens. In 1975, they reached the Stanley Cup finals but lost to the Flyers in six games. Buffalo has not made a trip to the finals since.

Blues right winger Frank St. Marseille faces off against North Star Mike Chernoff. St. Marseille notched 13 points in the 1970 playoffs to help St. Louis knock off both Minnesota and Pittsburgh.

Frosh Goalie Dryden
Stymies the Mighty Bruins
1 9 7 0 - 7 1

Judging by the preseason polls, 1970-71 was to be the year of the Boston Bruins. The defending Stanley Cup champions were believed to possess the armament for a dynasty. Some Boston dreamers suggested it would last for a decade. In reality, it didn't even last a year.

The Bruins were awesome during the 1970-71 regular season, though, as they knocked home 399 goals over a 78-game schedule. Boston went 57-14-7 and finished atop the East by a fat 12 points. For all intents and purposes, the Bruins eliminated the second-place New York Rangers two months before the season ended.

The Beantowners were so good that they often sleep-walked through their games. Thus, when the Buffalo Sabres upset the Bruins at Boston Garden one night late in the season, it really wasn't a great surprise. "We can get up for teams like Chicago and New York," said Bruins center Derek Sanderson, "but playing an expansion team is like a first-rate night club entertainer playing at a neighborhood bar."

In addition to Bobby Orr and Phil Esposito, there was Terrible Ted Green, the Bruins' bruising defenseman, who returned to the lineup following his infamous stick-swinging brawl in September 1969

with Wayne Maki of St. Louis. Wearing a helmet to protect his once-fractured skull, Green made a courageous comeback, although his speech remained impaired and the quality of his play had clearly deteriorated.

But Boston's power was so awesome that Green's errors were usually obscured by the avalanche of goals by Esposito (76), Johnny Bucyk (51), Ken Hodge (43), Orr (37), and Johnny McKenzie (31). Espo set an NHL record for both goals and points (152), while Orr set a new league mark for assists (102).

If the Bruins had any detectable flaws, they were in goal and behind

 Montreal went with rookie Ken Dryden in the 1971 playoffs, and he responded by beating the powerful Boston Bruins.

the bench. Boston goaltenders Gerry Cheevers and Ed Johnston combined for a 2.65 goals-against average, lagging behind Gilles Villemure and Ed Giacomin of New York (2.26) and Tony Esposito and Gerry Desjardins of Chicago (2.35).

Boston rookie coach Tom Johnson, who succeeded Cup-winning Harry Sinden, permitted discipline to break down toward the end of the season. As a result, his players were out of shape and ill-prepared for the playoffs. This would lead to Boston's disgrace in the opening round.

In New York, the Rangers had hoped to seriously challenge Boston during the regular season. "We never had a better balanced team," said manager/coach Emile Francis. "This club is capable of going as far as it wants." New York finished the season at 49-18-11, 12 points behind Boston.

The Blackhawks, who were transferred to the West Division in 1970-71 when Vancouver and Buffalo were admitted to the East, conquered their division easily. Chicago collected 107 points, 20 more than runner-up St. Louis. Then, as if to prove that the rest of the West sector was comprised of nothing more than minor-league clubs, the Blackhawks shellacked Philadelphia in four straight playoff games.

Champions of the East Division the previous year, Chicago developed an ideal balance between defense and scoring. Brothers Bobby and Dennis Hull scored 44 and 40 goals, respectively, while the defense, led by Pat Stapleton and Bill White, held the enemy in check. Typical of the Blackhawks was center Pit Martin, who combined potent offense with vigilant defensive play.

"I can't emphasize how important Martin is to this club," said coach Billy Reay. "I have great confidence in him individually and in any line on which he plays."

The Canadiens, who missed the

The Vancouver Canucks debuted in the NHL in 1970-71 and went 24-46-8. Despite the humble record, goalie Charlie Hodge was solid in net.

The NHL Players Association presented the Lester B. Pearson Award to the NHL in 1970-71. The award, which was named after a former Prime Minister of Canada, goes to the league's outstanding player, as voted by the players. Boston superstar Phil Esposito took the 1970-71 honor.

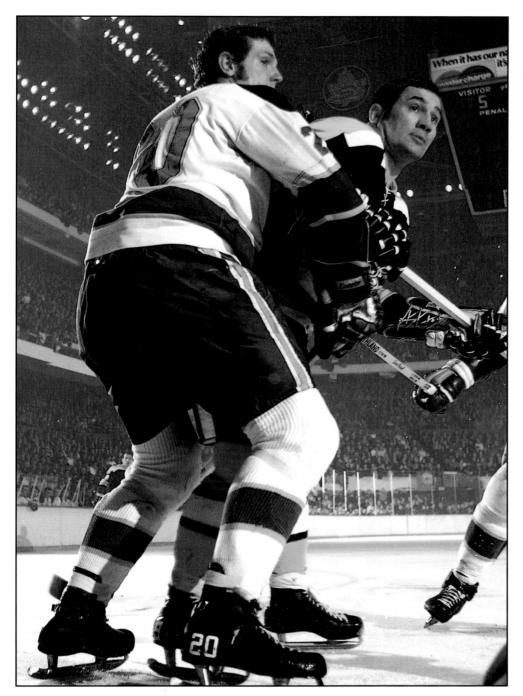

OAKLAND SEALS

The Oakland Seals joined the NHL for the 1967-68 season. Before they had played a game, press pundits predicted the Seals would be one of the first expansion teams to make the play-offs. They were dead wrong.

That first season was a debacle, as the Seals finished 15-42-17. The Seals' problems began at the top. Bert Olmstead, the team's feisty coach/general manager, couldn't stand losing, and he let his team and the press know it. One player remarked: "If Olmstead did public relations for Santa Claus, there wouldn't be any Christmas."

Another problem was attendance—there wasn't any. Prior to the 1970-71 season, the Seals were acquired by the notorious Charles Finley. Finley changed the team name to the California Seals and also changed the color of their jerseys and and made the players don white skates. No matter. The Seals finished with the worst record in the league (20-53-5). By 1972-73, they sunk to even worse depths (16-46-16).

In February 1974, the NHL purchased the Seals from Finley and everyone breathed a sigh of relief—prematurely. The Seals' attendance remained embarrassing, and in 1976 the franchise was relocated to Cleveland and renamed the Barons.

However, hockey will return to the Bay Area. San Jose has been awarded a franchise for the 1991-92 season.

Boston's Johnny Bucyk reached his peak in 1970-71, tallying 51 goals. In this Boston Garden setting, Bucyk rubs shoulders with North Star Tom Reid.

playoffs in April 1970 for the first time in 22 years, appeared to be sinking once more. Dissension had surrounded coach Claude Ruel ever since the opening of training camp, and veterans Ralph Backstrom and John Ferguson retired. Ferguson returned on November 14, but Ruel resigned on December 3. Montreal promoted assistant coach Al MacNeil to replace Ruel.

Thanks to the ineptitude of former heavyweights Toronto and Detroit, the Canadiens remained in playoff contention. It was obvious that Montreal needed new faces in order to climb higher. "I'm always open for trades," said Canadiens manager Sam

Pollock on January 5, 1971, "but I'm sure as hell not looking."

The Red Wings were looking, however, and on January 13, 1971, the Canadiens dispatched Mickey Redmond, Guy Charron, and Bill Collins to Detroit for superstar Frank "Big M" Mahovlich. A day later, the Big M scored his first Canadiens goal and Montreal was off and flying.

In March, Pollock produced his ace-in-the-hole, elevating a McGill University law student, Ken Dryden, from the minor leagues to play goal. "Use Dryden," advised Floyd Curry of the Canadiens' general staff, "and he'll win the Stanley Cup for you." Nobody

believed Curry until the seventh game of the opening playoff series with Boston.

Dryden had won each of his six regular-season games before taking on the vaunted Bruins. The insertion of this poetry-reading rookie against the defending Cup champions was hailed as one of hockey's most daring ploys. But amazingly, it worked.

Boston won the opener at home 3-1, though Dryden played well. In the second game, the Bruins bombarded him and amassed a 5-1 lead. But the Canadiens' spirit would not be squelched. Montreal fought back and won the game 7-5. "That game," said Dryden, "told us we had a chance to

The West won the 1970-71 All-Star Game 2-1. Here, Frank Mahovlich (27) and Gordie Howe (9) tangle with West defenseman Pat Stapleton.

Chicago's Dennis Hull enjoyed his best goal-scoring season in 1970-71 when he knocked in 40. Dennis's brother and teammate, Bobby Hull, scored 44.

PHIL ESPOSITO

Some say Phil Esposito is the finest center of all time. They point out that he regularly led the NHL in scoring; that he was consistently voted a first-team All-Star; and that the Boston Bruins' renaissance directly coincided with his arrival in 1967.

However, others say that Esposito "lost it" by 1973. They mention that he was knocked out of the 1973 Stanley Cup playoffs with a bodycheck from Ron Harris, a third-string New York Rangers defenseman. Phil-knockers say Esposito lost his scoring touch in the clutch when Boston skated in the 1974 and 1975 playoffs.

Nevertheless, few would doubt that Phil was a superstar. Just the fact that he recovered from his near-crippling 1973 knee injury to win the 1973-74 scoring title—his fifth in six years—is testimony to the man's superiority and gumption.

On November 7, 1975, the sensitive and emotional Esposito was shaken right out of his skates when he learned that, after eight seasons with the Bruins, he was being traded to the hated New York Rangers. In 1978, Fred Shero was hired as manager/coach and immediately put in a system that Phil could adapt to. Playing like the Esposito of old, he led the Rangers to the Stanley Cup finals, where they lost to the Montreal Canadiens in five games.

win the series."

Montreal won the third game 3-1, but the Bruins rebounded with 5-2 and 7-3 triumphs. On the brink of elimination, the Canadiens demolished the Beantowners 8-3 in Game Six.

The final game was all Dryden's. Boston scored first but the Canadiens rallied, took a 4-2 lead, and let their goalie do the rest. He held the Bruins at bay and recorded one of the most extraordinary upsets in the history of sports.

"Their entire team played well," said Phil Esposito, "but Dryden decided the series. He never cracked, never appeared to lose confidence or be bothered by the pressure. He beat us."

Montreal's Henri Richard, a veteran of nine Stanley Cup-winning teams, epitomized the feeling of his teammates. "This," said Richard, "is the greatest series victory of my career."

It was so great that the Canadiens suffered a near-fatal letdown in their semifinal series against the mediocre Minnesota North Stars. Montreal eventually won the series four games to two, but not before various members of the club openly criticized coach MacNeil.

The Stanley Cup finals pitted *Les Habs* and the Blackhawks. The Canadiens were still unsteady in the

first two games of the series, as the Blackhawks, led by Jim Pappin and Lou Angotti, won 2-1 and 5-3 at Chicago Stadium.

Back at the Forum, the Montrealers tied the series at two apiece. But their house still was not in order. After Chicago defeated them 2-0 for a three-two series lead, Richard blasted MacNeil, calling him "incompetent." Prior to the sixth game, threats were made against MacNeil's life and he required police protection throughout the game. Yet, with all the acrimony and dissent, Montreal's skaters came from behind in the third period to win the game 4-3.

In 1970-71, Phil Esposito tallied 76 goals and 152 points—demolishing both NHL records. Teammates Esposito, Bobby Orr (139), John Bucyk (116), and Kenny Hodge (105) finished one-two-three-four in the NHL in scoring. Boston rang up 399 goals, breaking the league record by 96.

Four of the NHL's best checking players converge during action at the Boston Garden. The Canadiens include Terry Harper (19) and Henri Richard. The Bruins are penalty-killers Ed Westfall (18) and Derek Sanderson. Montreal defeated Boston in the 1971 semifinals, winning Game Seven 4-2.

The final game was played in Chicago before 21,000 fans on May 18, 1971. If there was a more dramatic ending to an NHL playoff, few could remember it. Chicago leaped ahead 2-0 and appeared to have the Canadiens lined up for the knockout punch. The lead seemed safe until the last six minutes of the second period, when Montreal's Jacques Lemaire hurled a long, hard—but seemingly manageable—shot at goalie Esposito. The puck sailed over Esposito's shoulder and into the net, putting Montreal within a goal of Chicago.

A few minutes later, Lemaire shoveled a pass to Richard, who slipped one past Esposito to tie the score. At 2:30 of the third period, the Pocket Rocket buzz-sawed his way around defenseman Keith Magnuson and swerved hard toward Esposito. When Tony came out to meet the onrushing Canadien, Richard lifted the puck over the goalie's falling body, pushing Montreal ahead 3-2.

From that point on, Dryden turned back Bobby Hull and the rest of the Chicago shooters. The Blackhawks never scored again and Montreal won the Stanley Cup. MacNeil was hoisted on the shoulders of the very players who earlier had lambasted him. His job appeared secure.

However, on June 10, less than a month after his astonishing triumph, MacNeil quit the Canadiens to take a job as manager/coach of the new Nova Scotia Voyageurs of the AHL.

"I realized that coaching the Canadiens would be a tough position to hold," said MacNeil. "I don't think there's a future in it for me." The Canadiens hired Scotty Bowman to replace MacNeil.

For the second straight season, Orr was awarded both the Hart and Norris Trophies. Meanwhile, Gil Perreault of the Buffalo Sabres won the Calder Trophy and Bucyk of the Bruins took the Lady Byng prize.

Orr's the Difference as Bruins Topple Rangers

1971-72

For a change, logic prevailed in the NHL's division races. The Boston Bruins finished the season on top of the East Division with 119 points with a record of 54-13-11.

Stopping the Boston hockey machine was like Peter Puck trying to block a Zamboni. The Bruins not only finished ten points ahead of their nearest foe, the New York Rangers, but also shellacked the hated Blueshirts in five out of the six games they played during the regular season.

Defenseman Bobby Orr won the Hart Trophy for an unprecedented third straight season. Meanwhile, Phil Esposito, the other half of Boston's one-two punch, led the league in scoring with 133 points—16 more than runner-up Orr. Between them, Bobby and Phil scared the opposition just by stepping onto the ice.

So glittering were the Bruins' individual and collective performances that they overshadowed outstanding teams elsewhere. The Rangers, for example, enjoyed a superb season. They were led by All-Star defenseman Brad Park and the "GAG (Goal-A-Game) Line," which consisted of center Jean Ratelle, Rod Gilbert, and Vic Hadfield.

Until he was injured during the homestretch, Ratelle seemed like a good bet to win the scoring championship. Although he missed 15 games, the lean New York center managed to notch 46 goals for 109 points to finish third behind Esposito and Orr. Jean's reward was the Lady Byng Trophy. "Ratelle," said Emile Francis, "is a perfect gentleman and a perfect hockey player."

Ratelle's linemate, Hadfield, became the first Ranger ever to score 50 goals. He finished fourth in the NHL with

⚠ **Not even All-Star goalie Ed Giacomin could stop the high-powered Bruins offense in the 1972 finals. Here, Phil Esposito hones in on the New York netminder.**

106 points, while the line's third man, Gilbert, finished fifth with 97 points on 43 goals.

Injuries to each of the GAG Line aces hurt them in the playoffs. Nevertheless, the Rangers defeated Montreal in the first playoff round, four games to two, and went on to shellack Chicago in four straight games. Chicago had no alibi for its abysmal 1972 playoff effort. Having run away with the West Division championship for the second year in a row, coach Billy Reay's Windy City skaters were regarded as a solid Cup threat.

But playing in the weaker West Division had given Chicago a distorted view of the power of the East. After sweeping Pittsburgh in four straight in the opening Cup round, the Hawks were thoroughly demolished by the hobbled Rangers. Bobby Hull put the debacle in perspective when he said:

"It just seemed that the Rangers wanted the win more than we did."

Chicago's only consolation was that goalie Tony Esposito, playing in 48 games, had the best goals-against average (1.76) in the league. The combination of Esposito and substitute Chicago goaltenders Gary Smith and Gerry Desjardins posted a collective 2.12 goals-against average to win the Vezina Trophy for the Blackhawks.

The next biggest disappointment, after Chicago's playoff failure, was the performance of the 1971 Stanley Cup champion Montreal Canadiens. Fortified with new coach Scotty Bowman, who supposedly would lead them to the top, the Canadiens were never able to squeeze themselves out of third place in the East. Most of the time, they were saved by the heroics of goalie Ken Dryden, who won the Calder Trophy despite being the playoff hero the year before.

Bowman did obtain creditable performances from big left wing Frank Mahovlich, who finished sixth in the league in scoring with 96 points, and was heartened by the return of defenseman Serge Savard, who had suffered a severe leg injury the previous year. Although Montreal often played mediocre hockey during the regular campaign, many expected the Canadiens to flash their "mystique" in the playoffs and skate to the finals. But Bowman discovered that the Canadiens' mystique was not retroactive, and Montreal fell easy prey to the Rangers in six games.

One of the most exciting races in 1971-72 was for the fourth and final playoff spot in the East. The Detroit Red Wings, who dropped coach Doug Barkley and replaced him with Johnny Wilson early in the season, appeared capable of overtaking the Toronto Maple Leafs. Toronto seemed in

The Rangers' Gilles Villemure was one of hockey's best backup goalies. In 1971-72, he played 37 games, went 24-7-4, and posted a splendid 2.09 GAA.

GARY DAVIDSON

Gary Davidson, who with Dennis Murphy founded the World Hockey Association in 1972, was no newcomer to professional sports rivalries. In 1967, Davidson was instrumental in the formation of the now-defunct American Basketball Association.

"It has been conclusively proved by the players themselves that there is room in hockey for a second major league," declared Davidson. "That those players had the courage to follow the leadership of the WHA's equally courageous owners is ample testimony to our credibility."

Davidson, who also created the new and unique nonreserve clause in the standard player contracts of the new league, never saw the WHA become a stable entity. He departed in 1974 to try his hand in other sports. All of Davidson's attempts to set up these rivalries turned out to be colossal failures for the investors, but not for himself. From all accounts, Davidson did very well financially.

trouble when Leafs coach Johnny McLellan was sidelined with a nervous stomach late in the season. Just when it appeared the Leafs would collapse, ancient Hall of Famer King Clancy moved behind the bench and steered the Leafs into fourth.

"I used some good old Irish blarney to loosen them up," Clancy explained, "and some common sense."

Clancy led his Leafs against the powerful Bruins in the playoff's opening series. They startled the Bostonians with a sudden-death overtime win in Game Two on a goal by center Jim Harrison. "With a break here or there," said Clancy, "we might have taken the series. But we didn't get those breaks." The Bruins won the series in five games.

Meanwhile, the Minnesota North Stars—coaxing splendid seasons out of such oldtimers as Gump Worsley, Dean Prentice, Charlie Burns, and Doug Mohns—finished a solid second in the West Division, 19 points ahead of the third-place St. Louis Blues. But age took its toll against the North Stars in the playoffs, and the younger, speedier Blues upset Minnesota on Kevin O'Shea's dramatic sudden-death goal in the seventh game of the series.

The Blues then went up against the Bruins in one of the most one-sided series in playoff history. Boston swept St. Louis by embarrassing scores of 6-1, 10-2, 7-2, and 5-3. In so doing, the Bruins bombed three different St. Louis goalies—Jacques Caron, Ernie Wakely, and Peter McDuffe. "Our team

was awed by the Bruins," said St. Louis coach Al Arbour.

The Stanley Cup finals featured Boston vs. the Rangers, which was billed as a matchup made in heaven. The Big, Bad Bruins were renowned for their roughhouse style. By contrast, the lightweight Rangers were respected as a clean, short-passing team that stressed brains over brawn. The series was fueled by a controversial book, *Play the Man*, authored by Rangers defenseman Park.

In his book, Park criticized such Bruins as Esposito, Johnny McKenzie, and Ted Green and thoroughly enraged the Beantowners before the opener. "You have to give Park credit," said Boston coach Tom Johnson. "His book helped us a lot whenever we played

1971-72

Best Record
Boston
(54-13-11)

Stanley Cup Finals
Boston 4
New York 2

Art Ross Trophy
Phil Esposito
(66/67/133)

Hart Trophy
Bobby Orr
(37/80/117)

Vezina Trophy
Tony Esposito
Gary Smith

Calder Trophy
Ken Dryden

Norris Trophy
Bobby Orr

Lady Byng Trophy
Jean Ratelle

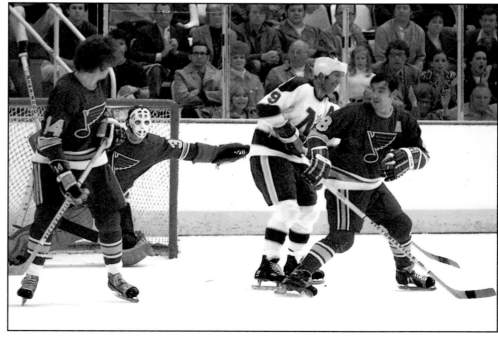

Barclay Plager (8) protects goalie Ernie Wakely from a Boston shot. The Bruins annihilated the Blues in the 1972 Stanley Cup semifinals.

Helmets came into vogue in the 1970s. North Star Charlie Burns (9), who had a plate in his head because of an injury, was one of the first to wear a helmet.

the Rangers. It gave our guys an extra incentive to beat them."

The series opened in Boston Garden on April 30, and for a time it seemed that Boston would run the New York Rangers right out of Massachusetts. The home team took a 5-1 lead, but the Blueshirts rallied to tie the score in the third period. The Rangers couldn't capitalize on their momentum, however, and Bruins utility forward Ace Bailey scored Boston's sixth and winning goal at 17:44 of the third period.

Boston won the second game of the finals 2-1, but the Rangers came back in Game Three at Madison Square Garden, as Park scored twice in the first period and New York won 5-2. Now, it appeared, the Broadway Blues might tie the series and stun the Bruins

with an upset, just like Montreal had done a year earlier.

But the Rangers, following their long-standing tradition, choked in the clutch. In the vital fourth game, goalie Ed Giacomin gave up two goals to Orr and one to Don Marcotte before the Rangers could marshall an attack. Boston held on to win 3-2.

The Bruins had hoped to wrap up the series at home on May 9, but they didn't reckon with little Gilles Villemure, Giacomin's understudy. Clearly the better of the two New York goalies over the regular season, Villemure came off the bench to play splendidly in the fifth game at Boston Garden. Meanwhile, his mates rallied from 1-0 and 2-1 deficits to win on a pair of third-period goals by little

speedster Bobby Rousseau. The series moved back to Madison Square Garden for Game Six.

The finale was a viciously played game that saw Orr send Boston in front 1-0, despite Villemure's acrobatics. Boston's Wayne Cashman scored twice in the third period to put his team up 3-0. That's how it ended, as goalie Gerry Cheevers proved impenetrable. Boston had won the Stanley Cup.

"Let's face it," said Bruins goalie Eddie Johnston. "We won every big game we had to win all season. That's the sign of a good club and that's why we won the Cup."

Rangers captain Hadfield had a better explanation. "We played them pretty even," he said, "but they had Bobby Orr and we didn't!"

BOBBY HULL

In the summer of 1972, Chicago Blackhawk Bobby Hull jumped to Winnipeg of the World Hockey Association. It was a major coup for the WHA, as Hull had led the NHL in goal-scoring seven times. For Bobby Hull, though, the jump only caused headaches.

First of all, in its desperate attempt to kill the WHA, the NHL attempted to bar Hull from playing by using every legal method at its command. A court injunction sidelined him for the first month of the campaign until, finally, that restriction was lifted. Hull was able to take Winnipeg to the 1973 finals of the WHA Avco World Cup, but they lost to New England.

During the 1977-78 season, Bobby staged a one-man, one-game strike, protesting against violence in hockey. He was particularly incensed at the way WHA officials were allowing intimidators to go after his Swedish linemates, Anders Hedberg and Ulf Nilsson.

In 1980, Hull was traded to Hartford where he teamed with Gordie Howe. Hull had played nine games when his female companion was involved in a near-fatal car accident. Rather than continue playing, Hull often visited her in the hospital and decided against finishing the season.

The rivalry between Bobby Orr (4) and Brad Park (2) reached full-boil in 1972. The two dropped the gloves during the Stanley Cup finals.

Soviets Shock the NHL;
WHA Raids Its Rosters

1 9 7 2 - 7 3

The 1972-73 hockey season seemed like it would never end.

When the Boston Bruins won the Stanley Cup and the annual draft meetings ended in the spring of 1972, the hockey season actually began again. Hockey remained on the front pages of the sports sections from June through October.

Two unusual happenings caused this state of affairs. The first was the emergence of a baby major league, the World Hockey Association. The second was the truly fabulous eight-game series between the Soviet National Hockey Club and the NHL-sponsored Team Canada.

Just days after the Bruins won the Cup in 1972, agents from the WHA began combing NHL rosters, looking to sign players for the new 12-team league. With each week, more and more NHL aces either threatened to, or actually did, jump to the new league. The biggest news occurred in June, when Chicago Blackhawks scoring leader Bobby Hull signed a ten-year, $2.75 million contract to play and coach the Winnipeg Jets. Hull's move made front pages across the continent,

The Soviets gave Team Canada more than it bargained for in the eight-game 1972 series. Here, Jean Ratelle is collared by the Soviet defense.

A tribute to Philly's Bobby Clarke, who won the Hart Trophy in 1972-73.

and it promptly forced the smug NHL owners to sit up and take notice—and to eventually take legal action.

By now, panic gripped the NHL front office. Fearful of being raided, the New York Rangers signed all of their better players to outlandishly high salaries, losing only defenseman Jim Dorey to the WHA's New England Whalers. The more frugal Bruins weren't as lucky. They lost Johnny McKenzie and Derek Sanderson to the Philadelphia Blazers and Ted Green to the Whalers. The New York Islanders, who had yet to play a single NHL game, lost Norm Ferguson and Garry Peters to the New York Raiders and Ted Hampson to the Minnesota Fighting Saints. The raiding continued through the summer.

Meanwhile, Team Canada went into training for the eight-game series— four in Canada and four in Russia— that supposedly would be a breeze for the NHL aces. "If we don't win this series in eight straight," said Montreal goalie Ken Dryden, "it will be a dark day for Canada, judging by the way people are talking."

It was a dark day for Canada. On September 2, 1972, the first game of the series was played at the Forum in Montreal and the Russians triumphed 7-3. "This," said one NHL official, "is the catastrophe of the century." The NHL skaters rebounded in the second game for a 4-1 win, but the third game ended in a 4-4 tie. Then in the final game of the Canadian tour, the Russians humiliated

Team Canada 5-3. Vancouver fans chased the NHL stars off the ice with a resounding chorus of boos.

When the series resumed in Moscow, Team Canada opened with a 3-0 lead that held up until the third period. But the astonishing Russians would not be denied and rallied for a stunning 5-4 victory. "The Russians," said Dryden, "are not 20 guys dependent on a star to bail them out. They have an organized plan of attack that pays off."

Now it was Team Canada's time to rally. Trailing in games 3-1-1, the NHL skaters suddenly came alive and took the next three games and the series. Toronto Maple Leafs forward Paul Henderson emerged as the hero, scoring the winning goals in the last minutes of

Eddie Shack was aptly nicknamed the "Entertainer." The former Toronto star played the 1972-73 season with the Penguins, scoring 25 goals.

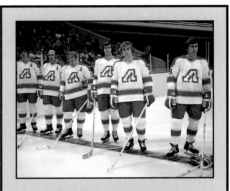

ATLANTA FLAMES

The Atlanta Flames franchise was born in 1972-73, with Bill Putnam serving as team president. He chose Cliff Fletcher to be his manager and named Bernie "Boom Boom" Geoffrion coach. Geoffrion got off to a winning start, and by midseason the Flames were astoundingly in the midst of a West Division pennant race.

Atlanta's goaltending was truly superior, with Dan Bouchard and Phil Myre splitting the duties. However, first-round draft choice Jacques Richard was a disappointment, and the club's scoring leader turned out to be a nobody named Bob Leiter. The defensive corps was anchored by journeymen Noel Price and Pat Quinn and the youthful Randy Manery.

For the 1973-74 season, the Flames added Calder Trophy runner-up Tom Lysiak at center and made the playoffs in just their second season. However, "playoff" was a dirty word in Atlanta. The Flames from the South would appear in a total of 17 playoff games, managing only two wins.

The Flames moved to Calgary for the 1981-82 season. In 1988-89, the franchise won its first Stanley Cup.

the seventh and eighth games. In the final game, Henderson rapped his own rebound past a fallen Soviet netminder with only 34 seconds remaining to win the Series for Canada. Despite the stirring comeback, hockey fans realized that the Soviet skaters were every bit as good as the North American professionals, if not better.

Once the Team Canada series ended, attention turned to the war between the NHL and the WHA. Lawsuits brought by the NHL sidelined Hull through the early part of the season, but a Philadelphia judge finally ruled in favor of the WHA. Hull joined the Winnipeg Jets as an active skater.

But the Golden Jet wasn't capable of filling all of the WHA rinks all the time. Within a month of the opening game, the league was hit with several problems. Despite the presence of Sanderson, McKenzie, and Bernie Parent, the Philadelphia Blazers were a bust at the gate. Attendance also was a problem in New York and Ottawa.

"We expected problems," said WHA President Gary Davidson, "and have contingency plans to handle them."

By December, the WHA had taken over operation of the debt-ridden New York franchise. In Philadelphia, Blazers owner Bernie Brown made several economic moves, including the axing of Sanderson. Eventually, Derek was granted a form of "severance pay" from the WHA and he returned to the Boston Bruins.

The WHA also saw some bright spots. Quebec proved to be a solid franchise, as did New England, Houston, and Winnipeg. Houston and Los Angeles did better than expected.

Despite raids and a lower quality of play throughout the league, the NHL enjoyed a financial bonanza in every one of its cities—except for Oakland. Owner Charles Finley's California Seals cut ticket prices in half to attract customers. Atlanta, which iced a surprisingly strong squad, took to hockey like gin takes to tonic. Likewise, the New York Islanders attracted a large and devoted following

In 1972, the WHA signed Bobby Hull (left) to a record-setting deal. Note the youngster behind the check—future Blues star Brett Hull.

Winnipeg Jets Bobby Hull and Larry Hornung tie up the New York Raiders' Ron Ward. In his 1972-73 debut season, Hull was the WHA's main superstar, scoring 51 goals in just 63 games. He also led his team to the Avco Cup finals.

1972-73

Best Record
Montreal
(52-10-16)

Stanley Cup Finals
Montreal 4
Chicago 2

Art Ross Trophy
Phil Esposito
(55/75/130)

Hart Trophy
Bobby Clarke
(37/67/104)

Vezina Trophy
Ken Dryden

Calder Trophy
Steve Vickers

Norris Trophy
Bobby Orr

Lady Byng Trophy
Gil Perreault

at Nassau Coliseum.

As for the races, the Rangers were favored in the East and the Blackhawks still rated high in the West, even though Hull was gone. But Emile Francis's Rangers proved to be the most disappointing team in either division. They not only missed first place for the 31st consecutive season, but they even relinquished second place to the Boston Bruins in the last weeks of the campaign.

Because they were in a rebuilding year, the Montreal Canadiens were not expected to win the Stanley Cup. But coach Scotty Bowman had them cracking early in the schedule, and soon it was clear that the Flying Frenchmen would win the Prince of Wales Trophy. "It reached a point," said Canadiens captain Henri Richard, "where each of our losses was like a disaster. There will be even more pressure for us in the playoffs." The "rebuilding" Canadiens finished 52-10-16.

In the West Division, Chicago's Blackhawks won the Clarence Campbell Bowl with a less impressive record (42-27-9). Still, they cleared second-place Philadelphia by eight points.

The WHA, considerably more balanced than the NHL, offered a stimulating race in its first season. Hull's Winnipeg Jets won the West and Green's New England Whalers were the class of the East. Not surprisingly,

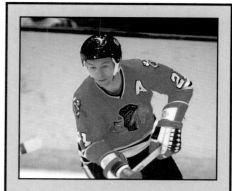

STAN MIKITA

If any single player can be described as the guts of a hockey team, Stan Mikita, the one-time shifty Chicago Blackhawk center, was precisely that man. The wily Mikita guided the Blackhawks to the Stanley Cup finals in 1973, before the Canadiens eliminated them in six games.

To purists, Mikita was the total hockey player. Coach Billy Reay said Stan had Rocket Richard's accuracy as a shooter, Gordie Howe's defensive mastery, Bobby Hull's speed and shot, and Jean Beliveau's stick-handling ability. "Mikita," added Reay, "does more with everything he's got than any player I've seen."

Before the 1972-73 season, Stan considered an offer from the Chicago Cougars of the World Hockey Association. After losing Bobby Hull to Winnipeg the previous season, the Blackhawks now stood to lose their second superstar in as many years.

But in the end, Mikita chose to stay put. "I just wanted to stay with the Blackhawks," Mikita said. "Everything doesn't revolve around money. After you play 12 or 13 years with that Indian head on your jersey, it means something."

In February 1974, Chicagoans displayed their appreciation for Mikita by throwing a "night" in his honor at Chicago Stadium. Stan played until the 1979-80 season before retiring.

Two of the best defensive centers of the 1970s were Chicago's Pit Martin and the Rangers' Walter Tkaczuk. Martin was a pretty good offensive threat too, as evidenced by his ten goals in the 1973 playoffs. In the '73 Stanley Cup semifinals, Martin's Hawks routed the Rangers in five games.

JEAN RATELLE

When coach Emile Francis took over the New York Rangers in 1966-67, he immediately inserted Jean Ratelle on a line with Vic Hadfield and Jean's boyhood chum, Rod Gilbert. Ratelle embarked on a string of three consecutive 32-goal seasons. But somehow, the hockey world failed to take full notice of Ratelle until the 1971-72 season.

On February 27, 1972, Ratelle became the first Ranger in history to notch 100 points in a season. Less than a week later, disaster struck. Jean's right ankle was fractured when it was struck by a slapshot. He was disabled for the rest of the regular season and made a brief appearance in the Stanley Cup finals.

On November 7, 1975, Jean was involved in what many considered the landmark trade in hockey history. Along with Brad Park and Joe Zanussi, Ratelle was shipped to the Bruins in exchange for Phil Esposito and Carol Vadnais. Ranger management considered Ratelle "over the hill" and regarded him as a "throw-in."

However, it didn't take long for "Gentleman Jean" to prove them wrong. In his first season with Boston, he led them in scoring with 90 points. The following year, Ratelle again led the team in scoring with 94 points. Quite an achievement for an "over-the-hill" hockey player.

▲ Defenseman Larry Robinson tries to stuff Dennis Hull into the net. The 6'3" Robinson was a key factor in Montreal's 1973 finals win over Chicago.

▲ Montreal's Serge Savard (18) eludes Dennis Hull during the 1973 finals.

the same teams met in the WHA playoff finals for the Avco Cup. Fortified with more former NHLers, New England won the championship four games to one.

The NHL's Stanley Cup playoffs gave the Rangers a chance to redeem themselves for their poor regular-season play. In the opening round, the Broadway sextet responded with an easy five-game rout of the defending champion Bruins.

In other rounds, Chicago knocked out St. Louis, as expected; Buffalo gave Montreal a scare before bowing four games to two; and Philadelphia eliminated Minnesota. As the semifinals got underway, the Rangers were favored

over Chicago while Montreal was expected to beat Philadelphia.

Both the Rangers and the Flyers won their opening games on enemy ice but never won again. Chicago stunned the Rangers with four straight triumphs, while the Canadiens skated past a hard-hitting Philadelphia club.

"We had to win," said Montreal's Richard. "After finishing first, our fans expected us to win the Cup. By the time we reached the finals, we had to win the Cup because, by then, they had forgotten that we finished in first place. When you are the Canadiens, you cannot make excuses."

Les Habs looked shaky in the finals, but they were clearly the better team

and ultimately beat Chicago in six games. "We made a great effort," said winning coach Bowman. "We had a great team and it was a great series."

Boston's Bobby Orr captured the Norris Trophy for a record-setting sixth consecutive season, while teammate Phil Esposito again led the league in both points and goals (130 and 55).

Flyer Bobby Clarke won the Hart Trophy on the strength of 37 goals and 104 points. New York Ranger Steve Vickers was awarded the Calder and Gil Perreault took the Lady Byng prize. Dryden helped bring the Vezina Trophy to Montreal with his 2.26 goals-against average.

Clarke and Philly
Bully Way to Stanley Cup

1 9 7 3 - 7 4

At the beginning of the 1973-74 season, slogans began popping up on hundreds of automobile bumpers in and around Philadelphia. Accompanied by a Philadelphia Flyers emblem, the message read: "THINK STANLEY CUP!"

And so for eight months, Philadelphians did some heavy wishful thinking. Many believed that coach Fred Shero and his swashbuckling band of stick-handlers could become the first expansion club to acquire Lord Stanley's storied mug. Real experts, though, predicted the Rangers to win the Stanley Cup. And if the Broadway Blueshirts failed, surely the defending champion Montreal Canadiens or the power-laden Boston Bruins would skate off with the prize.

The Rangers were the top choice because they had seemingly the most balanced team—from goalie Ed Giacomin to defensive whiz Brad Park to forwards Jean Ratelle, Walt Tkaczuk, and sophomore ace Steve Vickers. Besides, the Rangers hadn't copped the coveted Stanley Cup in 34 years!

"We had better do it this year," said defenseman Rod Seiling, "because there won't be any 'next year' for a lot of us if we miss."

Indeed, Madison Square Garden's management was fed up with a club sporting the highest team salary in hockey ($2 million) yet didn't boast any marquee names or championship trophies.

Ordinarily, the Canadiens would have been favored over the Rangers, but All-Star goalie Ken Dryden decided to forsake hockey for one season. He needed to be a law clerk in Toronto in order to obtain his law degree. Minus Dryden, the Canadiens were left with three inexperienced goaltenders—Michel Larocque, Wayne Thomas, and Michel Plasse—none of whom could fill Dryden's skates.

The Bruins had their own problems. Superstar center Phil Esposito had injured himself in the 1973 playoffs and would supposedly limp through the 1973-74 season. With Esposito sub-par and Bobby Orr liable to re-injure his tender knees at any time, the Bruins were on thin ice.

▲ The Jack Adams Award, given to the NHL's top coach, debuted in 1973-74.

▲ Four Broad Street Bullies, including goalie Bernie Parent and defenseman Barry Ashbee, stick it to Minnesota's J.P. Parise (standing).

Once the season started, favored New York did an immediate nosedive. Rookie coach Larry Popein became an embattled leader, as his players instigated a mutiny against him. While the Rangers floundered, the Bruins—paced by the seemingly healthy Esposito and Orr—moved right to the top of the NHL East, with the Canadiens in close pursuit.

The Rangers nestled themselves into third place. Only fourth place—contested by Buffalo and Toronto—seemed a question mark. The remaining East teams—the Red Wings, Islanders, and Canucks—were clearly outclassed.

In the West Division, the bullying Philadelphia Flyers were bashing everyone in sight. Throughout the season, the Flyers and Chicago engaged in a neck-and-neck battle for the Clarence Campbell Bowl. The Blackhawks made a determined bid for the top in the homestretch, but the Flyers prevailed, finishing with a 50-16-12 record. The other two positions produced surprise finishers.

Traditional losers, the Los Angeles Kings found themselves a new manager (Jake Milford) in midseason, arranged a couple of key trades, and galloped into the playoffs for the first time since 1969.

Even more surprising were the second-year Atlanta Flames. Coached by the effervescent Boom Boom Geoffrion, the Georgia sextet maintained a winning profile through the first half of the campaign. Then, when everyone figured they'd fold, Geoffrion revved them up again. Atlanta nosed into the playoffs ahead of Minnesota, Pittsburgh, St. Louis, and California.

The scoring race was less surprising, as Boston's Esposito again led the league in scoring (145 points on 68 goals). He was followed by three teammates—Orr (122 points), Ken Hodge (105), and Wayne Cashman (89). Their hot sticks shot Boston into a first-place finish in the East. Montreal was second, the Rangers third, and Toronto fourth.

Despite their relatively dismal third-place finish, the Rangers were given a good chance to win the Stanley Cup.

▲ **Goalie Wayne Thomas and the Canadiens tried their all in 1973-74, but they couldn't offset the loss of Ken Dryden.**

Coach Popein had been fired in midseason and Rangers GM Emile Francis seemed to have straightened his team's assorted problems. Sure enough, the Rangers rose to the occasion, defeating Montreal in a six-game opening round.

The Bruins routed Toronto in four straight, while Philadelphia did the same to Atlanta. Chicago needed five games to oust Los Angeles in the other West Division playoff.

Now the meaningful playoffs began. Chicago took on the Bruins and seemed to have them on the ropes with a quick win in Boston. But the Beantowners rallied and dispatched Billy Reay's club in six games.

The Philadelphia-New York

semifinal series was billed as a match between the "Ferocious" Flyers and the New York "Nice Guys." And ferocious the Flyers were, battling at every turn. The Rangers fought back and extended the series to a full seven games, but the high-flying Flyers ousted New York in the deciding contest.

If Philadelphia was to prevail in the Stanley Cup finals, it would have to stop the mighty one-two punch of Orr and Esposito. Coach Shero believed that Orr was more dangerous and spent long hours reviewing films and consulting with his aid, Mike Nykoluk. Finally, they came up with the formula.

"The idea," Shero explained, "was to make Orr work harder than he normally had to work."

RICK MARTIN

Fans at Buffalo's Memorial Auditorium began watching Rick Martin during the 1971-72 campaign. That year, he scored 44 goals, then a rookie record, and helped provide the Sabres with instant respectability. In 1973-74, Martin, as a member of the "French Connection Line" with Gil Perreault and Rene Robert, scored 52 goals in 78 NHL games.

"He's the greatest natural scorer I've ever coached," said Sabres boss Punch Imlach, who had coached for a long, long time.

Martin's critics had little to carp about except for one incident. In September 1972, Martin—along with Perreault, Vic Hadfield, and Josh Guevremont—walked out on Team Canada in the midst of its series with the Soviet National squad. Martin argued that he had been overlooked by Team Canada coach Harry Sinden. He said his abilities were rusting in Russia when they could have been better honed to sharpness in Canada.

"I was facing my second year in the NHL, where my career lies," explained Martin. "I needed the Sabres' training camp badly."

By 1979, Martin's scoring pace dropped off, as rumors of skirmishes between Martin and Perreault abounded. The Sabres' goal production dropped and the French Connection Line was soon disbanded.

Bobby Sheehan (on knees) was a speed demon who starred briefly for the WHA's New York Raiders. He's shown here against the Minnesota Fighting Saints.

In 1973-74, Gordie Howe played alongside sons Marty (center) and Mark (right) with WHA Houston. Marty was a solid defenseman but never developed into an All-Star like Mark.

So instead of sending one player in to forecheck the fleet and powerful Orr, Shero used his forward lines as flexible roadblocks. They didn't stop Orr, but they did slow him down significantly. One night, Ross Lonsberry pulverized Orr with a bodycheck that left Bobby crumpled on the ice.

"Seeing Bobby on the ice," said Lonsberry, "had to depress the Bruins."

They were even more depressed over Esposito's sudden scoring drought and apparent lack of vitality. Coach Bep Guidolin indirectly criticized Esposito when he said, "I wish we had a Godfather!"

The Flyers did. Baby-faced Bobby Clarke was deadly in the face-off circle, beating Esposito over and over again. "When Clarke loses a face-off," said Guidolin, "you don't move because he's got his stick between your legs or else he's grabbed your stick. He doesn't let you move until he moves. The kid's always thinking."

Boston won the opener, but Philadelphia stunned the Bruins at Boston Garden in Game Two. The Flyers then won twice at The Spectrum, only to drop the fifth match in Beantown. "For the first time," explained Shero, "we gave Orr too much room."

The mistake was corrected in the sixth and final match at The Spectrum, but not before the Flyers indulged themselves in a unique ritual—the playing of Kate Smith's rendition of "God Bless America." The Flyers entered the game with a 35-3-1 record when Miss Smith was heard, but normally they only played a recording of the tune. This time, Kate was there in the flesh.

"Couldn't you sing 'As the Caissons Go Rolling Along'?" Esposito asked wistfully. Miss Smith said sorry, she couldn't. Esposito and Orr then attempted to brush a little luck on themselves by shaking Kate's hand.

All the gesture got them was a 0-0 tie until 14:48 of the first period, when Flyer sophomore Rick MacLeish tipped an Andre Dupont shot past Bruins goalie Gilles Gilbert. That was all the Flyers needed, as Bernie Parent was

1973-74

Best Record
Boston
(52-17-9)

Stanley Cup Finals
Philadelphia 4
Boston 2

Art Ross Trophy
Phil Esposito
(68/77/145)

Hart Trophy
Phil Esposito

Vezina Trophy
Bernie Parent
Tony Esposito

Calder Trophy
Denis Potvin

Norris Trophy
Bobby Orr

Lady Byng Trophy
John Bucyk

Vic Hadfield (11) reached his NHL scoring peak in 1971-72 when he scored 50 goals for the Rangers. The 1973-74 season was his last in the Big Apple. He joined the Penguins in 1974-75.

TIM HORTON

On February 20, 1974, the Buffalo Sabres lost to the Toronto Maple Leafs. After the game, Buffalo manager Punch Imlach and defenseman Tim Horton took a stroll up Church Street in Toronto, near Maple Leaf Gardens. Tim had a badly bruised jaw and was depressed about the loss. The perennial optimist, Imlach tried to cheer up his old pal.

"You played only two periods," said Imlach, "and one shift in the third, yet you were picked as a star of the game. If all the guys had played so well, we'd have won going away."

Horton forced a smile. "Well, Punch," he said, "there's always tomorrow."

But for Tim Horton, there would be no tomorrow. Early the next morning, en route to Buffalo in his sports car, Tim lost control of his automobile and crashed on the Queen Elizabeth Way. He died instantly.

"There were defensemen you had to fear more because they were vicious and would slam you into the boards from behind," Bobby Hull once said. "But you respected Horton because he didn't need that kind of intimidation. He used his tremendous skill and talent to keep you in check."

Horton was posthumously inducted into the Hockey Hall of Fame in 1977.

▲ The 1974 finals witnessed one of the most vicious fights in playoff history, as Philly's Dave Schultz decisioned Boston's Terry O'Reilly.

▲ Flyer Rick MacLeish compiled 22 points during the 1974 playoffs.

playing his usual spectacular game in the Flyers goal. Miss Smith remained on hand to cast her beloved spell over the Flyers, who led until the final buzzer. The Flyers fans hailed their new champions and the Bruins lined up for the traditional post-series handshakes.

"The Bruins," said Orr, "are now No. 2. The Flyers are No. 1."

Esposito won the Hart Trophy for the second time in his career, while Orr captured the Norris Trophy for an amazing seventh consecutive season. Another Bruin, John Bucyk, became a two-time winner of the Lady Byng Trophy, while Denis Potvin of the New York Islanders was awarded the Calder award.

Unlike the NHL races, the WHA featured greater parity and relatively tight races. Bobby Hull, burdened by coaching and playing problems, was a major disappointment. The Houston Aeros lured 45-year-old Gordie Howe out of retirement for a couple of million dollars and also signed his sons, Marty and Mark. The Howe trio led the Aeros to the top of the Western Division. New England's well-balanced Whalers topped the Eastern Division and were favored again to win the Avco Cup.

But the Whalers were stunned by the underdog Chicago Cougars, who knocked them out of the opening round. Houston, Toronto, and Minnesota each advanced to the semifinals. Once again, Chicago

surprised everyone by eliminating Toronto in seven games, while Houston ousted Minnesota in a bitter six-game series.

The finals were terribly anticlimactic. Houston won the championship, pulverizing Chicago in four straight games. Gordie was voted the WHA's most valuable player, and his 18-year-old son, Mark, was the league's rookie of the year.

Gordie Howe said the triumphs were more satisfying than the four Stanley Cups he helped win during his 25 years with Detroit. "This one," he said, "means a little more because of the three of us playing together on the same team. I don't think I've ever had as much fun as I did this year."

Flyers Fight Off Sabres
for Second Straight Title

1 9 7 4 - 7 5

The success of the Philadelphia Flyers (a.k.a. the "Broad Street Bullies") was criticized by purists. But the Flyers adamantly defended their position—and still do. "Sure we hit hard," said Hall of Famer Bill Barber, "but there was also a high skill level on the team, from Bernie Parent in goal on out to Bob Clarke at center. You have to score goals to win hockey games,

and we did plenty of that too."

Like it or not, the Flyers picked up where they had left off the previous season, bulldozing their way to a 51-18-11 record. Parent's goaltending was good for a 2.03 goals-against average, which earned him the Vezina Trophy. The indefatigable Clarke delivered a league-tying 89 assists, though his 116 points were well behind Bobby Orr's

league-leading 135 mark. Orr also tallied 89 assists.

Although the WHA had made significant cuts into NHL rosters, the senior league continued to expand. Washington, D.C. and Kansas City were added to the NHL. The Washington Capitals signed former AHL star Jimmy Anderson to coach the team, while the Kansas City Scouts

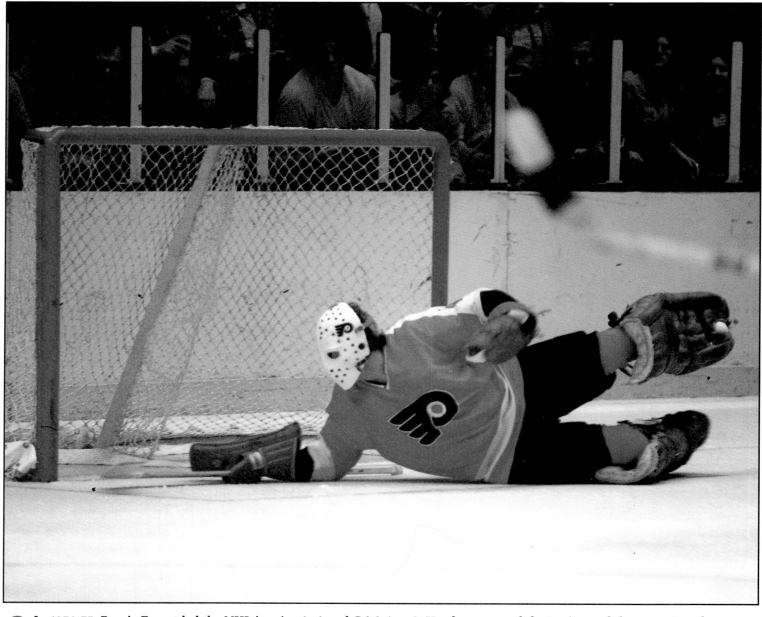

In 1974-75, Bernie Parent led the NHL in wins (44) and GAA (2.03). He also captured the Vezina and the Conn Smythe.

inked former Bruins coach Bep Guidolin as coach. The game of musical coaching chairs continued, as Don "Grapes" Cherry, a career minor-leaguer, was named to coach the Bruins. Finally, Floyd Smith took over for Joe Crozier in Buffalo.

The NHL decided to divide itself into a new 18-team, two-conference, four-division arrangement. One of the conferences was named the Prince of Wales Conference, and the other was called the Clarence Campbell Conference. The Campbell Conference contained the Lester Patrick Division (New York Islanders, New York Rangers, Philadelphia, and Atlanta) and the Conn Smythe Division (Chicago, Kansas City, Minnesota, St.

Louis, and Vancouver). The Prince of Wales Conference included the James Norris Division (Detroit, Los Angeles, Montreal, Pittsburgh, and Washington) and the Jack Adams Division (Boston, Buffalo, Toronto, and California).

While NHL attendance held up in most cities, the league was continually pressured by the pesky WHA. The rival league constantly produced publicity, creating stunts that confounded the senior circuit. One such event was an eight-game series between the cream of the WHA and a Soviet All-Star team. Though the Russians won the series, the WHA players gained considerable respect and even more ink. Moreover, Gordie Howe and his two sons, Marty and

BERNIE PARENT

Playing in 73 regular-season games in 1973-74, Bernie Parent produced a dazzling 1.89 goals-against average, best in the NHL. The veteran led the Flyers to the Stanley Cup finals against Boston and, in the sixth and final game of the series, shut out the high-scoring Bruins 1-0. Parent won the Conn Smythe Trophy as the most valuable player in the Stanley Cup playoffs.

As the Broad Street Bullies retained their heavyweight title in 1974-75, Parent again captured the playoff MVP award—the only player ever to win consecutive Conn Smythe Trophies.

Parent's brilliant career spanned from 1965-66 to 1978-79, but it ended in tragedy. Bernie was accidentally struck in the right eye by a New York Ranger stick. The stick actually found its way through the tiny opening in Parent's mask.

Bernie, who knew immediately that he was in trouble, was rushed to the hospital, where he spent the next ten days with both eyes bandaged. With injury to the retina and a dislocation of the lens, observers feared Parent's days as a netminder were over. At the conclusion of the 1978-79 season, the popular goalie announced his retirement.

Parent was inducted into the Hockey Hall of Fame in 1984.

One of the key Flyers during the mid-1970s was Rick MacLeish. MacLeish netted 38 goals in 1974-75 and tallied 11 more in the playoffs.

The Flyers' Fred Shero (*seated*) was the first NHL coach to actively employ assistant coaches. Here, he discusses strategy with aides Mike Nykoluk (*left*) and Barry Ashbee.

Mark, continued starring for the Houston Aeros, which embarrassed the NHL.

The WHA also upstaged the senior league when it came to signing European players. Two of the best were Ulf Nilsson and Anders Hedberg, who teamed up with Bobby Hull in Winnipeg. The Toronto Toros landed the highly regarded Czech Vaclav Nedomansky. Once the Europeans displayed their magnetism, the NHL followed suit and began signing them.

NHL leaders kept hoping the WHA would go away. But somehow the new league hung on. In 1974-75, Edmonton boasted former Red Wing ace Bruce MacGregor on right wing and Hall of Famer Jacques Plante in goal. Jake the Snake opened with a flourish, but his play cooled down and he finished with a 15-14-1 record and a 3.32 goals-against average.

"While it's true that Jacques didn't set the world on fire," said ex-WHA President Howard Baldwin, "it's also true that we landed another big name in our war with the NHL. Every time we signed a high-quality player like Plante, we moved closer to the NHL and, no less important, we won another skirmish on the publicity front."

On the NHL front, some teams— particularly the New York Rangers— began suffering from the "fat cat" syndrome. The Blueshirts, who many believed had the personnel to win the Stanley Cup, couldn't keep pace with the Flyers and found themselves closely pursued by two expansion teams— Atlanta and the Islanders. Once it became apparent that the Flyers had locked up first place in the Patrick Division, a splendid race developed for second, third, and fourth.

The Islanders, who had been a

laughing stock since their inception, made a major leap forward under the coaching of Al Arbour and GM Bill Torrey. By the midpoint of the 1974-75 season, Arbour's skaters displayed a marked improvement over the previous year. Though 19-41-18 in 1973-74, they rose to 33-25-22 in 1974-75.

Torrey still was not content with the results. He wanted more oomph up front and went to the NHL marketplace in search of scorers. To his amazement, he learned that Minnesota North Stars manager Jack Gordon was prepared to unload two crafty forwards with superb scoring credentials—J.P. Parise and Jude Drouin. Torrey acquired the pair in return for Ernie Hicke, Doug Rombough, and Craig Cameron, a trio of forwards who had made only a minimal contribution to the Islanders' cause.

Drouin was impressed with his new hockey club. "I hope that the guys here

1974-75

Best Record
Philadelphia
(51-18-11)

Stanley Cup Finals
Philadelphia 4
Buffalo 2

Art Ross Trophy
Bobby Orr
(46/89/135)

Hart Trophy
Bobby Clarke
(27/89/116)

Vezina Trophy
Bernie Parent

Calder Trophy
Eric Vail

Norris Trophy
Bobby Orr

Lady Byng Trophy
Marcel Dionne

The 1974-75 season belonged to Philadelphia center Bobby Clarke. He tied for the NHL lead with 89 assists, captured his second Hart Trophy, and captained his Flyers to their second straight Stanley Cup.

realize what a good team they've got," Drouin said. "They're not far from the big money."

True, but the Islanders weren't yet in the money. They lost three straight games in early March and were in danger of missing the playoffs. However, they beat the powerful Boston Bruins in Uniondale, as goalie Glenn "Chico" Resch yielded just one goal in what one observer termed "the biggest victory" of his NHL career. Despite a vigorous challenge from Atlanta, the Islanders made the playoffs—and very nearly won second place from the Rangers.

Thus, owner Roy Boe's faith, Torrey's insight, Arbour's patience, and the Islanders' vigor produced a playoff berth well before most observers thought it possible. Just two years earlier, they had finished 12-60-6.

Although they did not have a scorer among the Top Ten, the L.A. Kings totaled 105 points and finished second to the Canadiens in the Norris Division. Buffalo ran away with the Adams, finishing a full 19 points over Boston, while Vancouver topped the Smythe, edging St. Louis by two points.

For sheer David and Goliath drama, nothing could top the opening playoff round between New York's rivals—the Rangers and the Islanders. The Isles were as confident as a young team could be; still, they were somewhat awed by their cross-county counterparts.

"We know we're better than the Rangers," said Denis Potvin. "We're younger, stronger, and better. For some reason, though, we have too much respect for them. We treat them like gods. I guess we really have a bit of an inferiority complex, probably because we believe too much of what we hear and read about them."

DAVE SCHULTZ

No athlete ever received more media attention for less talent than Dave Schultz, a pugnacious forward who burst onto the NHL scene in 1971-72 for one game and became a regular a season later. Schultz was a key member of the ferocious Flyers during the era in which the "Broad Street Bullies" were bringing home the Stanley Cup. He worked hard to earn his nickname "The Hammer."

Schultz led the NHL in penalty minutes in 1972-73, 1973-74, and 1974-75 (garnering an astronomical record-breaking 472 minutes in 1974-75). In his first eight seasons as a pro, Schultz spent the equivalent of 57 games in the penalty box. In addition to his fighting ability, Schultz honed his hockey skills and netted 20 goals in 1973-74.

However, with a growing awareness around the NHL of excessive violence, and with the "intimidation" game becoming passe, Schultz became expendable and was dealt to the Los Angeles Kings in 1976.

The Hammer became somewhat of a journeyman hockey player, going to the Pittsburgh Penguins and then to the Buffalo Sabres before retiring in 1980.

Houston's Gordie Howe (right) was clearly one of the main attractions of the WHA. Here, he battles Winnipeg at Sam Houston Coliseum in Texas.

In 1975, Buffalo reached the finals for the only time ever. The Sabres beat Montreal in the semis, thanks largely to Gil Perreault (right).

The WHA's Avco Cup was sponsored by Avco Financial Services. The company paid $500 to the WHA for this right.

The Islanders beat the Rangers at Madison Square Garden 3-2 in Game One, but lost the second game at Nassau Coliseum 8-3. Most thought the Rangers would romp in the third game at the Garden. It would not happen.

The Islanders piled up a 3-0 lead midway through the second period and 17,500 Rangers fans seemed prepared to throw in the towel. However, the Rangers fought their way back on the strength of two Bill Fairbairn goals. Then, with the Islanders staggering, Steve Vickers sent the game into overtime by scoring with 0:14 remaining in regulation. After the intermission, however, Islander Parise shocked the Rangers by scoring 11 seconds into the extra period. The Islanders thus earned the title "Kings of New York."

Other playoff rounds were also filled with upsets. Toronto surprised the high-flying Kings while the Blackhawks dispatched the Bruins.

Continuing their unexpected play, the Islanders then pulled off one of the most remarkable comebacks in history. In their second-round series, the Isles lost their first three games to Pittsburgh, only to come back and win the next three. In Game Seven, New York captain Ed Westfall scored the series-winner in the third period. Suddenly, the Isles were in the semifinals against the defending champion Flyers!

New York lost three straight to the Flyers, but they again stormed back to win the next three. Could the Islanders pull off back-to-back miraculous comebacks? No. Philly won Game Seven 4-1 and skated into the Stanley Cup finals. Their opponent was the Buffalo Sabres, who knocked off Chicago in the first round and Montreal in the second.

It was appropriate that Philadelphia and Buffalo made it to the finals, as the two teams tied for the regular-season lead with 113 points. It also marked the first time two expansion teams met for the Cup. Buffalo featured the dazzling pass work of Rene Robert, Gil Perreault, and Richard Martin, who composed the "French Connection Line."

The Sabres put up a good fight, but could not cope with Bernie Parent's goaltending and Philadelphia's all-ice checking. Philly won in six games. It was symbolic that the Flyers' Cup-winning goal was scored by hard-nosed Bob "Hound Dog" Kelly.

Flyers ace Clarke won his second straight Hart Trophy. Orr, who beat teammate Phil Esposito for NHL scoring honors (135-127), took his eighth consecutive Norris Trophy. Detroit's Marcel Dionne nabbed the Lady Byng, Parent snagged the Vezina, and Atlanta's Eric Vail skated off with the Calder prize.

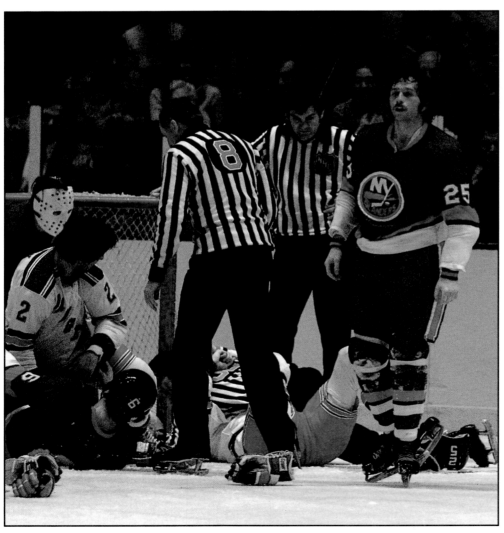

▲ **The 1975 playoffs sparked a heated New York-New York rivalry. The Islanders won this series, but it was not without its squabbles.**

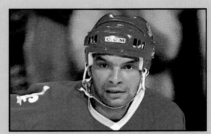

Tony McKegney

BLACKS IN HOCKEY

Quite a fuss was made when the NHL's Washington Capitals signed a black player, Mike Marson, to a 1974-75 contract. Only one black man had ever reached the NHL before Marson—Willie O'Ree. O'Ree played for Boston in 1960-61 after a two-game trial in 1957-58.

During the mid- and late 1940s, Sherbrooke of the Quebec Senior Hockey League used an entire black line, consisting of the Carnegie brothers (Ossie and Herbie) and Manny McIntyre. Herbie was believed to be the equal of most NHL stars, but couldn't crack the majors. Herbie hinted that his skin color had a lot to do with it.

However, Grant Fuhr has played magnificently during his long NHL career, and race has never been an issue with Grant. Recently, more and more black youngsters have taken up hockey, and with very positive results. The municipally operated ice-skating rink in Harlem (New York) has developed a full-scale hockey program.

Habs Outclass the Fightin' Flyers, Go All the Way

1 9 7 5 - 7 6

It has been a fact of hockey that the Stanley Cup champions dictate the style of play to which lesser teams aspire. In the late 1950s, for example, the five-time Cup-winning Canadiens established the explosive style of hockey that wore the enemy to a frazzle. Other teams adopted this approach.

And so it was in the mid-1970s, when the Philadelphia Flyers brawled their way to two straight Stanley Cups. The Flyers had popularized the use of the goon, and now many teams were adopting a similar strategy. However, one team conspicuously avoided that trend. The Montreal Canadiens, coached by Scotty Bowman, boasted too many stars and too much class, from goalie Ken Dryden on out.

Veteran Canadien Jim Roberts explained his team's mystique. "The Canadiens," said Roberts, "are not Montreal's team, not Quebec's team. They are Canada's team. The team is as cosmopolitan as the city. Montreal fans make you have more good games. The fans are critical; they know the game better than most since they play hockey themselves, and they expect

One of the most skillful defensemen during the Canadiens' dynastic era of 1976-79 was Guy Lapointe. Here, Lapointe breaks out of his own end, with New York's Phil Esposito in pursuit.

Gilles Gratton's mask was as colorful as his personality. Unfortunately for Gratton, his mask frightened few shooters. Gilles lasted just two years in the NHL, splitting time with the Blues and the Rangers.

good games every time."

In 1975-76, the Habs not only displayed world-class goaltending from Dryden but excellent defense from Serge Savard and Guy Lapointe. Guy had developed into one of the NHL's most accomplished backliners.

"Lapointe," said coach Bowman, "is much like Bobby Orr. He has talent and he's a hard worker. He skates hard in a game and he skates hard in practice. That means a lot to a coach."

As always, the Canadiens' forte was skating. Led by high-scoring forward Guy Lafleur, the Flying Frenchmen were really flying now. "They are so good as skaters," said Chicago Blackhawks coach Billy Reay, "that they don't need Henri Richard or Guy Lafleur. This is the best skating Canadiens team ever."

There were several reasons for this renaissance. Bowman's more relaxed attitude was important, but it was the young faces that really sparked the Canadiens. Yvon Lambert, Mario Tremblay, and Doug Risebrough, in particular, were the catalysts. They looked like a cross between the Three Musketeers and the Dead End Kids.

"You look at their production and their aggressiveness," said Bowman, "and you have to conclude that they gave us everything, more than we hoped. When we put them together, they just clicked."

The Maple Leafs were also undergoing a renaissance, due in large part to their brilliant Swedish defenseman, Borje Salming. "Salming," said Leafs exec King Clancy, "is the best defensive defenseman in the NHL."

Not so fortunate were the New York Rangers. The playoff loss to the Islanders the previous spring really hurt, and the hiring of Ron Stewart as new coach did little to help. On the plus side, the Rangers acquired two promising forwards—Pat Hickey and Wayne Dillon—who signed with New York after a stint with the WHA's Toronto Toros.

In a more sensational move, high-scorer Marcel Dionne left the Detroit Red Wings as a free agent and signed with the Los Angeles Kings. The Wings obtained defenseman Terry Harper and forward Dan Maloney as compensation.

The league's hopes of developing a California rivalry between L.A. and the San Francisco Bay Area continued to flounder, as the Oakland franchise won few fans and fewer games.

▲ In an effort to shake up the struggling Rangers, GM Emile Francis waived goalie Ed Giacomin, a former All-Star and a fan favorite. Giacomin caught on with the Red Wings. New York only got worse.

▲ Toronto's Borje Salming was the best defensive defenseman of the mid-'70s.

Marcel Dionne, who had starred with Detroit, demanded a trade after the 1974-75 season. Dionne wound up in L.A., and in 1975-76 he scored 40 goals.

BOBBY CLARKE

In 1972, Team Canada defeated the Soviet National Hockey Club. And Bobby Clarke, the diabetic kid from northerly Flin Flon, Manitoba, emerged as the most outstanding player in the eyes of Soviet hockey experts.

Clarke returned from the Soviet series and, as a member of the Flyers, won the coveted Hart Trophy for the 1972-73 season, a feat he repeated in 1975 and 1976.

Bobby was the heart of the up-and-coming Flyers. In the spring of 1973, the Flyers reached the Stanley Cup semifinals for the first time, before being eliminated by Montreal in five tough games. It was during this series that Clarke gained notoriety as a less-than-dainty combatant. He played the game extraordinarily hard, and by 1973-74 everybody knew it.

Captain of the Flyers, Clarke led them to Stanley Cup victories in 1973-74 and 1974-75. They reached the finals the following year but lost to the Canadiens.

After his 15-year playing career, Clarke became vice-president and general manager of the Flyers in 1984. During his six-year tenure, Philadelphia reached the Stanley Cup finals twice, both times losing to Edmonton.

Despite several different owners, the California Seals kept skating in mud. San Francisco magnate Mel Swig purchased the team and promised to move it to San Francisco when a new rink was built. However, San Francisco's civil leaders showed no inclination to accommodate Swig.

The WHA continued to lure NHL stars and, as a result, salaries continued to escalate. Moreover, the NHL saw a proliferation of agents who tried to help out the wealthy players. Some skaters, such as Phil Esposito, rejected WHA offers simply because they felt more comfortable in the senior league. "I signed for two-and-a-half times less than an offer I had from the WHA," said Esposito.

The Esposito-Orr combination crumpled when Orr's troublesome knee acted up and he went under the knife for the fourth time. When Orr was fit enough to play, he netted five goals and 13 assists in ten games. However, he aggravated the knee again and still more surgery was needed.

Meanwhile, the expansion Islanders and Flyers battled each other for the Patrick Division crown. Philly remained a power thanks to the leadership of captain Bobby Clarke, who had a league-leading 89 assists, and right wing Reggie Leach, whose 61 goals led the league. Because of a Bernie Parent injury, Wayne Stephenson took over in goal and fit in neatly. He went 40-10-13 with a 2.58 goals-against average.

The Islanders were powered by a number of excellent draft picks, including big left wing Clark Gillies,

hard-hitting center Bryan Trottier, and feisty right wing Bobby Nystrom.

Emile Francis's Rangers continued to flounder, and the Blueshirts boss resorted to desperate tactics. First off, Francis waived long-time favorite goalie Ed Giacomin. The Red Wings immediately claimed Giacomin, who returned to New York with his new team and whipped the Rangers 6-4. So angry were Ranger fans that, two nights later, Francis required a police escort to escape the Nassau Coliseum after a game at the Islanders' rink.

Francis continued his shake-ups. He dealt defenseman Brad Park, center Jean Ratelle, and rookie Joe Zanussi to Boston for Carol Vadnais and Esposito. Espo was stunned by the trade and grudgingly trotted off to New York. "There should be a rule," Esposito

The expansion Islanders, improving every year, knocked off Buffalo in six games in the 1976 playoffs. Here, Gary Howatt *(left)* stations himself in front of Sabres goalie Gerry Desjardins.

1975-76

Best Record
Montreal
(58-11-11)

Stanley Cup Finals
Montreal 4
Philadelphia 0

Art Ross Trophy
Guy Lafleur
(56/69/125)

Hart Trophy
Bobby Clarke
(30/89/119)

Vezina Trophy
Ken Dryden

Calder Trophy
Bryan Trottier

Norris Trophy
Denis Potvin

Lady Byng Trophy
Jean Ratelle

insisted, "protecting veterans from trades after a player has been with a team five or seven years."

While the trade couldn't keep the Rangers out of last place, the Bruins greatly benefited from the deal, moving ahead of Buffalo in the Adams Division. For a few games, Boston was able to use ace defensemen Orr and Park on the power play. Bruins veteran John Bucyk showed he hadn't lost his scoring skill, netting his 500th career NHL goal on October 30, 1975.

The season saw two Soviet teams—Central Red Army and the Soviet Wings—play an eight-game exhibition series with NHL teams. The highlight was a New Year's Eve match at Montreal's Forum, which resulted in a 3-3 tie between the Canadiens and the Red Army. Critics rated it one of the

most artistic and thrilling games of the decade. Although the Canadiens outclassed the Russians offensively, Soviet goalie Vladislav Tretiak was exceptional in goal.

As the NHL season wound down, hockey moralists viewed the campaign as a battle between wrong (the Broad Street Bullies) and right (any one of a few teams who played a cleaner, classier game). In the end, Philadelphia annexed first place in the Patrick Division (118 points) with the Islanders 17 points behind in second.

The Blackhawks won the Smythe with just 82 points, while Boston topped the Adams with 113. Montreal led all teams with 127 points (58-11-11). Lafleur topped the NHL in both goals (56) and points (125).

Nevertheless, Flyers captain Clarke

won the Hart Trophy. Ratelle nabbed the Lady Byng award, while Islanders defenseman Denis Potvin was given the Norris Trophy. The Bruins' boisterous leader, Don "Grapes" Cherry, grabbed the Adams Award as best coach.

Despite the Canadiens' paucity of silverware, the Montrealers entered the playoffs as formidable challengers to the champion Flyers. The Habs' first encounter was with the Blackhawks, whom they smoked in four straight. Dryden was brilliant in goal, as the Hawks mustered just three goals in the series. By contrast, the Flyers were nearly upset by an upstart Toronto club. The Leafs extended Philadelphia to a full seven games before bowing 7-3 in the final match.

In the semifinals, Philadelphia took

KEN DRYDEN

Ken Dryden began his NHL career in the limelight. Elevated by the Canadiens late in the 1970-71 season, Dryden played in only six regular-season games. Then, as the Canadiens captured the Stanley Cup, Dryden won the Conn Smythe Trophy as the most valuable player in the playoffs.

Dryden posted a 2.24 goals-against average in 1971-72, his official rookie season, and was awarded the Calder Trophy. The next season, his average climbed a hair to 2.26, and Dryden carted home the Vezina Trophy.

It was then that Ken dropped the big verbal bomb. He announced he was quitting pro hockey to take a $7,000-a-year job as a law clerk in Toronto. He was willing to work for peanuts as a law clerk because the Habs weren't willing to meet his financial terms.

Dryden sat out all of 1973-74 before re-signing with Montreal on May 24, 1974. The contract was one of the highest ever for a goalie, estimated at well over $100,000 a year. But Ken had a mediocre year in 1974-75, as the Canadiens were wiped out of the Stanley Cup playoffs by Buffalo.

Dryden played until 1978-79, posting a career 2.24 GAA.

△ **Guy Lapointe (right) battles Bobby Clarke in the 1976 finals. With a four-game sweep, Montreal supplanted the Flyers as the dominant team of the NHL.**

on Boston while Montreal met the up-and-coming Islanders. Cherry's Bruins thumped the Flyers in their opening game with a 4-2 victory at The Spectrum. And it was thought that the Flyers, wearied by their long opening series, would fall. However, they rallied for an overtime 2-1 win in Game Two and breezed to victories in the next three games.

The Canadiens made it seven straight playoff wins by taking the Islanders in the first three games of their series (3-2, 4-3, and 3-2). The Nassau men managed one victory, 5-2 in Game Four, but bowed out in the next contest 5-2. Thus, the stage was set for a climatic final series between the league's two best teams who displayed dramatically contrasting styles.

The finals opened in Montreal. The

game was tied 2-2 until Flyer Larry Goodenough scored at 5:17 of the third period. But the Canadiens would not be denied. Jacques Lemaire tied the score in the middle of the period and, with less than two minutes remaining, Lapointe scored the winner for a 4-3 decision. The Canadiens took the second game 2-1, and the teams flew to the City of Brotherly Love for Game Three.

Again, Montreal edged the Flyers. Leach's two goals gave Philadelphia a 2-1 lead after the first period, but Steve Shutt tied it for Montreal in the second. In the third stanza, low-scoring defenseman Pierre Bouchard beat Stephenson for the winner.

More important to the NHL's public relations department was that the "good guys" were prevailing over the bullying Flyers. The Canadiens

whizzed by such intimidators as Dave Schultz, Moose Dupont, and Bob "Hound Dog" Kelly. And when push came to shove, the Canadiens stood their ground courageously. Habs defender Larry Robinson scored a decisive knockout versus Schultz, letting it be known that Montreal would not play patsies to the Broad Street Bullies.

The Flyers opened Game Four with a goal by Leach in the first minute of play. Montreal later tied the score at 3-3 with an Yvan Cournoyer goal at 19:49 of the second period. Lafleur and Peter Mahovlich banged in goals late in the third period and the Canadiens grabbed the Stanley Cup from the Flyers. Nobody knew it at the time, but yet another Canadien dynasty was in the making.

Montreal Wins 60 Games and 20th Stanley Cup

1 9 7 6 - 7 7

On paper, the 1976-77 Canadiens were not as awesome as previous Montreal squads. Sure, they boasted many top-of-the-line players, including the following: Steve Shutt, Guy Lafleur, Yvon Lambert, Bob Gainey, Doug Risebrough, Doug Jarvis, Yvan Cournoyer, Mario Tremblay, Larry Robinson, Guy Lapointe, Serge Savard, and Ken Dryden. But as a group, they lacked the overwhelming firepower of Montreal's dynasty teams of the 1950s.

Yet coach Scotty Bowman melded a remarkably cohesive unit that dominated as few teams ever have. The Canadiens' prime concern was not as much the foe from without, but the enemy within. As champion, Montreal had to fight off complacency. "Success can do strange things to championship teams," said Bowman. "There was always the possibility that some of the boys might get lazy."

Many Canadiens were coming off the Canada Cup tournament, which involved teams from six countries—Canada, Czechoslovakia, Finland, the Soviet Union, Sweden, and the United States. The host team won the tourney, defeating the Czechs in the finals.

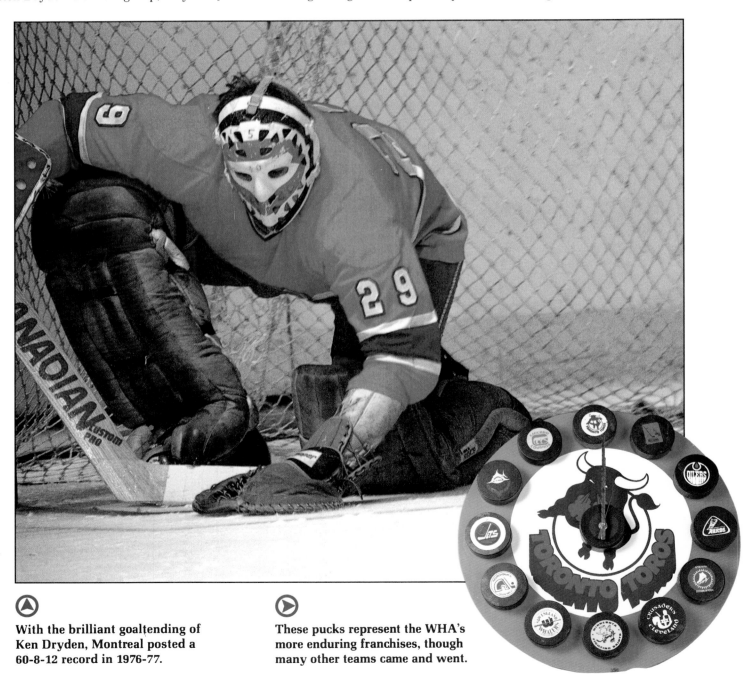

⬆ **With the brilliant goaltending of Ken Dryden, Montreal posted a 60-8-12 record in 1976-77.**

▶ **These pucks represent the WHA's more enduring franchises, though many other teams came and went.**

240

Bobby Orr was named the outstanding player, although Denis Potvin played equally well.

Orr, who had been Boston's golden boy since the late 1960s, sent shock waves through Beantown when he signed as a free agent with the Chicago Blackhawks. Windy City hockey fans hoped that Orr's gimpy knees would hold up. As it turned out, Bobby's limbs failed him. He was unable to play more than 20 games for Chicago in a tragic countdown to a stupendous ten-year NHL career.

Having been dethroned as champions, the Flyers attempted to regroup. They moved right back to the top of the Patrick Division, thanks largely to Rick MacLeish, who totaled 97 points (on 49 goals) to finish fourth in the league. Lafleur led the league in scoring for the second year in a row (136 points on 56 goals). Linemate Shutt led the NHL in red lights with 60.

Financially, the NHL was being bled white by the WHA, which simply would not go away. To stay alive, the WHA continued to add new cities, including one in Birmingham, Alabama. These new teams, though, seemed to come and go. In all, 26 cities iced WHA teams; 22 of them were eventually abandoned.

WHA rosters were even more unstable. Only one Edmonton player, Al Hamilton, was with the club from the start in 1972 to the WHA's finish in 1979. Norm Ferguson paid the price for his loyalty. He launched his WHA career with the New York Raiders, who later became the New York Golden Blades, the Jersey Knights, and the San Diego Mariners. All four teams folded.

Analysts offer many reasons for the WHA's instability. Winnipeg Jets owner Ben Hatskin had this theory: "In the end, it wasn't arena troubles, money troubles, or the NHL which hurt the league. It was circumstances. In 1974, when the WHA made up Team Canada and played the Soviet Union, if we had won that series, we would still be around. We would have been accepted as a big-time league. Then things got really bad when we lost the Vancouver Blazers, Toronto Toros, and Phoenix."

The Oilers suffered considerable

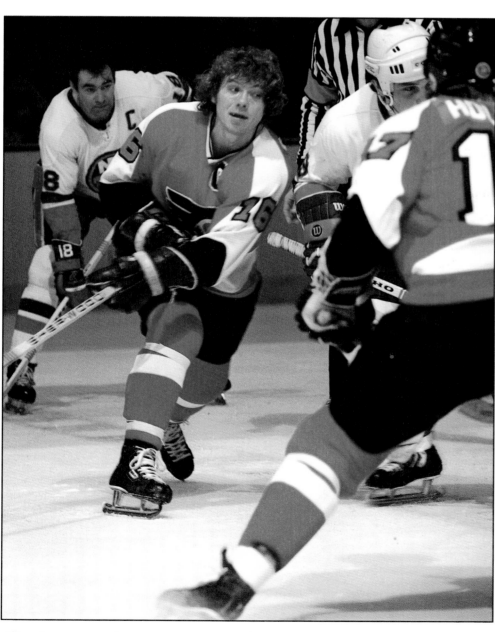

The 1976-77 Flyers went 48-16-16 and scored a whopping 323 goals. Captain Bobby Clarke (16) again led the attack, tallying 63 assists and 90 points.

LARRY ROBINSON

Defenseman Larry Robinson was an integral part of the Canadiens' glorious run of four consecutive Stanley Cups (1976-79). And despite his advanced age, he played a major role in the Habs' surprise Cup win in 1986. "That last one," Robinson recalled, "was the most satisfying to me and the most fun."

Until the 1974-75 season, the only fame Robinson attained was from an incident on February 17, 1974. That day, Larry clipped the wings—and the ego—of Flyers brawler Dave Schultz before a delighted Montreal crowd.

Most Canadiens fans who witnessed the one-sided fight were convinced that head-knocking was Robinson's destiny. What they didn't realize was that this big fellow was a rugged, talented defenseman who would soon become the cornerstone of Montreal's impenetrable defense.

Robinson established his ability as a strong, rushing puck-carrier. He also could lug the rubber and engineer the offense in clutch situations.

Robinson, who played three years in L.A. before retiring in 1992, and who holds the NHL record for playoff games (227), became head coach of the Kings in 1995.

turbulence at the top. Bill Hunter, once the darling of Edmonton, was eventually pushed out of his job, as the Oilers continued to flounder. In 1976-77, real estate entrepreneur Nelson Skalbania began running the show. Skalbania, in turn, added millionaire Peter Pocklington to the masthead as an equal partner.

"Nobody knew it at the time," said Jim Browitt, former administrator of the WHA, "but Pocklington's arrival would herald a complete turnabout in Edmonton's hockey fortunes. Peter was followed by two of the biggest and most important names in the business—Glen Sather and Wayne Gretzky."

While the WHA barely kept itself

afloat, the NHL finally abandoned Oakland and moved the California Golden Seals to Richfield, Ohio, a distant suburb of Cleveland. In 1976-77, the Seals became the Cleveland Barons—though they still suffered on the ice and at the gate. The equally troubled Kansas City Scouts left Missouri and pitched their tent in

Chicago's Stan Mikita resisted temptations to play in the WHA. His loyalty paid off on February 27, 1977, when he scored his 500th NHL goal.

The new Colorado Rockies went 20-46-14 in 1976-77, though veteran Doug Favell (1) often shined between the pipes.

Denver, where their name was changed to the Colorado Rockies. Finally, attendance in Atlanta was starting to dwindle. Hockey, apparently, couldn't grow in the deep South.

As the 1976-77 NHL season unfolded, the imbalance in quality became acutely apparent. Not a team in the Smythe Division finished above

the .500 mark. In the Norris Division, Detroit finished at 16-55-9, while Montreal went a phenomenal 60-8-12. The Canadiens set an NHL record for both wins and points. In the other two divisions, Boston, Buffalo, Philadelphia, and the Islanders all reached 100 points.

For a change, the Canadiens were

not overlooked when it came to awards. The glamorous Lafleur won the Hart Trophy while Robinson took the Norris. Teammates Dryden and Michel "Bunny" Larocque earned the Vezina. Atlanta's Willi Plett was named rookie of the year.

Among the milestones was Stan Mikita's 500th goal on February 27,

 A growing rivalry between the Flyers and Islanders often led to fistfights. This fracas involved Islanders Gerry Hart (2) and Denis Potvin (5).

BRAD PARK

Though often overshadowed by fellow defenseman Bobby Orr, Brad Park was one of the game's greatest backliners. The consummate contemporary defenseman, Park was the master of the hip check as well as an exceptionally accurate shooter. Park could develop an attack and then retreat in time to intercept an enemy counter-thrust.

His game was embellished by a fluid skating style that often underplayed his speed. He also had a storehouse of power that proved deceptive because of his modest size.

Park captained the modestly successful New York Rangers of the late 1960s and early 1970s, but he never tasted the Stanley Cup champagne. After his trade to the Boston Bruins, he did his best to keep a declining team competitive. Brad was voted to the First All-Star Team in 1970, 1972, 1974, 1976, and 1978.

Park's own spirits were occasionally deflated by Orr's presence. Playing second fiddle to a superstar like Orr wasn't the easiest thing in the world, but Park made the adjustment.

"If I have to be No. 2," Brad explained, "I might as well be No. 2 to a super player like Orr."

Brad finally obtained the recognition he deserved in June 1988, when he was elected to the Hockey Hall of Fame.

Team Canada's Guy Lafleur is thwarted by a pair of Czechs in a Canada Cup game. The Czechs have traditionally excelled in international play.

1977. Jean Ratelle and Rod Gilbert each passed the 1,000-point level, and Toronto's Ian Turnbull set a record for defensemen by scoring five goals in a 9-1 victory over Detroit on February 2, 1977.

While the Canadiens prepared for their Cup defense, the Flyers loomed as the most distinct playoff threat. In the first playoff round, Philly conquered Toronto in six games and was hungry to regain the mug. The Canadiens, meanwhile, looked even better than they had a year earlier. They overwhelmed St. Louis in four straight (outscoring the Blues 19-4) to reach the semifinals.

Philadelphia lost its semifinal match with Boston. The Bruins opened the series with two overtime wins in The Spectrum (4-3 and 5-4), and then swept the series with two wins at home. Meanwhile, Montreal won its semifinal match by dusting off the Islanders in six games.

For the second year in a row, a "good vs. evil" scenario unfolded. Like the Broad Street Bullies, Don Cherry's Big, Bad Bruins played a truculent brand of hockey. But Boston, like Philadelphia, could not intimidate the great Canadiens.

The tone of the finals was set in the opening game, as the Habs jumped into a 3-1 lead in the first period and won 7-3. In the second game, Dryden shut out Boston while Peter Mahovlich, Risebrough, and Shutt scored for the Canadiens.

Even friendly Boston Garden couldn't help the Bruins. Montreal scored three first-period goals and won 4-2. Boston scored first in Game Four, but Jacques Lemaire tied the count in the second period; the game eventually went into overtime. Lemaire scored the winner at 4:32 of sudden-death, giving Montreal its second straight Stanley Cup and its 20th overall.

GIL PERREAULT

Gil Perreault was the first pick in Buffalo Sabres history in 1970. He didn't disappoint, as he captured the Calder Trophy in the 1970-71 season and immediately took over as leader of Buffalo's hockey club.

Perreault's finest season was in 1975-76, when the classy forward totaled 44 goals and 113 points in leading the Sabres to the Stanley Cup finals, where they lost to the Flyers in six games. Gil centered on the famed "French Connection Line" with wingers Rick Martin and Rene Robert.

In a sense, Perreault most resembled Beliveau when Jean was having his finest years with the Montreal Canadiens. "Like Beliveau," said Emile Francis, at the time general manager of the Rangers, "Gil has all the moves and great range. There's no way to stop him if he's coming at you one-on-one."

Perreault retired in 1987 and is currently eighth on the all-time point-scoring list. In 1990, Gil was inducted into the Hockey Hall of Fame.

Montreal defenseman Larry Robinson took the Norris Trophy in 1976-77 and also helped the Canadiens to the Stanley Cup. Montreal routed the Bruins in the finals, winning in four. Montreal's Jacques Lemaire scored in overtime of the finale to clinch the Cup.

NHL Lords Fidget
as WHA Team Signs Gretzky

1 9 7 7 - 7 8

In pursuit of their third straight Stanley Cup, the Canadiens attempted to plug their few weak spots with players who had developed in the farm system. Young defensemen like Brian Engblom and Bill Nyrop saw more action. However, the nucleus of stars remained the same, with Guy Lafleur heading the galaxy. His linemates, Steve Shutt and Jacques Lemaire, were at the very top of their game, helping Lafleur to 60 goals and 132 points—both league-leading marks.

As the NHL-WHA war continued, more and more NHL lords wanted to accommodate or merge with the WHA. One of the most significant steps in that direction was taken when Clarence Campbell—a hard-line WHA foe—resigned. He was replaced by John A. Ziegler Jr., a Detroit lawyer who had been chairman of the NHL's Board of Governors. Ziegler was ready to bargain with the WHA.

In the meantime, the WHA stayed in business—but just barely. In Indianapolis, for example, the Racers were projecting losses of $1.3 million for the new season. On the other hand, Indianapolis was doing what NHL teams could not do. It signed a kid who was being touted as the greatest prospect in history. His name? Wayne Gretzky.

By sheer coincidence, Gretzky joined the WHA precisely when the NHL was conducting its annual meeting in Montreal. When the news of Wayne's signing reached Montreal, it drew a mixed reaction from the old guard. Some tried to ignore the event as if it had transpired in some mythical land beyond the sea. Others pooh-poohed its significance. Some said they couldn't blame the lad one bit.

In 1977-78, the WHA scooped the NHL by signing the greatest prospect in history—17-year-old Wayne Gretzky.

1977-78

Best Record
Montreal
(59-10-11)

Stanley Cup Finals
Montreal 4
Boston 2

Art Ross Trophy
Guy Lafleur
(60/72/132)

Hart Trophy
Guy Lafleur

Vezina Trophy
Ken Dryden
Michel Larocque

Calder Trophy
Mike Bossy

Norris Trophy
Denis Potvin

Lady Byng Trophy
Butch Goring

"You can't blame the kid for getting a big offer and taking it," said Bruins general manager Harry Sinden. "But you have to wonder what effect it will have on his overall hockey career. Gretzky is 17 with one year of major-junior experience. He has great talent, but he's not that big. He's going to take a pounding in pro hockey."

Gretzky's stint in Indianapolis was brief. Racers owner Nelson Skalbania was running out of money and sold the youngster to Peter Pocklington, owner of the WHA's Edmonton Oilers.

Although they pretended otherwise, many NHL moguls kept looking over their shoulders at the WHA and in particular at Gretzky. The WHA, still struggling for survival—and hoping fervently for a rapprochement with the NHL—exploited Gretzky for all he was worth. For example, *The Hockey News* ran a WHA ad that included a large photo of Gretzky accompanied by the caption: "Many of the brightest young stars in hockey are thrilling fans in WHA arenas."

The kid was catching on and drawing large crowds. The WHA paraded him around as if he were the

league's mascot. At one point, the WHA shipped Gretzky and his boyhood idol, Gordie Howe, to Manhattan for a midtown press conference—just to show off their jewel.

The WHA had other jewels in its firmament. Bobby Hull still was a major attraction with Winnipeg, while the Howe family—Gordie and sons Mark and Marty—moved to the New England Whalers. The Howes' presence helped establish Hartford as a viable franchise. Behind the scenes, negotiations between the NHL and

New York's Bryan Trottier flattens Toronto's Borje Salming (21) and goalie Mike Palmateer during the 1978 playoffs.

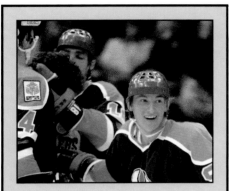

EDMONTON OILERS

Hockey fans on the Canadian prairie got their first taste of major-league hockey in 1971. That year, the Edmonton (then Alberta) Oilers became an original member of the World Hockey Association. Bill Hunter, a prominent Edmonton entrepreneur, was instrumental in starting the franchise, and he took the post of vice-president and general manager.

Hunter has been responsible for many changes in Edmonton. Among them was opening the $13 million, 16,000-seat Northlands Coliseum, replacing the team's old rink which had a seating capacity of only 5,200.

Midway through the 1976-77 WHA season, Glen Sather took over the coaching duties and led the Oilers to the first of their 14 straight WHA and NHL playoff appearances. Three years later, when the club entered the NHL, Sather took on the added responsibilities of president and general manager.

Led by the great Wayne Gretzky, the Oilers won four Stanley Cups in the 1980s. Despite trading Gretzky, Edmonton won the Cup in 1989-90.

WHA intensified as the 1977-78 campaign unfolded.

Throughout the season, Montreal remained the dominant team with Boston and the Islanders right behind. While the Canadiens' artistry dazzled the fans, Don Cherry's Bruins captivated Boston with their blue-collar style of play. The very vocal Cherry lacked a headliner like Lafleur, but made due with the likes of two-fisted Terry O'Reilly and feisty Bobby Schmautz.

Quite often, Cherry himself got more headlines than his players, as he promoted fighting, challenged his more

conservative coaching opponents, and otherwise socked the staid hockey establishment. But his players loved him. As high-scoring Peter McNab put it, "Grapes was the definitive player's coach."

The Islanders were another attention-getting club, thanks to the emergence of a powerful line that featured Bryan Trottier at center, towering Clark Gillies on left wing, and rookie sharpshooter Mike Bossy on the right. Bossy would score 53 goals and add 38 assists for 91 points. The Isles displayed a splendid goaltending

tandem featuring talkative Glenn "Chico" Resch and bombastic Billy Smith. The latter became notorious for battling with enemy forwards.

On defense, the Islanders had a new version of Bobby Orr in the versatile Denis Potvin. Potvin was better in his defensive end than Orr ever was, hit harder than Orr, and did many of the same things up front. The Isles wasted no time challenging Philadelphia for first place, and this time they actually surpassed the powerful Flyers. New York finished at 48-17-15.

The NHL lords had hoped the

Rangers would emerge in the Patrick Division. They figured that a strong team on Broadway would bolster the league's selling power. Unfortunately, the Rangers finished in the basement for the third year in a row.

But even the Rangers weren't as bad as the Washington Capitals (17-49-14), who brought up the bottom of the Norris Division; nor were they as lowly as the Cleveland Barons (22-45-13), who were dead last in the Adams. The newly transplanted teams were in bad shape. The Barons drew precious few fans to the Richfield Coliseum, and

Denver was less than enthused about its Rockies.

Though the Canadiens were the class of Canada, another team was making noise in Toronto. Coach Roger Neilson conducted the overture and high-scoring Darryl Sittler (45 goals) and Lanny McDonald (47) banged the drums. More than that, Neilson iced a mean machine led by Dave "Tiger" Williams and heavy-hitting Jerry Butler.

After the final regular-season game was played, the division leaders were Montreal, Boston, the Islanders, and Chicago. Lafleur captured his second

straight Hart Trophy. Bossy took the Calder while Ken Dryden and Bunny Larocque earned the Vezina. Potvin won the Norris and Montreal's Bob Gainey was the first to win the Frank Selke Trophy, awarded to the best defensive forward.

Montreal's Cup defense was predicated on Dryden's superlative goaltending, a well-balanced defense, and, most of all, Lafleur's timely goals. Montreal reached the semifinals by overpowering a mediocre Detroit team. The Big, Bad Bruins swept Chicago in four straight, and Philadelphia

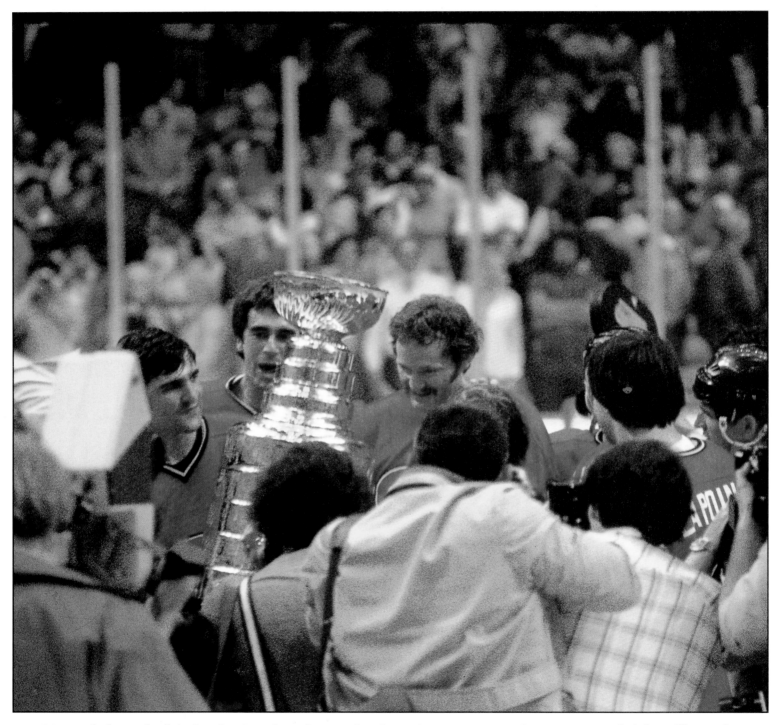

Montreal players bask in Stanley Cup glory after ousting the Bruins at Boston Garden. Serge Savard (left), Gilles Lupien (second from left), and Larry Robinson (right of Cup) admire the mug.

disposed of the Sabres four games to one.

A major upset developed in the Toronto-Islanders matchup, one of the most viciously played of all time. The Leafs' top defenseman, Borje Salming, left the series after being accidentally clobbered by New York's Lorne Henning. Moreover, the Islanders lost Bossy after he was rammed into the boards by Butler. After trailing in the series three games to two, the Leafs bludgeoned their way to a 5-2 win at home and then won the series at Nassau Coliseum, netting the decisive goal in overtime.

But the upstart Leafs were no match for the champs. The Canadiens grounded them out of the semifinals in four games. In the other semifinal series, Boston dispatched the Flyers in five games.

In the finals, the Bruins provided Montreal with some real competition. After the Habs took 4-1 and 3-2 decisions at home, Boston counter-attacked with 4-0 and 4-3 wins at their arena. But in the fifth game, the contenders from Boston looked more like pretenders; the Canadiens scored four straight goals and coasted to a 5-1 win. After the Bruins netted a first-period goal in Game Six, Montreal put together four unanswered scores for the Cup.

The Canadiens had now won three straight Stanley Cups, making them only the fourth team ever to turn the trick. Montreal had clearly developed a dynasty.

"In order to have a dynasty," said Boston's Sinden, "you have to have strong goaltending. Montreal has that and a lot more. They're going to be tough to stop."

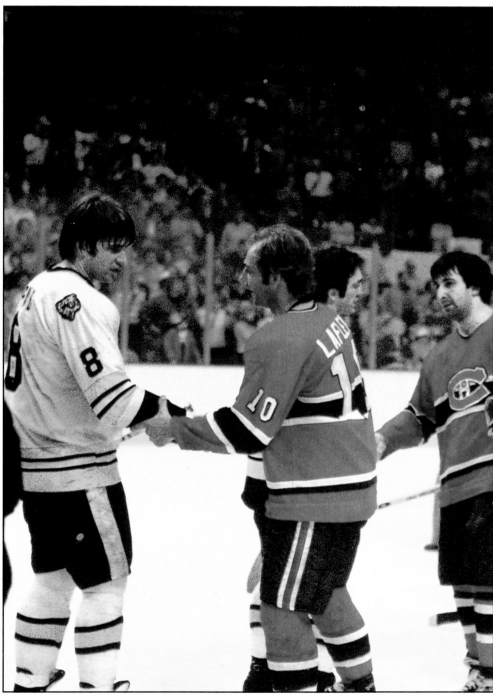

For the second straight year, Montreal defeated Boston in the finals, this time in six games. Peter McNab (8) congratulates Guy Lafleur (10) in the traditional post-game, hand-shaking parade.

SCOTTY BOWMAN

A severe head injury, suffered in 1951-52 while playing junior hockey, completely altered Scotty Bowman's career. He joined the Montreal Canadiens organization, where he spent 16 years scouting, troubleshooting throughout the farm system, and coaching at the junior and minor-league professional level.

In 1967, Bowman was hired as the first coach of the expansion St. Louis Blues and led them to the Stanley Cup finals in each of his first three seasons. Poor relations with the Blues' owners forced Bowman to leave Mound City for Montreal, where he coached from 1971 to 1979. Bowman led the Canadiens to five Stanley Cup titles, including four straight (1976-79).

In 1979, Scotty was named coach of the NHL All-Stars in the Challenge Cup series against the Soviets, but he was terribly disappointed as his team went down in defeat.

In '79, Bowman took over as director of hockey operations, general manager, and coach of the Buffalo Sabres. On December 19, 1984, in Chicago, the Sabres defeated the Blackhawks 6-3, giving Scotty his 691st coaching win and making him the winningest coach in NHL history.

In 1991-92, Scotty became coach of Pittsburgh and led the Penguins to the Stanley Cup. Still not through, Bowman took control of the Red Wings and turned them into a powerhouse.

NHL and WHA Unite; Montreal Wins Fourth Straight

1 9 7 8 - 7 9

An era ended early in the 1978-79 campaign, as Bobby Orr hung up his skates after playing only six painful games for the Chicago Blackhawks. No less painful to the league were the Cleveland Barons. The Barons were in such bad financial shape that they merged with the lowly Minnesota North Stars. The new team remained in Minnesota. Despite the addition of Cleveland's players, the North Stars finished the season at 28-40-12.

Over in New York, the Rangers were starting to fly—thanks to Madison Square Garden's big bankroll. With their plentiful bucks, the Blueshirts pried Swedish stars Anders Hedberg and Ulf Nilsson away from the Winnipeg Jets. In addition, Garden boss Sonny Werblin imported Fred Shero from Philadelphia to become general manager and coach. The additions were enough to lift the Rangers to a 40-29-11 record.

Meanwhile, the NHL and WHA were discussing a merger. It was becoming apparent that the senior league would absorb four of the six WHA franchises—Edmonton, Quebec, Winnipeg, and Hartford. (Cincinnati

▲

Guy Lafleur (left) and Bob Gainey (right) led Montreal to one more Cup in 1978-79.

▶

Pictured are Wayne Gretzky's bronzed feet, as well as his first pair of hockey skates.

and Birmingham were cut adrift.) Winnipeg Jets owner Ben Hatskin predicted a merger all along.

"I always thought we'd merge," Hatskin said. "Let's face it. The people in Edmonton, all over the West, are NHL people at heart. When you've been watching *Hockey Night in Canada* for 25 years and all you've heard is NHL, you don't want to be part of something secondary.

"This merger, first and foremost, isn't a victory for the WHA. It's a victory for Canadian hockey.... There would not be NHL hockey in Quebec City, Edmonton, and Winnipeg next season if it wasn't for the WHA."

Although he was a Peter-come-lately, Edmonton Oilers owner Peter Pocklington was also a major factor in the merger. He knew he could produce a lucrative NHL team and he was able to prove it. Before the 1978-79 season ended, the Oilers sold 14,200 NHL season tickets in a four-day period.

"Let's face it," said Pocklington. "There's a lot of disposable income in this city and sports is one of the few items it can be spent on."

While power brokers from both leagues were ironing out merger details, the power structure of the four divisions remained about the same. Montreal, the Islanders, Boston, and Chicago repeated as division winners. The Islanders actually notched more points than Montreal (116-115). Boston finished at 43-23-14, while Chicago won the Smythe with an embarrassing 29-36-15 mark.

The Isles' success was rooted in their balance. Bryan Trottier led the league in points (134 on 47 goals) and captured the Hart Trophy. His sidekick, Mike Bossy, led the league in red lights with an eye-popping 69. Left wing Clark Gillies notched 91 points while defenseman Denis Potvin tallied 101.

The Islanders—the first expansion team ever to lead the league in points—took dead aim at the Stanley Cup. They got off to a heartening start in the opening round of the playoffs, as they broomed the Blackhawks in four games. The defending champion Canadiens also swept their opening foe, Toronto, though the Leafs pushed them into overtime in

GUY LAFLEUR

When he was in his prime, Guy Lafleur skated with a blend of power and grace that was unmatched among his peers. Despite a seemingly frail physique by hockey standards, Lafleur generated one of the most dynamically accurate shots in NHL history.

From 1975 to 1979, when the Canadiens thoroughly dominated the NHL while capturing four consecutive Stanley Cups, Lafleur was their ace in the hole. When the game hung in the balance, the Habs would call Lafleur's number and he would invariably deliver.

Lafleur first established himself as an offensive force in the 1974-75 season, when he potted 53 goals and added 36 assists. The following year marked the first of three consecutive scoring titles for Lafleur, the only Canadien in history to accomplish such a feat.

Guy Lafleur retired in 1984. With his angular features and blond mane flying behind him, Montreal's ace earned a spot in the Hockey Hall of Fame.

"Hockey," said Lafleur, "is like a drug for me. I am hooked. I can't do anything about it." He proved it by coming back in 1988 to play for the Rangers and contribute 18 goals. He moved on to Quebec for the 1989-90 and 1990-91 seasons.

Flyer Reggie Leach owned one of the most terrifying shots in the NHL. Leach, who scored 61 goals in 1975-76, tallied 34 in 1978-79.

the final two games.

Unobtrusively, the Rangers began a relentless march. They started with a swift preliminary-round triumph over Los Angeles and a quarterfinal-round victory over the Flyers. The semifinals featured two of the most intense rivalries in the game: Rangers vs. Islanders and Canadiens vs. Bruins.

In the New York-New York series, the Rangers won the curtain-raiser 4-1 at Nassau Coliseum. The Isles rebounded for an overtime win in the second game, although they were outplayed again. Coach Shero's strategy was to smother Potvin, the man who spearheaded the Isles defense and triggered the offensive attack.

When the series resumed at Madison Square Garden, the Rangers won the game 3-1 and established themselves as the superior club. The Isles squeaked out a 3-2 overtime win in Game Four, but no matter. The Rangers rallied for a 4-3 triumph on Long Island and clinched the series with a 2-1 win at home.

The Bruins were also smelling an upset, as they played Montreal even for the first six games of their series. The action heated up in Game Seven at the Forum, as Boston clung to a 4-3 lead with time running out. But incredibly, Boston coach Don Cherry and his players suffered a communication lapse at a critical time—somehow, the Bruins were left with an extra man on the ice. After a painfully long grace period, the referee

1978-79

Best Record
New York I.
(51-15-14)

Stanley Cup Finals
Montreal 4
New York R. 1

Art Ross Trophy
Bryan Trottier
(47/87/134)

Hart Trophy
Bryan Trottier

Vezina Trophy
Ken Dryden
Michel Larocque

Calder Trophy
Bobby Smith

Norris Trophy
Denis Potvin

Lady Byng Trophy
Bob MacMillan

Prior to Wayne Gretzky, Marcel Dionne was the most productive scorer in Los Angeles Kings history. Nicknamed "Little Beaver," Dionne notched 59 goals and 71 assists in 1978-79.

After brilliant success with Philadelphia, Fred Shero moved his coaching act to New York in 1978-79. In his first season, Shero resurrected a weak Rangers team and led it to the Stanley Cup finals.

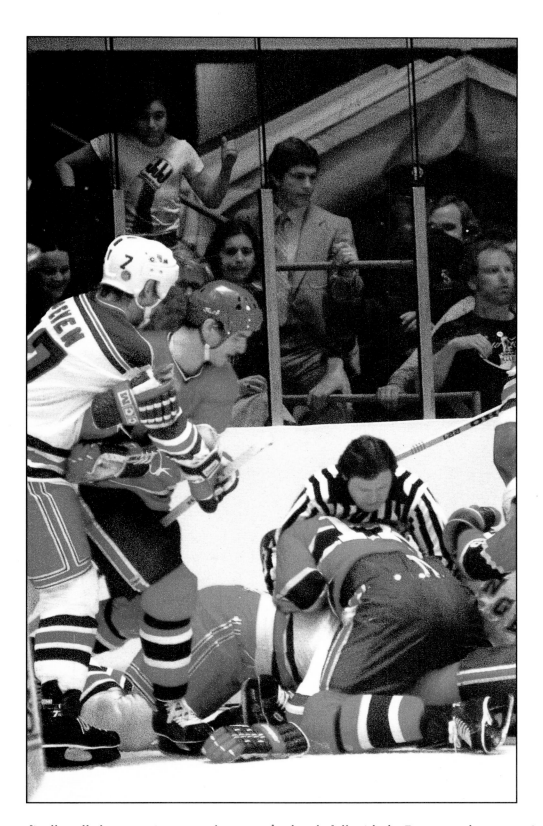

Montreal clearly outmatched New York in the 1979 finals. Here, a Canadien rubs a Ranger's face into the ice.

Gordie Howe

THE HOWE FAMILY

Between the years of 1946 and 1971, Gordie Howe won the Hart Trophy six times. His artistry, versatility, and durability earned him legendary status.

"He was not only the greatest hockey player I've ever seen," said former teammate and Hall of Famer Bill Gadsby, "but also the greatest athlete."

Gordie remained a major factor in the NHL until his retirement. Then, to everyone's amazement, he surfaced again, this time in 1973 in the World Hockey Association. Gordie returned to the ice at age 45, and his sons, Marty and Mark, signed to skate alongside Pop with the Houston Aeros.

When Houston bowed out of the WHA, Gordie and family moved north to the New England Whalers for the 1977-78 campaign. The Whalers were admitted to the NHL in 1979. The Howes made NHL history on March 12, 1980, against the Red Wings; Marty was inserted into the starting lineup as the right wing on a line with his father at center and brother Mark at left wing.

Mark Howe went on to have a stellar career with the Flyers, making the First All-Star Team three times.

finally called a two-minute penalty against Boston.

Boston desperately tried to kill the penalty, but Montreal wouldn't die. A Guy Lafleur shot beat goaltender Gilles Gilbert, sending the game into overtime.

The Bruins had chances to dispose of the Habs, but Ken Dryden was impenetrable. Eventually, Montreal got the break it needed and Yvan Lambert beat Gilbert at 9:30 of the sudden-death.

In the finals, the Canadiens had their hands full with the Rangers, who whipped them 4-1 in Game One at the Forum. Shockingly, the Rangers took a 2-0 lead in the first period of the second game. But the Canadiens had too much power. Their counter-attacks produced a 6-2 win in Game Two. From that point on, the champs were undaunted. They won the next three games—4-1, 4-3, and 4-1—for their fourth straight Stanley Cup.

Canadiens fans were soon dreaming of a fifth straight Cup, but two postseason events dimmed their hopes. For starters, Scotty Bowman had gotten restless behind the bench and wanted to move up to the general manager's office. But when this was denied him, he abandoned Montreal and became GM of the Buffalo Sabres. Another blow to the Canadiens was Dryden's decision to retire and pursue other interests.

The Montreal dynasty had been rocked to its very foundation as it prepared for its drive for five.

THE GRETZKY YEARS

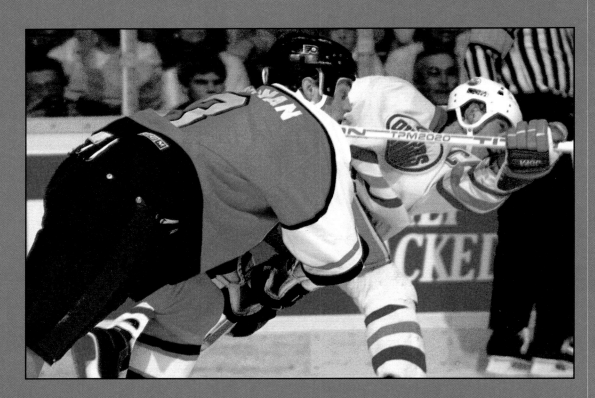

During the 1980s,
the Great One captures nine
Hart Trophies and four
Stanley Cups.

During the 1980s, Wayne Gretzky notched 86 goals and 188 assists in the playoffs. At left, he releases a devastating slapshot during the 1987 finals against Philadelphia. Above, he hoists the Stanley Cup after winning the title in 1985.

THE 1980s

With the WHA finally out of the way, the NHL began the 1980s with a clean slate. The league hoped to recoup its financial losses and regain some of its stability and prestige.

This was not simple, largely because of floundering hockey clubs in Atlanta and Denver. Though the league hated relocating franchises, it had no choice with these two teams. For the 1980-81 season, the Flames moved to Calgary, Alberta, to play in the new 20,000-seat Saddledome. In 1982-83, the Rockies relocated to the Brendan Byrne Arena in East Rutherford, New Jersey; they were renamed the Devils.

In 1979-80, four former WHA teams entered the NHL. The Quebec Nordiques made the quickest impact thanks to a cloak-and-dagger move, in which they snatched Czechoslovakian brothers Peter and Anton Stastny from behind the Iron Curtain.

The Edmonton Oilers also started impressively. They were blessed with youngsters such as Mark Messier, Kevin Lowe, Paul Coffey, and, of course, Wayne Gretzky. The Winnipeg Jets and Hartford Whalers didn't do as well, although Hartford briefly showcased Bobby Hull and Gordie Howe.

The 1980s saw a dramatic shift in the league's power structure. During the decade, nine of the ten Stanley Cups were won by expansion teams. The Islanders opened the '80s with four consecutive championships (1980-1983). They proved to be one of the greatest teams of all time, as they won 19 consecutive playoff series.

The league's power pendulum then swung over to Edmonton, as the Oilers won four Cups (1984, 1985, 1987, 1988). The Canadiens broke Edmonton's streak in 1986, and the expansion Calgary Flames finished the decade with a Cup win in 1989.

During the 1980s, the style and structure of NHL hockey changed considerably. The battling, bruising style of the Flyers had become passe. In the early 1980s, the model team became the Islanders, who could fight or play with finesse. The role model then became the Oilers, who dazzled opponents with their speed and offensive firepower.

In February 1980, the world witnessed the incredible gold-medal performance of the U.S. Olympic team in Lake Placid, New York. The U.S. players soon decorated several NHL teams, and by mid-decade many U.S.-born players were jumping from college campuses to the NHL.

At the start of the 1980s, Howe finally hung up his legendary skates; and by the start of the '90s, Gretzky had broken nearly all of Howe's scoring records. Edmonton traded Gretzky in 1988 in one of the biggest swaps in sports history, but it didn't hamper Wayne's effectiveness. Between 1980 and 1989, the Great One had accumulated nine Hart Trophies.

Islanders Skate to First-Ever Stanley Cup

1 9 7 9 - 8 0

Though the four WHA teams were glad to enter the NHL, they had to weather an expansion draft that basically decimated their clubs. First, the players from the defunct Birmingham Bulls and Cincinnati Stingers were dispersed throughout the NHL, with 28 players going to the four former WHA teams. Then, the NHL got to claim 43 former WHA players whom they had previously drafted but who had chosen to play WHA hockey instead.

In the final stage of the draft, the Nordiques, Jets, Oilers, and Whalers were only allowed to protect two goaltenders and two skaters. Meanwhile, the 17 NHL clubs could protect two goalies and 15 skaters. Under the circumstances, it's amazing the new teams remained competitive.

With the addition of the four new teams, the league had to reorganize its divisions. The Whalers moved into the Norris Division and the Caps moved out, switching to the Patrick. The Nordiques became the fifth team in the Adams Division and the Oilers and Jets were placed in the Smythe, which now had six teams.

Before the 1979-80 season began, Los Angeles sports king Jack Kent Cooke sold his empire. Cooke peddled the Forum, the L.A. Kings, and the National Basketball Association's L.A. Lakers to Jerry Buss for almost $68 million.

The off-season also saw several major changes behind the benches. Scotty Bowman left the Canadiens to manage the Buffalo Sabres; Bowman was replaced in Montreal by Bernie Geoffrion. Punch Imlach, who had been fired as GM by Buffalo, was hired for the same capacity by the Toronto Maple Leafs. Imlach named Floyd Smith as coach, replacing Roger Neilson, who then went over to Buffalo to assist Bowman!

The abysmal Colorado Rockies attempted to reverse their fortunes by hiring flamboyant coach Don Cherry. Former goalie Eddie Johnston became the Blackhawks' new coach, and Al MacNeil replaced Fred Creighton in

The Islanders won the 1980 Stanley Cup finals, but they had to fight off the Flyers to do it.

Atlanta. Creighton then became coach of the Bruins, whom Cherry had just left.

Signaling the end of an era for the Montreal Canadiens, goaltending phenom Ken Dryden hung up his mask after eight NHL seasons, five Cups, and five Vezina Trophies. Then, shortly before the season began, Habs captain Yvan Cournoyer also announced his retirement. After two operations on his ailing back, the Roadrunner knew it was time to step down.

Former Blackhawk and WHA star Bobby Hull decided to un-retire after being claimed by the Winnipeg Jets. "His return is a great bonus for the people of Canada," said Jets GM John Ferguson, "and fans in the NHL cities will be able to see Bobby play again."

The helmet became an essential part of the hockey wardrobe, as the NHL made helmets mandatory for the 1979-80 season. Only players who had signed pro contracts prior to June 1, 1979, and had signed special waivers would be exempted from the rule.

In 1979-80, hockey was fraught with contract disputes. St. Louis' Garry Unger threatened to begin an antitrust suit against the NHL unless he was traded to another team. Atlanta bought his rights, sending Red Laurence and defenseman Ed Kea to St. Louis. Unger, reportedly asking less than $200,000 a year from the Blues, signed with Atlanta for $1 million over five years. Meanwhile, Atlanta was reputed to be losing close to $2 million a year!

On the other hand, with a minimum of fuss and fighting, the Islanders signed young star Bryan Trottier to a six-year contract. Including bonuses, the pact was reportedly worth $2 million.

Once the season got underway, records began toppling almost nightly. Phil Esposito became only the second player in NHL history to score 1,500 points, joining Gordie Howe. Howe finished the season, and his career, with 801 goals, the last of which he scored in his final game. The Kings' Charlie Simmer scored goals in 13 straight games, and Unger ended his

On February 22, 1980, the U.S. Olympic team upset the Soviet Union to advance to the gold-medal round. Two days later, the U.S. beat Finland to pull off the famed "Miracle on Ice." Two major defensive contributors for the U.S. were Ken Morrow (3) and Mike Ramsey (5).

Several members of the 1980 U.S. Olympic team graduated to the NHL. Among them were Gary Suter (foreground) and Ken Morrow (background), who played for the Flames and Islanders, respectively.

1979-80

Best Record
Philadelphia
(48-12-20)

Stanley Cup Finals
New York I. 4
Philadelphia 2

Art Ross Trophy
Marcel Dionne
(53/84/137)

Hart Trophy
Wayne Gretzky
(51/86/137)

Vezina Trophy
Bob Sauve
Don Edwards

Calder Trophy
Ray Bourque

Norris Trophy
Larry Robinson

Lady Byng Trophy
Wayne Gretzky

Bernie Geoffrion coached Montreal for a mere 30 games in 1979-80.

▲ The Islanders won the 1980 Cup on a Game Six overtime goal by Bob Nystrom, who's being hugged along the boards. Lorne Henning and Bob Lorimer join in.

BRYAN TROTTIER

Bryan Trottier's career embraced many phases. In the first, he became a productive forward even though he entered the league with few advance notices. In the second phase, he emerged as one of the NHL's foremost centers and key to the Islanders' 1980-83 dynastic run.

The leading scorer in the 1980 playoffs (29 points, 12 goals), Trottier paced the Islanders to Stanley Cup triumphs in 1980, 1981, 1982, and 1983. He won the Calder Trophy as the NHL's rookie of the year in 1976; made the First All-Star Team at center twice; won the Hart Trophy in 1979, the same year he led the NHL in scoring (134 points on 47 goals); and was voted the Conn Smythe Trophy in 1980.

Trottier played with seemingly no emotion, yet he was merely masking his feelings. He actually played with an intensity rare among his colleagues or foes, and was invariably one of the first players to the puck. Hall of Fame referee Bill Chadwick called him the best hockey player he ever saw.

In the summer of 1990, the Islanders informed Bryan that his services were no longer needed. Trottier chose not to retire. He instead signed with Pittsburgh, where he earned two more Stanley Cup rings.

NHL iron-man streak at 914 games (he hadn't taken a breather since 1968).

The Philadelphia Flyers finished with the best record in the NHL (48-12-20). In doing so, they racked up the longest streak without a loss in NHL history. Over a 35-game period, the Flyers went 25-0-10. On November 28, Isles goalie Billy Smith also entered the record books. Against the Rockies, Smith flipped a pass down the ice; the puck didn't touch anybody and, believe it or not, it actually slipped into the Colorado net. Smith, a goalie, was credited with a goal.

By season's end, Wayne Gretzky became the youngest NHLer ever to score more than 100 points. However,

Gretzky was deprived of the Calder Trophy, as the league decided he was not a first-year player because he had played in the WHA. Gretzky ended the season with 137 points, tied with L.A.'s Marcel Dionne for the lead. Gretzky also lost out on the Art Ross Trophy since Dionne scored two more goals than he did (53-51).

Wayne did manage to cop two trophies, as he won the first of nine Harts he would acquire in the decade. He also took the Lady Byng. The rookie of the year was Boston defenseman Ray Bourque, who set a Bruins rookie record with 65 points. Montreal's classy Larry Robinson gained his second Norris Trophy.

Buffalo's goaltending duo of Bob Sauve and Don Edwards earned the Vezina.

Montreal's Guy Lafleur enjoyed his last great season, as he scored 50 goals and finished third in the NHL with 125 points.

When the regular season had finished and the playoffs began, four teams were given a chance to win the Cup: the Canadiens, who were looking to duplicate their five-in-a-row record of the 1950s; the Flyers, who were the regular-season champs; the still-powerful Bruins; and the dark-horse Sabres.

After blowing their chances in the semifinals against the Rangers in 1979 and struggling all season this year, few

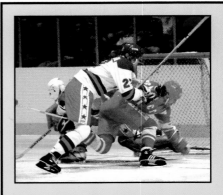

Former Montreal coach Scotty Bowman jumped to Buffalo in 1979. In 1979-80, Bowman led the Sabres to the best record in the Wales Conference—47-17-16.

Long in need of a strong second-line center, the Islanders finally found their man in March 1980. Butch Goring helped the Isles to the Stanley Cup.

1980 U.S. OLYMPIC TEAM

All the world loves an underdog, and that explains why the 1980 U.S. Olympic team thrilled the masses with its gold medal victory at Lake Placid, New York.

Coach Herb Brooks's team was seeded seventh among the 12 teams in the tournament, but no matter. In the opening game against Sweden, the U.S. got a goal from Billy Baker with 0:27 remaining to tie it 2-2. In its next battle, the U.S. surprisingly dominated Czechoslovakia, en route to a 7-3 victory. The Americans followed with wins against Norway, Rumania, and West Germany to advance to the medal round.

The run for the gold began on Friday, February 22, as the United States faced the Soviet Union. The Americans played them even until the third period, when U.S. captain Mike Eruzione netted the goal "heard 'round the world." The shot gave the U.S. an incredible 4-3 victory over the Soviets.

Two days later, all they had to do was beat Finland to capture the gold medal. A shorthanded goal by Mark Johnson late in the third period gave the Americans a 4-2 lead. As the final seconds ticked off the clock, ABC commentator Al Michaels screamed: "Do you believe in miracles? Yes!"

expected the New York Islanders would get past the semis. But Isles GM Bill Torrey still thought the club could win it all. On March 10, the day of the trade deadline, he made a blockbuster move that would spark his team to the Cup. Torrey traded defenseman Dave Lewis and former first-round draft choice Billy Harris to Los Angeles for spunky forward Robert "Butch" Goring. Goring, along with newly arrived Olympian Kenny Morrow on defense, gave New York that little extra it needed.

In order to generate as much playoff revenue as possible, the NHL allowed 16 of its 21 teams to make the playoffs. The new system pitted the team with the

best season record against the club with the 16th best record. The second best team played the 15th best, third best played 14th best, and so on.

The league's top team, Philadelphia, opened up against the Oilers, who squeaked into the playoffs with 69 points. The Flyers swept Edmonton in three straight. Meanwhile, second-place Buffalo did away with Vancouver in four; third-place Montreal swept Hartford in three; and fourth-place Boston took five games to eliminate Pittsburgh.

Minnesota erased Toronto in four games; Chicago swept St. Louis; and the Rangers took out Atlanta in four. The fifth-place Isles took four games to

eliminate the Kings and, in the process, Trottier became the first NHL player in playoff history to score two shorthanded goals in the same period.

In the quarterfinals, the Sabres needed only four games to do away with Chicago, making Bowman the winningest coach in Stanley Cup playoff history. In other quarterfinals, the Flyers thumped the Rangers and the Islanders dumped Boston. The upset came when the North Stars eliminated Montreal. In Game Seven, Al MacAdam scored with only 86 seconds left in regulation to put Minnesota over the top.

In the semifinals, the North Stars again surprised the hockey world when they won Game One against Philadelphia at The Spectrum. That would be their last gasp, however, as the Flyers flew back to win four straight, earning them the right to face . . . the Islanders. For the first time in their brief existence, the New York Islanders entered the Stanley Cup finals, having defeated the Sabres in six semifinal games.

Game One of the finals opened at The Spectrum, as the Islanders edged Philadelphia with a Denis Potvin goal at 4:07 of overtime. Philly evened the series by pounding the Isles 8-3 in Game Two. New York returned the compliment in Game Three by whipping the Flyers 6-2—which

included five New York power-play goals. Game Four went to the New Yorkers 5-2, and the upstart Isles were looking for a Cup win in The Spectrum. But it was not to be, as the Flyers fought back to a 6-3 victory. The series returned to Nassau Coliseum for Game Six.

In the sixth game, Philadelphia's Reg Leach opened the scoring at 7:21 of the first. Moments later, Potvin tied the game with a shot that the Flyers protested, claiming Potvin's stick was above his shoulders. The goal remained, however, and the two teams ended the first period tied 2-2.

In period two, goals from Mike Bossy and Bobby Nystrom gave the

Islanders a two-goal margin. But in the third, goals from Flyers Bob Dailey and John Paddock again tied the game and the teams were now faced with overtime. At 7:11 of the first extra period, Nystrom received a beautiful relay from big John Tonelli, redirecting the puck past Philly goalie Pete Peeters. The tally gave the New York Islanders their first Stanley Cup.

As the Islanders quaffed champagne, it was announced that the Atlanta Flames—the team that had joined the NHL the same season as the Isles—had been purchased by Nelson Skalbania, a Vancouver businessman. Skalbania would move the team to Calgary, Alberta.

The Islanders won their first Stanley Cup on May 24, 1980, defeating the Flyers in six games. Winger Bryan Trottier consoles Bill Barber (7) while Bob Dailey waits in line.

Howe Hangs 'Em Up; Gretzky Breaks Scoring Record

1 9 8 0 - 8 1

In the summer of 1980, coaches again were playing musical chairs. Johnny Wilson was fired by the Penguins and replaced by Eddie Johnston, who had just been fired by Chicago. Don Cherry was ousted by the Rockies, which caused an uproar among Colorado's Cherry boosters. Don's reaction? "I spend six months trying to put a team together," he said, "but it's pretty tough to fly like an eagle when you're mixed up with turkeys."

Cherry was replaced by Billy MacMillan, while Gerry Cheevers took over the Bruins. Jacques Demers resigned as Nordiques coach, prompting Quebec GM Maurice Filion to moonlight behind the bench.

In June 1980, Gordie Howe, 52, ended a playing career that spanned five decades and eight U.S. presidents. Gordie became director of player development for the Hartford Whalers. Almost simultaneously, the most penalized player in NHL history, Dave Schultz, decided to hang up his gloves after only nine seasons. Schultz, with 2,294 penalty minutes, had helped the Flyers battle and brawl their way to two Stanley Cups, but bounced around

Six Sutter brothers have skated in the NHL, including Brent (21, Islanders), Brian (11, St. Louis), Rich (15, Vancouver), Darryl (27, Chicago), and Duane (12, Chicago). Ron's jersey is not shown.

the league after that.

"I tried to prove I could skate and score too," said Schultz, "but all they ever wanted me to do was fight."

In Quebec, the Nordiques stunned the hockey world when they brought defectors Peter and Anton Stastny to North America. The Stastnys, former stars on the Czech National Team, helped boost the Nords out of the Adams Division basement and into the playoffs. Peter, obviously the more talented brother, set a pair of records for rookies with 70 assists and 109 points; he also won the Calder Trophy.

Throughout the season, coaches continued to come and go. Oilers GM Glen Sather fired Bryan Watson, Tommy McVie became the fourth Winnipeg coach to be fired in one season, and Hartford's Don Blackburn was replaced by Larry Pleau. Fred Shero resigned as Rangers coach and was replaced by Craig Patrick, grandson of Ranger builder Lester Patrick.

A near-tragedy occurred in a game between Hartford and the Islanders. During the game, Whalers star Mark Howe was checked into the net. The net lifted up and Howe landed on one of the sharp spikes that held the net in place. The metal drove into Howe's buttock and within a half-inch of his spine. Howe's injury eventually led to the redesign of the hockey net. Despite the horrifying incident, Howe recovered rapidly and was playing again by February.

JARI KURRI

The discovery of Jari Kurri—a star for the Edmonton Oilers—was a combination of smarts and luck. Kurri was spotted in a training camp in Finland, where, it just so happened, the Oilers were scheduled to play some exhibition games. An Edmonton scout was impressed with Kurri and, upon his advisement, the Oilers selected him in the 1980 Entry Draft.

Kurri spent ten seasons in Edmonton and contributed mightily to their five Stanley Cup championships. Jari posted Hall of Fame numbers during his tenure with the Oilers. He totaled 474 goals and 1,043 points in only 754 games.

Kurri's most incredible season came in 1984-85, when he set an NHL record for a right wing with 71 goals, then netted a record-tying 19 goals in the playoffs for a full total of 90 red lights. He led the league with 68 goals the next year.

After the Oilers' Stanley Cup victory in 1990, Kurri signed with a team in Italy. "I think a lot of players could figure it out during the season that I might not be coming back," Kurri said.

But Kurri did come back. After one season with the Milan Devils, he rejoined Wayne Gretzky, moving to the Los Angeles Kings, where he has continued his excellent two-way play since 1991-92.

The prime weapon of the dynastic Islanders was right wing Mike Bossy, who led the NHL with 68 goals in 1980-81. At the time, only Phil Esposito and Bossy himself had ever reached such heights.

At midseason, Phil Esposito decided to retire from the game, leaving with a career total 1,590 points, second only to Howe's mark (1,850). Just days later, in a game against Quebec, Islander right wing Mike Bossy became only the second player in NHL history to score 50 goals in 50 games, tying Maurice Richard's feat of the 1944-45 season.

In the meantime, Wayne Gretzky was revising the record books almost daily. He finished the season with 164 points, breaking Espo's single-season mark of 152. Gretzky's 109 assists broke Bobby Orr's record. Needless to say, Wayne won his first Art Ross Trophy and his second Hart.

The St. Louis Blues put forth a surprising season and nearly finished on top of the league. However, the Islanders finished with a flourish, including a 13-game unbeaten streak, and topped the Blues by three points. After the Isles' 110 points and the Blues' 107, Montreal was the only other team to break the 100-point plateau (103). Winnipeg finished in the league basement (9-57-14), while the faltering Detroit Red Wings limped into 20th place with only one victory in their last 21 games.

In the best-of-five preliminary round of the playoffs, the youthful Oilers upset the Montreal Canadiens in just three games, leading a stunned Claude Ruel to retire from coaching forever. Three-game sweeps were all the rage, as the Isles blanked Toronto, Minnesota upset the Bruins, Buffalo

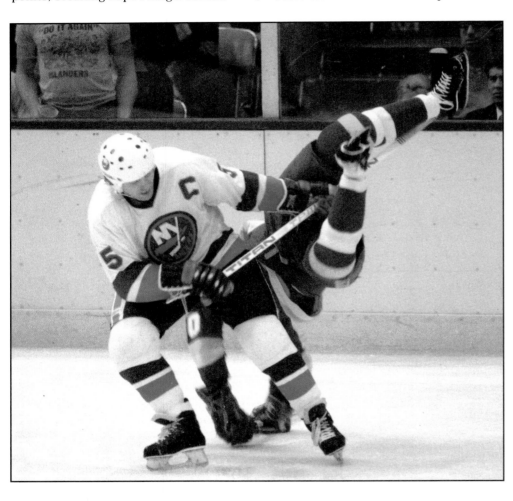

The Islanders won their second straight Stanley Cup in 1981, beating Minnesota in the finals in five games. Here, Denis Potvin topples a North Star with a vicious bodycheck.

Minnesota goalie Don Beaupre smothers the puck during a scramble in the 1981 Stanley Cup finals. Islander Clark Gillies pins an unidentified North Star to the ice.

1980-81

Best Record
New York I.
(48-18-14)

Stanley Cup Finals
New York I. 4
Minnesota 1

Art Ross Trophy
Wayne Gretzky
(55/109/164)

Hart Trophy
Wayne Gretzky

Vezina Trophy
Richard Sevigny
Denis Herron

Calder Trophy
Peter Stastny

Norris Trophy
Randy Carlyle

Lady Byng Trophy
Rick Kehoe

swept Vancouver, and Calgary squelched Chicago. The New York Rangers took four games to eliminate the Kings, while St. Louis and Philadelphia needed the full complement of five games to take out Pittsburgh and Quebec, respectively.

The quarterfinal, best-of-seven round saw Edmonton stretch the Islanders to six games before yielding. The Rangers upset St. Louis in six; Minnesota took out Buffalo in only five games; and Calgary shocked Philadelphia in seven.

In the semifinals, the plucky North Stars pulled their third straight upset, as they eliminated the Calgary Flames in six games. Meanwhile, in a New York-New York series, the Islanders overwhelmed the Rangers in four straight games. The finals would showcase the North Stars and the Cup-defending Isles.

There would be no more upsets for the North Stars, however, as the Islanders handily won the first three games, icing Minnesota 6-3, 6-3, and 7-5. Minnesota fought back in Game Four at home to win 4-2, which forced a fifth game in Nassau Coliseum. The Islanders stormed onto the ice to score three goals by 10:03 of the first period, two of them by Butch Goring. New York breezed to a 5-1 win, thus capturing its second consecutive Stanley Cup.

With ten playoff goals to his credit, Goring copped the Conn Smythe Trophy. Other award winners included

▲ **Second-line center Butch Goring won the Conn Smythe Trophy in 1981. Goring scored ten playoff goals, including two in the fifth and final game of the Stanley Cup finals.**

DENIS POTVIN

Denis Potvin retired in April 1988, secure in the knowledge that he was one of the NHL's most significant players. Whether he was better than Bobby Orr has been a matter of considerable debate.

It was Potvin's misfortune, even before he set foot in the NHL, to be labeled "the next Bobby Orr." At the time of the comparison, in the early 1970s, Orr was the king of hockey.

"I didn't like being compared with Orr," said Potvin, "because we were different personalities with different playing styles."

Remarkably, Denis proceeded to justify the lofty comparisons. He won the Calder Trophy in 1974, and he was named to the First All-Star Team in 1975, 1976, 1978, 1979, and 1981. In addition, he was voted the Norris Trophy winner in 1976, 1978, and 1979.

Potvin could score and create attacking opportunities in the Orr manner, but he added a dimension to his game that never was part of the Orr repertoire: He could deliver crushing bodychecks behind the blue line—and often did.

Denis was the cornerstone of a New York Islanders team that won four straight Stanley Cups in the early 1980s. He finished his 15-year career with 310 goals and 1,052 points, setting records for an NHL defenseman.

Rick Kehoe of Pittsburgh, who took the Lady Byng, and Randy Carlyle of Pittsburgh, who took the Norris. Montreal's goaltending trio of Richard Sevigny, Denis Herron, and Michel "Bunny" Larocque earned the Vezina. It was the first time ever that three names were inscribed on the Vezina for one season.

Montreal's Bob Gainey won the Selke Trophy for the fourth straight year. And avid hockey devotee Charles M. Schulz, creator of the "Peanuts" cartoon series, was awarded the Lester Patrick Trophy for service to hockey in the United States.

Almost before the teams could pack up their gear, the coaching changes began again. In a surprise move, Kings coach Bob Berry resigned and, two weeks later, surfaced as the Canadiens' coach. Tom Watt, assistant to Vancouver coach Harry Neale, was chosen by Winnipeg GM John Ferguson to head the Jets' bench.

Finally, Rangers GM Patrick hired none other than Herb Brooks to coach the Blueshirts. Ironically, Patrick had been Brooks's assistant coach for the 1980 U.S. Olympic club. Pundits theorized that Brooks, a veteran college coach, would find it constricting to take orders from a younger man who had once been his aide.

The hiring of Brooks would signal yet another change in the NHL. Brooks was known as a proponent of European-style hockey, and he would be on the lookout for speedy players with a penchant for puck-handling and passing.

WAYNE GRETZKY

Wayne "The Great" Gretzky's list of achievements is unprecedented. Since the age of 18, when Gretzky made his NHL debut, he has accomplished the following:

• Led Edmonton to four Stanley Cup championships.

• Won nine Hart Trophies.

• Led the league in scoring from 1980-87 and in 1989-90, 1990-91, and 1993-94.

• Set an NHL record of 215 points (52 goals, 163 assists) in 1985-86.

• Scored 92 goals in 1981-82, shattering Phil Esposito's record of 76.

• Broke Gordie Howe's career records for goals, assists, and points.

Gretzky was age 17 when he signed a four-year, $875,000 contract with the WHA's Indianapolis Racers. When the Racers folded, Oilers owner Peter Pocklington bought Gretzky's contract for $850,000 and moved him to Edmonton.

From the moment he set skate in Northlands Coliseum, Gretzky ensured that all 17,300 seats would be filled. By January 1982, Wayne had become such an attraction that scalpers were demanding $200 a ticket for a regular-season game in Toronto—the fans wanted so desperately to see the Great One.

"The NHL needs someone to hang its hat on, and Gretzky looks like a hat tree," said Howe.

In August 1988, Gretzky was traded to L.A. in one of the greatest trades in sports history. In 1995, he took the Kings to the Cup finals but could not push them past Montreal. In 1996, he was traded to St. Louis.

 Islander captain Denis Potvin enjoys a Stanley Cup joy ride.

Gretzky Lives Up to Nickname, Knocks Home 92

1 9 8 1 - 8 2

Big news was made in the June 1981 draft. First off, Winnipeg GM John Ferguson chose Dale Hawerchuk as the first pick in the first round. "I knew I wanted Dale," said Ferguson, "from the moment I first saw him in juniors two years ago."

Another first was Bob Carpenter, chosen third overall by the Washington Capitals. Carpenter became the first American ever drafted in the first round. Edmonton had the eighth pick and it spent it on Grant Fuhr, a goaltender from the Victoria Cougars. Fuhr became the first black ever drafted in the first round, as well as the first goaltender drafted in the initial go-around in 16 years.

Once again, the NHL realigned all of its teams, hoping to create more regional rivalries. The Patrick Division now contained Philadelphia, Washington, Pittsburgh, New York, and New York. The Adams boasted Montreal, Boston, Buffalo, Hartford, and Quebec. The Smythe Division included Edmonton, Vancouver, Calgary, Colorado, and Los Angeles. And the Norris contained Minnesota, Winnipeg, St. Louis, Chicago, Toronto, and Detroit.

As if that wasn't enough, the NHL also rearranged its divisions. The Patrick and Adams Divisions now composed the Prince of Wales Conference, while the Smythe and

Norris now made up the Clarence Campbell Conference. The Wales Conference now contained teams from the East, while the Campbell housed clubs from the West.

The league also opted for an unbalanced schedule—with teams playing many more intra-divisional games—and it revised the playoff structure. Now, four teams from each division would make the playoffs. These teams would face each other in the first two rounds until one emerged as a division winner. The four division winners would enter the semifinals, and the winners of the semis, of course, would meet in the Stanley Cup finals.

Several more Czech players entered

In 1981-82, Mike Bossy (*left*) posted 64 goals, while Wayne Gretzky (*right*) netted an NHL record 92.

the league for the 1981-82 season. Quebec brought yet a third Stastny brother—26-year-old Marian—into the country. The Nords then signed Miroslav Frycer, this time legally, after the NHL and the Czech Ice Hockey Federation agreed that veterans from the Czech National Team could be acquired by NHL teams through a special draft.

Frycer was one of four players permitted by the CIHF to come over. However, Vancouver signed two Czech vets, Ivan Hlinka and Jiri Bubla, before the "draft" ever took place. After the Canucks started the season poorly and the media began to lay the blame at the feet of the Czechs, outspoken

Vancouver coach Harry Neale called the press "racist."

In Washington, the Caps began the season by dropping 12 of their first 13 games, causing owner Abe Pollin to fire almost his entire front office. GM Max McNab, coach Gary Green, and assistant coach Mill Mahoney all got the ziggy. This left assistant GM Roger Crozier, who had a long history of nervous disorders left over from his goaltending days, temporarily in charge of the whole shooting match. Much to Crozier's relief, Pollin soon hired Bryan Murray to coach the Caps.

Several lucrative contracts were inked and/or renegotiated. Wayne Gretzky was the big winner, as he

renegotiated a deal that would net him a reported $20 million over 15 years. Mike Bossy's new contract called for $4.5 million dollars over seven years.

Trade activity was fairly high during the 1981-82 season. Buffalo GM Scotty Bowman sent goalie Bob Sauve, Jim Schoenfeld, Derek Smith, and Danny Gare to Detroit for Dale McCourt, Mike Foligno, Brent Peterson, and future considerations. The Leafs dispatched Ian Turnbull and his hefty salary to the Kings for Billy Harris and John Gibson. Moreover, Toronto virtually gave veteran Darryl Sittler to the Flyers, receiving a college player, a 1982 second-round pick, and future considerations.

Dave "Tiger" Williams was the most penalized player of all time, as he spent 3,966 minutes (the equivalent of a long weekend) in the penalty box. In 1980-81, the Vancouver left wing was penalized for 343 minutes. In 1981-82, he sat for another 341 minutes.

1981-82

Best Record
New York I.
(54-16-10)

Stanley Cup Finals
New York I. 4
Vancouver 0

Art Ross Trophy
Wayne Gretzky
(92/120/212)

Hart Trophy
Wayne Gretzky

Vezina Trophy
Bill Smith

Calder Trophy
Dale Hawerchuk

Norris Trophy
Doug Wilson

Lady Byng Trophy
Rick Middleton

Bryan Trottier

ISLANDERS DYNASTY

The Islanders of the early 1980s were clearly one of the greatest teams of all time. They succeeded in winning 19 consecutive playoff series, beginning in 1980 and concluding in 1984. No other team can make that statement.

In that period, the team coached by Al Arbour and managed by Bill Torrey won four straight Stanley Cups. They did so with the best balanced club of the post-expansion era.

The Isles featured one of the premier snipers in Mike Bossy, the best two-way hitting center ever in Bryan Trottier, the best clutch goaltender in Bill Smith, the leadership of captain Denis Potvin, and more significant role players than any other team in the era. Bob Bourne was the NHL's fastest forward; Clark Gillies was the most productive fighting left wing (when provoked); and Butch Goring was a fleet second center who doubled as a penalty-killer and a checker-of-stars.

There were no weak links in the line-up. "They could play you any way you wanted to play them," recalled Herb Brooks, who coached the rival Rangers at the time. "They had skilled players like Bossy, Trottier, and Potvin and tough guys like Garry Howatt and Bobby Nystrom. They could finesse with anyone or grind with the best of them."

▲ **Chicago's Doug Wilson scored 39 goals and won the Norris in 1981-82.**

Later in the season, Quebec traded their new Czech, Frycer, and a late-round draft pick to Toronto for Wilf Paiement. And Pittsburgh sent Mark Johnson (who had been the leading scorer on the 1980 U.S. Olympic team) to Minnesota for a second-round selection.

As in the previous two seasons, records began to fall throughout the NHL. By beating Colorado on February 20, the Islanders won their 15th straight game, which broke the NHL record set by the Bruins in 1929-30. Meanwhile, Edmonton set a record for goals in a season (417), while Pittsburgh netted a record 99 power-play goals.

Winnipeg's Hawerchuk became the first true rookie to tally both 40 goals and 100 points in a season, as he helped the Jets finish at .500. (Remember, they posted a 9-57-14 record the year before.)

But the young Edmonton center they called the "Great One" broke the most records the most often and apparently with the greatest of ease. Gretzky finished the 1981-82 season with a mind-boggling 92 goals, a jaw-dropping 120 assists, and a record ten hat tricks. His 92 red lights broke the NHL record by 16, while his 212 points broke his own NHL record by 48.

Only three teams passed the century mark in points, as the Islanders topped

the league with 118, Edmonton shot up to second with 111, and the Canadiens amassed 109.

Only the lowly Colorado Rockies had fewer than 20 wins, with a record of 18-49-13. At season's end, the Rockies would be sold to an East Coast consortium that included Houston Astros owner John McMullen and former New Jersey Governor Brendan Byrne. The team would be known henceforth as the New Jersey Devils, and they would open the 1982-83 season in the brand-new Brendan Byrne Arena in Jersey's Meadowlands Sports Complex.

In the first round of the Adams Division playoffs, Montreal was

▲ **Mike Bossy outflanks Canuck goalie Richard Brodeur in the 1982 finals. Bossy won the 1982 Conn Smythe Trophy.**

expected to sweep the fourth-place Nordiques. Thus, the hockey world was surprised when Quebec won the series at 0:22 of overtime in Game Five. After the Boston Bruins defeated the Buffalo Sabres in four games, they took the inspired Nordiques to seven. But Boston lost at home and the Nords became Adams Division champs.

In the Patrick Division, the Pittsburgh Penguins took the favored Islanders to the limit. The Isles finally took Game Five thanks to the heroics of big John Tonelli, who tied the game late in the third period and then gave his team the win in overtime. The Rangers beat Philadelphia in four games, setting up another New York-

New York matchup. Again, it was a rough and hard-fought series, but the Islanders finally overcame the Broadway Blueshirts in six.

The favorite in the Norris Division was Minnesota, which had gone all the way to the Stanley Cup finals the previous season. But Minnesota ran into a hot Chicago sextet that burned the Stars in four. Likewise, St. Louis knocked off the Jets in four. In the division finals, Chicago left St. Louis singing the blues after six games.

The biggest upset of all occurred in the Smythe Division, where Los Angeles, which had finished 17th in the league overall, whipped the mighty Oilers in five games. The Kings beat

Edmonton at its own game, outscoring them 10-8 in the first game and 7-5 in Game Five. In the meantime, the Canucks stunned the favored Flames in three games. Vancouver then continued its surprising ways by knocking off the Kings in five.

In the best-of-seven Campbell Conference championship, the hot Hawks ran into the even hotter goaltending of Richard "The King" Brodeur, as Brodeur and the Canucks polished off Chicago in five contests. During that one loss, referee Bob Byers disallowed a Canucks goal and Vancouver coach Roger Neilson and his entire team waved white towels in "surrender." This bit of sarcastic showmanship cost the Canucks $11,000 in fines. It must have been worth it, as Vancouver advanced to the Stanley Cup finals for the first time ever.

In the Prince of Wales championship, the New York Islanders didn't allow Quebec a single victory, as they swept the exhausted Nords in four games. Hockey pundits predicted that the fierce Islanders would simply devour the Canucks in the finals. They were right.

Although they extended the Islanders to 6-5 and 6-4 in the first two games, the Canucks were blanked in Game Three 3-0. Vancouver managed only a single tally in Game Four, as New York won 3-1. The Isles thus became the first U.S. team ever to win the Cup three years running, and only the third franchise in NHL history (along with Montreal and Toronto) ever to do so. Despite being doggedly and savagely battered by Canucks left winger Tiger Williams, Mike Bossy

scored 17 playoff goals to earn the Conn Smythe Trophy.

Gretzky again won the Art Ross and Hart Trophies. Hawerchuk took the Calder while Boston's Rick Middleton nabbed the Lady Byng. Blackhawk Doug Wilson snagged the Norris.

The league struck a new trophy in memory of Bill Jennings, who had been governor and president of the New York Rangers for many years. The William M. Jennings Trophy was to be awarded to "the goaltender(s) having played a minimum of 25 games for the team with the fewest goals scored against it." The Vezina would now be awarded to the "goalkeeper adjudged to be the best at his position as voted by the general managers of the 21 clubs."

The first winners of the Jennings Trophy were Rick Wamsley and Denis Herron of Montreal. The Vezina, now an individual trophy, was awarded to Bill Smith of the Islanders.

Charlie Simmer

KINGS VS. OILERS, 1982

On the night of April 10, 1982, the Los Angeles Kings and Edmonton Oilers locked up in Game Three of the Smythe Division semifinals—one of the most remarkable games in NHL history.

The Kings trailed 5-0 after two periods and had been thoroughly humiliated. When Wayne Gretzky tapped in a short shot to make the count 5-0, his celebration contained a little extra showboating. His antics fired up the Kings as the teams opened the third period.

Grant Fuhr's shutout was broken early in the third on Jay Wells's tally, but that was only the beginning. Doug Smith and Charlie Simmer closed the deficit to 5-3. And with four minutes left in regulation, Mark Hardy put in a rebound past the beleaguered Fuhr. Incredibly, with only five seconds left, Steve Bozek slammed a rebound over Fuhr's shoulder to knot the score.

The Kings carried their emotional high into overtime, and they didn't disappoint. At 2:35, Daryl Evans slapped a face-off blast past Fuhr for the victory.

Los Angeles took a 2-1 series lead and eventually won the series in five games. This upset was a shocker—Edmonton had outdistanced L.A. by 48 points in the regular season. The Oilers only had themselves to blame, as one period of lackluster hockey cost them a chance to advance.

Bob Nystrom scores in the 1982 Stanley Cup finals. The Canucks, who were 30-33-17 on the season, were clearly no match for the Isles.

The final buzzer has sounded at Pacific Coliseum on May 16, 1982, concluding the Islanders' four-game sweep of the Canucks.

Islanders Broom Edmonton
for Fourth Straight Cup

1 9 8 2 - 8 3

In the summer of 1982, the NHL gave final approval for the sale of the Colorado Rockies to the syndicate headed by John McMullen. For the privilege of playing at the new Brendan Byrne Arena in New Jersey's Meadowlands Sports Complex (which included Giants Stadium and Meadowlands Race Track), the New Jersey Devils franchise had to pay upwards of $30 million. This money included indemnity to the New York Rangers, New York Islanders, and Philadelphia Flyers for "invading" their territories.

The Devils would join the Patrick Division, while the Winnipeg Jets agreed to move into the high-flying Smythe Division to replace the former Rockies. The Patrick would now be the only division with six teams.

In the Motor City, pizza baron Mike Ilitch purchased controlling interest in the Red Wings for a mere $7 million, ending a half-century of control by the Norris family. Ilitch also pried Jimmy Devellano away from the Islanders and named him GM. Devellano then hired Nick Polano, a former minor-leaguer, to coach the Wings—the team's 16th

Isles goalie Bill Smith, the 1983 Conn Smythe winner, completely defused the Oiler offense in the finals. Here, he guards his crease while Dave Lumley and Ken Linseman wait for a shot.

coach in 15 seasons.

As always, there were coaching changes all over the place. Larry Kish took over the bench chores for Hartford from Larry Pleau—though after 49 games, Kish would resign and Pleau would once again take over the coaching. The Blackhawks hired Orval Tessier as head coach, and Buffalo's Scotty Bowman added Red Berenson to his staff as an assistant coach.

In Washington, the Caps took Roger Crozier off the job as GM and hired Calgary's assistant GM, David Poile, to take over that role. The Flames' new ice general became Bob Johnson, a hugely successful coach at the University of Wisconsin. Two of the coaching changes worked wonders, as both Chicago and Washington improved dramatically.

In the Entry Draft, Boston had the first pick but entered into an unusual arrangement with the Minnesota North Stars (who were scheduled to pick second). The Stars were dying to get the draft's hottest prospect, Brian Bellows. And in order to make sure they could get him, they sent two players (Brad Palmer and Dave Donnelly) to Boston with the agreement that Bruins GM Harry Sinden would pass Bellows by.

Sinden took Minnesota's two players and then spent his first pick on defenseman Gord Kluzak—which he later said he would have done anyway! The North Stars grabbed Bellows, who never lived up to their expectations. The acquisition of Kluzak allowed Sinden to deal blue-liner Brad McCrimmon to Philadelphia for goalie Pete Peeters. Peeters would oblige the Bruins by setting a record streak of 31 games without a loss.

In the 1982 off-season, the Flyers orchestrated another major trade, as they acquired defenseman Mark Howe from the Whalers for centerman Ken "Rat" Linseman, left winger Greg Adams, and their first-round pick in 1983. Hartford, in turn, dealt Linseman and Don Nachbaur to the Oilers for backliner Risto Siltanen and 18-year-old left winger Brent Loney.

In Montreal, veteran forward Doug Risebrough had asked to be traded and

Boston's Norm Leveille *(left)* suffered a brain hemorrhage in 1982 and remained partially paralyzed. Here, he sits with Montreal's Larry Robinson.

BOB GAINEY

While the Montreal Canadiens were winning four straight Stanley Cups from 1976-79, Bob Gainey emerged as the best two-way player in hockey. Although he didn't score as many goals as teammate Guy Lafleur, the ones he did get were invariably clutch tallies.

In 1979, in the Stanley Cup finals between Montreal and the New York Rangers, Gainey demonstrated how a timely bodycheck could help win a game and a series. The husky winger leveled New Yorker Dave Maloney with a monumental check, and then set up a pivotal goal that deflated his opposition.

A swift skater, Gainey became the quintessential defensive forward. He was so good, in fact, that he won the Frank Selke Trophy in the award's first four years of existence.

Bob Gainey, in time, was named captain of the Canadiens and helped the Montrealers to a surprise Stanley Cup win in 1986. His game declined thereafter, and in 1989 he hung up his skates to become a player/coach in France. Prior to the 1990-91 season, he was named head coach of the Minnesota North Stars.

the Canadiens obliged, sending him to Calgary for a couple draft picks. But Montreal's biggest swap was with the Caps, as it packaged Rod Langway, Brian Engblom, Doug Jarvis, and Craig Laughlin to Washington for defenseman Rick Green and forward Ryan Walter. It was a trade that shocked the NHL, as Langway alone was considered to be worth more than Walter and Green combined. The move would definitely help the Caps become a contender in the Patrick Division.

On October 5, 1982, the New Jersey Devils debuted in the Meadowlands, skating to a 3-3 tie against Pittsburgh. Another first occurred when the Hartford Whalers, featuring former Olympic star Mark Johnson, met the Calgary Flames, who were coached by Mark's father, Bob. Never before in the history of the NHL had a son played against a team coached by his father.

Between the first and second periods of a Bruins-Vancouver game on October 23, promising Boston rookie Norm Leveille suffered a brain hemorrhage that doctors claimed had nothing to do with the game itself. Tragically, Leveille would remain partially paralyzed for the rest of his life.

Although the league has since instituted severe penalties for brawling and stick-swinging, the 1982-83 season was marred by several ugly incidents. Linseman received a four-game suspension for drilling his stick into Toronto's Russ Adam—and this was only in the exhibition season! Whaler Blaine Stoughton sat out eight games after a vicious cross-check on Pittsburgh's Paul Baxter.

Vancouver's Tiger Williams got a seven-game suspension for stick-dueling with Isles goalie Bill Smith. After whacking Red Wings goalie Greg Stefan, North Star Willi Plett was awarded an eight-game suspension. Finally, Kings tough guy Jerry Korab sat out six games after out-smacking equally tough Dale Hunter of the Nords.

As for the record books, Kings veteran Marcel Dionne became the ninth NHLer to score 500 career goals;

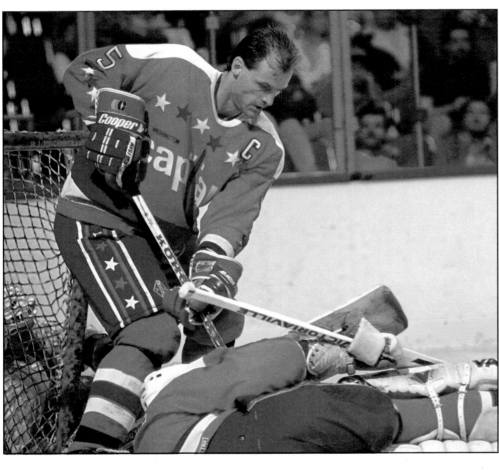

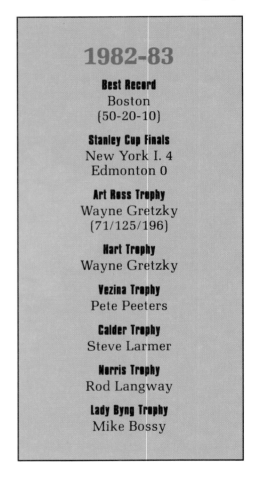

Washington acquired Rod Langway in 1982 and he led the Caps to their first-ever playoff in 1983. Despite scoring just three goals in 1982-83, Langway won the Norris Trophy.

The new New Jersey Devils, 17-49-14 in 1982-83, were the joke of the NHL. Here, goalie Chico Resch looks right while Islander Bob Bourne is apparently tapping one in on the left.

MIKE BOSSY

In 1977, a brilliant ray appeared on the hockey horizon—Mike Bossy, the "Goal Machine."

The genius of Bossy was evident from his rookie season, when he set an NHL freshman record with 53 goals, but it was not fully realized until 1980-81. That season, he equaled Rocket Richard's accomplishment of scoring 50 goals in 50 games.

Bossy got off to a hot start early in that campaign. He then brought more attention upon himself by stating that scoring 50 goals in 50 games would be his deepest personal achievement.

Game 50 was at Nassau Coliseum against the Quebec Nordiques. Bossy needed two goals to tie the mark, but he didn't score through the first 55 minutes of the game. With a little more than five minutes left to play, Quebec took a penalty. Bossy converted on the power-play opportunity with 4:10 remaining in the game. Amazingly, he netted his 50th with 1:29 left.

In 1980-81, Bossy notched 68 goals and 51 assists. The next year, he totaled 64 goals and 83 assists. Despite a debilitating leg injury, he choreographed the Isles to their third straight Stanley Cup in May 1982 and was named MVP of the playoffs.

Bossy was an effective scorer for several more seasons before a chronic back problem led to his retirement.

In 1982-83, Chicago's Steve Larmer won the Calder on the strength of 43 red lights. At the time, only four rookies had ever scored more goals.

he finished the season as the league's sixth highest point scorer with 1,270. Flyer Bobby Clarke passed the 1,100-point barrier, while Mike Bossy became the first NHL player to score 50 or more goals in his first six seasons—and the first to score more than 60 goals in three consecutive years. The Rangers' Mark Pavelich became the first U.S.-born player to score five goals in one game (against the Whalers), and Wayne Gretzky set an assist record with 125.

Wayne's team also set an NHL record for goals with 424, as they finished the year with 106 points. Three other teams reached the century mark, including Boston (110),

Philadelphia (106), and Chicago (104). The Hawks actually improved by 32 points over the year before.

The Islanders finished a disappointing sixth in the overall standings, but proceeded to get their act together for the playoffs. Boasting so many playoff-tested players (Bryan Trottier, Denis Potvin, Bossy, Smith, etc.), a fourth straight Stanley Cup was certainly attainable.

In the Patrick playoffs, the Isles ousted Washington (which made the playoffs for the first time ever) in four games. At the same time, the mediocre Rangers swept the Flyers in three. The Islanders needed six games to defeat an injury-decimated Rangers club and

gain their fifth straight Patrick Division title.

In the Adams Division, the Bruins trounced the Nordiques in four contests and then took the full seven games to defeat the Buffalo Sabres, who had upset the Canadiens in three straight.

Boston was favored to take the Wales title, with Peeters performing beautifully in the nets and forwards Rick Middleton and Barry Pederson scoring goals virtually at will. Against the Islanders, the Bruins constantly shadowed Bossy, which worked only temporarily. Mike eventually broke free to score seven goals in two high-scoring Islander home victories, 8-3 and 8-4. The Isles entered the Stanley

Cup finals for the fourth consecutive time.

Edmonton won the Smythe by sweeping Winnipeg and then clubbing Calgary in five games (the Flames had beaten Vancouver). Chicago ruled in the Norris, as it took the Blues in four and the North Stars in five (Minnesota had defeated Toronto). The Campbell Conference finals were a mismatch, as Edmonton skated by the Hawks in four straight.

As was typical of Gretzky & Co., several records were broken along the way. Wayne scored an unprecedented seven points in one playoff game (against Calgary), and his Oilers tallied a record 34 goals in one series

(also against the Flames).

Amazingly, the Oilers were totally outmatched by the Islanders. New York defeated the talented, speedy, Oilers in four straight games with an exhibition of defense stymieing offense. In Game One, Smith actually shut out Edmonton, as New York won 2-0. In Game Two, the Islanders beat the Oilers at their own game, scoring three goals in the first period and eventually winning 6-3.

In Game Three, the Isles again shut down the Edmonton machine, taking the game 5-1. Game Four saw the New Yorkers score three goals in the first period—all within a minute and 37 seconds. Edmonton came as close to

tying as they had all series, but Smith held the score to 3-2 in the third period, executing some saves that left the crowd breathless.

The New York Islanders became the first U.S.-based team to win four consecutive Stanley Cups—and only the third team ever to win four in a row. Smith emerged as the Conn Smythe Trophy winner, as he held the Oilers to seven goals in the final series.

Other trophy winners included Gretzky, who took the Art Ross and the Hart, and Chicago's Steve Larmer, who annexed the Calder. Peeters earned the Vezina while Bossy accepted the Lady Byng. The Norris went to Washington's Langway.

LANNY McDONALD

Lanny McDonald, one of the most popular players to ever lace up a pair of skates, announced his retirement as an active player of the Calgary Flames on August 28, 1989. He remained with the Flames in a management capacity.

McDonald completed an outstanding 16-year career that saw him go directly from the Western Hockey League (Medicine Hat) to the NHL (Toronto Maple Leafs) in the fall of 1973. Lanny totaled 500 goals and 1,006 points in 1,111 career games.

Twice McDonald was a second-team All-Star right wing. He won the Bill Masterton and King Clancy Memorial Trophies. And he was named Bud Man of the Year in 1989.

Elected in 1992 to the Hall of Fame, McDonald holds the Flames record for most goals in a season (66 in 1982-83). He also scored 40 or more goals in six seasons and 33-plus goals in nine seasons. Lanny notched the winning goal in Calgary's 1989 Cup finale win at Montreal.

Currently, McDonald is vice-president of corporate and community relations for the Flames. He is also involved in many charities, especially the Special Olympics.

Islander Duane Sutter, a top performer in the 1983 finals, is verbally assaulted by Wayne Gretzky. Ken Linseman sticks up for his Oiler teammate.

It's Out with the Isles and In with the Oilers

1 9 8 3 - 8 4

The 1983-84 season would see the ascendancy of the Edmonton Oilers and the beginning of the end for Islander dominance. Ironically, the Islanders would drive their way to the top of the Patrick Division in 1983-84, win three more rough playoff series (bringing their total to 19), and enter their fifth straight Stanley Cup finals as the favorite.

Prior to the season, the NHL held a landmark Entry Draft—five U.S. natives were picked in the first round. In all, 65 Americans were chosen in the draft, along with 35 Europeans and 144 Canadians. The first pick overall was New Jersey native Brian Lawton, who went to the North Stars. The Whalers selected Canadian Sylvain Turgeon while the Islanders spent their third pick on a Detroit native, Pat LaFontaine.

One team, the St. Louis Blues, were not allowed to draft players that year, a factor that would haunt the club for years afterward. The Blues were paying a penalty for an incident that occurred during the 1982-83 season. Here's what happened: The Blues had been losing money and their owner, Ralston Purina, was considering selling the team. Bill Hunter, a promoter from Edmonton who had been involved with the inception of the WHA, proposed to buy the club and move it to Saskatoon, Saskatchewan, and construct a new arena.

The NHL governors voted the proposal down, however, and Ralston Purina launched a lawsuit against the NHL. The league countered by sueing Ralston Purina, claiming the company was in "a breach of trust with the citizens of St. Louis." The upshot of the whole mess was that St. Louis was not allowed in the 1983 draft because of

 Grant Fuhr's sensational puck-stopping helped Edmonton beat the Islanders for the 1984 Stanley Cup.

the litigation. And although the Blues were soon purchased by California-based entrepreneur Harry Ornest for a mere $3 million, they began the 1983-84 season with no new draft selections.

They also began the season with a new coach, Jacques Demers. Other new faces behind the benches were Jack Evans in Hartford, Lou Angotti in Pittsburgh, and Bill Mahoney in Minnesota. Soon afterwards, Winnipeg replaced Tom Watt with Barry Long, and Montreal ousted Bob Berry in exchange for Jacques Lemaire. After the New Jersey Devils lost 18 of their

first 20 games, they axed GM/coach Billy MacMillan. MacMillan was replaced by Tom McVie as coach and Max McNab as GM.

At one point during the Devils' losing streak, Edmonton obliterated the little demons 13-4. After the game, Wayne Gretzky quipped that the Devils "are putting a Mickey Mouse operation on the ice." Gretzky had inadvertently done the franchise a big favor. The next time the two teams met, Byrne Arena was a sea of Mickey Mouse ears and chanting fans. It didn't immediately produce victories for the

club, but the controversy did begin to draw fans to the cavernous rink.

The Devils were involved in another controversy during the 1983-84 season. The club's president, Bob Butera, accused Patrick Division rival Pittsburgh of aiming to win the first draft pick for the 1984-85 season, rather than trying to win games. Everyone knew that the next Entry Draft would feature the young center Mario Lemieux, who was scoring about two goals a game in the Quebec Junior League.

Pitt GM Eddie Johnston offered an

Chicago native Chris Chelios, a graduate of the 1984 U.S. Olympic team, signed with the Montreal Canadiens and emerged as one of the best defensemen in the NHL. Chelios helped Montreal to the Wales Conference finals in the spring of '84.

Scott Stevens, a power behind the Washington blue line, developed into one of the league's tougher defensemen. Stevens helped the 1983-84 Capitals to 48 wins, the most they ever had.

BILL SMITH

In the decade spanning 1975-85, the New York Islanders were one of the NHL's premier teams. They couldn't have done it without goalie Bill Smith. In that ten-year span, Smith dazzled New York with his artistry, durability, and unquenchable thirst for victory.

Smith accumulated four Stanley Cup rings over his career. In his play-off debut in 1975, he orchestrated the Islanders to an opening-round upset over the Rangers. Furthermore, "Bad Billy," as he was known to the foe, totaled 88 playoff wins, won the Conn Smythe Trophy (1983), the Vezina Trophy (1982), and shared the Jennings Trophy (best goals-against average, 1983) with then-teammate Roland Melanson.

To his opponents, Smith was a Darth Vadar on skates, a misanthrope who thought nothing of crippling Wayne Gretzky or attempting to remove Lindy Ruff's eye. Unfortunately, Smith's bluster and occasional block-busting often clouded the artistic aspects of his goaltending.

Smith helped the Isles to a Patrick Division regular-season title in 1987-88. Even though he was 37 years old, Smith played in 38 games and posted a respectable 3.22 goals-against average. In 1988-89, Billy moved into eighth place on the all-time wins list for goaltenders with 305 victories. He retired prior to the 1989-90 season.

Bob Gainey (23) and the Canadiens almost dethroned the Islanders in the 1984 semis, as they won the first two games. But New York swept the next four games to reach its fifth straight Stanley Cup finals.

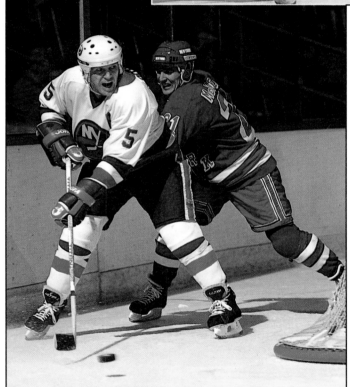

Islander Denis Potvin outraces Ranger George McPhee in Round One of the 1984 playoffs. The Blueshirts nearly eliminated their hated rivals, but the Islanders eventually won the series three games to two.

---

enraged rebuttal to Butera's remarks but, nevertheless, the Pens lost eight of their last ten games. They finished last in the league, three points behind the wimpy Devils, and thus won the right to pick first. They would indeed draft Lemieux, who would go on to become a goal-scoring machine.

After three years of struggling in the tiny Stampede Corral, the Calgary Flames finally moved into their brand-new arena, the Olympic Saddledome (which was built for the 1988 Winter Olympics). With their big, new home, the Calgary franchise skated out of red

ink and into the black.

To add a little excitement, the league voted to re-institute overtime in regular-season games. The extra period would last five minutes; if neither team scored in the five-minute stanza, then the game would end in a tie. (Overtime had been a normal feature of the regular season until 1942, when the league canceled it because of travel restrictions imposed by the rigors of World War II.) In the 1983-84 season, 140 games entered overtime; 54 of them—more than a third—resulted in wins.

Several major trades took place during 1983-84. First off, Minnesota shipped Bobby Smith to Montreal for Mark Napier and Keith Acton. L.A. swapped Larry Murphy to the Caps for Brian Engblom and Ken Houston. Quebec shuffled Real Cloutier and a first-round pick off to Buffalo for Tony McKegney, Andre Savard, Jean-Francois Sauve, and a third-round pick.

Detroit packaged Willie Huber, Mike Blaisdell, and Mark Osborne to the Rangers for Ed Mio, Ron Duguay, and Eddie Johnstone. Winnipeg dealt Dave Christian to the Caps for young Bobby

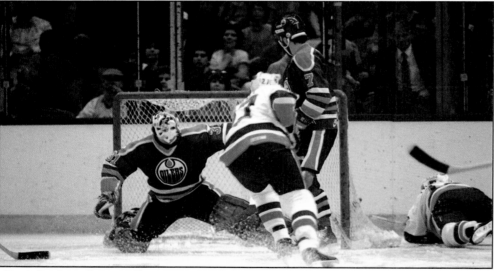
Oiler Dave Lumley and Islander Butch Goring face off in the 1984 finals.

Islander John Tonelli tests Grant Fuhr in the 1984 finals.

PAUL COFFEY

Paul Coffey needed all the support he could get during his rookie season with the Oilers. Plucked in the first round of the 1980 Entry Draft, Paul traveled to Alberta with great expectations. But by the time he reached Edmonton, Coffey lost his confidence. Luckily, coach Glen Sather was willing to be patient, and soon Coffey found himself.

By 1988, Coffey had compiled three Stanley Cup rings, two Norris Trophies, and a goal-scoring record for defensemen (48 red lights in 1985-86). Yet Coffey, after seven years as an Oiler, was dispatched to the Pittsburgh Penguins in autumn of 1987. The trade was instigated by a contract squabble in the summer of '87. Coffey didn't like Edmonton's offer and ultimately walked out on the team. "Coffey's trade wasn't easy," said Sather, "but it certainly was necessary."

Coffey was injured for most of his first season with the Penguins. But in 1988-89, he scored 30 goals and added 83 assists in helping Pittsburgh to the playoffs for the first time in seven years. He then helped the Penguins win the Stanley Cup in 1990-91.

Coffey reunited with Wayne Gretzky in L.A. before his trade to Detroit, where he took the Red Wings all the way to the Stanley Cup finals and won his third Norris Trophy in 1995. Coffey is the highest-scoring defenseman in NHL history.

Dollas. And the Penguins bussed Randy Carlyle to Winnipeg for a 1984 first-round pick.

The season began with Marcel Dionne, 32 years old, passing Rocket Richard on the all-time goal-scoring list, as he netted No. 545. In December, Guy Lafleur scored his 500th goal, joining a very select NHL group. The Oilers set yet another scoring record (446 goals). And Edmonton's Paul Coffey broke Bobby Orr's record for points by a defenseman, as he pocketed 126.

Gretzky again led the league in scoring with 205 points (including 87 goals), steering the Oilers to a league-best 57-18-5 record. Boston edged Buffalo (104 points to 103) to win the Adams Division, while the Islanders took the Patrick with 104 points. Minnesota, with 88 points, posted the only winning record in the Norris. This division would be a bastion of mediocrity for the remainder of the decade, prompting a *Sports Illustrated* headline to read: "How They Bore Us in the Norris."

In the Norris playoffs, the Stars ousted the Blackhawks in five games, while coach Demers rallied his Blues past Detroit in three. Minnesota took seven games to eliminate St. Louis.

Over in the Smythe, Edmonton swept the Jets while Calgary defeated Vancouver in four. In the division championship, the Oilers and Flames set the nets afire; Edmonton won the series with a 7-4 shootout in Game Seven. In the Campbell Conference finals, the high-powered Oilers blew past Minnesota in four games.

Over in the Adams Division, Montreal broomed the Bruins in the first round, despite starting kid goalie Steve Penney. Quebec also swept

Buffalo in three. Montreal then ousted Quebec in six games, the last of which was one of the most fight-ridden contests in playoff history.

In the Patrick Division, the Caps swept the Flyers, but the Islanders took the full five games to eliminate the Rangers. It took the Isles the same number of games to skate past the Caps for the division title and the chance to meet Montreal in the Wales finals.

The Canadiens looked like they would finally end the Islanders' record number of series wins, as they won the first two games. But the seasoned Long Islanders gathered their forces one more time and won the next four

straight, thus winning their fifth consecutive conference title.

The Stanley Cup finals saw a changing of the guard—out with the Islanders, in with the Oilers. New York goalie Billy Smith was upstaged by Edmonton's acrobatic puck-stopper, Grant Fuhr. Though the Isles were known for their great defense, the Oilers proved that they too could play tough D. And with scoring talents like Gretzky, Jari Kurri, Glenn Anderson, and Mark Messier, the Oilers simply wore out the Islanders.

Edmonton blew past New York in five games to win the Stanley Cup. For the Islanders, this would be their last

hurrah. The Oilers? They were just warming up.

Gretzky again took the Hart Trophy, while teammate Messier was voted the Conn Smythe. Sabres rookie Tom Barrasso won both the Calder and the Vezina. Mike Bossy, who tallied 50 goals for a record-breaking seventh season, was again awarded the "consolation" prize of the Lady Byng.

Washington personnel won several awards. Bryan Murray won the Jack Adams Award as coach of the year; Al Jensen and Pat Riggin won the Jennings Trophy for the lowest GAA; and Doug Jarvis took the Selke as the best defensive forward.

1983-84

Best Record
Edmonton
(57-18-5)

Stanley Cup Finals
Edmonton 4
New York I. 1

Art Ross Trophy
Wayne Gretzky
(87/118/205)

Hart Trophy
Wayne Gretzky

Vezina Trophy
Tom Barrasso

Calder Trophy
Tom Barrasso

Norris Trophy
Rod Langway

Lady Byng Trophy
Mike Bossy

Wayne Gretzky falls into Islanders goalie Bill Smith during the 1984 Stanley Cup finals. The Oilers proved their might by scoring 19 goals in the last three games of the series. Gretzky scored 13 times in the 1984 playoffs while Jari Kurri topped everyone with 14 tallies.

Oilers Quaff Champagne as Flyers Beg for Water

1 9 8 4 - 8 5

The Edmonton Oilers had six good reasons to believe they could repeat their Stanley Cup triumph: Wayne Gretzky, Jari Kurri, Paul Coffey, Grant Fuhr, Mark Messier, and Kevin Lowe.

"All the talent was in place," said Lowe. "The challenge was to get everyone to play to potential, develop maturity, and not get cocky or overconfident. We knew there were

some pretty good challengers out there."

Best of all were the Philadelphia Flyers, who would actually out-point the Oilers, 113-109, over the 80-game season. A major difference between the clubs was in the number of productive stars. While Gretzky and Kurri led all NHL scorers with 208 and 135 points, respectively, the Flyers' top point-getters were Tim Kerr (in 18th place

with 98 points) and Brian Propp (in 19th place with 96 points). Philadelphia relied on teamwork, solid defense, and splendid goalkeeping from Pelle Lindbergh.

Before the season even started, discussion focused on rookie Mario Lemieux, who, the year before, had tallied 133 goals and 149 assists in the Quebec Junior League. Drafted first

Glenn Anderson sprays champagne after his Oilers doused the Flyers in the 1985 Stanley Cup finals.

overall by the Pittsburgh Penguins, Lemieux fulfilled all of his advance notices. Despite a huge frame, Mario moved majestically, passing and shooting with wonderful precision. He finished his rookie season with 100 points on 43 goals.

Other standout rookies included two members of the 1984 U.S. Olympic team—Chris Chelios of the Canadiens and Pat LaFontaine of the Islanders. Although he was a defenseman, Chelios finished the season with 64 points. The speedy LaFontaine tallied just 54 points but flashed exciting potential.

"What it showed," said Calgary Flames coach Bob Johnson, "is that Americans are going to be more and more of a factor in major-league hockey."

The biggest factor of all in hockey was, of course, Gretzky. He not only led the league in scoring, but he also led in the plus/minus rating (plus-98). Gretzky was tops in goals (73), assists (135), shorthanded goals (11), and shots (358). Many were claiming that the Great One was better than his idol, Gordie Howe. Gretzky diplomatically replied, "There'll never be another Gordie Howe."

The surprise team of the year was the Washington Capitals, who finished third overall with 101 points and featured two 50-goal scorers in Bobby Carpenter (53) and Mike Gartner (50).

"It was a positive development, all right," said Capitals GM David Poile. "I suppose now the problem is that too

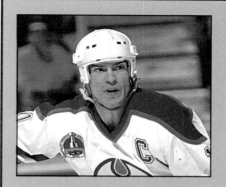

MARK MESSIER

Edmonton Oilers boss Glen Sather would never publicly admit it, but those close to Sather insist his favorite player of all time is Mark Messier, whom he nurtured as an awkward Oiler in 1979. Messier emerged as one of the most gifted shooters of the 1980s and, arguably, the best clutch player of his era.

In 1989-90, Messier notched 45 goals and 84 assists in capturing the Hart Trophy. He helped lead the Oilers to their fifth Stanley Cup championship in seven years.

Mark was also the hero of the 1984 Stanley Cup finals, in which Edmonton upset the mighty Islanders. After splitting the first two games of the series, the two teams headed to Edmonton for Game Three.

In Game Three, with Edmonton trailing by a goal, Messier stormed the Islanders' zone, skating one-on-one with New York defenseman Gord Dineen. He faked the Islander into a knot and then delivered a mighty shot that handcuffed goalie Billy Smith.

The goal ignited an Oilers rally that sent them to a 5-2 victory. Edmonton won its first Stanley Cup and Messier (not Wayne Gretzky, mind you) won the Conn Smythe Trophy.

In 1991-92, Messier joined the New York Rangers, and in 1994 he became the first man in NHL history to captain two different teams to Stanley Cup championships.

Chicago's Doug Wilson eludes Islander Patrick Flatley at Nassau Coliseum. Wilson, one of the NHL's best rushing defensemen, tallied 22 goals and 54 assists in 1984-85. His Hawks advanced to the Campbell Conference finals, where they fell to the mighty Oilers.

Philadelphia's Pelle Lindbergh blossomed into the NHL's top goalie of 1984-85. The Swedish netminder went 40-17-7 and was awarded the Vezina Trophy. His work in the net helped the Flyers to the Stanley Cup finals.

In 1984-85, the Penguins unveiled rookie sensation Mario Lemieux, who tallied 43 goals to win the Calder Trophy. A year earlier in junior hockey, Lemieux terrorized opponents by amassing 133 goals and 149 assists in 70 games.

The Winnipeg Jets finally found a star in Dale "Ducky" Hawerchuk. In 1984-85, the talented center garnered 53 goals and 77 assists to lead the Jets to a 43-27-10 record—by far their best ever.

1984-85

Best Record
Philadelphia
(53-20-7)

Stanley Cup Finals
Edmonton 4
Philadelphia 1

Art Ross Trophy
Wayne Gretzky
(73/135/208)

Hart Trophy
Wayne Gretzky

Vezina Trophy
Pelle Lindbergh

Calder Trophy
Mario Lemieux

Norris Trophy
Paul Coffey

Lady Byng Trophy
Jari Kurri

much of our scoring is concentrated in these two people. Ideally, you ought to have some secondary threats just to make things more complicated for defenses around the league."

The most exciting divisional race took place in the Adams, as Montreal, Quebec, and Buffalo battled to the wire. Montreal finally won the division by three points over the Nordiques and four over the Sabres. "We were down three points in the standings from the year before, and that made the difference," said Quebec president Marcel Aubut.

Another success story was the St. Louis Blues, a club that nearly had

moved to Saskatoon. Under the baton of GM Ron Caron and coach Jacques Demers, the Blues climbed to first place in the Norris (37-31-12). The Blues won on the strength of hard work and the leadership of captain Brian Sutter. "With a captain like Brian Sutter, a coach has all the security he'll ever need," said Demers. "He's a great leader. When other guys see a player working as hard as he does, they can't do any less. They'd be ashamed of themselves if they did."

That the Chicago Blackhawks finished second in the Norris Division was a tribute to the virtuosity of Denis Savard (105 points) and the eventual

coaching of GM Bob Pulford, who fired head coach Orval Tessier in midseason. "Obviously, being GM is a job in itself," said Pulford, "but it appears we get our best results when I take a hand in the coaching. So that's the way it's got to be."

Stanley Cup finalists only a year earlier, the New York Islanders began showing signs of wear and tear, finishing at 40-34-6. The Isles got another big year out of Mike Bossy (58 goals, 117 points), while young Brent Sutter emerged as a new star (42 goals, 102 points). But the Islanders were no longer an intimidating team. When the playoffs started, Edmonton was

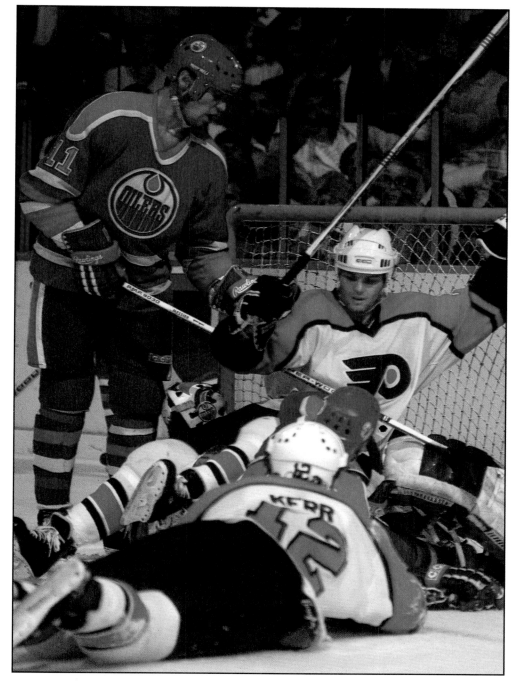

Grant Fuhr does his darnedest to keep the puck, two Flyers, and a teammate out of the net during the 1985 Stanley Cup finals.

PAT LaFONTAINE

Pat LaFontaine, a member of the 1984 U.S. Olympic team, accomplished a great deal in seven seasons with the New York Islanders. But his greatest moment of all came in the 1987 playoffs.

The Islanders were facing the Washington Capitals in the opening round. Game Seven, at the Capital Centre, was tied at the end of regulation. They played three gut-wrenching overtimes and still there was no winner. Finally, at 8:47 of the fourth O.T., LaFontaine ended it with a turnaround slapshot from just inside the blue line.

"We were all pretty beat at the time," LaFontaine recalled. "I had just come off the bench when Gordie Dineen circled the net and took a shot. I was actually laying back covering up for him when the puck bounced off a Washington player and rebounded to me. I took a swipe at it and hoped for the best.... It caromed off the post and into the net. It was the most memorable moment in my hockey life."

In 1991, LaFontaine was traded to Buffalo, where he helped Alexander Mogilny to a 76-goal year in 1992-93 (while scoring 53 goals of his own). Despite some crippling injuries, LaFontaine has been the Sabres' sharpest weapon during the 1990s.

favored to repeat.

Once the postseason began, the Oilers swept through their divisional foes, beating Los Angeles three straight and then taking out Winnipeg in four. They advanced to the semifinals to take on the Blackhawks, who defeated a sorry lot of Norris Division foes.

In the Adams, both Montreal and Quebec won their opening rounds, setting up an exciting matchup between the two provincial rivals. The series went the seven-game limit and wasn't settled until 2:22 of overtime when Peter Stastny scored for Quebec. Philadelphia blew through the Patrick

playoffs, disposing of the Rangers in three games and the Islanders in five.

In the conference finals, Edmonton easily knocked off Chicago while Philadelphia outclassed the Nordiques. The Oilers and Flyers were clearly the best two teams in hockey, and they would meet in the Stanley Cup finals. For Philly, it was their first trip to the finals since 1980, when they lost to the Islanders. For Edmonton, this was their third straight finals appearance.

The series opened at The Spectrum and the Oilers knew it wouldn't be easy, mostly because Philadelphia had swept the season series with Edmonton three games to none. In

Game One of the finals, Gretzky & Co. skated as if they were in quicksand; the Flyers won 4-1. The next day, coach Glen Sather walked into the meeting room and told his Oilers, "It was so bad last night, I don't even want to show you guys the films."

For Game Two, Sather shook things up a bit when he inserted young Finn Esa Tikkanen into the lineup, placing him alongside Gretzky. Philly hung tough but the Oilers held a 2-1 lead right down to the wire. Edmonton scored an empty-netter to clinch it.

The series resumed at Northlands Coliseum and Edmonton won 4-3—but it wasn't easy. For the first two-thirds of the game, the Oilers followed their game plan and built a 4-1 lead. But in the third period, Edmonton became unglued and almost lost the game.

Flyers coach Mike Keenan tried to thwart Edmonton's scoring by going with four defensemen. This strategy may have worked at first; but as the series wore on, the backliners were getting tired and they simply couldn't cope with the Oilers' speed.

In Game Four, the Flyers jumped out to a 3-1 first-period lead. But in the second period, Glenn Anderson tied the score at 3-3. Goalie Fuhr made a spectacular play, stopping Philly's Rick Tocchet cold on a breakaway.

Gretzky then scored two goals to put Edmonton ahead to stay.

By this point, the Flyers were exhausted. In fact, the Flyers wanted water bottles placed on top of the nets so that goalies could get a drink during the respites. The Oilers thought it was a ridiculous idea, suggesting that if Philly wanted water bottles, then why not make it a whole picnic lunch—some fried chicken or cheese and crackers?

In Game Five, the Oilers ran away from the Flyers, but tempers became frayed near the end and even the coaches, Keenan and Sather, did quite a bit of jawing. By the time the fighting had ended, the final score was 8-3. The

Edmonton Oilers sipped champagne for the second straight year.

"I figure we had to repeat as Stanley Cup winners before a lot of people would realize how good we really were," said Gretzky, winner of the Conn Smythe Trophy. "Having proven ourselves, we've begun to get the respect we deserve."

Besides winning the Smythe and Art Ross Trophies, Gretzky captured his sixth straight Hart Trophy. Teammate Coffey took the Norris for the first time, while Oiler Kurri won his first Lady Byng. Lemieux ran away with the Calder while Vezina honors went to the Flyers' Lindbergh.

As the Oilers ran away with the 1985 finals, Philly players became rather testy. Here, Flyers Derrick Smith and Ed Hospodar (right) vent their frustrations on Edmonton's Mike Krushelnyski (26).

What more can a guy ask for? Edmonton right wing Jari Kurri celebrates with a cigar, a beer, and a Stanley Cup. Kurri scored an astronomical 90 goals on the year, including 19 in the playoffs. The 19 tallies tied an NHL playoff record, set by Flyer Reggie Leach in 1976.

MARK HOWE

There has been only one thing "wrong" with this speedy, deft-passing defenseman who comes from Detroit—his last name is spelled H-O-W-E. Had Mark Howe been anyone but the son of the inimitable Gordie Howe, he would have been acknowledged as a genuinely superior hockey player in his own right and a future Hall of Famer.

At age 16, Mark was a member of the 1972 silver medal-winning U.S. Olympic team. At 17, he starred for the Toronto Marlboros, winners of the 1973 Memorial Cup. At 18, and again at 19, Mark starred alongside his father and brother Marty as a member of the Avco Trophy-winning Houston Aeros of the World Hockey Association.

Mark suffered a scary injury with the Philadelphia Flyers in 1980, when his backside landed on one of the bayonet-like prongs that held the goal net in place. He returned to action about a month afterwards. Mark later helped Philly to the Stanley Cup finals in both 1985 and 1987. His best season, numerically, was 1985-86, when he totaled 24 goals and 58 assists.

A four-time member of the NHL's First All-Star Team, Howe signed in 1992 with Detroit, where he played three more seasons before retiring.

Oilers Beat Themselves; Canadiens Beat Calgary

1 9 8 5 - 8 6

One more time, the Edmonton Oilers dominated the NHL. The Oilers completed the regular campaign with 119 points—nine more than the second best team, the Philadelphia Flyers. Wayne Gretzky, seemingly bored with scoring goals, allowed his teammates to light the lamp. The Great One dished off an NHL record 163 assists, while chipping in 52 goals of his own.

While the media focused on Gretzky, Oilers defenseman Paul Coffey was posting his own astounding numbers. In 1985-86, Coffey scored 48 goals, breaking Bobby Orr's record for most goals in a season by a defenseman.

More than that, Coffey fortified the argument that he was the greatest offensive defenseman of all time.

"Speed is the biggest asset you can have in this game, and nobody's got more than Paul Coffey," said Minnesota GM Lou Nanne.

"Coffey's skating ability is the equal of Orr's when Bobby was in his prime, but Orr was more creative when he had the puck," said Brad Park, who played against both. "Bobby would create more plays than Paul does. Bobby would take the puck, go around the net, and slip it out—come up with all kinds of plays. Orr was better than Coffey."

Thanks to Gretzky and Coffey, the Oilers surpassed 400 goals for the fifth straight season; no other NHL team has ever reached that mark in even one campaign. With other super-snipers, like Jari Kurri and Glenn Anderson, it's not surprising that Edmonton scored five or more goals in 60 percent of its 80 games.

Few could imagine the Oilers not winning the Cup in 1985-86, but several other teams would give them a hard time. One was the Calgary Flames. Despite losing ten straight games in midseason, coach Bob Johnson's Flames finished the season

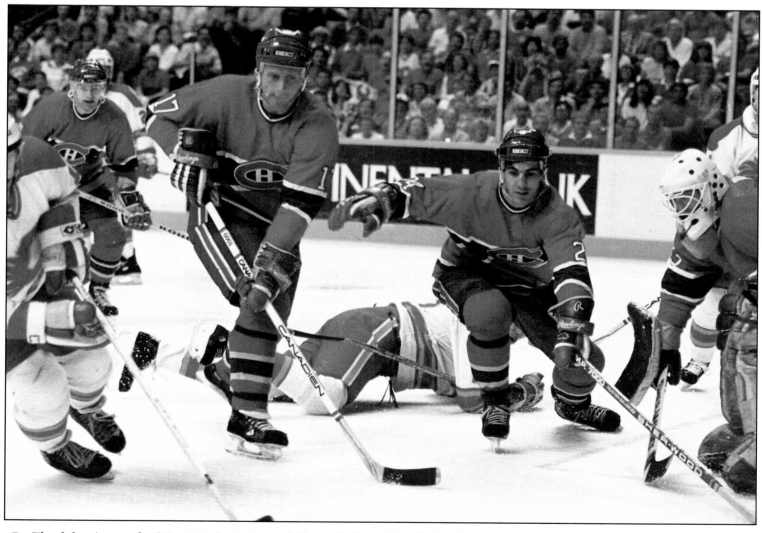

▲ The defensive work of Craig Ludwig (17) and Chris Chelios (right) helped Montreal oust Calgary in the 1986 finals.

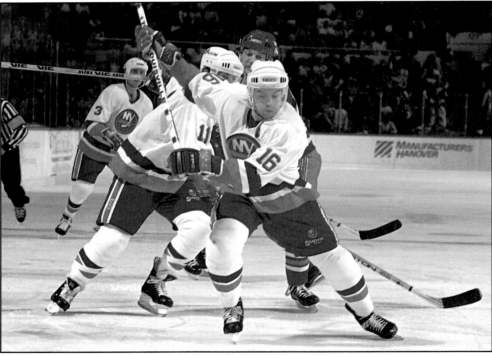

1985-86

Best Record
Edmonton
(56-17-7)

Stanley Cup Finals
Montreal 4
Calgary 1

Art Ross Trophy
Wayne Gretzky
(52/163/215)

Hart Trophy
Wayne Gretzky

Vezina Trophy
John Vanbiesbrouck

Calder Trophy
Gary Suter

Norris Trophy
Paul Coffey

Lady Byng Trophy
Mike Bossy

with a solid 89 points (40-31-9). Calgary seemed to feed on bad teams, and having three such clubs—Los Angeles, Vancouver, and Winnipeg—in its own division didn't hurt.

The player expected to supply the scoring clout for the Flames was Hakan Loob. In January, coach Johnson placed Eddie Beers and Steve Bozek onto a line with Loob, providing him with speedier mates. It helped, but not enough. Management decided to shake up the team by trading Beers, Gino Cavallini, and Charlie Bourgeois to St. Louis for Joey Mullen, Terry Johnson, and Rik Wilson. Management thought

that Mullen was the big-time scorer the team needed.

Calgary also counted on Lanny McDonald and Doug Risebrough—both of whom were acquired through trades. Well along in hockey years, they brought a wealth of experience and smarts. Late in the season, Calgary GM Cliff Fletcher orchestrated another deal. He shipped Rich Kromm and Steve Konroyd to the Islanders for veteran left winger John Tonelli. The Flames were hoping to amass enough weapons to beat Edmonton in the playoffs.

Another formidable squad was developed in Philadelphia. For the

third time in the last four years, the Flyers finished first in the Patrick Division. The team was fourth in scoring (335) and topped the NHL in defense, allowing 31 fewer goals than runner-up Washington (241-272).

Philly suffered a terrible blow when star goaltender Pelle Lindbergh died in a car crash on November 10, 1985. At the time of the death, the Flyers were 12-2-0. The hockey world expected the team to falter or even to fold. But the Flyers didn't miss a step, as they won their next three straight and seven out of nine following the tragedy. Bob Froese, who had been the backup

Patrick Roy took over as the Canadiens' goalie in 1985-86 and became an instant star. The 20-year-old won 15 out of 20 playoff games and led the Habs to an upset Stanley Cup victory.

Glen Sather was the coach, GM, and architect of the Edmonton dynasty. Assistant John Muckler (*left*) took over the coaching reins in 1989.

Scott Stevens

SOARING SALARIES

Hockey players traditionally have been the most underpaid professional athletes. Maurice Richard, the Babe Ruth of the game, never earned more than $25,000 in a season. Hockey's greatest star, Gordie Howe, didn't earn six figures until the birth of the WHA in the early 1970s.

The salary spiral turned upward for stick-handlers in the mid-1960s with the formation of the NHL Players Association. But it took its biggest leap when the WHA challenged the NHL in the 1970s.

The competition provided by the new league sent salaries soaring. Soon, $100,000 salaries were scorned as chump change. In 1990, St. Louis signed Scott Stevens to a four-year contract worth $5.145 million. On his 27th birthday, Mario Lemieux signed a seven-year deal with Pittsburgh worth $42 million.

In September 1993, a published list of top annual salaries described just how far the NHL had come from its "good old days," with Lemieux at the top at $5 million, followed by Eric Lindros at $3.55 million, Wayne Gretzky at $3 million, Steve Yzerman at $2.7 million, and Mark Messier at $2.53 million. Per year, that is. There were more than 25 million-dollar players at the time, and the number was only expected to grow.

goalie, took over masterfully, leading the league in shutouts with five.

The Philadelphia defense, although it lacked depth, played with grit and determination. The Flyers forwards helped the defense with their almost maniacal back-checking. Coach Mike Keenan seemed to have an endless supply of back-checking forwards, including Ron and Rich Sutter, Rick Tocchet, and Peter Zezel. A host of Flyers stopped the enemy by checking, spearing, slashing, or getting in someone's hair.

A surprise team was Quebec, which topped the tough Adams Division. The

Nords started the season at 7-0-0, slumped badly after that, and then picked up the pace to finish 43-31-6.

The Nords got an unexpected lift from goalie Clint Malarchuk. Here was a fellow who came into the season with a career goals-against average of 4.43 in 40 NHL games. He opened the 1985-86 campaign in the minors and looked like he would stay there—until Richard Sevigny broke his hand. Clint came up and responded with a tremendous season, finishing with a 3.21 GAA and turning in quality outings regularly.

At playoff time, the experts

predicted Edmonton would win its third straight Stanley Cup—provided that coach Glen Sather maintained a modicum of discipline. It seems the Oilers had become a thoroughly wild bunch of hockey players.

Nevertheless, Edmonton breezed past Vancouver in the first round of the Smythe playoffs. Meanwhile, Calgary ousted Winnipeg. The Flames would meet the Oilers in the series they were waiting for.

The Oilers opened at home feeling very confident, and with good reason: They had won 18 straight playoff games in the friendly confines of

Northlands Coliseum. But the Flames were unimpressed. In Game One, McDonald put Calgary ahead at 1:27 of the first period, as the Flames breezed to a 4-1 victory. The Flames pushed Edmonton into overtime in Game Two, but the Oilers won it 6-5 on an Anderson goal.

The series extended to a full seven games with the finale staged in Edmonton. The score was tied 2-2 in the third period when one of the most publicized events in hockey took place.

It began innocently enough as Oiler Steve Smith—a big, young defenseman —stood behind his net with the puck,

looking to send it up ice. Unfortunately for the Oilers, Smith bobbled the puck and never got a handle on it. When he tried to pass the rubber ahead, the puck just sputtered off his stick. It hit the back of goalie Grant Fuhr's left leg and rebounded into the Edmonton net. Flames goaltender Mike Vernon withstood a barrage of Oilers shots in the final minutes to preserve the Calgary win. Edmonton was out of the playoffs.

Meanwhile, another epic upset was taking place in the Patrick Division. The New York Rangers—who had finished in fourth place—stunned a

sold-out Spectrum crowd in Game One with a 6-2 thrashing of the Flyers. The next night, Rangers goaltender John Vanbiesbrouck performed magnificently, stopping 42 of 44 shots—many very difficult—in a losing effort. The Blueshirts managed only 12 shots at Flyer netminder Froese and scored once.

The teams split the two games back at Madison Square Garden and returned to The Spectrum for the fifth and deciding game. The Rangers had not won a final game in a playoff series since 1928, losing ten straight deciding contests.

◀

The spectacular goaltending of John Vanbiesbrouck, shown here stopping Flyer Dave Poulin, helped the Rangers upset Philly in the 1986 playoffs.

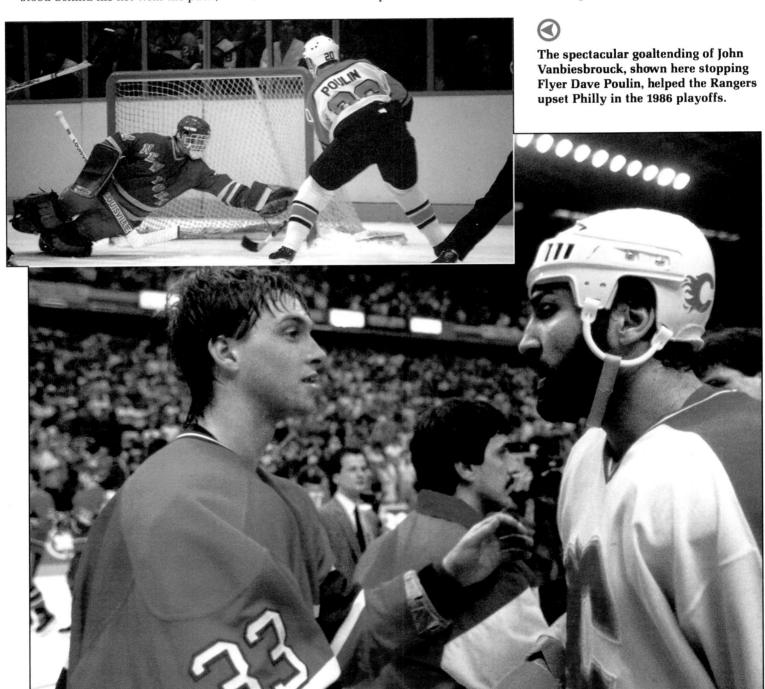

▲ **After falling to Montreal in five games in the 1986 finals, Calgary's John Tonelli congratulates Canadien goalie Patrick Roy. Tonelli had already won four Stanley Cups with the Islanders.**

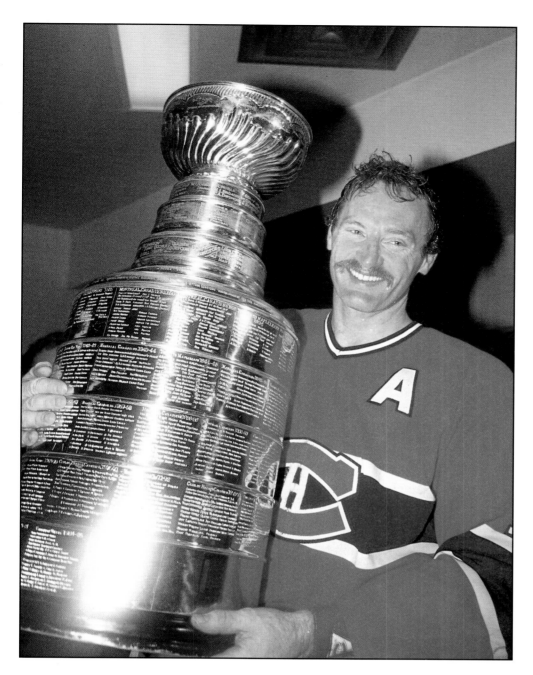

After defeating Calgary in the 1986 finals, defenseman Larry Robinson hoists the Stanley Cup. This was the sixth Stanley Cup for Robinson, who had won five mugs with Montreal in the 1970s.

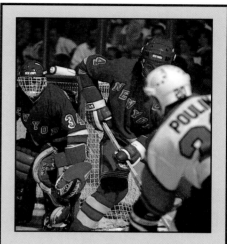

1986 PLAYOFF UPSETS

More than any other year in the 1980s, the 1986 playoffs provided the most exciting and unpredictable action for hockey fans. All four division winners were eliminated by the second round, and just when fans thought they had seen everything, another shocking upset made the headlines.

What made this year so special, besides the galvanic underdog triumphs, was the number of unique stories that unfolded during April and May. Goalie John Vanbiesbrouck singlehandedly guided the Rangers to the semifinals, stunning the mighty Flyers and Capitals along the way.

The Hartford Whalers, in the playoffs for the first time in six seasons, swept past the Adams Division champion Quebec Nordiques and pushed the Montreal Canadiens to the limit in seven tension-filled games. Kevin Dineen scored the key goals for the underdog Whalers.

Out West, the Calgary Flames ousted the invincible Edmonton Oilers in seven games. Edmonton's Steve Smith accidentally knocked one into his own net, which ultimately eliminated his own team.

The Montreal Canadiens utilized a cast of obscure youngsters to storm to their 23rd Stanley Cup, headed by goaltender Patrick Roy, who won the Conn Smythe Trophy. Not to be outdone, rookie Claude Lemieux fired in ten playoff goals, including the overtime series-winner against Hartford.

Pierre Larouche pushed New York to a 1-0 first-period lead, but Ilkka Sinisalo tied the score and the audience anticipated a Flyers surge. However, goals by Willie Huber and Mark Osborne lifted the Rangers to a 3-1 advantage and the Flyers fizzled under the relentless checking of the Ranger forwards. New York added two empty-net goals to clinch the series, winning Game Five by a score of 5-2.

The Rangers then knocked off the Washington Capitals in six games to reach the conference finals for the first time in seven years. The Blueshirts would meet the Montreal Canadiens, who had escaped the Adams Division with a hard-fought win in a seven-game series against the Hartford Whalers. New York was no match for the Canadiens, who disposed of the Rangers in five games. In the other

conference finals, Calgary bested a feisty St. Louis team in seven games.

Thus, the Stanley Cup finals pitted the fabled Canadiens vs. the Johnny-come-lately Flames, who were making their first-ever finals appearance. The Flames looked like Cup champions in Game One at the Saddledome, where they decisively handled the Habs 5-2. However, Montreal buckled down and played like the Canadiens of yesteryear. Montreal won the next four games—3-2, 5-3, 1-0, and 4-3—for their first Stanley Cup championship since 1979.

Habs rookie goalie Patrick Roy won the Smythe Trophy, allowing one goal or less in eight of his 20 games. Gretzky, of course, took the Hart Trophy, his seventh in a row. The Calder was awarded to Calgary's Gary Suter, while the Rangers' Vanbiesbrouck captured the Vezina Trophy.

Stars Rendez-Vous in Quebec;
Fans Cheer in Alberta

1 9 8 6 - 8 7

An eventful 1986-87 season was highlighted by an exhibition played in the middle of winter. Rendez-Vous '87 was a two-game series played between the NHL All-Stars and the Soviet National Team, which took place in Quebec City during Winter Carnival week. The NHLers won the first game 4-3 on February 11, then lost the finale 5-3 on Friday, February 13.

But to summarize Rendez-Vous '87 as such is like calling Wayne Gretzky an okay hockey player. Rendez-Vous '87 was a spectacle—a real "happening," to use '60s jargon. The event was years in the planning, had a cast of thousands, included events that stretched over a week, and necessitated a five-day hiatus in the NHL regular-season schedule.

The games themselves featured exhilarating hockey played by the best in the game, included some chauvinist officiating, and proved virtually nothing about whether the Russians or the NHLers were better. But, almost everyone had a great time.

In Calgary, however, fans were more interested in their Flames. Could Calgary again upset the mighty

 Rendez-Vous '87 featured two games between the NHL All-Stars and the Soviet National Team. The series opened with a ceremonial face-off between Wayne Gretzky (*left*) and Viacheslav Fetisov.

Edmonton Oilers and return to the Stanley Cup finals? The Flames may have gone 1-6-1 against Edmonton in the 1985-86 regular season; but after beating Edmonton in the 1986 playoffs, the Flames gained a psychological edge on the Oilers. In 1986-87, Calgary went 6-1-1 against Edmonton.

Calgary was a solid, stable outfit. Cliff Fletcher had been general manager for the franchise since its Atlanta days, and "Badger" Bob Johnson had been coach for five seasons. The Flames were big and strong and quick, had the best power play in the NHL, and boasted excellent goaltenders in young Mike Vernon and Reggie Lemelin.

Calgary's only problem was that

Edmonton was still in the same division. Whenever the Oilers were mentioned, the first word that popped up was "offense." The most impressive characteristic of the Oilers' attack was its efficiency. Sixteen other teams took more shots on goal during 1986-87, yet the Oilers scored more goals than any other team.

Gretzky led the NHL in scoring for the seventh straight season, tallying 183 points on 62 goals. League runner-up, linemate Jari Kurri, was 75 points behind; Kurri notched 54 goals and 54 assists. Teammate Mark Messier finished one point behind Kurri with 107 points (on 37 goals). This trio powered Edmonton to a 50-24-6 record, the best in the NHL.

PETER STASTNY

In a between-periods interview during the 1987-88 season, Peter Stastny was dumfounded when the broadcaster suggested he would certainly be voted into the Hockey Hall of Fame. "I'm flattered," said Stastny. "I had never thought about it before." Yet, many others have given it considerable thought. And for good reason.

After coming over from Czechoslovakia, Stastny won the Calder Trophy in 1980-81, setting rookie records for the most points and assists in a season (109 and 70). From that point on, Peter and kid brother Anton virtually carried the Quebec Nordiques through the 1987-88 campaign.

Quebec never won a Stanley Cup with Stastny, but it was surely no fault of Peter's. In 64 playoff games with Quebec, he totaled 81 points. Stastny was traded to New Jersey in 1989-90 and retired while with St. Louis in 1994-95.

If Stastny could be compared in style to any other NHL superstar, it would be Islanders great Bryan Trottier. Each was creative with the puck, industrious to a fault, and able to score goals as well. Peter proved to be both consistent and productive. He surpassed 1,000 points during his tenth NHL season.

Whalers Coach Jack "Tex" Evans turned Hartford into a major player in 1986-87. The Whalers captured the tough Adams Division, though they lost to Quebec in Round One of the playoffs.

Edmonton's Glenn Anderson breaks through the Iron Curtain in Rendez-Vous '87 action. The NHLers won the first game of the two-game series 4-3, but lost the second 5-3.

While they were no match in the scoring department, the hard-working Philadelphia Flyers did tally 100 points on the season. They received splendid goaltending from turbulent Ron Hextall and superior coaching from Mike Keenan. And as always, the Flyers played it tough. With relentless checking and tight defense, the Flyers allowed the second fewest goals in the NHL (245).

Some thought Keenan was too tough on his players. In one instance, center Ron Sutter was upset with his coach, claiming that Keenan had rushed him back into action too soon after his back injury. Other players were reportedly upset over Keenan's kamikaze tactics.

Wrote Walt MacPeek of Newark's *Star-Ledger:* "Some Flyers, believe it or not, do not like the way their coach sends them out on the ice with instructions to fight or 'get' players from opposing teams. The insult to their professionalism is just that much more hard to accept when he makes an assistant, usually Paul Holmgren, relay the orders."

Criticism or not, Keenan kept Philadelphia No. 1 in the Patrick Division. He proved adroit in fitting goalie Hextall into the lineup, even though others believed the youngster was being rushed.

One of the NHL's up-and-coming teams was the Hartford Whalers, a

club that had built through the draft. Centerman Ron Francis was Hartford's best offensive player (93 points, 30 goals), although he slumped in April for the second season in a row. Paul Lawless, a speedy left winger, achieved career highs with 22 goals and 54 points, despite missing 12 games as a result of injury. Left winger Sylvain Turgeon, a quick and classy forward, was injury-prone; he missed the first 39 games.

Right wing Kevin Dineen (79 points, 40 goals) turned out to be the Whalers' biggest and most pleasant surprise. As a third-round pick, he didn't classify as a sleeper but nonetheless outperformed original projections. The

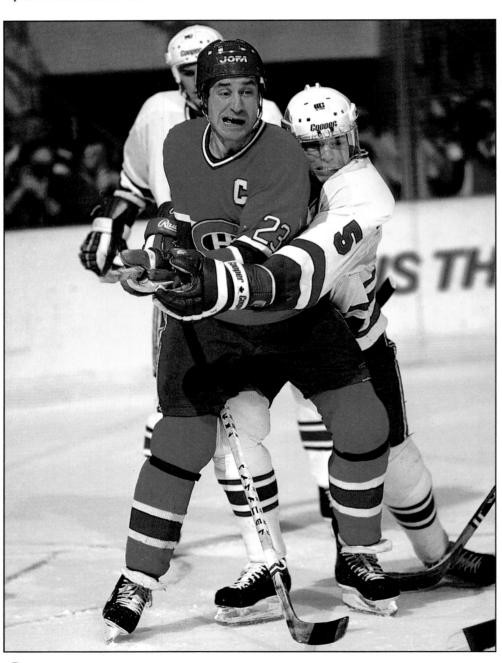

 Hartford defenseman Ulf Samuelsson tangos with Montreal's Bob Gainey.

1986-87

Best Record
Edmonton
(50-24-6)

Stanley Cup Finals
Edmonton 4
Philadelphia 3

Art Ross Trophy
Wayne Gretzky
(62/121/183)

Hart Trophy
Wayne Gretzky

Vezina Trophy
Ron Hextall

Calder Trophy
Luc Robitaille

Norris Trophy
Ray Bourque

Lady Byng Trophy
Joe Mullen

During the 1980s, U.S. First Lady Nancy Reagan promoted a "Just Say No" to drugs campaign. This is the hockey stick she used for several public service television announcements.

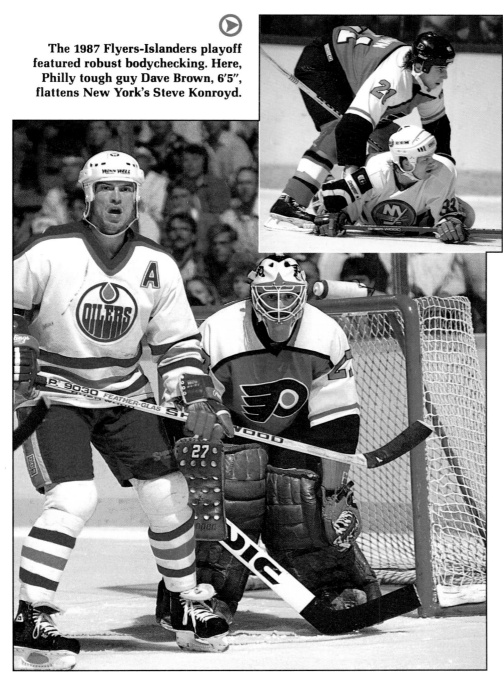

The 1987 Flyers-Islanders playoff featured robust bodychecking. Here, Philly tough guy Dave Brown, 6'5", flattens New York's Steve Konroyd.

Rookie goalie Ron Hextall, the 1986-87 Vezina Trophy winner, appeared in 26 playoff games that spring, going the full route in 25 of them.

ISLES VS. CAPITALS, 1987

Those who came to the seventh and deciding game of the 1987 Patrick Division semifinal—pitting the New York Islanders and Washington Capitals at the Capital Centre—expected an exciting game. When they left over six hours later, they had witnessed the most memorable hockey game of the 1980s—a four-overtime thriller in which the Isles prevailed 3-2.

Consider the final statistics after six-plus periods: 132 total shots on goal, 75 by Washington. And it wasn't just the outrageous numbers. It was the number of quality chances that Isles goalie Kelly Hrudey and Caps goalie Bob Mason turned away.

Both netminders matched each other save for save. A spectacular Hrudey glove save on a Bobby Gould slapper was answered by Mason's point-blank stops on Bob Bassen and Duane Sutter. Mason even had his helmet knocked off during a goalmouth flurry in the second overtime, and he still managed to thwart two close-in shots.

Finally, at 1:56 a.m. on Easter Sunday, Pat LaFontaine's blue-line slapshot ended the Caps' misery. The Islanders lost their next series to the Flyers, but the talk of the 1987 playoffs was definitely the "Easter Epic."

club's real sleeper was Ray Ferraro (59 points on 27 goals), a fifth-round pick in 1982.

Ulf Samuelsson was a mainstay of the Hartford defense, earning the best plus/minus mark and the most penalty minutes among the backliners. Samuelsson was outstanding at keeping the ice clear around the Hartford slot and crease areas.

Perhaps the most enigmatic Whaler was coach Jack Evans. Just a season earlier, the fans at Hartford Civic Center hung banners from the rafters that cried, "JACK MUST GO!" Yet the stoic Evans stayed, and in 1986-87 there were no anti-Evans banners. And for good reason. The Whalers won the

Adams Division with a 43-30-7 record, one point ahead of the legendary Montreal Canadiens.

"If Jack isn't coach of the year," quipped his boss, Emile Francis, "then I'm a monkey's uncle." Evans wasn't voted the Adams Award as top coach... nor did he fare well in the playoffs.

In the first round of Adams playoff action, Quebec upset Hartford in six games, while Montreal swept Boston in four. In the Norris, first-place St. Louis was instantly knocked out by Toronto, which had finished fourth. And the Detroit Red Wings, who had been so feeble for so many years, opened the playoffs by sweeping Chicago.

The Calgary Flames, who had hoped

to meet Edmonton in the playoffs again, never quite made it. In the first round of Smythe action, Winnipeg doused the Flames in six games. Edmonton crowned the Kings in five.

In the Patrick, Philadelphia ousted the Rangers in six games. But by far the most exciting first-round matchup featured the Islanders and Capitals. The series lasted a full seven games and wasn't settled until the finale's fourth overtime! Early on Easter Sunday morning, New York's Pat LaFontaine beat goalie Bob Mason for the win, ending 128 minutes and 47 seconds of nail-biting action.

In the division championships, Edmonton blew by Winnipeg while

Young Kelly Buchberger served as Edmonton's enforcer in the 1987 finals.

GRANT FUHR

Grant Fuhr, never a media darling, was always overshadowed by such Edmonton teammates as Wayne Gretzky, Mark Messier, and Jari Kurri. But Fuhr was extraordinary in net—the preeminent goaltender of the late 1980s.

Fuhr's achievements speak more eloquently than the netminder himself. He played on five Stanley Cup championship teams and was a member of the NHL's First All-Star Team.

Fuhr has been special in many ways. He's led the league in miraculous saves, as he's pulled puck after puck out of nowhere. He was also the NHL's first black goalie, although he said he never felt any discrimination.

For several years, Fuhr shared goaltending duties with Andy Moog during the regular season, but Grant invariably got the nod in big games. In the fall of 1987, Moog opted to play for the Canadian Olympic team, and Fuhr was burdened with the heaviest workload of his life. He played in a record 75 games and produced a 3.43 average. In the playoffs, Grant was in goal for every one of Edmonton's 18 games, as the Oilers marched to their fourth Cup triumph in five years.

In the 1990s, Fuhr has played for Toronto, Buffalo, L.A., and St. Louis, and he was still going strong for St. Louis in 1995-96.

Montreal eliminated Quebec. The Isles took Philadelphia to seven games but were beaten by Philadelphia 5-1 in the finale. The Toronto-Detroit series was another thriller; the Wings won the finale 3-0 and entered the semifinals for the first time in 21 years.

Detroit didn't last long, though, as Edmonton dismantled the Wings in five games. The Flyers, employing brawn as well as style, knocked off the Habs in six. Edmonton entered the Stanley Cup finals as the favorite, though Philadelphia hoped to muscle its way to the title.

Oilers coach Glen Sather, aware that the Flyers would use force, inserted hulking rookie Kelly Buchberger into

the lineup for Game One. Buchberger's job was to neutralize Philly bruiser Dave Brown and thereby open the ice for Gretzky & Co.

Other Oiler heavies also delivered their message early, namely Kevin McClelland and Marty McSorley. Consequently, Brown and the Flyers played more like lambs than lions. Nevertheless, Philly still managed to extend the series to seven games. How? Gretzky offered a partial answer.

"We could have won the series in four straight," said the Great One, "if we hadn't gotten careless in the third game. Remember, we were up 3-0 (and also two games to none). If we had concentrated all the way, we'd have

taken the game and, I'm sure, wrapped it up in four."

The Oilers overwhelmed Philly in Game Seven but were unable to open more than a one-goal gap. They finally moved ahead by two goals in the dying moments of the game, as Glenn Anderson unloaded a tremendous slapshot past an exhausted (and screened) Hextall. The Oilers had regained the Stanley Cup.

Besides his third Stanley Cup and seventh Art Ross Trophy, Gretzky won his eight consecutive Hart Trophy. Calgary's Joe Mullen earned the Lady Byng while Boston's Ray Bourque took home the Norris for the first time. Hextall walked off with the Vezina.

Troubled Oilers Drop Coffey, Hang On to the Cup

1 9 8 7 - 8 8

By the late 1980s, the theme around the NHL went, "As Wayne Gretzky goes, so go the Edmonton Oilers." When the Great One was in great condition, he led the NHL in scoring and the Oilers were invincible. When he suffered injury, the Oilers were noticeably inferior.

The 1987-88 season was a perfect example, as the defending champions lost their captain for 16 games and also lost first place to the Calgary Flames. But Edmonton had many other problems, starting with training camp.

The headaches began when former Norris Trophy-winning defenseman Paul Coffey quit the team in a contract hassle with management. Rather than bend to his ace's wishes, Glen Sather first let Coffey brew alone; he then shipped him to the Pittsburgh Penguins in an elaborate deal that brought sniper Craig Simpson to Edmonton.

Backup goalie Andy Moog gave Sather another migraine. Moog, a proven talent, was tired of playing second fiddle to starter Grant Fuhr. He went to play for the Canadian Olympic team and later was traded to the Boston Bruins. Without Coffey and Moog, and with an injured Gretzky, the Oilers seemed more vulnerable than they had been in years.

To make matters worse, grumblings were heard from the Edmonton locker room. Some Oilers didn't like the manner in which owner Peter Pocklington was handling some of his players, including Gretzky. The rumblings would become louder later in the season and finally would explode the following summer with a Gretzky-led mutiny.

The Oilers were not the only team with problems. Because he had chopped down Kent Nilsson during the 1987 Stanley Cup finals, Flyers goalie Ron Hextall was suspended for the first eight games of the 1987-88 campaign. Although it wasn't apparent at the time, Hextall's suspension would have a long-range effect on the Flyers—and would lead to the ousting of coach Mike Keenan.

Marty McSorley (*left*) and Rick Middleton battle through a fog at Boston Garden during the 1988 finals.

After a contract dispute with the Oilers, defenseman Paul Coffey (right) was traded to Pittsburgh in November 1987. Despite numerous clubhouse squabbles in 1987-88, Edmonton's GM and coach Glen Sather (left) kept his troops in line. The Oilers accumulated 99 points on the year and skated all the way to the Stanley Cup.

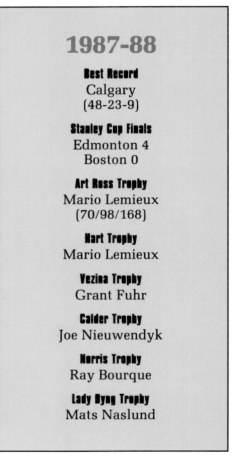

1987-88

Best Record
Calgary
(48-23-9)

Stanley Cup Finals
Edmonton 4
Boston 0

Art Ross Trophy
Mario Lemieux
(70/98/168)

Hart Trophy
Mario Lemieux

Vezina Trophy
Grant Fuhr

Calder Trophy
Joe Nieuwendyk

Norris Trophy
Ray Bourque

Lady Byng Trophy
Mats Naslund

Early in the season, Philadelphia's primary bully, Dave Brown, pole-axed Tomas Sandstrom of the New York Rangers. The episode, which took place at Madison Square Garden, reverberated across the continent and transcended the hockey world. For the Flyers, it created the most adverse publicity since the Dave Schultz Era.

The Flyers got off to a miserable start, which was difficult to digest for a team accustomed to winning. This led to a tension-filled locker room. Keenan feuded with Rick Tocchet; Brad McCrimmon could not come to terms with Philadelphia and was dealt to Calgary—a move that irked Flyer

Mark Howe; and Hextall, ironically, became a marked man.

Hextall's aggressive tactics, while intimidating to many forwards, began inspiring counter-attacks. "More guys on the opposition seemed to think I was 'fair game' and were going after me," said Hextall.

Like most of their Patrick Division opponents, the Flyers ebbed and flowed like the tides. By Christmas 1987, they played like avenging Cup finalists and moved toward the top of their division. "We looked good enough to go all the way," said catalyst Peter Zezel, "then the injuries just wiped us out." The most notable casualty was

goal-scoring giant Tim Kerr, whose season was ruined by a series of shoulder surgeries.

By season's end, Philly posted a 38-33-9 record (85 points). Amazingly, all six teams in the Patrick finished with between 81 and 88 points.

Over in Calgary, the Flames were without coach Bob Johnson, who left to become chief amateur hockey guru in the United States. Without Badger Bob, many predicted that the Flames were headed for the southern portion of the Smythe Division.

The Flames had other problems as well. John Tonelli had slowed to a crawl and seemed to have lost his zip.

Lanny McDonald had lost just about everything but his Yosemite Sam moustache, while Hakan Loob seemed to have his heart in Sweden. Then there was rookie coach Terry Crisp, who had a loud mouth and no NHL coaching experience to back it up.

If that wasn't bad enough, the Flames lost top defenseman Jamie Macoun for the year after he suffered an off-season automobile accident. Finally, potential All-Star Paul Reinhart suffered the effects of a chronic bad back. Some thought the Flames would fall to last place. And yet, when the curtain fell in April, Calgary boasted the best record in

hockey, 48-23-9. How did they do it?

"We've been very, very fortunate the way our new players have turned out," said Flames GM Cliff Fletcher. "Joe Nieuwendyk, Brian Glynn, and Brett Hull, who we eventually traded for a pretty good return. Add to that the way Brad McCrimmon plugged a big hole on defense."

The biggest change of all for Calgary was behind the bench. The outspoken Crisp was a 180-degree turnaround from his predecessor, Johnson. Crisp didn't keep notepads or hold intense skull sessions, as was the case with Johnson. But Crisp got through to his players, particularly Nieuwendyk. Joe

was expected to score somewhere between 25 and 30 goals; but under Crisp, he finished the campaign with an astonishing 51 tallies. He won the Calder Trophy and was as much a reason as anyone why the Flames burned brightly.

Less serene were the Montreal Canadiens, who experienced a turmoil-filled season that affected them more off the ice than on it. The following are a list of disturbing incidents that hindered the Habs:

● During a game at Chicago, Chris Chelios got into a shouting match with coach Jean Perron on the team bench.

● According to rumor, the team's

RAY BOURQUE

Just as Denis Potvin was overshadowed by defenseman Bobby Orr, Ray Bourque was burned by Paul Coffey's press clippings. It wasn't until the 1986-87 season that Bourque became the top banana of the NHL blue-line bunch.

Ray has not only annexed five Norris Trophies, but he has also demonstrated many of Bobby Orr's qualities. And the comparisons to Orr do have a certain validity. Clearly, Bourque's biggest asset on the ice is his skating ability. He has speed and agility that is almost unmatched in the NHL.

Ray can also play the physical game with the best of the NHL backliners. He is not afraid to use the body, and his play in the corners is often fearsome. Bourque's upper-body strength also allows him to fire a rocket from the point.

Because of his skill and durability, Bourque was frequently asked to log extra ice time. Eventually, fatigue did set in, and Ray seemed tired and less effective in the Bruins' 1988 and 1990 Stanley Cup finals losses to Edmonton.

There's very little that Ray Bourque can't do. He is surely the most dangerous player on the Boston Bruins, and one of the best blue-liners in NHL history. He was named to either the First or Second All-Star Team in each of his first 16 years.

▲ Defenseman Chris Chelios was one of the Canadiens who bickered with coach Jean Perron. Despite the in-fighting, Montreal went on to win 45 games.

▲ Canadiens coach Jean Perron (pointing) got the axe in 1988.

veteran defensemen planned to convince Perron to go with only five backliners and eliminate young defenseman Mike Lalor.

• Perron angered his French-speaking players by declaring that some francophone Canadiens thought they were big shots and needed to be cut down to size.

• Winger Chris Nilan openly criticized Perron, asked to be traded, and was dealt to the New York Rangers.

• Veteran defenseman Larry Robinson told friends he was tired of all the politics on the team, and he also took Perron to task. Eventually, Perron was fired.

Through the whole ugly mess, the Habs managed to fight off a determined bid by the Boston Bruins and secure first place in the tough Adams Division.

For a time, it looked like Buffalo would win the Adams. Under new coach Ted Sator, the Sabres did so well that by mid-January Neil Campbell of *The (Toronto) Globe and Mail* wrote: "They should name Ted Sator coach of the year right now, before his Sabres melt away." Buffalo did melt a little, but they still finished with 85 points, 21 more than the year before.

The most romantic team of 1987-88 was the New Jersey Devils, who struggled until coach Doug Carpenter was fired on January 26, 1988. Rookie GM Lou Lamoriello replaced Carpenter with former NHL defenseman Jim Schoenfeld. The Devils got a huge boost after the 1988 Winter Games when Canadian Olympic goalie Sean Burke joined the team. Suddenly, the Devils got hot and began reeling off win after win. They visited Chicago on the last day of the season needing a victory to clinch a playoff berth. Stunningly, they got it on John MacLean's goal in overtime.

The Jerseyites rode their magic into the playoffs, disposing the Islanders in the opening round and then stretching Washington to seven games in the division finals. Game Seven was tied late in the third period when MacLean

The Devils knocked off both the Islanders and Capitals in the 1988 playoffs. Here, David Maley (8) and Brendan Shanahan (11) tie up Capitals defenseman Kevin Hatcher.

The Devils celebrate a goal at Byrne Arena in the 1988 playoffs. Washington netminder Pete Peeters picks the puck out of the net, while New Jersey's Tom Kurvers goes to celebrate with his mates. The Devils won the series in seven games to advance to the Wales Conference finals.

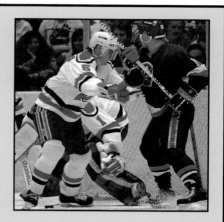

DEVILS PLAYOFF RUN, 1988

Perhaps the biggest Cinderella story of the 1980s was the 1988 New Jersey Devils—the "Mickey Mouse" team that needed overtime of game No. 80 to make the playoffs and came within one game of reaching the Stanley Cup finals.

The arrival of Canadian Olympic goalie Sean Burke sparked the team in March, as he went 10-1. Still, the Devils needed to beat Chicago in the season finale in order to make the playoffs. They did, as John MacLean rifled home a shot in overtime.

New Jersey split the first four games of the opening round against the first-place Islanders. But the Devils prevailed on Long Island in Game Five and clinched the upset with a thrilling 6-5 nail-biter at Byrne Arena. The Washington Capitals provided a formidable opponent in the Patrick Division finals, but the Devils' mystique continued. They edged the Caps in seven. During that series, Swedish star Patrik Sundstrom set an NHL playoff record when he notched eight points in a 10-4 victory over Washington.

New Jersey faced Boston in the Wales Conference finals, and, amazingly, pushed the series to seven games. Boston led Game Seven 3-0, only to see the Devils close to within a goal. However, the Bruins put the game away midway through the third period with a 6-2 victory.

The Cinderella run had ended for the Devils, but their trip to the ball provided the best story of the 1988 postseason.

did it again, redirecting a shot past Pete Peeters. MacLean's heroics gave the Devils a startling 3-2 win and put them in the Wales Conference finals.

In other playoff action, a surprisingly strong Detroit team emerged victorious in the Norris. Calgary met Edmonton in the Smythe Division finals, but the Oilers swept the Flames in four straight. Finally, Boston fought off its opponents in the Adams Division.

In the Wales Conference finals, Boston was expected to obliterate New Jersey. The Devils did extend the series to a full seven games, but they eventually succumbed to the Beantowners.

In the Campbell Conference finals, Edmonton zipped past the Red Wings in five games in a series that was marred by a mini-scandal. On the night before Game Five, a half-dozen Red Wings—including noted alcohol abusers Bob Probert and Petr Klima—went out drinking. The Wings played horribly the next day, which triggered public outrage in the Motor City.

The Stanley Cup finals were a huge letdown, as Edmonton thumped the Bruins in Games One, Two, and Three. Game Four was tied 3-3 at Boston Garden when, believe it our not, the lights went out. Nobody could turn them back on and the game was suspended. They played Game Five in Edmonton, where the Oilers turned out the Bruins' lights with a 6-3 win. The Oilers skated off with their fourth Stanley Cup in five years.

Mario Lemieux, who dethroned Gretzky as leading scorer by tallying 70 goals and 98 assists, earned the Hart Trophy. Ray Bourque won his second straight Norris Trophy, Fuhr annexed the Vezina, and Montreal's Mats Naslund was awarded the Lady Byng prize. Gretzky didn't go home empty-handed, as he walked away with the Conn Smythe Trophy.

However, just a few months later, Gretzky's unhappiness with the Oilers would percolate to the surface, and he would be traded to the Los Angeles Kings.

Gretzky Crowned a King in Greatest Trade Ever

1 9 8 8 - 8 9

The simmering unhappiness that had brewed between the Edmonton Oilers and team general manager Glen Sather erupted into the most monumental trade in sports history. Wayne Gretzky, who had been regarded as the least likely player ever to be traded, was dealt to the Los Angeles Kings on August 9, 1988. The Oilers sent Gretzky, Mike Krushelnyski, and Marty McSorley to L.A. for young scoring whiz Jimmy Carson, Martin Gelinas, the Kings' first-round choices in the 1989, 1991, and 1993 Entry Drafts, and a staggering $15 million.

Kings owner Bruce McNall was gambling that Gretzky could transform Los Angeles hockey into a marquee sport. "When you get the greatest player who ever lived," said McNall, "you know the fans will respond."

He was right. The outpouring of enthusiasm was instantaneous and immense. Fans gobbled up tickets, and for the first time in the club's history, the Kings sold out on opening night. In his Los Angeles debut against Detroit, Gretzky—with his usual dramatic flair—scored the game's first goal en route to a Kings victory.

▲ In the "Deal of the Century," Wayne Gretzky was dealt from Edmonton to L.A. on August 9, 1988. Here, Gretzky takes the podium in Tinseltown to explain why he's happy to be a King.

Gretzky did everything expected of him, filling the Forum, igniting unprecedented hockey interest in Los Angeles, and turning the Kings into a contender. By season's end, the Great One had turned in another superb scoring performance, with 54 goals, 114 assists, and 168 points. Carson rang up 49 goals and 100 points but the rookie Gelinas was a nonfactor.

Indeed, the loss of Gretzky adversely affected the Oilers, who stumbled throughout the season. Without Gretzky, the Edmonton offense was carried by Carson, Jari Kurri, and Mark Messier, but none could compensate for the loss of hockey's most productive scorer. The Oilers dropped to third place in the Smythe Division, only four games above the .500 mark.

Despite his productive season, Gretzky was bypassed in the scoring race for the second straight year. More commanding than ever, Mario Lemieux ran away with the scoring race, reaching 85 goals and 199 points. He shared the league lead in assists with Gretzky (114). The Kings' Bernie Nicholls was living proof of Gretzky's powerful influence, as he finished second in the NHL in goals with a personal best 70 red lights in 79 games.

For the first time, another name entered the Golden Circle. Detroit's multi-talented Steve Yzerman crowded Gretzky in the scoring race and topped the Great One in goals (65-54). The Red Wings captain finished with 155 points, pacing the Wings to a first-place finish in the Norris Division. For his excellent work, Yzerman took home the Lester B. Pearson Award as the outstanding player of the year, as voted by his peers in the players' association.

Unquestionably, the league's biggest disappointments were the New York Islanders and the New Jersey Devils, each of whom had made the playoffs a year earlier. The Isles slipped under coach Terry Simpson, who was fired in midseason and replaced by Al Arbour. The Isles tumbled from first to last in one year. Meanwhile, the Devils' rousing playoff run in 1988 did little for them in the new season. Coach Jim Schoenfeld managed to keep his job, but

▲ **Red Wing heartthrob Steve Yzerman tallied 155 points in 1988-89.**

▲ **In 1988-89, Guy Lafleur came out of retirement to play for the Rangers.**

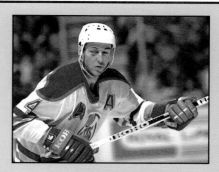

KEVIN LOWE

For years, Edmonton's Kevin Lowe was overshadowed by such flamboyant characters as Wayne Gretzky, Mark Messier, and Glenn Anderson, as well as his dynamic blue-line teammate, Paul Coffey.

Lowe has been a keep-my-own-end-clean brand of back-liner since his NHL debut in 1979. There has always been a bite to his bodychecks and a mean streak that all the great defensemen possess.

Lowe's importance to the Oilers was never more evident than during the 1987-88 season. He played the best defense of his life following the Coffey trade, but suffered a serious arm injury during the homestretch. Medical sources said he would be unable to return for the 1988 playoffs.

Never fear. The gritty Lowe returned to the lineup before the playoffs began. Bedeviled with a cast and limited in his range, Kevin nevertheless became an inspiration for the Oilers, who went on to win the Cup.

Noted Gretzky: "I'd hate to think where the Edmonton Oilers would be without Kevin Lowe." The Rangers, for whom Lowe has played since 1992-93, feel the same way.

none of the magic worked a second time around. New Jersey finished a dismal fifth in the six-team Patrick Division.

As scenarios go, none was more bizarre than the one involving the New York Rangers. Under turbulent coach Michel Bergeron, the Rangers were a force in the Patrick Division through most of the season. But Bergeron and general manager Phil Esposito feuded endlessly, and only days before the season ended Esposito pushed the panic button. He fired Bergeron and put himself behind the bench. Entering the playoffs in the midst of managerial chaos proved to be the kiss of death for the Rangers, whose quest for a Stanley Cup neared the 50-year mark. In a display of sheer collapse, the club was swept in four games by Pittsburgh.

The Pittsburgh club, already dangerous thanks to the work of Lemieux, was bolstered in goal with the midseason acquisition of goalie Tom Barrasso. The Pens landed Barrasso in exchange for former first-round draft pick Doug Bodger, an outstanding defenseman who would help Buffalo immeasurably in years to come. Meanwhile, on the bright side for the Blueshirts was the rapid development of Brian Leetch as a dominant defenseman. Leetch won the Calder Trophy, edging Vancouver's Trevor Linden and fellow Ranger Tony Granato, and became the anchor of the Ranger power play.

The Rangers weren't the only Patrick Division team in deep playoff trouble. The Capitals, who finished atop the division in the regular season, and who bolstered their offense with the acquisition of dynamic Dino Ciccarelli, fell to the Flyers in six first-round games. The blockbuster deal bringing Ciccarelli to D.C. cost the Caps dearly, as Mike Gartner and Larry Murphy headed to the North Stars.

The best coaching job in the NHL was turned in by newcomer Pat Burns, who led Montreal to a first-place finish (53-18-9). Amazingly, not a single Canadien could be found among the top 24 scorers in the league, although Montreal defenseman Chris Chelios finished fourth in scoring among the backliners. Defense was the Canadiens' forte and, not surprisingly, Patrick Roy won the Vezina Trophy.

Montreal, a team known for

L.A. defenseman Dale Degray bangs Edmonton's Glenn Anderson into the glass during the 1989 playoffs. The Kings ousted the Oilers in seven.

Calgary defenseman Rob Ramage pesters Montreal's Brian Skrudland during the 1989 Stanley Cup finals.

Flames captain Lanny McDonald had been a big-leaguer since 1973, but it wasn't until his retirement season, 1988-89, that he played for a Stanley Cup winner.

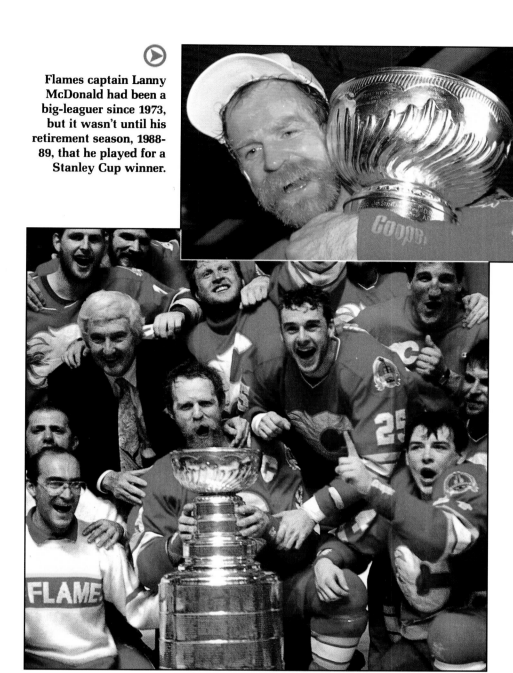

The Flames pose for a team picture immediately after winning the Cup. The silver-haired gent on the left is GM Cliff Fletcher.

THE GRETZKY TRADE

In the biggest sports trade in history, Edmonton hero Wayne Gretzky was traded to the L.A. Kings in August 1988. In the deal, Edmonton swapped Gretzky, Mike Krushelnyski, and Marty McSorley for Jimmy Carson, Martin Gelinas, three first-round draft picks, and $15 million.

It seems Oilers owner Peter Pocklington was inspired by the $15 million more than anything else. But what impact did Wayne's wife, actress Janet Jones, have on the move? Insiders believed she inspired Wayne to look to L.A. when it became apparent that Pocklington was determined to trade him.

By winning the Stanley Cup in 1990, the Oilers proved something by doing it without Wayne, although they still felt attached to the "Great One." During the Cup celebration, Oiler Kevin Lowe said, "Mark Messier and I looked at each other and said: 'This one's for the G-man because he's still such a big part of our team.'"

Meanwhile, the Gretzky-led Kings have enjoyed some success. They knocked off the defending champion Calgary Flames in the opening round of the 1990 playoffs, only to be halted by the Oilers in the division finals.

swinging deals that bordered on highway robbery, did it to the woeful Toronto Maple Leafs early in the year. They swapped the pugnacious John Kordic to Toronto in exchange for unhappy Russ Courtnall, a speedster with a rifle shot. Courtnall regained his scoring touch (23 goals) while Kordic amassed penalty time (198 minutes) and wore out his NHL welcome.

More and more American-born players were emerging in the NHL. Among rookie scoring leaders, three out of the first four—Leetch, Granato, and Craig Janney—were born in the USA. While hockey continued to be a young man's game, oldtimers still made their mark—especially Guy Lafleur, the former Montreal star who had been inactive for more than three

seasons. Esposito lured him out of retirement and Lafleur responded with a commendable season, notching 18 goals and 45 points in 67 games with the Rangers. Enthusiastic chants of "Guy, Guy, Guy" resounded throughout the league.

No team, apart from the Kings, attracted more attention than the Gretzky-less Oilers. Edmontonians just couldn't get No. 99 out of their minds. On his first visit to Northlands Coliseum since the trade, Gretzky was hailed as a conquering hero. Fans carried banners proclaiming "DOWN THE DRAIN WITHOUT WAYNE" and many wore Los Angeles jerseys.

The Oilers' first tour of the NHL produced a turnout of media anxious to compare the 1988-89 edition with

the Cup winners. Over and over, players such as Gretzky, Messier, and Kevin Lowe answered the questions, but some of the best replies came from opponents like the Calgary Flames.

"Without Wayne," said Flames goalie Mike Vernon, "the Oilers look like they're trying to fly a plane without the pilot."

Defenseman Gary Suter added, "Gretzky symbolized the Oilers for a lot of years. His absence has taken away some of the mystique, but it would be foolish to say they'll be pushovers just because he's gone. They still have more pure talent than anyone in the league."

One of those talents was tenacious Finn Esa Tikkanen, who had an uncanny ability to antagonize any foe.

He accomplished this with errant elbows, sticks to the ribs, and considerable oratory. "I know I'd hate to play against me," laughed Tikkanen. Esa soon became Gretzky's *bete noire*. Esa relished the idea of shadowing the NHL's best players, and he worked over the Great One just as vigorously as he did Lemieux and Yzerman. "These are the best players in the world," said Tikkanen, "which is why I enjoy checking them."

The Gretzky-Edmonton confrontation reached its climax on April 5, 1989, in L.A., when the Oilers and Kings faced off in the opening playoff round. Game One saw the Kings get on the board just 61 seconds into the game on a goal by Chris Kontos, a journeyman pro whose playoff performances far

outshined his regular-season play. But Tikkanen and Craig Simpson scored goals 67 seconds apart in the third period to lift Edmonton past Los Angeles 4-3.

The Oilers eventually opened a three-games-to-one lead in the series, before the Kings staved off elimination in Game Five at home. Now Edmonton returned to the Northlands Coliseum to, presumably, finish off Gretzky and his Kings. However, L.A.'s Kontos, who had been playing in Europe earlier in the year, scored his seventh goal in six playoff games. And with Kelly Hrudey playing the best goal of his life since coming to the club from the New York Islanders in a midseason trade, the Kings won the game 4-1 and sent the series back to Los Angeles.

Game Seven saw the Kings take command early, outshooting Edmonton in the first period 16-8, yet they only led by one goal, 2-1. The Oilers fought back in the second period, however, and eventually tied the score 3-3.

The Oilers' downfall would be a sequence of penalties late in the second period, leaving them two men short. Gretzky orchestrated the power play, delivering a magnificent pass to Nicholls in the slot. Bernie skirted to Grant Fuhr's right before depositing the puck in the twine, giving the Kings a 4-3 lead after two periods.

In the third period, the ebb and flow of the skaters had fans shuddering for nearly 15 minutes, but neither Fuhr nor Hrudey allowed a score. Then it happened. Kings defenseman Dale

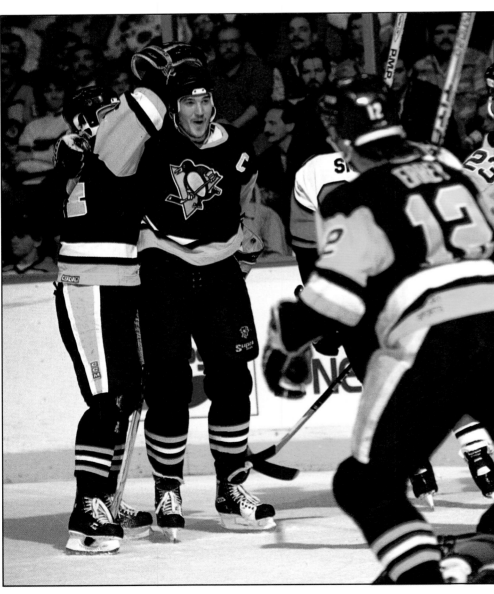

In 1988-89, Mario Lemieux led the NHL with 85 goals (third most in history) and 199 points, though he finished second to Wayne Gretzky in MVP voting.

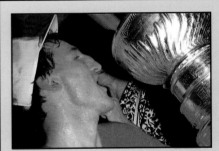

Tim Hunter

CANUCKS VS. FLAMES, 1989

It was David vs. Goliath played to perfection: the defensive-minded Vancouver Canucks against the powerful Calgary Flames in the first round of the 1989 playoffs. But although they were heavy underdogs, the Canucks pushed Calgary to seven games.

In Game Seven, Saddledome fans felt confident after two periods of play, as Joe Mullen's fluke goal put Calgary up by one. However, when Doug Lidster slipped a short shot past Mike Vernon to tie the score, the arena fell deathly silent.

The intensity reached tumultuous heights as the teams moved into overtime. Calgary goalie Mike Vernon made three amazing blocks—a kick save and two brilliant glove stops. Canucks netminder Kirk McLean saved the day himself with a miraculous paddle save on Mullen's sure goal.

Finally, at 19:21 of the first O.T., Flame Joel Otto deflected a centering pass past a helpless McLean. For the Flames, the thrilling match inspired them to capture the Stanley Cup.

Craig Janney, a Connecticut native and a U.S. Olympian, tallied 62 points for the Bruins in 1988-89. The rookie center dittoed his performance the following year before ringing up 92 points in 1990-91.

Ranger rookie Tony Granato was one of the new wave of U.S. natives emerging in the NHL. In 1988-89, Granato earned Calder consideration thanks to his 36 goals.

Degray, a castoff like Kontos, drilled a 50-foot power-play shot past Fuhr with 5:46 left in the period to give Los Angeles a two-goal cushion. Finally, Gretzky nailed the Oilers' coffin shut with an open-net score. The Forum erupted into a frenzy as the champions were dethroned.

"I have mixed emotions about the win," Gretzky admitted afterward. "There were a lot of personal emotions involved and, for that reason, I didn't enjoy the series as much as I might have."

Meanwhile, Calgary's opening playoff series against Vancouver went the full seven games, proving to be one of the most exciting in recent history.

It was climaxed in overtime of Game Seven when goalie Vernon rescued his club with heart-stopping heroics, including an unforgettable glove save on a Stan Smyl breakaway. Joel Otto enabled the Flames to advance by scoring in overtime. A shot from the point glanced off his leg and eluded Canuck goalie Kirk McLean.

Calgary, after being one goal away from elimination, marched all the way to the Stanley Cup finals, as they swept the Kings in the division finals and then disposed of the Chicago Blackhawks in five in the conference finals.

The Flames went on to meet the Montreal Canadiens who, in beating Hartford, Boston, and Philadelphia,

lost a total of just three games. Calgary successfully avenged their 1986 Cup loss to Montreal by knocking off the Habs in six closely contested games. It was a storybook ending for Calgary's Lanny McDonald, who scored a pivotal goal in Game Six at Montreal. The goal helped Calgary win its first Stanley Cup in franchise history. Ironically, it was the last goal McDonald ever scored.

McDonald's teammate, Al MacInnis, earned the Conn Smythe Trophy on the strength of his 24 playoff assists. Another Flame, Joe Mullen, won the Lady Byng, while Montreal's Chelios took the Norris. Gretzky took home the Hart Trophy, his ninth of the decade.

NEW SENSATIONS

**The NHL opens its doors to
new teams, new cultures, and
a new wave of superstars.**

St. Louis' Brett Hull *(left)* and Pittsburgh's Mario Lemieux *(right)* stole the limelight in the early 1990s. In three years, Hull scored 228 goals while Lemieux won two Stanley Cups and two Conn Smythes.

THE 1990s

Early in the decade, the 1990s showed all the signs of being a renaissance period for the NHL. The league had seen the birth of a new Stanley Cup power in Pittsburgh, where Mario Lemieux was simply the game's most dominant player; a revival of the New York Rangers as Stanley Cup champions after a 54-year drought; and, of course, the ubiquitous presence of the Montreal Canadiens in the championship hunt.

Teams who'd been down on their luck in recent years, such as Chicago, Detroit, Vancouver, and the New Jersey Devils, showed signs of life. The league also underwent major expansion, bringing five new teams to the circuit: San Jose, Anaheim, Ottawa, Tampa Bay, and (South) Florida.

The NHL also saw a new crop of scoring aces, many with exotic names. Along with Brett Hull, Kevin Stevens, and Gary Roberts, the league welcomed Teemu Selanne from Finland, the quartet of Alexander Mogilny, Sergei Fedorov, Pavel Bure, and Alexei Zhamnov from Russia, Jaromir Jagr from Czechoslovakia, and Mikael Renberg from Sweden as new Top Ten scorers.

But all the news was not good. There was labor turmoil between management and the NHL Players Association. Negotiations for a new collective bargaining agreement collapsed and caused a temporary work stoppage during the tail end of the 1991-92 season, delaying the start of the playoffs.

Then, after talks went nowhere during the off-season following the 1993-94 campaign, the owners instituted a lockout, threatening to cancel the season if they did not see a restructuring of salaries, free agency, and other revenue sharing. The lockout lasted more than three months and ultimately resulted in a 48-game schedule.

The lockout could not have come at a worse time. The NHL was at an all-time high in popularity. Television ratings were up, fan interest was raging in Southern California (where hockey was once seen as a dying ember), and the game seemed to be enjoying a new level of legitimacy among the four major professional sports.

But the league was under new leadership by now. John A. Ziegler was replaced by Gil Stein in 1992, and Gary Bettman took over as commissioner in 1993. Bettman, who came from the National Basketball Association, took an active role both in forcing the lockout as well as by later pressing the two sides to save the season and resolve their differences. On January 20, 1995, the NHL finally played the first game of its season.

The players who cruise the NHL circuit continue to be bigger, faster, and more talented each year. The game itself is reaching into markets previously thought to be barren of interest. New stars emerge each season, and parity appears to be a genuine reality for the future.

Glasnost Hits NHL;
Oilers Grab Back the Cup

1 9 8 9 - 9 0

One of the most progressive events in international hockey history developed during the summer of 1989. In a move led by New Jersey Devils owner John McMullen, a wave of Soviet hockey stars made their way to North America and signed with NHL teams.

"I had hoped to get them a lot sooner," said McMullen, "but I'm delighted that we finally were able to bring them over." In the case of the Devils, the players were defensemen Viacheslav "Slava" Fetisov and Sergei Starikov. The two were welcomed at a gala press conference that attracted world-wide attention.

Meanwhile, other NHL teams were busily signing their Soviets. The Vancouver Canucks inked Vladimir Krutov (whose nickname, "Tank," would take on new meaning after he arrived in British Columbia overweight) and Igor Larionov, while the Calgary Flames welcomed Sergei Makarov. The most controversial of the Russians was 20-year-old Alexander Mogilny, who, unlike his comrades, defected to the United States at the beginning of what promised to be a sensational career. Despite objections from the Soviet authorities, Mogilny was allowed to remain with the Buffalo Sabres.

The Soviets attracted an inordinate amount of publicity. The cover of *Sports Illustrated*, for example, featured Fetisov and Starikov amid the tall weeds of the New Jersey Meadowlands. Starikov, brought over essentially to "keep Fetisov company," failed to last with the Devils, but Fetisov, regarded as the Denis Potvin of the international hockey scene, remained.

In midseason, New Jersey added still another Soviet player, Alexei Kasatonov. Ironically, the only two Russian-speaking players on the team did not talk to each other. Fetisov had been angry at Kasatonov because of a dispute that dated back to their days on the Soviet National Team. Many of the players on those great Soviet teams had

 Oiler Bill Ranford snares a Boston shot in the 1990 finals. Randy Burridge moves in for the rebound that never came.

viewed Kasatonov as a mole for the coach, Viktor Tikhonov. Nevertheless, the pair worked efficiently together on the Devils defense.

The season was also marked by other dramatic personnel changes. General manager Phil Esposito was fired by the Rangers and replaced by youthful Neil Smith, who had come from the Detroit organization. Smith, in turn, hired veteran Roger Neilson to coach the club.

Smith then packaged a pair of talented, gritty wingers in Tomas Sandstrom and Tony Granato to Los Angeles for Bernie Nicholls, who was coming off a career year. The Blueshirts also shipped hard-working Ulf Dahlen

to Minnesota for Mike Gartner, bringing the speedy sniper back to the Patrick Division, where he had starred as a Capital for so many years. The moves paid immediate dividends, as the Rangers finished on top of their division for the first time since 1942.

Another new bench boss was Boston Bruins coach Mike Milbury who, armed with Ray Bourque and Cam Neely, turned a team of "plumbers" into the best team in the league (46-25-9). With 101 points, the Bruins finished two points better than the Calgary Flames.

Despite Boston's superior record, coach-of-the-year honors went to Bob Murdoch of the Winnipeg Jets. Despite a

modest lineup, Murdoch guided the Jets to a 37-32-11 record and a third-place finish in the Smythe Division. Ironically, Winnipeg's Dale Hawerchuk tallied just 81 points—the fewest of his nine-year career and a direct result of Murdoch's team-first approach.

The Chicago Blackhawks, who snatched premier left winger Michel Goulet from Quebec for three nondescript players, finished atop the Norris Division even though iron-fisted coach Mike Keenan continually battled with his players—Denis Savard in particular. The Hawks were most closely pursued by the St. Louis Blues who, for the first time in club history,

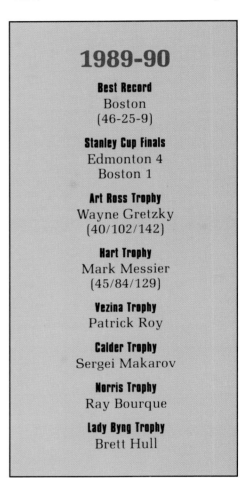

On October 15, 1989, Wayne Gretzky broke Gordie Howe's all-time scoring record of 1,850 points. These are the last 14 pucks Gretzky netted to break Howe's record.

Proof that Americans can produce gifted scorers is Boston-bred Jeremy Roenick. Roenick played so well in 1989-90 that Chicago was able to trade star center Denis Savard.

After being a Canadien since 1973, defenseman Larry Robinson jumped to Los Angeles for the 1989-90 season. Unfortunately, Robinson showed only flashes of his former brilliance.

BRETT HULL

Maurice Richard learned how difficult it was to raise hockey players after his illustrious career. One of the Rocket's sons tried hockey and failed. "There was too much pressure on him," said Richard.

The same could have been said by Bobby Hull, the "Golden Jet." His son Brett, in choosing hockey as a career, knew he would be thrust into the limelight.

"It was a tough act to follow," said St. Louis Blues GM Ron Caron, "but you have to remember that Brett is a very special athlete."

Brett's first NHL stint with the Flames was less than overwhelming. His coach, Terry Crisp, considered him lazy, and the Flames dealt him to St. Louis in 1988. Under coach Brian Sutter, Brett's natural scoring talents surfaced and he more and more resembled his dynamic old man.

In no time, he was nicknamed the "Golden Brett," and he started to terrify goalies with a shot that approached 100 mph. But it was not until the 1989-90 season that Hull reached a new plateau, netting 72 goals. One year later, he scored a mind-boggling 86 goals, then followed with years of 70, 54, and 57. Pressed about his scoring prowess, Hull explained, "It must be in the genes."

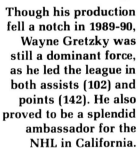

Though his production fell a notch in 1989-90, Wayne Gretzky was still a dominant force, as he led the league in both assists (102) and points (142). He also proved to be a splendid ambassador for the NHL in California.

featured a full-fledged star. Young Brett Hull, the son of the great Bobby Hull, led the league with 72 goals, most ever by a right wing.

The Blues benefited from a deal with Detroit, in which they received Adam Oates and Paul MacLean for Bernie Federko and Tony McKegney. Wings coach Jacques Demers wanted Federko and McKegney for their experience, but in reality they hardly helped the club. Oates, on the other hand, went on to notch 79 assists with St. Louis.

Meanwhile, Red Wings enigmatic enforcer Bob Probert was suspended for the season after being arrested on drug charges. The Red Wings, further

burdened by poor goaltending, finished last in the Norris (28-38-14), costing Demers his job. Not even a 62-goal performance by Steve Yzerman helped. Jimmy Carson was the only "happy" man in Detroit. After a miserable year in Edmonton as "the man for whom they traded Gretzky," Carson convinced the Oilers to trade him again, this time to his hometown club. He used the tactic of quitting the team as his final strategy. Carson finished the year with 21 goals and a lot to prove.

What looked to be an exciting scoring race between Wayne Gretzky and Mario Lemieux never materialized. Afflicted by a career-threatening back injury,

Lemieux was forced to sit out 21 of the Pens' final 22 games. Gretzky also had back trouble but missed only seven games and managed to win the scoring title with 142 points on 40 goals. Nevertheless, his effort could not turn the Kings into a winner. They finished below .500 (34-39-7) and in fourth place in the Smythe. Both Sandstrom and Granato were plagued by injuries as well, limiting their production.

A contender from the start, the Buffalo Sabres played vibrant hockey under rookie coach Rick Dudley. Their 98 points (45-27-8) were the third highest total in the league. It would have been better had Mogilny not

Edmonton's Craig Muni (center) guards Boston's Bob Sweeney during the 1990 finals. Edmonton goalie Bill Ranford (right) played all of the Oilers' 22 playoff games, won 16 of them, and captured the Conn Smythe Trophy.

The Islanders made the 1990 playoffs on the last game of the season, but they were quickly ousted by the rival Rangers in the first round. Here, Islander star Pat LaFontaine (right) tangles with Ranger defenseman Milo Horava.

suffered from a fear of flying. Mogilny missed 15 games and was a disappointment to the Sabres.

Montreal finished third in the Adams Division. The Canadiens witnessed the emergence of the mercurial Stephane Richer as a star in the old Montreal tradition of Guy Lafleur and Jean Beliveau. Richer, a 50-goal scorer in 1987-88 who fell to 25 goals the following year, returned to form. He scored 51 goals and had the second best plus/minus record in the league (plus-35).

For most of the season, it seemed highly unlikely that the Edmonton Oilers would win anything. One year

removed from Gretzky, the Oilers had a new head coach in John Muckler and were burdened with problems from the start. As mentioned, they had to deal with the Carson problem. Also, goalie Grant Fuhr was conspicuously absent due to a shoulder injury. Bill Ranford filled in for Fuhr and was an admirable 24-16-9.

Edmonton GM Glen Sather rebuilt his squad through some slick moves. With Gretzky gone, Sather and Muckler focused the offense around Mark Messier. "Moose" responded with a career-best 129 points and won the Hart Trophy. Sather also improved his team's speed by sending the

disgruntled Carson and Kevin McClelland to the Red Wings for Petr Klima, Joe Murphy, Adam Graves, and Jeff Sharples (later dealt to New Jersey for Reijo Ruotsalainen).

Edmonton still couldn't stop the great Gretzky. Facing off against his old mates on October 15, 1989, Wayne was one point behind Gordie Howe's all-time point-scoring mark of 1,850. With an assist in the first period, he tied the mark. Then, with only 53 seconds left in the third period—and his Kings trailing by a goal—Gretzky broke the record by backhanding a dramatic goal past Oiler goalie Ranford. Adding a thrilling touch to the evening, No. 99 netted the overtime goal that lifted Los Angeles to victory, 5-4.

What Howe had accomplished in 26 seasons, Gretzky had surpassed in just 11. Howe, who contemplated a one-game comeback to play with Wayne, was on hand to witness the milestone.

Gretzky's magic continued in the postseason, as his Kings upset the defending champion Calgary Flames in the first round. Though many experts considered Calgary to be a dynasty in the making, they were crushed when Mike Krushelnyski ended the series with a goal in the second overtime of Game Six. As a result, Calgary coach Terry Crisp was fired in favor of Doug

Risebrough. The Kings, meanwhile, were unable to capitalize on their good fortune and lost the Smythe finals to the Oilers in four games.

In the Patrick Division, the Rangers opened up against the crosstown Islanders, who had qualified for the playoffs on the last game of the season. The Rangers defeated the Isles in five games while the Washington Caps ousted New Jersey in six.

Powered by John Druce, who had all of 16 NHL goals to his credit, the Caps beat the Rangers in the Patrick finals. Druce netted an overtime goal in Game Five to knock the Rangers out of the playoffs; he finished the postseason

with 14 tallies. Coach Terry Murray, who had replaced his brother, Bryan, in midseason, guided the Caps to the Stanley Cup semifinals for the first time in franchise history.

In the Adams, the Boston Bruins were extended to seven games by the Hartford Whalers in Round One. The Whalers were game in the finale but lost 3-1 at Boston Garden. The Montreal Canadiens took out Buffalo in six games. However, the Habs were no match for the Bruins, losing to Boston in five in the division finals.

Over in the Norris, the first-place Chicago Blackhawks withstood challenges from the Minnesota North

 Late-season pick-up Brian Propp helped Boston sweep Washington in the 1990 Wales finals. Here, he tangles with defenseman Bob Rouse.

STEVE YZERMAN

In the late 1980s, Steve Yzerman was being touted as one of the top three centers in the NHL, classed with such megatalents as Wayne Gretzky and Mario Lemieux. And the accolades were well deserved. Yzerman was, for a time, the entire Detroit Red Wing offense, wrapped into a neat 5'11" package.

"He was the reason this team won or lost most nights," said his coach, Bryan Murray.

More recently, however, with the addition of Soviet ace Sergei Fedorov and future Hall of Famer Paul Coffey to the Red Wings roster, Yzerman has been able to share the load.

A first-round pick in the 1983 draft, Yzerman scored 39 and 30 goals in his first two seasons in the NHL before a knee injury sidelined him in 1985-86. Upon his return, the club adorned him with the captaincy and, in effect, asked him to lead them to Stanley Cup contention. Yzerman responded well to the challenge.

In 1987-88, he began a string of four consecutive seasons in which he scored at least 50 goals (50, 65, 62, and 51). In 1991-92, the graceful, hard-shooting Yzerman led the club in scoring with 45 goals and 103 points—his fifth straight 100-point season. In his first 12 NHL campaigns, Yzerman has amassed 1,160 points in 862 games.

Stars and the St. Louis Blues, outlasting both teams in two tough seven-game series.

In the semifinals, Edmonton eliminated Chicago in six games, blowing them out 8-4 in Game Six. The other semifinal was even a bigger mismatch, as Boston swept the Caps in four.

The Stanley Cup finals offered a rematch of the 1988 championship, when Boston lost to Edmonton in four straight games. Once again, the Bruins were no match for the faster skating, offensively superior Oilers, who nearly engineered another sweep. Boston managed to steal a game in Edmonton,

but that was all. Former Bruin goalie Ranford outplayed former Edmonton goalie Andy Moog in every game, earning himself the Conn Smythe Trophy as playoff MVP. The Oilers won their fifth Stanley Cup in seven years— and they did it without Gretzky.

In the midst of the Oilers' locker room celebration, Gretzky could not be forgotten. Veteran Kevin Lowe said, "Mark Messier and I looked at each other and said: 'This one's for the G-man because he's still such a big part of our team.'"

Other individual award winners included Ray Bourque, who copped his third Norris Trophy, and St. Louis'

Hull, who took the Lady Byng. Montreal goalie Patrick Roy annexed the Vezina Trophy for the second straight year. And in a controversial decision that brought closure to a season of change and innovation, Calgary's Makarov became the first Soviet player to win an NHL award.

Despite his "advanced" age (32) and experience (11 years with the Red Army team), Makarov was voted the league's top rookie, thus capturing the Calder Trophy. The outcry against this choice resulted in a change of the rules, which henceforth would disqualify players over 26 years of age from eligibility in this category.

Mark Messier, the 1989-90 Hart Trophy winner, holds the Stanley Cup aloft after Edmonton's win over Boston. It marked Messier's fifth Cup triumph.

Sergei Makarov and Viacheslav Fetisov

SOVIET INVASION

The NHL has long eyed the Soviet hockey system as a talent source. However, it wasn't until *glasnost* arrived that Russian players became available. In 1989, nine Soviets signed with NHL clubs.

These included Viacheslav Fetisov, Alexei Kasatonov, and Sergei Starikov with New Jersey; Alexander Mogilny with Buffalo; Vladimir Krutov and Igor Larionov with Vancouver; Helmut Balderis with Minnesota; Sergei Mylnikov with Quebec; and Sergei Makarov with Calgary.

The most successful was Makarov, who won the Calder Trophy in 1990. Two Soviets had problems adjusting. Krutov came to camp overweight and played with little enthusiasm during the season. And while Mogilny would go on to great things, he initially had trouble with airsickness.

As the 1990s progressed, more and more teams added former Soviet stars. The Red Wings signed Sergei Fedorov, a tremendous weapon, while Vancouver inked fleet-footed Pavel Bure, who had once played on a line with Fedorov and Mogilny on the Soviets' Central Red Army team.

Somewhat less dramatic but equally effective were Winnipeg's Alexei Zhamnov, who would prove a brilliant playmaker and finisher, and Sergei Zubov, a defenseman who led the Rangers in scoring in 1993-94.

Europeans, Americans Skate into Canadian Territory

1 9 9 0 - 9 1

In the spring of 1990, the Edmonton Oilers celebrated their fifth Stanley Cup championship. In the fall, they woke up with a hangover.

The defending champions suffered an endless spell of headaches. To begin, standout goalie Grant Fuhr confessed that he had once been a drug abuser, dabbling in cocaine. Fuhr was suspended by NHL President John Ziegler.

Next to take center stage in the growing soap opera was veteran right wing Glenn Anderson, who sat out the beginning of the season in a contract dispute with GM Glen Sather—a recurring theme in Alberta. On top of it all, reigning NHL MVP Mark Messier subsequently missed much of the season with a knee injury that inspired some to wonder aloud if Messier was reaching the end of the road.

Edmonton's problems didn't end there. Vladimir Ruzicka, for whom the Oilers spent $200,000 just to lure out of Czechoslovakia, fell out of coach John Muckler's favor. Ruzicka was dealt to the Boston Bruins for defenseman Greg Hawgood, who had similarly run afoul of the Beantown management staff. And Jari Kurri, then the world's most prolific right wing, quit Edmonton to play for an Italian

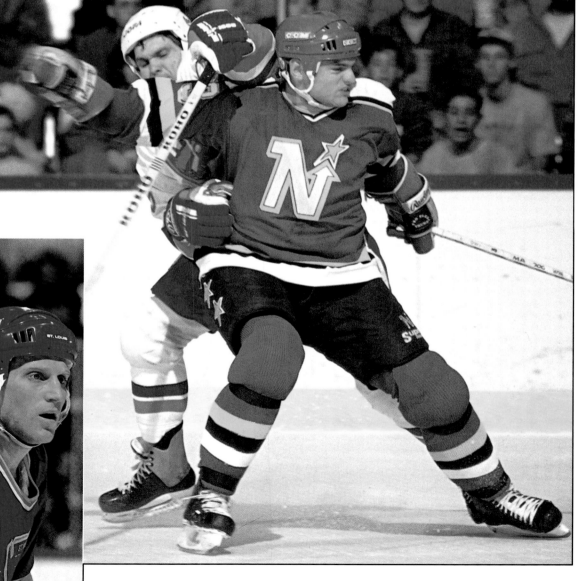

Despite a 27-39-14 record, the North Stars stormed all the way to the Stanley Cup finals, where they fell to Pittsburgh. Minnesota center Brian Bellows led the incredible surge, as he netted ten goals in the playoffs.

St. Louis' superstar Brett Hull cranked up the volume in 1990-91, netting 86 goals. On the year, Hull scored 35 goals more than anyone else.

team based in Milan. The Italians made the 30-year-old Kurri an offer he couldn't refuse: a higher salary and a shorter schedule—only 30 games.

Edmonton wasn't the only NHL team affected by European hockey. In fact, many clubs were influenced by the outstanding hockey programs—and the players being produced—across the Atlantic.

The Detroit Red Wings, for example, caused a major stir when they signed Central Red Army star Sergei Fedorov despite the protests of Soviet officials. Fedorov, just 20 years old at the time, jumped the Russian National Team before the 1990 Goodwill Games in Seattle. It was an unauthorized move that left the Soviets fuming. "This is a kind of stealing," said Georgi Oganov,

a spokesman for the Soviet Embassy in Washington.

At first, the Soviets threatened to retaliate by canceling the season's business with the NHL. But they relented, allowing the Minnesota North Stars and the Montreal Canadiens to tour the USSR in September 1990. They also consented to send three Soviet teams on a 21-game tour of NHL cities later in 1990-91. They needed the dollars, Canadian and American.

Another intercontinental series took shape in West Germany, where the St. Louis Blues and the Edmonton Oilers played a three-team tournament with a Dusseldorf, East Germany, squad.

Meanwhile, Czechs made nearly as much NHL news as the Soviets. In Hartford, the Whalers signed highly

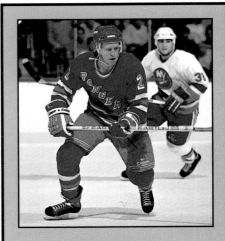

BRIAN LEETCH

At one time, few American players made it to the NHL. However, the Americans' gold medal in the 1980 Olympics changed all that. Olympians such as Mark Johnson, Mike Ramsey, Dave Christian, and Ken Morrow easily made the jump to the big leagues, and soon NHL scouts were combing American rinks for additional talent.

One of the prize prospects of the late 1980s was Brian Leetch, who launched his career at a private school in New England called Avon Old Farms. After a year at Boston College, Leetch made the 1988 U.S. Olympic team. He was immediately signed thereafter by the New York Rangers.

"In some ways," said former Ranger general manager Phil Esposito, "Brian is reminiscent of Doug Harvey. And there were few better puck-handling defensemen in the 1950s than Doug."

Leetch stepped into the NHL without missing a step. In 1988-89, he scored 71 points in 68 games and won the Calder Trophy. His skating is effortless, his shot deadly accurate, and his passes practically perfect.

The Rangers have grown to rely on Leetch. Brian won the Norris Trophy in 1992 and helped New York to the Stanley Cup in 1994, winning the Conn Smythe Trophy with 34 playoff points.

The Blackhawks made the deal of the year when they traded Denis Savard for Chris Chelios (pictured). Chelios's outstanding defense helped the Hawks to the best record in the NHL (49-23-8).

regarded winger Bobby Holik, relying heavily upon the influence of tennis star Ivan Lendl, who, as a member of the Whalers board of directors, helped convince Holik of the many benefits and rewards awaiting him in Connecticut.

At the same time, across the continent in Vancouver, top draft pick Petr Nedved signed with the Canucks after one very successful season with Seattle of the Western Junior Hockey League (65 goals in 71 games). And in New Jersey, Slovak ace Zdeno Ciger inked a deal with the Devils.

Not only was hockey expanding globally, but it was extending its roots throughout the United States. The NHL announced that a new franchise, the San Jose Sharks, would begin operations in 1991-92. Two more clubs

would hit the ice in 1992-93—the Ottawa Senators and the Tampa Bay Lightning.

Hockey in Florida? No joke. An exhibition game in St. Petersburg drew a crowd of 25,581, the largest in history. It was played at the Florida Suncoast Dome, a new domed stadium built for baseball. Top ticket prices were $99 and $66—the numbers Wayne Gretzky and Mario Lemieux wore on their backs.

Overall, the NHL was considering adding seven franchises by 1999. Some even speculated that the league would extend its reach across the Atlantic and organize a European division before the new century began.

Trading was again heavy in the NHL. Before the season even began, the Canadiens and Blackhawks

swapped superstars, as Denis Savard left the Windy City for his hometown of Montreal and former Norris Trophy defenseman Chris Chelios returned to his hometown of Chicago. The Red Wings cajoled New Jersey into giving them Paul Ysebaert, a minor-leaguer, in exchange for much-traveled defenseman Lee Norwood. Ysebaert would later blossom into a major scoring ace for Detroit.

Toronto, suffering through another endless, hopeless season, tried everything but with little success. They traded Ed Olzcyk and Mark Osborne to Winnipeg for defenseman Dave Ellett and effectively reduced an already depleted offensive attack. They then swapped the speedy Al Iafrate, a talented full-speed-ahead backliner, to Washington for Peter

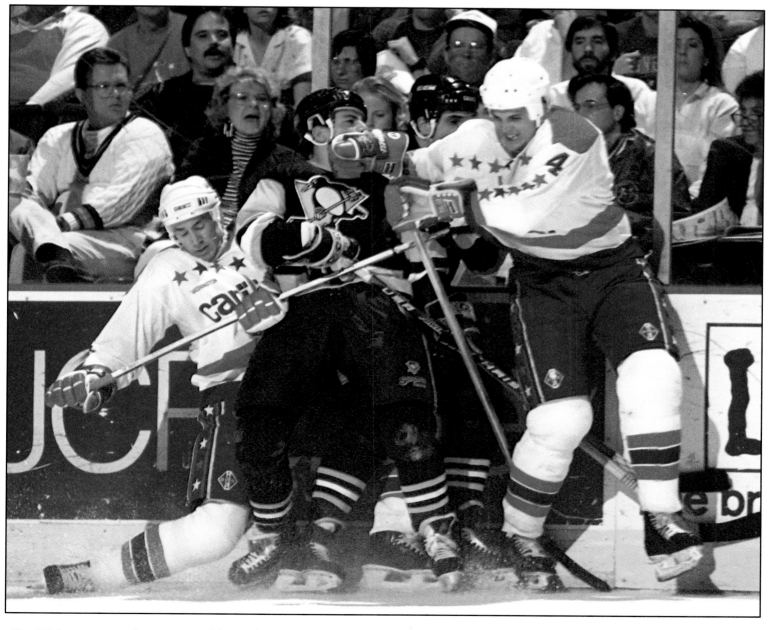

With one strong forearm, Washington's Kevin Hatcher pins Mark Recchi and two others into the boards. Recchi's Penguins beat the Capitals in the 1991 Patrick finals, then ousted Boston for the Wales title.

JEREMY ROENICK

On an unseasonably warm night in February 1990 at the L.A. Forum, Chicago rookie Jeremy Roenick's performance left everyone in awe.

With Al Secord and Denis Savard nursing injuries, the undermanned Blackhawks took the play away from the Kings. Late in the second period, Roenick skated through the slot toward the right hash marks. With everyone in the building expecting him to shoot, he slid a pretty pass to Jocelyn Lemieux on the left side of the net. Lemieux tapped it in past a startled Mario Gosselin. It is not every day that 20-year-old rookies set up goals in that fashion.

"Jeremy reminds me of a young Dale Hawerchuk," Hawks coach Mike Keenan said after the game. "Or Rick Tocchet in Philadelphia. They were players who wanted more of a leadership role on my teams."

Roenick finished his initial season with 26 red lights and 40 assists. In 1990-91, J.R. upped his production to 41 goals, then began a streak of three straight 100-point campaigns, scoring 53, 50, and 46 goals. A serious knee injury curtailed his 1994-95 season.

Though favored by some to win the Cup, Bernie Nicholls and the Rangers were trampled in Round One by Stephen Leach and the Capitals.

Zezel, a diligent worker whose discipline and leadership balanced a somewhat lax scoring punch.

The Minnesota North Stars endured a tumultuous 1990. The team owners, George and Gordon Gund, threatened to move the team elsewhere (to San Jose, in fact) if they did not find a buyer willing to pay them $50 million dollars. At the 11th hour, with the Twin Cities torn apart by emotional upheaval, Howard Baldwin and then Norm Green pulled together the resources and purchased the team. The old regime, headed by Jack Ferreira and Pierre Page, was replaced by a new one featuring Bob Clarke as GM and ex-Montreal hero Bob Gainey at coach.

Clearly, there was a changing of the guard underway in the NHL and new teams—namely U.S. teams—were

emerging as powers. Two such clubs were the Los Angeles Kings and the Pittsburgh Penguins, each of whom won their first-ever division titles in 1990-91. Not surprisingly, the teams were powered by the best pair of hockey players in the world—Gretzky and Lemieux, respectively.

The Kings got 122 points from Gretzky and edged Calgary by two points in the Smythe Division (102-100). And although Pittsburgh lost superstar Lemieux for 54 games due to a back injury, the Penguins still won the Patrick Division. Right wing Mark Recchi (113 points) and defenseman Paul Coffey (93) led an explosive Pittsburgh attack.

The Norris Division featured the two winningest teams in hockey—Chicago (106 points) and St. Louis (105). The

Blackhawks boasted the stingiest defense in the league, thanks to defenseman Chelios and rookie-of-the-year goalie Ed Belfour. Belfour led the league with 74 games played, 43 victories, and a skimpy 2.47 goals-against average.

In St. Louis, it was the Hull and Oates show. Brett Hull solidified his spot as the NHL's No. 1 superstar, as he netted 86 goals, the second highest total in NHL history. Hull's pivotman, Adam Oates, chipped in 25 goals and established himself as one of the game's slickest playmakers, dishing off 90 assists.

Boston captured the Adams Division on the strength of defenseman Ray Bourque and the one-two combination of centerman Craig Janney and right winger Cam Neely. Bourque led the

▲ Korea native Jim Paek (*center*) scored his first NHL goal in the 1991 playoffs. Here, the Pittsburgh rookie sticks it to Minnesota's Mark Tinordi.

◀

Pittsburgh's Kevin Stevens battles Minnesota defenseman Chris Dahlquist in the 1991 Cup finals. Stevens, who scored 40 goals during the season, pumped in 17 in the playoffs—the second best mark ever. He would score 54 goals in 1991-92.

club in scoring with 94 points, Janney followed with 92, and Neely had 91 in 69 games.

Quebec finished last in the Adams and last in the NHL, thus earning the right to draft mega-prospect Eric Lindros. Lindros, whose boyhood idol was Mark Messier, was projected to become even better than the superstar. Lindros, however, refused to play for the Nordiques and his status with the team and the league is still up in the air.

As the playoffs began, all eyes were on the Minnesota North Stars. Minnesota, which finished with a meager 27-39-14 record, knocked off the top two teams in hockey in the first two rounds. Led by new coach Gainey and center Brian Bellows, the Stars upset Chicago in six games and then eliminated the Blues in six.

Meanwhile, over in the Smythe Division, Edmonton upset both the third and fourth best teams in hockey. Though they had to undergo six overtime games, the Oilers skated past Los Angeles in Round One and Calgary in Round Two.

Pittsburgh, thriving under the tutelage of coach Bob Johnson, took the Patrick rather easily, beating Washington in five games in the division finals. The Bruins won the Adams, though the Canadiens pushed them to seven games in their division finals.

In the battle of the upstarts, Minnesota faced Edmonton for the Campbell Conference title. Minnesota hadn't won at Edmonton in over 11 years, but no matter—the North Stars opened with a 3-1 victory in the Oilers'

rink. After Edmonton whipped them 7-2 in Game Two, the Stars played at the Oilers' up-tempo pace and beat them 7-3 in Game Three and 5-1 in Game Four. In Game Six, Bobby Smith's third-period goal gave Minnesota a 3-2 win and a spot in the finals.

The Wales Conference finals featured a milder upset. Pittsburgh welcomed Lemieux back to the lineup and they sped by the plodding, defensive-minded Bruins in six games. Boston's Neely scored 16 playoff goals, but he couldn't outgun the potent Pittsburgh offense. Adding injury to insult, a solid check against Neely by Ulf Samuelsson—which some deemed a dirty cheap shot—sent the burly winger to the sidelines and reduced the Bruins' chances even further.

So the Stanley Cup finals pitted two

surprise American teams—Pittsburgh, which had made the playoffs only once in the previous eight years, and Minnesota, which finished the regular season with the sixth worst record in the NHL.

The teams split the first two games before Minnesota took Game Three 3-1. Goalie Jon Casey, who had been brilliant in the playoffs, held the Penguins in check, while Lemieux sat out the match with recurring back spasms.

To the chagrin of North Stars checkers—who had so successfully shut down Jeremy Roenick, Brett Hull, and Mark Messier in previous rounds—Lemieux returned to the lineup in time for Game Four and the Penguins' offense kicked into high gear. Behind "Super Mario," the Pens took control of the series with a pair of victories, 5-3 and 6-4.

With a three-games-to-two advantage, the Penguins went for the jugular in Game Six. Joey Mullen, a veteran whose career had been given up for dead earlier in the year, proved his worth by scoring two clutch goals in the early going. Lemieux stole the show with four points, and Pittsburgh embarrassed the shell-shocked Stars

8-0. It was the most lopsided Cup-winning game in NHL history.

The Penguins, who were on the verge of celebrating a quarter-century in the league, thus captured their first Stanley Cup. Lemieux, who had brooded impatiently and unapologetically in the shadow of Wayne Gretzky for seven long seasons, now skated into the spotlight, shining as brilliantly in his moment of glory as any Stanley Cup hero ever had. For his 16 playoff goals and his immeasurable inspiration, Lemieux was voted the Conn Smythe Trophy as the playoff MVP.

Hull was elected the regular-season MVP, making him one-half of the only father-son team ever to be so honored. Brett also won the Lester B. Pearson Award as player of the year. Chicago netminder Belfour captured the Calder Trophy and Vezina Trophy—the first such double winner since Tom Barrasso turned the trick with Buffalo back in 1984.

Gretzky, who won the scoring race with 41 goals and 122 assists, earned his second Lady Byng Trophy (he won his first as a rookie). The Bruins' Bourque took the Norris Trophy for the fourth time in five years.

PATRICK ROY

Patrick Roy made one of the most spectacular NHL debuts in recent memory when he joined the Canadiens in 1985-86. Though his regular-season stats were merely adequate, he was absolutely brilliant in the playoffs. He won 15 games and boasted a 1.92 GAA. At just 20, he carried the Canadiens to the Stanley Cup and won the Conn Smythe Trophy.

In the years that followed, Roy established himself as one of the game's great netminders. In 1986-87, he shared the William Jennings Trophy with teammate Brian Hayward, for the first of three straight years, as the goalies on the NHL team that allowed the fewest goals.

In 1988-89, Roy won his first GAA title with a 2.47 mark—good enough to earn him his first Vezina Trophy. He held the title the following year as well, finishing that season with a league-high 31 victories and a 2.53 GAA. In 1991-92, Roy led the league with a 2.36 average, earning him his third Vezina Trophy in four years.

In the 1993 playoffs, Roy survived the highest pressure imaginable, winning ten games in overtime—including three in the finals against Los Angeles. The Habs ultimately beat the Kings in five games to win Stanley Cup No. 24—and 16-game winner Roy earned his second Conn Smythe Trophy.

Bob Errey celebrates a goal in the decisive Game Six of the 1991 Cup finals. Pittsburgh beat the North Stars 8-0—the biggest Cup-clinching rout in NHL history.

◀

Minnesota right wing Stewart Gavin up-ends Pittsburgh's Joe Mullen in Game Six of the Cup finals. In 1990-91, Gavin tallied 13 of his 21 points in the playoffs.

Penguins Win Again
But League Strikes Out

1 9 9 1 - 9 2

The Cinderella story surrounding the 1990-91 Stanley Cup champion Pittsburgh Penguins was barely off the sports pages when tragedy struck in Steeltown. News that coach Bob Johnson had brain cancer shocked and saddened the hockey world. In his one year behind the Pittsburgh bench, Johnson had been to the Penguins' team psyche what Mario Lemieux was to the Penguins' offense. The leading force.

The prospect of defending their league title would be difficult enough under normal circumstances. For the Penguins, the challenge of overcoming the loss of their revered bench leader seemed overwhelming.

Elsewhere, the season began with a No. 1 draft pick who thumbed his nose at the NHL team that selected him first overall, as well as the unveiling of a new franchise in California. There was also an unprecedented string of major roster changes, as teams scrambled to improve their chances of conquering the talented Penguins. And looming overhead was the threat of an NHL players strike.

The Eric Lindros Saga began in June when the Quebec Nordiques, against the advice of Lindros himself, announced their No. 1 pick at the 1991 draft. Unlike his predecessors throughout hockey history, Lindros refused to don the Nords jersey for the customary media photo, and he was quite adamant in his refusal to negotiate with Quebec.

As time went on, nothing changed to soften his views: "Look how many times they've finished last," he said later. "They haven't treated their players with any respect. Their owner (Marcel Aubut) just doesn't want to win at all. I don't know if he has political ambitions or if he just wants to sell the team, but he just doesn't want to win."

The New York Rangers, more than 50 years removed from their last Stanley Cup title, pulled out all the stops and lured Mark Messier away from Edmonton—Messier's hometown and the site of his many glorious years. In exchange for Mess, the Blueshirts surrendered Bernie Nicholls and minor-league prospects Louie DeBrusk and

▲ **League President John Ziegler (*third from left*) and other NHL brass discuss the strike's status with the media. Ziegler, who many thought did a poor job handling the strike, retired in June 1992.**

Steven Rice. Nicholls, whose wife was expecting twins, balked at the idea of leaving Broadway and refused to report to the Oilers until mid-December.

Labor unrest was rampant around the NHL. General managers tested age-old free-agent restrictions, and "untouchable" players of yesteryear were packaged like so much bacon. When the St. Louis Blues signed free agent winger Brendan Shanahan to a lucrative contract, the Devils demanded arbitration. NHL arbiter Edward J. Houston took New Jersey's point of view, apparently, and awarded the Devils the contract of defenseman Scott Stevens. It was a stunning blow to the Blues who only a year before had paid a hefty price to sign Stevens away from Washington.

In Alberta, Grant Fuhr, whose goaltending exploits helped the Oilers to four of their five Stanley Cups, was shipped to Toronto with malcontent winger Glenn Anderson. In exchange, Edmonton received scoring ace Vincent Damphousse, Luke Richardson, and Peter Ing.

The Montreal Canadiens followed up their Denis Savard-Chris Chelios swap of the previous year with a more promising deal, sending the unpredictable Stephane Richer to New Jersey for Devils captain Kirk Muller. Meanwhile, Jari Kurri had been enticed to return to the NHL when the Oilers traded him, via Philadelphia, to the Los Angeles Kings. In Los Angeles, Kurri joined his old buddy Wayne Gretzky.

In November, the Buffalo Sabres got into the act as well. The Sabres acquired Pat LaFontaine, Randy Wood, Randy Hillier, and future considerations from the New York Islanders in exchange for Pierre Turgeon, Uwe Krupp, Benoit Hogue, and Dave McLlwain. LaFontaine proved his worth quickly. Despite missing the month of October as a holdout and six weeks during November and December with a broken jaw, the speedy center finished the year with 46 goals and 93 points in only 57 games.

Behind the most inspirational player the club had ever known, the Rangers followed Messier to the top of the NHL. They finished with a league-leading 50-25-5 record and their first regular-

▼ Former Soviet defector Sergei Fedorov helped Detroit to a first-place finish in the Norris in 1991-92 (43-25-12). The speedy Fedorov was one of three top-notch Red Wing centers, the others being Steve Yzerman and Jimmy Carson.

▲ After his 86-goal performance in 1990-91, Brett Hull tallied 70 in 1991-92. Hull's output was not enough to help the St. Louis Blues, who finished at 36-33-11 and lost to Chicago in the first round of the playoffs.

season title in 50 years. Rookie Tony Amonte led all freshmen in scoring (35-34-69) and defenseman Brian Leetch was the highest scoring defenseman in the game (22-80-102). Leetch became the first backliner in team history to reach the 100-point mark.

St. Louis Blues sniper Brett Hull followed up his 86-goal season of 1990-91 with a mere 70-goal performance in 1991-92. Meanwhile, the NHL welcomed a spate of new members to the 50-goal club, including Pittsburgh's Kevin Stevens (54), Chicago's Jeremy Roenick (53), and Calgary's Gary Roberts (53).

The Devils lost their most dangerous goal-scorer when Johnny MacLean underwent season-ending surgery on his right knee. However, former Canadien Claude Lemieux enjoyed a career season, tallying 41 goals for New Jersey.

Out West, the addition of young Soviet wizard Pavel Bure helped the Vancouver Canucks grab the top spot in the Smythe Division. Bure, who sued the Soviet Red Army team for release from his arrangement with them, citing that his Red Army contract had been signed under duress, gained his freedom. He joined the NHL club and finished the season with 34 goals in 65 games.

On November 26, 1991, what had begun as a sad story ended in tears shed around the hockey world. Bob Johnson, who only months earlier had won the Stanley Cup, died of cancer at age 60.

John Ziegler

THE STRIKE

In April Fool's Day, 1992, the NHL Players' Association announced that it had gone on strike. Was this some kind of joke, a cruel hoax to torment hockey fans everywhere? Unfortunately, no.

For ten days, there was no NHL hockey. Instead, players and owners traded offers, swapped threats, and relayed proposals back and forth. Eventually, when it appeared that the playoffs might be lost—which would adversely affect the owners more than the players—an agreement was reached.

More than a dozen key issues were decided, with the players making modest gains in free agency. With the agreement, players could become unrestricted free agents at age 30, rather than 31. Also, teams now losing younger free agents would no longer be compensated as much as they were before.

Players also won on such issues as trading card revenue and playoff money. The owners were able to lengthen the season to 84 games and, if they chose, reduce their rosters to 19 players. The agreement, though, would expire in September 1993, leading to another work stoppage.

▲ **The Capitals boasted the second best record in the league in 1991-92 (45-27-8) and they did it behind Dino Ciccarelli, who scored 38 goals.**

◄ **For the first time in 50 years, the New York Rangers had the best record in the NHL in 1991-92 (50-25-5). Their success was credited to the leadership skills of wily Mark Messier. His 107 points also came in handy.**

"I'll remember Bob as the most optimistic, bright, intelligent, and positive man, with a heart that wouldn't give up," said Bryan Trottier, a member of the 1991 champion Penguins. "His will was contagious and I think his spirit will be contagious for a long time. He has left a mark on Pittsburgh."

The season was also marked by several disturbing developments. The FBI probed into the business practices of the NHL players union during the years of Alan Eagleson's reign—from the union's creation in 1967 until his resignation in December 1991. Among the areas targeted for examination were the handling of the pension, insurance payments, client fee structures, money management, and conflict-of-interest charges leveled at Eagleson by his critics. Eagleson refuted charges that he had mismanaged funds and had, he said, "played on both sides of the fence."

Meanwhile, the NHLPA's new boss, Bob Goodenow, was embroiled in a major contract squabble with owners over a new collective bargaining agreement. Negotiations threatened to result in a players strike if certain economic issues were not resolved by the March 30 deadline set by the players.

A hockey strike? Unheard of. It'll never happen. Such were the sentiments around the hockey community as spring approached. But on April 1, after the deadline passed and no accord had been reached, the players agreed by a nearly unanimous vote to strike.

For more than a week, the two sides made offer and counter-offer, threat and counter-threat. When it appeared the playoff season was in jeopardy of being canceled, the owners and players finally found common ground and

Not in their 21-year history had the Vancouver Canucks won 40 games, but they did it in 1991-92. Right wing Trevor Linden led the team offensively with 31 goals and 75 points.

1991-92

Best Record
New York R.
(50-25-5)

Stanley Cup Finals
Pittsburgh 4
Chicago 0

Art Ross Trophy
Mario Lemieux
(44/87/131)

Hart Trophy
Mark Messier

Vezina Trophy
Patrick Roy

Calder Trophy
Pavel Bure

Norris Trophy
Brian Leetch

Lady Byng Trophy
Wayne Gretzky

When he wasn't in the penalty box, Gary Roberts was Calgary's biggest weapon, scoring 53 goals. Nevertheless, the Flames finished 1991-92 in fifth place in the Smythe Division.

ERIC LINDROS

There have been few players who have come to the NHL with the kind of advance notice that accompanied Eric Lindros in 1991. After dominating the Ontario league with great scoring and a belligerent style, he was dubbed "The Next One," an homage to Wayne Gretzky, "The Great One." However, although he was the first choice in the 1991 Entry Draft when Quebec selected him, Lindros made it clear he had no intentions of playing for the lowly Nordiques.

Big, strong, and fast on his skates, Lindros showed he could play hard ball. Rather than giving in to the NHL powers, he spent the 1991-92 season with his Oshawa junior team and the Canadian National Team, scoring five goals at the 1992 Winter Games.

On June 30, 1992, Lindros was traded to both Philadelphia and the Rangers in a frenzy of activity that temporarily stymied league officials. Ultimately, the Quebec-Philadelphia trade won precedence, and Eric joined the Flyers in exchange for six players, a draft choice, and $15 million in cash.

Lindros battled injuries in his first two seasons yet still scored 41 and 44 goals. In 1994-95, he tied Pittsburgh's Jaromir Jagr for the league lead in points (70) and won the Hart Trophy as MVP and the Lester B. Pearson Award as the players' top choice.

Vancouver's first-place finish in 1991-92 could be credited to outstanding defense. Kirk McLean did the job between the pipes, posting 38 wins and a 2.74 GAA.

agreed to finish the regular season and the playoffs.

More than a dozen key issues were settled. The owners agreed to increase the players' playoff revenue; to increase the players' share of trading card profits; and to revamp the draft-pick compensation structure as applied to free-agent movement. The players agreed to lengthen the season to 84 games.

During the season, more blockbuster trades swept across the league. Among the most notable was a ten-player swap, the largest in league history, involving Toronto and Calgary. The Leafs unloaded Gary Leeman, Craig Berube, Michel Petit, Alexander Godynyuk, and Jeff Reese to Calgary for Doug Gilmour, Ric Nattress, Jamie Macoun, Kent Manderville, and Rick Wamsley. By all accounts, the Leafs got the better deal.

In St. Louis, Adam Oates left the Blues after disputing with management over his salary. He was traded to Boston for crafty Craig Janney, a deal that helped both teams.

Another huge trade involved three teams. Los Angeles acquired Paul Coffey from Pittsburgh, while Philadelphia got Brian Benning from the Kings and Mark Recchi from Pittsburgh. The Penguins landed Rick Tocchet, Ken Wregget, and Kjell Samuelsson from Philly and Jeff Chychrun from the Kings.

Montreal and Buffalo swapped defensemen, with Petr Svoboda heading to the Sabres and youngster Kevin Haller trekking north. The Philly Flyers were somehow able to snare Kevin Dineen from Hartford in exchange for Murray Craven (and later replaced coach Paul Holmgren with Kevin's father, Bill Dineen).

The playoffs, though belated, got off to a rousing start. In both the Adams

During the 1991-92 season, Boston traded for assist machine Adam Oates, who had been unhappy in St. Louis. Oates helped the Bruins sweep rival Montreal in the Adams finals, but they ran out of luck against Pittsburgh. Troy Loney and the Penguins swept Boston in the Wales Conference finals.

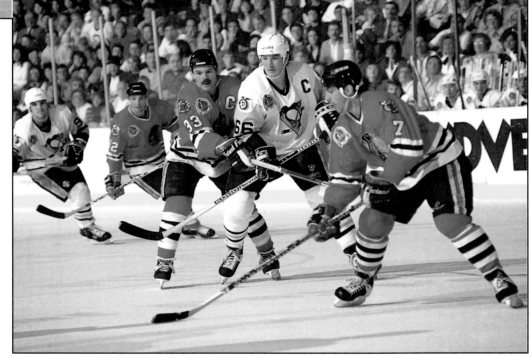

Chris Chelios (7), Mario Lemieux (66), and Dirk Graham (33) do the hokey pokey with the hockey puck during Game One of the 1992 Stanley Cup finals. Pittsburgh won the game 5-4 to end Chicago's string of 11 consecutive playoff wins. The Penguins would also win 11 straight in the postseason.

and Patrick Divisions, each first-round series was forced to seven games, with the Rangers, Pittsburgh, Montreal, and Boston prevailing.

Detroit survived through seven games in its series with Minnesota, as did Vancouver, which fought back from a three-games-to-one deficit to eliminate Winnipeg. Chicago and Edmonton were six-game winners over St. Louis and Los Angeles, respectively. (Not surprisingly, St. Louis' Brian Sutter and L.A.'s Tom Webster were the first coaches fired once their teams were finished.)

The Blackhawks made quick work of Detroit in the division finals, outscoring the offensive Red Wings 11-6 in a four-

game sweep. Vancouver dropped out of the postseason festivities after a 3-0 loss to the Oilers in Game Seven of their division finale. Boston avenged years of failure against their rivals from Montreal by eliminating the Canadiens in four straight games.

The most dramatic second-round series was fought between the heavily favored Rangers and defending-champion Penguins, who had struggled all year with problems (not only did Johnson pass away, but the team was sold midway through the season). The Rangers took two of the first three games. During Game Two, Mario Lemieux was the victim of a violent slash from Adam Graves, a blow that

left the Penguins star with a broken bone in his left hand. The Pens rallied behind their ace netminder, Tom Barrasso, and took the next three games and the series, laying waste to another Ranger season.

Meanwhile, the Chicago Blackhawks, winners of seven straight playoff games, continued an awesome postseason display thanks to the goaltending of Eddie Belfour. In the semifinals, the Hawks needed only four games to shed the nuisance of Edmonton from their Stanley Cup hopes. In sweeping the Oilers, Chicago tied an NHL record for consecutive postseason victories (11) and outscored Edmonton 21-8.

Pittsburgh got a huge boost when Lemieux returned to the lineup ahead of schedule. Mario scored a pair of goals in Game Two of Pittsburgh's semifinal series against Boston, putting the Pens ahead two games to none. Lemieux scored twice more in the clinching fourth game, including the game-winner, as the club marched back to the finals.

Chicago's consecutive-game winning streak came to an end in Game One of the championship round. Lemieux, with another two-goal performance, powered Pittsburgh to a 5-4 victory. In the next contest, it was Mario's scoring magic again that spelled doom for the outclassed Hawks. Lemieux broke a 1-1 tie with yet another two-goal night and gave Pittsburgh a 3-1 victory, placing Chicago squarely behind the eight ball.

After a remarkably lackluster 1-0 shutout victory in Chicago by red-hot goalie Tom Barrasso in Game Three, the Pens iced their second straight Stanley Cup championship in a wild 6-5 shootout in Game Four. In so doing, they matched the consecutive-win record (11) earlier reached by the Blackhawks. Lemieux, who netted his 16th playoff goal, earned his second Conn Smythe Trophy and put the rest of the NHL on warning.

"The type of team we have," he said, "we can play any type of game." And win. Convincingly.

Lemieux's artistry and dominance in the playoffs elevated him to another plateau. Teammates and foes have united in unanimous praise of the Penguin superstar. All agree, he is the best player in the world. If he survives the rigors of NHL warfare, the 1990s will be the decade of Mario Lemieux.

JAROMIR JAGR

Midway through his rookie NHL season in 1990-91, Jaromir Jagr was the topic of conversation among players and journalists who watched a spirited morning skate. Pittsburgh's Joe Mullen simply shook his head when asked about the 18-year-old right winger.

"Jaromir is going to be awesome in this league," Mullen said. "Just watching him skate, watching what he can do with the puck, watching him shoot from anywhere at anytime, you know he's going to be one of the great ones."

Drafted fifth overall by the Penguins in the 1990 draft, Jagr left his homeland in Kladno, Czechoslovakia. He knew very little English but had a world of talent. During his rookie season, his size (6'2", 208 pounds) allowed him to outmuscle many opponents, and his speed and grace provided yet another way to victimize the enemy. With 27 goals and 57 points, Jagr finished fourth among all NHL freshmen in scoring.

Only 22 years old and playing in his fifth NHL season, Jagr faced a huge challenge in 1994-95 when Penguins leader Mario Lemieux was out for the year. In 48 games, Jagr scored 32 goals and 70 points, winning his first NHL scoring title. Still improving each year, Jagr should be a dominant force well into the next millennium.

Pittsburgh's Shawn McEachern is hounded by Chris Chelios *(left)* and Stephane Matteau (32) during the Stanley Cup finals. Despite the Pens' sweep, this series was tight. The four games were decided by a total of five goals.

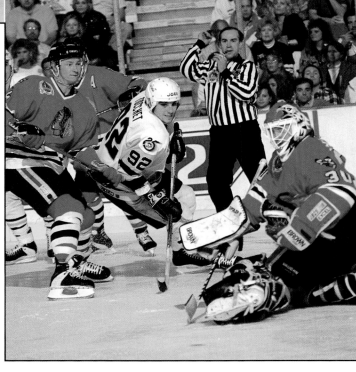

Pittsburgh's Rick Tocchet goes in on Chicago goalie Eddie Belfour in the 1992 Cup finals. The Penguins burned Belfour for six goals in the decisive Game Four, winning the game 6-5.

Canadiens Still Standing
After 11 Sudden-Deaths

1 9 9 2 - 9 3

In an enthusiastic burst of optimism, the NHL grew from 22 teams to 24 with the start of the 1992-93 season, welcoming old friends—the Ottawa Senators—back to the fold and establishing brand-new operations in central Florida. If anyone worried that hockey wouldn't fly in the sunny South, the Tampa Bay Lightning struck that notion to the ground by selling out their inaugural home opener against Chicago.

However, despite the great fervor that accompanied these new teams into the NHL, both clubs were destined to suffer typical first-year doldrums. The Senators managed to win just ten games—including a thrilling 5-3 debut at home against Montreal and a single victory on the road against the Islanders. Meanwhile, Tampa Bay rode a 42-goal performance from Brian Bradley and chalked up 23 victories, but still finished third worst

overall, ahead of only Ottawa and second-year San Jose.

In Philadelphia, the Flyers premiered 19-year-old Eric Lindros, whom they'd acquired from Quebec on June 30 in a blockbuster deal that sent six players (Ron Hextall, Kerry Huffman, Mike Ricci, Steve Duchesne, Chris Simon, and Peter Forsberg) plus a first-round draft pick (Jocelyn Thibault) and $15 million to the Nords. After missing the playoffs for

⊿ **Winger Ed Ronan and the Montreal Canadiens showed no mercy in the 1993 Stanley Cup finals, slaying Los Angeles three straight times in sudden-death.**

the previous three seasons, the Flyers placed the weight of the world on Eric's broad shoulders. Though he responded impressively with 41 goals, Lindros missed 23 games due to injuries, and the Flyers—still not ready for prime time—again missed the postseason.

In the midst of the campaign, the NHL also witnessed the arrival of a new league boss, as interim President Gil Stein was shuffled out of the deck and Gary Bettman, a highly respected former member of the NBA's high command, took over in the newly designated office of "commissioner." Bettman would soon put his mark on the game, as the collective-bargaining-agreement stalemate between the owners and the players union was reaching crisis levels.

Meanwhile, teams from coast to coast scrambled to fill gaping holes. In a quiet but important deal, the Sabres acquired goalie Dominik Hasek, once an All-Star in Europe, from Chicago for seldom-used Stephane Beauregard. Hasek settled into a rotation with Daren Puppa and later Grant Fuhr, who came from Toronto in a midseason trade, but ultimately "Dominik the Dominator" would survive his competitors and acquire No. 1 status in Buffalo's nets.

At the same time, the Oilers were still reeling without Mark Messier to guide them. From a Stanley Cup title in 1990, they had fallen from grace. In search of grit and leadership, they swapped high-scoring winger Vincent Damphousse to the Canadiens for tough guys Shayne Corson and Brent

MARIO LEMIEUX

If Wayne Gretzky owned the 1980s (and he did), the '90s have belonged to Mario Lemieux, one of the best and most courageous players ever to skate in the NHL.

Plagued by chronic back pain, Lemieux has been a battered but rarely conquered warrior. After winning the scoring championship in both 1988 and 1989, he won the title again in 1992 and 1993. In the spring of 1991, Lemieux accomplished what some thought was impossible: He brought the Stanley Cup to Pittsburgh, a city that nearly lost NHL hockey in the mid-1980s. Lemieux repeated this feat in 1992 with a second Cup (and another playoff MVP award).

But his greatest achievement was yet to come. In 1992-93, Lemieux was leading the NHL in scoring when he was diagnosed with Hodgkin's disease and forced to undergo strenuous radiation treatment. He missed two months of the NHL season, yet he returned in time to win his fourth scoring title, with 160 points in 60 games.

He took the 1994-95 season off, then, in 1995-96, he made one of the most remarkable comebacks in sports history, immediately reclaiming his place atop the league scoring chart.

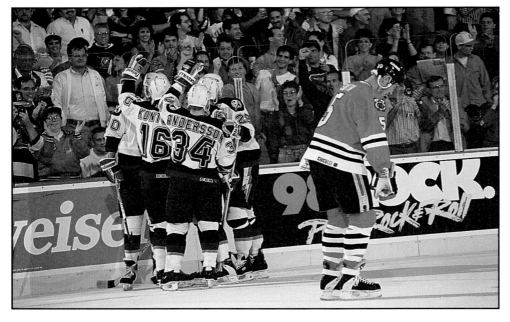

In 1992-93, Kings port-sider Luc Robitaille tallied 63 goals while setting an NHL record for points by a left winger (125).

Chris Kontos (16) and Mikael Andersson (34) of the expansion Tampa Bay Lightning celebrate a goal against Chicago. Tampa Bay won 23 games and impressed fans with their gutty play.

Gilchrist and promising winger Vladimir Vujtek. But the move would prove futile as the Oilers continued to fade, missing the playoffs for the first time since joining the NHL in 1979. In a season of league-wide, record-breaking offensive achievement, the Oilers' top scorer, Petr Klima, finished with a meager 48 points.

In New Jersey, despite his heroic play in the 1988 playoffs, goalie Sean Burke was *persona non grata* among fans and management. After a year of exile with the Canadian Olympic Team, Burke officially left the Devils for Hartford in a trade for center

Bobby Holik, a former first-round draft pick who brought a rugged style that subtly began to transform New Jersey's on-ice character.

In Pittsburgh, where the Penguins were looking very strong for a third straight Cup, their leader, Mario Lemieux, wasted no time getting right back on the war path, beguiling goalies and bearing down hard on his fourth scoring title. With his back moderately healthy and his touch as sweet as ever, "Super Mario" led all scorers through early January with 39 goals and 104 points in just 40 games, an average of 2.6 points per night. His

Penguins controlled the Patrick Division and looked like an excellent bet to win a third playoff title.

But on January 11, 1993, the roof caved in. Lemieux, plagued throughout his career with injuries, was diagnosed with Hodgkin's disease, a form of lymph cancer. Before, the worst he'd faced was the threat of early retirement because of his cranky back. Now, at just 27, he faced his own mortality. With a strenuous plan of radiation therapy ahead, Mario quit the game he had loved and dominated. His departure left a huge hole in the hearts of all hockey fans.

1992-93

Best Record
Pittsburgh
(56-21-7)

Stanley Cup Finals
Montreal 4
Los Angeles 1

Art Ross Trophy
Mario Lemieux
(69/91/160)

Hart Trophy
Mario Lemieux

Vezina Trophy
Ed Belfour

Calder Trophy
Teemu Selanne

Norris Trophy
Chris Chelios

Lady Byng Trophy
Pierre Turgeon

A year after shattering his jaw, Buffalo's Pat LaFontaine scored 53 goals in 1992-93 and was second in the NHL in points with 148, a record for an American.

The expansion Ottawa Senators were a miserable lot in 1992-93, finishing 10-70-4 overall, going 1-40-0 on the road, and yielding nearly twice as many goals as they scored.

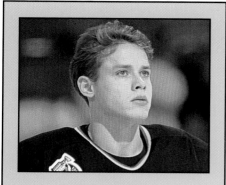

PAVEL BURE

There was a time when it looked like Pavel Bure would never play for the Canucks. Drafted by Vancouver in 1989, he was briefly ruled ineligible by former NHL boss John Ziegler. The Canucks sued the league and won, bringing the Moscow-born youngster to Vancouver in 1991.

After winning the Calder Trophy in 1991-92, Bure used his sophomore season to rewrite the Canucks' record books. He scored 60 goals and 110 points to shatter the club's old marks. Vancouver fans, who remembered the disappointment of Vladimir Krutov, soon nicknamed Bure "The Russian Rocket."

In 1993-94, his third year, he carried the Canucks to the Stanley Cup finals with his second straight 60-goal season. In the playoffs, he finished second in scoring to playoff MVP Brian Leetch.

A brilliant skater with a surgeon's touch and a rocket-launcher for a shot, Bure had it all going for him when he was felled with torn knee ligaments early in 1995-96. The injury came right after Vancouver acquired Bure's buddy, Alexander Mogilny, from Buffalo.

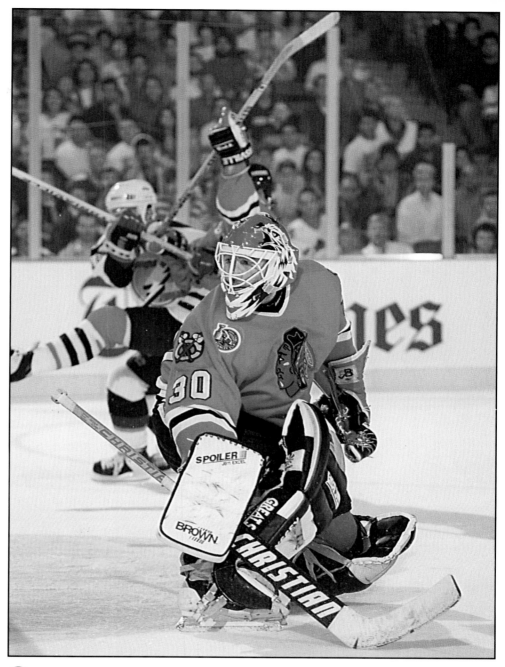

▲ Vezina-winning Eddie Belfour puck-stopped Chicago to the Norris title.

"I'll be back," he told his legion of admirers, "when I'm 100 percent and when I'm cured. If I come back in six weeks or eight weeks or next year, that's not important right now. My health is more important than playing hockey. As soon as I'm ready to come back, I'll be there. Hopefully, I'll be able to help us win another Stanley Cup. But first things first."

While Lemieux retreated to attend to his immediate health concerns, a young Finnish winger for Winnipeg was tearing up the league. Jets rookie Teemu Selanne, drafted in 1988 from Jari Kurri's old Jokerit club, was blistering pucks past goalies at a furious pace. In early March, he shattered Mike Bossy's rookie goal-scoring record (53), and by season's end he had locked up the Calder Trophy, establishing a new record with 76 goals. This should have earned Selanne the goal-scoring title, but this year it only tied him with Buffalo sniper Alexander Mogilny (the first Russian ever to strike for 50 goals). Mogilny also turned on the red light 76 times, thanks largely to the work of his clever set-up man, Pat LaFontaine.

On March 2, 1993, after two months off, Lemieux made a triumphant return to the Penguins lineup. At the time of his comeback, he was fourth in the league scoring race, trailing LaFontaine, Steve Yzerman, and Adam Oates. But in the last 20 games of the season, Lemieux scored 30 goals and collected 26 assists for 56 points. In the final week of the season, he recorded the second five-goal game of his career when he helped Pittsburgh humiliate the Rangers 10-4 at Madison Square Garden. Not only did Lemieux catch the pack, he shifted into overdrive and passed them all— including LaFontaine, who finished with 148 points to Mario's 160. Lemieux earned his fourth Art Ross Trophy as well as the Hart Trophy, the Bill Masterton Trophy, and the Lester B. Pearson Award.

The Penguins captured their first regular-season title with 119 points, winning the Patrick Division by 26 points. The Rangers, who'd taken the

Presidents' Trophy just a year before, toppled to the bottom of the division and missed the playoffs altogether, as injuries and personnel strife plagued the organization. Before the final buzzer sounded on their dreadful season, GM Neil Smith announced that Mike Keenan would take over as coach for the following season, replacing Roger Neilson, with whom team captain Messier apparently did not get along.

In Boston, powered by Adam Oates (142 points, a league-high 97 assists) and rookie Joe Juneau (102 points), the Bruins overcame the loss of goal-scoring giant Cam Neely, whose injured leg kept him out of all but 13 games. The Bruins outlasted the Nordiques, whose Mats Sundin notched points in 30 straight games, the fourth-longest streak in NHL history.

Vancouver stunned the West by winning the Smythe Division, thanks to a 60-goal performance from Pavel Bure, the first Canuck (and the second Russian) ever to reach the 50-goal plateau. In a season of uncharacteristic offensive prowess, the Canucks boasted six skaters with at least 25 goals as they amassed 346 tallies, a franchise record. Wayne Gretzky's L.A. Kings trailed Vancouver by 13 points in the standings, but their best was yet to come.

In the "black and blue" Norris Division, the Blackhawks proved to be the toughest defensive team in the league. Led by goalie Ed Belfour, winner of his second Vezina Trophy with a 2.59 GAA, and Chris Chelios, who won his second Norris Trophy, the Hawks matched timely goal-scoring with stingy defense to win 47

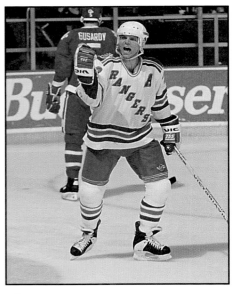

History was made on January 23, 1993, when the Rangers' Mike Gartner scored his 30th goal of the season. In so doing, he became the first player to register 14 straight NHL seasons with at least 30 goals.

Boston center Adam Oates, combining smartly with rookie forward Joe Juneau, notched 45 goals and a league-high 97 assists in 1992-93.

Toronto center Doug Gilmour set club records for assists (95) and points (127) in 1992-93. He also won the Frank Selke Trophy and was runner-up to Mario Lemieux for league MVP honors.

In 1992-93, Manon Rheaume became the first woman to play professional hockey, as she tended goal for the International League's Atlanta Knights for two games.

Capitals and Islanders go at it during the 1993 playoffs after Washington's Dale Hunter viciously blindsided Pierre Turgeon. The Caps lost the game and the series, and Hunter was suspended for the first 21 games of the 1993-94 season.

ALEXANDER MOGILNY

In 1989-90, the NHL threw open its doors to players from the Soviet Union. While many teams stocked up on players in the twilight of their careers, the Sabres signed 20-year-old right winger Alexander Mogilny, a young phenom in the dawn of his stardom.

However, despite his breathtaking speed and precision puck control, the Khabarovsk native languished through his rookie season. He scored only 15 goals while he battled an acute fear of air travel and several bouts of homesickness.

After raising his goal totals to 30 and 39 in subsequent seasons, the more mature fourth-year pro exploded for 76 goals in 1992-93 while playing with Pat LaFontaine. After suffering a broken leg in the 1993 playoffs, Mogilny's production declined in 1993-94. However, that year he became the first Soviet player to wear the captain's "C" in the NHL, filling in when LaFontaine was injured.

Traded to Vancouver in 1995-96, Mogilny briefly reunited with former Red Army linemate Pavel Bure (who missed most of the year with an injury). In Vancouver, Mogilny regained his scoring touch.

games. The Hawks held off a serious challenge from Detroit, which got another brilliant performance (58 goals, 137 points) from Steve Yzerman and 41 goals from "washed up" winger Dino Ciccarelli.

Overall, it was a tremendous year for skill and finesse as 21 players reached the 100-point plateau, setting a new league standard. Buffalo's fleet-footed LaFontaine reached the 50-goal plateau (53), as did the man for whom he was traded, New York Islander Pierre Turgeon, who scored 58 goals en route to the Lady Byng Trophy.

Veteran slot master Dave Andreychuk, who split the year between Buffalo and Toronto, made excellent use of his new Leafs center, Doug Gilmour, and joined the 50-goal club, though most of his 54 goals were scored from within two or three feet of the net. Philadelphia's Mark Recchi joined this elite group with 53 goals but, like Chicago firebrand Jeremy Roenick (who enjoyed his second straight 50-goal campaign), didn't even make the Top Ten list.

As the playoffs began in mid-April, upsets were in vogue. In the Adams Division, fourth-place Buffalo took only four games to sweep division-champion Boston, winning three games in overtime, including Game Four. Third-place Montreal dropped its first two games to second-place Quebec before winning four straight to take that series in a mini-upset.

In the Patrick Division, Pittsburgh skated past New Jersey in five games, outscoring the Devils 23-13, while the heavily favored Capitals could not suppress an energetic Islanders team that won three games in overtime and stole Game Six at home. During the dying moments of that match, Washington's feisty Dale Hunter pitchforked Turgeon heavily into the boards from the blind side, effectively ending Turgeon's playoffs and earning himself a 21-game suspension to start the 1993-94 season.

In the Norris Division, upsets continued. St. Louis rocked the

TEEMU SELANNE

Not since Jari Kurri skated the starboard wing on Wayne Gretzky's line in Edmonton has a Finnish-born skater dominated NHL goalies as Teemu Selanne did during his brilliant rookie year (1992-93). He shattered Mike Bossy's rookie goal-scoring record (53) with 76 red lights and also broke Peter Stastny's freshman scoring record (109) with 132 total points.

Like Kurri, Selanne hails from Helsinki and played his pre-NHL hockey at Jokerit in the Finnish senior league before he joined Winnipeg, which drafted him tenth overall in 1988. He also shares Kurri's skating and shooting artistry.

Voted the NHL's top rookie in 1993, Selanne endured the worst kind of sophomore jinx when he suffered a severed Achilles tendon and missed 33 games of the 1993-94 season. He bounced back with 22 goals and 48 points in the shortened 1994-95 campaign.

Teamed with American-born Keith Tkachuk and Moscow native Alexei Zhamnov, Selanne is one-third of the game's most talented "international" line, averaging well over a point per game.

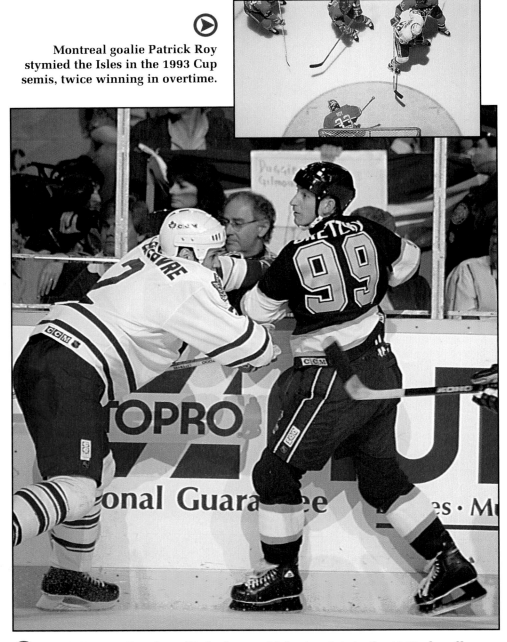

Montreal goalie Patrick Roy stymied the Isles in the 1993 Cup semis, twice winning in overtime.

L.A.'s Wayne Gretzky tallied a league-high 40 points in the 1993 playoffs.

Blackhawks with four straight wins as Brett Hull and Craig Janney scored two game-winners apiece. The hard-fought series between Toronto and Detroit lasted seven games and beyond regulation time before Leafs winger Nik Borschevsky netted an O.T. goal.

In the Smythe Division, fourth-place Winnipeg teased Vancouver for six games before falling to the offensively superior Canucks. An interesting series was fought between the Kings and Calgary. Tied at two games apiece after four matches, the Kings—with Gretzky at the controls—exploded for 18 goals in the next two games, shellacking the Flames by scores of 9-4 and 9-6 to move on.

In the second round, only Montreal had it "easy," if you could call it that.

The Sabres, who lost their top two weapons (LaFontaine and Mogilny) to injuries in Game Three, lost three times in sudden-death, and Montreal completed its sweep while winning all four games by scores of 4-3.

In the Patrick Division, the Isles and Penguins waged a David vs. Goliath battle. Isles goalie Glenn Healy was magnificent as the series went seven games. Lemieux, who appeared exhausted as the series progressed, was not a factor in the playoffs. In Game Seven, the Isles got a huge break when Ray Ferraro and David Volek broke in two-on-one against Tom Barrasso in the sixth minute of overtime. Ferraro drew Barrasso out of his net and slid the puck across the slot to Volek, who tapped home the

winner and sent the underdog Islanders to a conference matchup with Montreal.

In the Norris Division final, a closely fought battle between goaltenders Curtis Joseph of the Blues and Toronto's Felix "The Cat" Potvin derailed in Game Seven. Before a home crowd of 15,700 fans, the Leafs bombarded St. Louis and built a 4-0 first-period lead on their way to a 6-0 series-ending win. The Smythe final between L.A. and Vancouver was tied 2-2 when the Kings won Game Five in double overtime and Game Six to clinch.

As the semifinals began, nobody gave the Islanders a chance against Montreal. Patrick Roy had been brilliant in goal, remaining cool in the face of constant sudden-death pressure. After a 4-1 home win to open the series, Montreal continued its magic by surviving a double-overtime thriller in Game Two when Stephan Lebeau scored at 6:21 of double O.T. If the Islanders felt doomed, they didn't show it in Game Three on their own ice. The dramatic return of Turgeon paid dividends as the wounded warrior gave New York a 1-0 lead, but the Habs tied the game late. In overtime, the Habs held the upper hand, and at 12:34 Guy Carbonneau scored to give Montreal a three-games-to-none advantage.

Roy's 11-game winning streak ended in Game Four as the Isles scratched out a 4-1 win, but they accomplished little more than prolonging their agony. Montreal scored in the first minute of Game Five and built a 5-0 lead before the Isles managed a goal. The final score was 5-2 for the Habs,

earning them a trip to the finals against the winner of the Toronto-Los Angeles series.

By now, Gretzky's Kings had developed the haughty notion that they could win a Stanley Cup. No strangers to sudden-death, the Kings staved off elimination with a 5-4 O.T. win in Game Six after losing Game Five in sudden-death. On May 29, the Kings and Leafs faced off in Game Seven in Toronto while the Canadiens watched at home on television.

In many ways, it was Gretzky's finest hour. Though he had four Stanley Cups to his credit with Edmonton, he'd had a far superior supporting cast with the Oilers. These Kings were a team that learned to win by watching "The Great One." And in Game Seven, Gretzky set the most stunning example, scoring a hat trick against Potvin and putting the game out of reach, 5-3, with his third goal of

the match with less than four minutes to play. The Leafs made it close in the final moments, but the Kings held on to win 5-4 and earn their first-ever trip to the Stanley Cup finals.

After their dramatic semifinal series, it was no surprise that the Kings rolled over the Habs in Game One of the finals, winning 4-1. But the magic wasn't on the side of the Kings after that night. The Canadiens won the next three games in overtime—giving them ten sudden-death triumphs in 11 playoff games. By the time the teams returned to Montreal for Game Five, the Kings' spirit was exhausted, and the Habs skated to a 4-1 win as Kirk Muller scored the Cup-clinching goal early in the second period to seal the Kings' fate. Roy, who finished the playoffs with a 2.13 GAA, was awarded a much-deserved Conn Smythe Trophy, and the Habs hoisted their 24th Stanley Cup.

There was no stopping Montreal's John LeClair in the 1993 Stanley Cup finals, as the energetic winger netted overtime goals in Game 3 (at 0:34) and Game 4 (14:37).

Left winger Vincent Damphousse gave Montreal an edge through four tough playoff series, as he netted three game-winning goals and led the club with 23 playoff points.

Finally! Rangers Quench Their 54-Year Thirst

1 9 9 3 - 9 4

Expansion and realignment were all the rage as the NHL prepared for the 1993-94 season. Teams and players moved around at a furious rate. The league added two more franchises, in Anaheim and Florida, bringing the number of teams in the league to 26. The Disney Corporation joined the NHL with the Mighty Ducks, while business magnate H. Wayne Huizenga (owner of the Blockbuster Video chain) debuted his Panthers out of the Miami Arena.

Meanwhile, despite a rise in fan support, another team was on the move. Having played their last home game at the Met Center on April 13, 1993, the Minnesota North Stars packed up and headed south on Interstate 35 to their new home in Dallas.

Under new Commissioner Gary Bettman, the NHL took on a more mainstream profile and abandoned its traditional division names. The Adams Division became the Northeast Division, the Patrick Division became the Atlantic Division, the Norris was now the Central Division, and the Smythe was renamed the Pacific Division. Gone too were the Wales and Campbell Conferences, renamed simply the Eastern and Western Conferences, respectively.

In Chicago, Steve Larmer's consecutive-game streak ended at 884, not because of an injury but because the veteran right winger declined to continue his career with the Blackhawks, preferring a trade to a new team and a new challenge after 11 full seasons in the Windy City. He was not the only player with a jersey change in his near future. From August 3, 1993, through the May 21, 1994, trading deadline, nearly 120 deals were cut and 200 players relocated. The activity was dizzying:

Prior to the start of the season, the Jets unloaded talented but expensive defensive ace Phil Housley to St. Louis for Nelson Emerson and Stephane Quintal. After missing the first month of the season in his holdout, Larmer ended up on Broadway in a three-team deal that saw him go from Chicago to Hartford

▲ Copping their coveted Cup wasn't easy for the Rangers. Game Seven of the Eastern Conference finals went to double overtime, and Game Seven of the finals was a tight 3-2 affair.

with Bryan Marchment for Eric Weinrich and Patrick Poulin, then on to the Rangers with Nick Kypreos and Barry Richter for James Patrick and Darren Turcotte. Patrick was later shipped to Calgary with Zarley Zalapski and Michael Nylander for Gary Suter, Paul Ranheim, and Ted Drury. One day after that deal was completed, Suter was transferred to Chicago with Randy Cunneyworth for Frantisek Kucera and Jocelyn Lemieux.

Jimmy Carson's fall from grace continued, as his stay in L.A. ended in January 1995 when the Kings traded him to Vancouver for untested youngster Dixon Ward. Meanwhile, Marty McSorley, who'd been swapped from L.A. to Pittsburgh in August, was returned to the Kings (with Jim Paek) in February for Tomas Sandstrom and Shawn McEachern, the player for whom he was originally traded.

Late in the year, Boston sent Joe Juneau to Washington for Al Iafrate in a deal that would eventually backfire for both clubs, as Iafrate would be plagued by knee injuries and Juneau's effectiveness would mysteriously go into decline. Craig Janney, who'd been awarded to Vancouver as compensation when the Blues signed free agent Petr Nedved in March 1994, was traded back to St. Louis a week later for Jeff Brown, Bret Hedican, and Nathan Lafayette in a deal that would help the Canucks go all the way to the Stanley Cup finals.

The revitalized Rangers, gearing up for another run at the playoffs, sent Mike Gartner (a chronic playoff dud) to Toronto for money winger Glenn Anderson, shipped future star Tony Amonte to Chicago for grinders Stephane Matteau and Brian Noonan, and dispatched rookie speedster Todd Marchant to Edmonton for the leadership of three-time Stanley Cup champ Craig MacTavish.

And the players weren't the only ones whose lives were in upheaval. On November 15, the on-ice officials, who'd been in year-long negotiations for a new collective bargaining agreement, walked out in the first-ever

SERGEI FEDOROV

Imagine a player in Detroit so great that fans are heard asking "Steve who?" in regard to future Hall of Famer Steve Yzerman.

Sergei Fedorov, who once played on a line with Pavel Bure and Alexander Mogilny when the three were teenagers on the Central Red Army squad, is one of the greatest two-way players in NHL history—as dangerous in an offensive role as he is while back-checking.

Drafted by Detroit in 1989, the fleet-footed center scored 31 rookie goals in 1990-91, then 32 and 34 in his next two years. He also demonstrated his tremendous back-checking skills, consistently finishing among the best plus/minus players in the league.

In 1993-94, he chased Wayne Gretzky for the scoring title, finishing second with 120 points. He also had the best rating (plus-48) among NHL forwards. When trophies were distributed at season's end, Fedorov was a three-time winner, becoming the first Russian in league history to win the Hart Trophy, Frank Selke Trophy, and Lester B. Pearson Award.

Vancouver's "Red Rocket," Pavel Bure, pocketed 60 goals in 1993-94 and won his first goal-scoring title.

Calgary finished atop the Pacific Division thanks to defenseman Al MacInnis and his booming slapshot.

John Vanbiesbrouck earned Hart Trophy consideration in 1993-94 after puck-stopping the expansion Florida Panthers to 33 victories.

The Kings' Wayne Gretzky celebrates his NHL record-breaking 802nd goal on March 23, 1994. Gretzky rifled one past Vancouver goalie Kirk McLean on a set-up from Marty McSorley to break the record of Gordie Howe, Wayne's boyhood idol.

strike of their union. Replacements were brought in—to resounding discontent among players and management.

One player offered the following reaction after the first week of the walkout: "That's enough. Give (the replacements) their jerseys, let them enjoy their few minutes of glory, and get them out of there. We need the old guys back." By the end of November, the union zebras were back in place.

The Dallas Stars found a warm reception awaiting them in Texas, and they responded with 42 wins and a third-place finish behind Detroit and Toronto in the powerful Central Division. The Red Wings were paced by Sergei Fedorov, who scored 56 goals and 120 points (second in the

league). Fedorov, a brilliant skater and defensive player, recorded a sterling plus-48 rating. When awards were handed out at season's end, Fedorov walked away with the Hart Trophy, the Frank Selke Trophy, and the Lester B. Pearson Award. The Leafs, who roared to the best start in NHL history with ten straight wins, finished just two points behind Detroit.

In the Pacific Division, the Flames got 40 goals each from Robert Reichel and Theo Fleury and 41 from Gary Roberts en route to the regular-season division title. The Canucks, with another 60-goal show from franchise player Pavel Bure, took second. San Jose surprised everybody with 33 wins to finish third, as first-year coach Kevin Constantine coaxed 30 goals

from veteran Red Army hero Sergei Makarov and 30 wins from Latvian goalie Arturs Irbe. Anaheim finished ahead of both L.A. and Edmonton but failed to qualify for the playoffs in the new set-up, as only the top eight teams in each conference earned postseason berths.

In the Northeast Division, the Penguins continued to prove they could win with or without Mario Lemieux. Though their courageous leader was limited to just 22 games due to failing health, the Pens finished four points ahead of the Bruins for the division title. In Boston, injured hero Cam Neely scored 50 goals despite playing in only 49 games. Neely won the Masterton Trophy for perseverance following this tremendous comeback.

Montreal squeaked into third place in the Northeast, one point ahead of Buffalo, whose brilliant goalie Dominik Hasek won the Vezina Trophy and was runner-up for the Hart Trophy as well. Hasek finished with a 1.95 GAA, a .930 save percentage, and seven shutouts, all league bests. Quebec dropped from second to fifth in the division race, though a high point came on February 17, 1994, when the Nordiques' Mike Ricci burned the Sharks for five goals in a 8-2 romp.

The Presidents' Trophy went to the Rangers, top team in the Atlantic Division, who finished with a 52-24-8

record. Blueshirts goalie Mike Richter led the league with 42 wins under new coach Mike Keenan. Left winger Adam Graves set a franchise record with 52 goals, and Soviet defenseman Sergei Zubov led the team in scoring with 89 points. New Jersey, with a new coach of its own, Jacques Lemaire, finished second as rookie goalie Martin Brodeur emerged as a star, finishing with the second-best GAA in the league (2.40). Brodeur took the Calder Trophy, beating out a wonderful crop of freshmen that included Philly's Mikael Renberg (38 goals), Edmonton's Jason Arnott (33), and Ottawa's Alexei Yashin (30).

Lemaire, who instituted a tight defensive style known as the "neutral-zone trap" (which would prove highly successful as well as bitterly controversial), was named coach of the year. Washington placed a distant third, with few highlights to its season. One came late in the year when Peter Bondra connected for five goals in a February win over Tampa Bay.

On March 20, 1994, Wayne Gretzky scored the 801st goal of his career, tying his hero, Gordie Howe. Three nights later against Vancouver, he scored No. 802 to become the top goal-scorer of all-time. This was the

The Mighty Ducks of Anaheim, owned by Walt Disney Company CEO Michael Eisner and named after the hit Disney movie, debuted in 1993-94 with 33 victories, a record for an expansion team.

Toronto's Dave Andreychuk, a lumbering winger with remarkably soft hands around the net, blasted home 53 goals in 1993-94 and helped jump-start Toronto to a 10-0-0 start.

MIKE GARTNER

No player in NHL history has achieved what Mike Gartner achieved when he built a streak of 15 consecutive 30-goal seasons, starting with his rookie season (1979-80) when he ripped 36 goals, and ending with the 34 goals he scored in 1993-94.

A speedy skater with a rocket-launcher shot, Gartner began his streak with Washington. In 1984-85, he had his best season, reaching the 50-goal and 100-point marks for the only time in his career. Traded to the North Stars in 1989, he then moved on to the Rangers in 1990. He scored 49 goals on Broadway in 1990-91, then was traded to Toronto late in the 1993-94 season.

Gartner had to play the early part of his career in the shadows of brilliant right wingers Guy Lafleur, Mike Bossy, and Jari Kurri, and yet he joins them, statistically, as one of the most productive snipers in league history. With consistency and durability, Gartner has placed himself in that group even though he has never won a single major NHL award.

Following the 1994-95 season, he ranked as the fifth all-time leading goal-scorer with 629 career tallies. The only right winger in history to score more goals than Gartner is Gordie Howe.

record—among his more than 60 scoring marks—that meant the most.

"By far," he emphasized. "There is no comparison. The ones that are the best are the hardest ones to break. Somebody is going to have to play 16 years at 50 goals a year (to catch me)."

The Great One finished the season with 130 points to win his tenth Art Ross Trophy (as well as the Lady Byng Trophy, his fourth), but it wasn't enough to get the Kings into the postseason. Boston's Raymond Bourque led all NHL defensemen in points (91) and earned his fifth Norris Trophy, edging Devils captain Scott Stevens (whose plus-53 rating led the league). Only Bobby Orr (eight) and Doug Harvey (seven) had won the Norris Trophy more times than Bourque.

For the second year in a row, the playoffs began with a major upset as Detroit, a heavily favored team, lost a stunning opening-round series to San Jose in seven games. Also in the Western Conference, Vancouver staged a thrilling comeback over Calgary in seven games, winning the last three matches in overtime (Game Seven ended in double overtime thanks to Bure). Toronto snubbed the Blackhawks in six while St. Louis was swept by Dallas.

In the East, the Rangers shellacked the Isles in four straight while

1993-94
Best Record
New York R.
(52-24-8)
Stanley Cup Finals
New York R. 4
Vancouver 3
Art Ross Trophy
Wayne Gretzky
(38/92/130)
Hart Trophy
Sergei Fedorov
(56/64/120)
Vezina Trophy
Dominik Hasek
Calder Trophy
Martin Brodeur
Norris Trophy
Ray Bourque
Lady Byng Trophy
Wayne Gretzky

With a 3-1 victory over Tampa Bay in February 1994, Detroit coach Scotty Bowman recorded his 1,000th NHL victory, including regular-season and playoff games. Only one other coach had won more than 800 games (Al Arbour, 902).

Sweden won the 1994 Olympic gold medal in spectacular fashion. Tied 2-2 after regulation in the final game, Sweden and Canada engaged in the first-ever Olympic shootout. Peter Forsberg netted the winner for the Swedes.

Washington upset Pittsburgh in six. Despite his seven points, Mario Lemieux was obviously not in top form as the Pens went down. Meanwhile, the Habs and Bruins staged an epic war that lasted seven games before Boston prevailed, and the Devils also needed seven games to outlast Buffalo.

In the second round, the Rangers continued to dominate the opposition, crushing the Caps in five games.

Vancouver also needed only five games to eliminate the Stars. New Jersey took six games to squash the Bruins, and Toronto was extended to seven before finally landing the pesky Sharks.

In the Western Conference finals, Toronto beat Vancouver in Game One at home on Peter Zezel's O.T. marker 16:55 into the extra session, but it was all the Leafs could muster. The Canucks roared back to win four

CHRIS CHELIOS

Tough, ornery, talented, and determined to win. These are just a few of the words and phrases used to describe Chicago's native son. Chris Chelios began his NHL career in Montreal, carving his name on the 1986 Stanley Cup and winning the 1989 Norris Trophy, then was traded to his hometown Blackhawks in 1990.

Chelios was a collegiate star at the University of Wisconsin before joining the Habs late in the 1983-84 season. Growing slowly into a leadership role under the tutelage of Larry Robinson, Chelios became an All-Star-caliber player in the late 1980s. In Chicago, he quickly became the team's inspirational leader.

In 1993, following his third season in Chicago, he earned his second Norris Trophy with a 73-point, 282-PIM season. During the 1994-95 lockout, Chelios directed some unfortunate comments at NHL boss Gary Bettman, but he later apologized and vowed to clean up his act. He became a man of his word in 1995, when he earned his third First All-Star Team berth and finished the year with 38 points and just 72 PIM in 48 games.

Boston's Ray Bourque skated off with his fifth Norris Trophy in 1993-94. Bourque was named a first- or second-team All-Star in each of his first 16 seasons, a feat no other NHL player in history can claim.

Former Czech goalie Dominik Hasek filled in for the injured Grant Fuhr in 1993-94 and wowed Buffalo fans with his spectacular 1.95 goals-against average. It was the first time in 20 years that an NHL goalie had a GAA under 2.00.

END OF THE CURSE

It couldn't last forever, though some Rangers fans feared it might. "It," of course, is "The Curse," the 54-year Stanley Cup drought that made the Rangers the longest-suffering team in the NHL—until 1994, that is, when they beat the Vancouver Canucks in seven thrilling games. The 19,785-day wait was finally over.

The drought was agonizingly long considering there were only six teams in the league from 1942-67. The Rangers had reached the finals three previous times since 1940, but they fell to Detroit in seven games in 1950 (when no games were played in New York because ice wasn't available), six games to Boston in 1972, and five games to Montreal in 1979.

Some hockey zealots blamed The Curse on John Reed Kilpatrick, former owner of both the Rangers and Madison Square Garden. When the Garden's mortgage was finally paid off in 1941, Kilpatrick had the audacity to burn the papers in the Stanley Cup.

In the 1980s, Islanders fans humiliated Rangers faithful with chants of "Nineteen-forty! Nineteen-forty!" But now Blueshirt boosters had revenge. Said one fan's sign in the stands: "NOW I CAN DIE IN PEACE."

Nothing and no one could penetrate Kirk McLean's net during the 1994 Western finals. McLean notched two shutouts as Vancouver knocked off Toronto in five games.

straight as goalie Kirk McLean tossed a pair of shutouts, ending the series on Greg Adams's O.T. winner in Game Five.

Meanwhile, the Rangers and Devils engaged in a stirring battle, as New Jersey won Game One in sudden-death at the Garden only to have the Blueshirts shut them out in Game Two. The Rangers then returned the earlier favor and beat the Devils in New Jersey in O.T. to take a 2-1 series advantage. But the Devils fought back to tie and move ahead with a Game Five victory at the Garden. In a classic moment, Rangers captain Mark Messier announced emphatically to newspaper reporters that his team would win Game Six. He then went out and scored a hat trick to spark a come-from-behind win and send the series to Game Seven.

On their home ice, the Rangers held a 1-0 lead until the final seconds of the game before New Jersey's Valeri Zelepukin poked home a rebound in a goalmouth scramble and tied the game with only eight seconds on the clock. Through the first overtime period, the teams played all-out, and the Rangers out-shot the Devils 15-7 without luck. Then, in the sixth minute of double overtime, Rangers winger Matteau curled around the back of the Devils' net and unleashed a tricky wrap-around that Brodeur lost in his skates. With that goal, the Rangers earned their first trip to the finals since 1979.

The Stanley Cup finals continued where the semifinals left off, as sudden-death was the fashion of the day. In Game One, after the Rangers and Canucks ended regulation tied at 2-2, the teams played almost a full

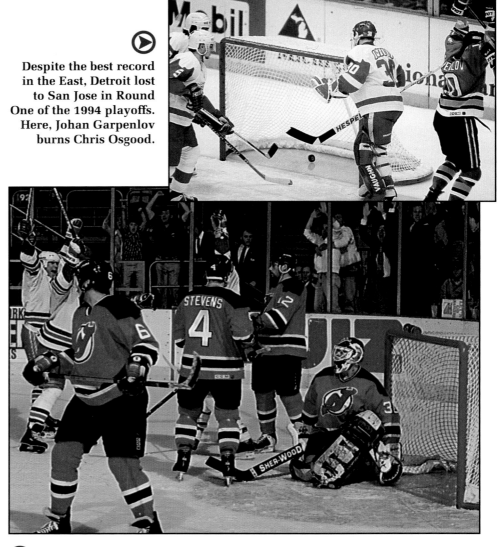

Despite the best record in the East, Detroit lost to San Jose in Round One of the 1994 playoffs. Here, Johan Garpenlov burns Chris Osgood.

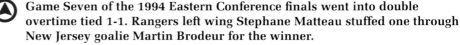

Game Seven of the 1994 Eastern Conference finals went into double overtime tied 1-1. Rangers left wing Stephane Matteau stuffed one through New Jersey goalie Martin Brodeur for the winner.

period of overtime. With only 34 seconds to play, the Rangers let Vancouver's Adams beat Richter and take away the Rangers' home-ice advantage.

The Blueshirts rebounded with a dramatic 3-1 win in Game Two before traveling west, where they blasted five goals past McLean, including a pair from Brian Leetch, en route to a 5-1 win in Game Three. Shut out of Stanley Cup glory for 54 years, the New Yorkers moved within one win of the championship when they erased an early two-goal deficit to win Game Four 4-2, with Leetch scoring once and assisting on the Rangers' other three goals.

But the Canucks proved worthy adversaries. Leading 3-0 in Game Five in New York, they let down long enough for the Rangers to tie the game

before scoring three more times themselves to win 6-3 and send the series back to Vancouver. The Canucks handily won Game Six 4-1, and the curse that had plagued the Rangers for more than five decades seemed well in place as the teams returned to Madison Square Garden for the Game Seven showdown.

Leetch, though, got the Rangers started at 11:02 with his 11th goal of the playoffs, and Graves ended a ten-game scoring drought with his tenth playoff goal less than four minutes later to build a 2-0 first-period lead. The Canucks pulled to within 3-2 with 15 minutes to play in the third period, but Rangers goalie Richter was a brick wall and the Broadway Blueshirts survived to capture the Stanley Cup.

The Rangers hoisted the fabled mug for the first time in 54 years, two

months, and one day. Leetch was named MVP of the playoffs with 34 points in 23 games, and Messier became the first man ever to captain two NHL franchises to Stanley Cup championships.

Within weeks, coach Keenan left New York for St. Louis in a contract dispute. Worse yet, Mario Lemieux—still feeling the effects of back surgery and radiation therapy for Hodgkin's disease—announced that he would not play the following season.

And though the NHL enjoyed its brightest hours with the thrilling playoff action, darkness loomed ahead. Fear and frustration built throughout the summer of 1994, as the owners and players marched toward a collective bargaining stalemate that would result in the first extended work stoppage in league history.

Rangers winger Joey Kocur, shown sliding past Vancouver goalie Kirk McLean in the Stanley Cup finals, mustered just two playoff points. Kocur, though, was well-respected for his toughness and leadership skills.

Brian Leetch's first-period goal sparked the Rangers to victory in Game Seven of the 1994 Cup finals. Leetch led all playoff scorers (34 points) en route to the Conn Smythe Trophy, then spoke on the phone to U.S. President Bill Clinton immediately after the Rangers won the Stanley Cup.

Owners Lock Out Players;
Devils Trap the Wings

1 9 9 4 - 9 5

As hard as it is to believe, there almost wasn't any hockey in 1994-95, even in the afterglow of Lord Stanley's belated visit to Broadway and the national upswing in the game's popularity. When October arrived, no games were being played. No games in November or December either. Frustration and public misperception was rampant as the NHLPA and the owners set deadline after deadline, made "final offer" after "final offer," and seemed, at times, to be fatally locked in a quagmire of ill will and mistrust.

However, unlike the players' strike that shattered the 1994 major-league baseball season, the NHL players did not go on strike in 1994-95. It was the unified ownership that chose—when a new collective bargaining agreement appeared not to be forthcoming—to lock the players out as training camp neared its conclusion. The most pressing issues separating the two sides were free agency, salary arbitration, entry-level salaries, the imbalance between the U.S. and Canadian dollars, the Entry Draft, revenues and revenue sharing, and

discipline (fines accompanying suspensions).

As in any civil war, brothers occasionally ended up on opposite sides of some issues. Among the hottest issues causing differences of opinion was the high-dollar salaries being paid to rookies coming out of junior hockey. With recent record deals signed by the likes of Eric Lindros, Alexandre Daigle, and Paul Kariya, some veterans were shaking their heads.

Bernie Nicholls, a 13-year veteran who made use of his free-agent status

▲ Not even the quick-footed Sergei Fedorov could escape New Jersey's neutral-zone trap in the 1995 Stanley Cup finals. The Devils dismissed Detroit in four straight games.

to sign a new contract with Chicago during the off-season, viewed a salary cap on rookie salaries as just fine. "I sure as hell don't want to go on strike for a kid who has never played a game in this league and is asking for a million dollars."

On October 1, 1994, the NHL announced it would "postpone" the start of the season, after the owners rejected the players' offer to play as negotiations continued.

Chicago defenseman Chris Chelios directed his unhappiness at the new league boss. "If I were Gary Bettman, I'd be worried about my family," he stated. "I'd be worried about my well-being now. Some crazed fans, or even a player—who knows?—they might take matters into their own hands and figure they get him out of the way and things might get settled." Chelios apologized for his outburst soon after, but it was obvious that his frustration

was shared by his brothers in the players union.

After two weeks, it was clear that the process had bogged down. Players began to flee to Europe, or back to juniors, or to minor pro teams, to stay sharp during the interim. Many NHL front-line regulars found jobs in other venues, including NHLPA representative Marty McSorley, who was singled out for criticism when he joined Wayne Gretzky's "Team 99" European tour while insisting that his fellow NHLers stay home.

Some players not in demand from European teams became jealous of NHL brethren who were now earning big bucks overseas. Edmonton's Jason Arnott, who had narrowly missed winning the 1994 Calder Trophy, was outspoken. "I don't think it's right. We're getting locked out. We're part of a union; we should get locked out together."

THE LOCKOUT

After the 103-day tug-of-war that was the 1994-95 lockout, neither side could claim complete victory. But when the whistle had finally blown, the owners were the ones who had tugged the most.

With salaries spiraling out of control, Commissioner Gary Bettman and the owners had felt a need to play hardball with the players. They wanted a salary cap—or at least a tax system that would penalize teams with high payrolls. The players weren't about to put a limit on their salaries, and the stalemate began.

The lockout was long and nasty, wiping out 468 games. The owners never did get their salary cap or luxury tax, but the players—desperate to return to the ice—yielded ground in many areas: A rookie salary cap of $850,000 was now imposed; players with less than three years experience could no longer become restricted free agents; players with less than five years experience would not be eligible for arbitration; and players could not become unrestricted free agents until the ripe old age of 32.

With the new agreement, the owners wouldn't be able to completely control salaries, but at least they could keep them somewhat in check.

Commissioner Gary Bettman (center) and the other NHL power brokers twiddled their thumbs too long to please hockey-starved fans.

One of the few who made a living during the lockout was this ice shoveler at the Islanders' Nassau Coliseum.

After 103 days of foot-dragging, posturing, threatening, whining, pleading, and even some actual bargaining, the NHL and the players union finally devised a plan that everyone could live with. On January 11, 1995, with more than three months of the calendar wasted, the warring sides stood shoulder to shoulder and peered down the barrel of a totally lost season (and the potentially fatal damage that such a circumstance would mean to their sport) and agreed to blink together.

On Friday the 13th, the agreement was ratified by the members of the union. Said Bettman: "We all believe the future of the game is as bright as it has ever been. It's time for the entire NHL family to come together."

With the end of the lockout came a renewed vigor among the 26 teams to make a dash for the finish line in a 48-game schedule that would be played completely within each team's own conference. Deals that had been made in the summer had to pay off immediately.

In Detroit, the Red Wings had made a serious move toward a championship when they traded steady defenseman Steve Chiasson to Calgary for goalie Mike Vernon. The acquisition was in response to neophyte goalie Chris Osgood's heartbreaking loss to San Jose in the previous season's playoffs. While Osgood remained the "goalie of the future," the Red Wings knew their time was now.

Similar thinking in Quebec sparked the rapidly improving Nords to trade Mats Sundin to Toronto for Wendel

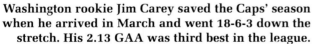
Washington rookie Jim Carey saved the Caps' season when he arrived in March and went 18-6-3 down the stretch. His 2.13 GAA was third best in the league.

Theo Fleury, a pint-sized dynamo with a nasty side, led Calgary in scoring in 1994-95 (29-29-58) and sparked the Flames to the Pacific Division title.

Pittsburgh center Ron Francis, wearing the captain's "C" while Mario Lemieux sat out the season, helped lead the Penguins to a sparkling 29-16-3 record.

▲ **Penguin Jaromir Jagr copped his first Art Ross Trophy in 1994-95 (32-38-70).**

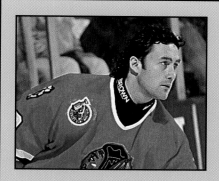

ED BELFOUR

Aptly nicknamed "The Eagle," goalie Ed Belfour soared from virtual obscurity as an over-aged junior to an award-winning NHL star in a span of five years.

When Belfour, a Manitoba native, was tending goal for Winkler (MJHL) in 1985-86, there was little reason to think he'd ever see the light of the NHL. Ignored in the draft, he won a chance to play at the University of North Dakota in 1986-87. After earning WCHA First All-Star status, he was signed by the Blackhawks, who sent him to the farm. He won IHL rookie-of-the-year honors in 1988.

After spending the 1989-90 campaign stopping pucks for the Canadian National Team, he became the Blackhawks' regular starter in 1990-91. And what a year it was. Belfour led the league in games (74), wins (43), and GAA (2.47) en route to both the Calder Trophy and the Vezina Trophy, joining Frank Brimsek, Tony Esposito, and Tom Barrasso as the NHL's only Calder-Vezina winners.

The Eagle took Chicago all the way to the Stanley Cup finals in 1992 and won his second Vezina Trophy in 1993. He's also earned three William Jennings Trophies.

▲ **Rookie Peter Forsberg helped power Quebec to the best record in the East.**

Clark, the heart and soul of the Leafs even during the recent tenure of super-squirt Doug Gilmour. Hartford signed banging winger Steven Rice from Edmonton in August and then lost coveted defenseman Bryan Marchment as compensation. The Whalers also acquired Glen Wesley from Boston at the high price of three No. 1 draft picks.

The Flames traded defenseman Al MacInnis to St. Louis for defenseman Phil Housley in July. The Habs sent high-salaried Guy Carbonneau to the Blues, who appeared to be collecting huge contracts; they led the NHL in payroll at around $23 million. The

Islanders, who had made Ron Hextall their sacrificial lamb in the 1994 playoffs against the Rangers, rewarded him by trading him back to Philadelphia, where they actually play defense in front of their goalies.

Once the collective bargaining agreement was signed, teams resumed their wheeling and dealing. The Stars shipped Mark Tinordi to Washington for Kevin Hatcher, who was reunited with his kid brother, Derian. The Caps also sent goalie Don Beaupre to Ottawa for a draft pick, opening a slot that would eventually be filled by an eye-opening rookie with "savior" written all over him.

The Flyers and Canadiens pulled off a major trade in February as Mark Recchi went to the Habs for Eric Desjardins, John LeClair, and Gilbert Dionne. In the 1993 playoffs, it was Desjardins and LeClair—with overtime goals in Games Two, Three, and Four—who did so much damage in the Finals against L.A. The deal would prove monstrous, as LeClair joined Eric Lindros and sophomore fitness freak Mikael Renberg to form the Legion of Doom Line, one of the deadliest in the league.

Isles GM Don Maloney pulled the trigger on an April blockbuster that brought Kirk Muller, Mathieu

1994-95

Best Record
Detroit
(33-11-4)

Stanley Cup Finals
New Jersey 4
Detroit 0

Art Ross Trophy
Jaromir Jagr
(32/38/70)

Hart Trophy
Eric Lindros
(29/41/70)

Vezina Trophy
Dominik Hasek

Calder Trophy
Peter Forsberg

Norris Trophy
Paul Coffey

Lady Byng Trophy
Ron Francis

The captain of the Flyers and the center of Philly's feared Legion of Doom Line, Eric Lindros was voted the NHL's most valuable player for 1994-95. The hard-charging Lindros tied for the league scoring title with Jaromir Jagr.

Schneider, and Craig Darby from Montreal for Pierre Turgeon and Vladimir Malakhov. But Muller, known for his leadership, went in the tank, and so did the Isles.

With such a short season, teams were in a perpetual scramble to find remedies and produce instant results. During a mid-April match, Jeremy Roenick locked legs with Derian Hatcher and was lost for the regular season with a severe knee injury, which impelled Chicago to reacquire Denis Savard. The slick veteran regained his touch and filled in for Roenick splendidly. The Leafs, who hadn't accomplished much since winning the first ten games of the

1993-94 season, made a series of trades, including a disastrous swap in which highly regarded goaltending prospect Eric Fichaud went to the Isles for Benoit Hogue, who promptly went into a scoring slump just when Toronto needed some goals.

As the season progressed in its abbreviated form, one of the most interesting stories took place in Pennsylvania, where Flyers center Eric Lindros and Penguins winger Jaromir Jagr staged a two-horse race for the scoring title. While leading his Flyers to the top of the Atlantic Division, Lindros potted 70 points in 46 games. Jagr's Pens finished second in the Northeast Division behind the

Nordiques. Jagr played in all 48 games and also recorded 70 points. Though Lindros had a higher points-per-game average, the Art Ross Trophy went to Jagr based on goals (he outscored Eric 32-29).

Lindros got his revenge later when he copped both the Hart Trophy and Lester B. Pearson. Meanwhile, Jagr's linemate, Ron Francis—who finished fifth overall in points—captured both the Frank Selke and Lady Byng Trophies for his excellent two-way play and sportsmanship.

Detroit was the class of the league, winning the Presidents' Trophy with 70 points. Paul Coffey was the team's leading scorer (58 points) en route to his third Norris Trophy. Calgary rode the back of Trevor Kidd in goal and tiny Theo Fleury up front (58 points) to a first-place finish in the Pacific Division.

Washington's Peter Bondra led the league in goals (34), while the Jets' Alexei Zhamnov quietly finished third overall in points (65)—though he made some very loud noise on April Fools' Day when he scored five times against L.A. On March 8, playing in his 983rd NHL game, the Rangers' Steve Larmer notched his 1,000th career point. He would finish with 1,012 before calling it quits at season's end.

In the Eastern Conference playoffs, the Rangers, who barely made it to the postseason, faced top-ranked Quebec, led by Joe Sakic, rookie sensation Peter Forsberg, and Owen Nolan. However, with a burst of offensive strength, the Rangers eliminated the Nordiques in six. Philadelphia hosted Buffalo and solved goalie Dominik Hasek to win in five games. The Penguins outlasted the Caps, who had been the recipients of a season-saving performance from first-year goalie Jim Carey (who had come up from the minors in mid-March and turned a 3-10-5 start into a 22-18-8 finish). The Devils had little trouble dispatching the Bruins, winning the series in five games.

In the West, Toronto blew a two-game lead and lost to Chicago in seven games, while Vancouver outlasted the Blues and the Sharks again shocked their first-round opponents, this year the Flames, in seven contests. The only series to end quickly was Detroit's five-game destruction of Dallas.

In Round Two, the Cup-champion Rangers gave up their crown with almost no fuss, losing four straight to Philly, while the Devils had only marginally more trouble with Pittsburgh, winning their series in five. San Jose's dream ended quickly, as the Sharks were annihilated by the Red Wings, outscored 24-6 over four games. Meanwhile, the Blackhawks got to the semifinals with a four-game sweep of the Canucks.

 Aided by his teammates' suffocating defense, New Jersey's Martin Brodeur went 16-4 with a 1.67 GAA in the 1995 playoffs.

DINO CICCARELLI

Dino Ciccarelli has never been fleet afoot, nor has he been big or flashy. As a junior skating for London in the OHL, he suffered a badly broken leg during the 1978-79 season and watched his draft stock plummet. When draft day came in 1979, Dino was totally ignored. Some youngsters would have given up.

Not Dino. Not only did he fight his way back into playing shape, he scored 50 goals in 1979-80, earned a free-agent contract with the Minnesota North Stars, and embarked on an NHL career that would last more than 15 years and feature a pair of 50-goal seasons (55 in 1981-82 and 52 in 1986-87).

Playing for Minnesota (nine years), Washington (three-plus years), and Detroit (four years and counting), Ciccarelli has proven to be a relentless goalmouth sniper, absorbing severe beatings at the hands of bigger, stronger defensemen to hold his ground in front of the net. Dino banged home his 500th career goal on January 8, 1994.

Ciccarelli has been beating the odds since the very beginning. Betting against his admission into the Hall of Fame would not be too wise.

Detroit's Paul Coffey, the all-time leading scorer among defensemen, still had it in 1994-95, copping the Norris for his exceptional scoring (58 points) and leadership skills.

Forward Slava Kozlov, the youngest of Detroit's Russian contingent, won the decisive Game Five of the Western finals with a double-overtime goal against Chicago.

NEW JERSEY DEVILS

In East Rutherford, New Jersey, they still remember the November night in 1983 when the Edmonton Oilers put a 13-4 licking on the Devils. Jari Kurri scored five goals that night and Wayne Gretzky called the struggling team "a Mickey Mouse" organization. It was the worst of times.

Now, those loyal fans have enjoyed full vindication. It took a dozen years, but in 1995 the Devils raised the Stanley Cup at center ice at Meadowlands Arena, the first title in the 21-year existence of the team.

Starting out as the Kansas City Scouts in 1974-75, then shifting to Colorado as the Rockies in 1976-77, the team struggled mightily for many years, eventually moving to New Jersey in 1982. Slowly, trades and draft picks built the club into a powerhouse. In 1993-94, the Devils added the final piece of the puzzle when they hired Jacques Lemaire as coach.

Lemaire installed the neutral-zone trap and the Devils launched their Stanley Cup-bound juggernaut. In a shocking example of their precise execution, they swept the Red Wings in the 1995 Stanley Cup finals and caused the NHL to change some rules to minimize the clutch-and-grab epidemic.

In the Cup semis, the Devils showed their neutral-zone trap to Philadelphia, and the Flyers skated right into it. Time and again, waiting and counterpunching, New Jersey held the Legion of Doom in check, then exploited openings in the Philly defense to score timely goals. After winning the first two games in Philly, the Devils lost Game Three at home in overtime and Game Four in regulation. But then the curtain came down on the Flyers, who dropped the next two games and the series.

Meanwhile, the Red Wings took advantage of their superior arsenal—and luck—and beat Chicago in five, taking Games One, Three, and Five in

sudden-death. Only one contest in the series was decided by more than one goal.

The Stanley Cup finals pitted Detroit, the league's third-best offensive team, against New Jersey, one of the top defensive teams. The Red Wings were 40 years removed from their last Stanley Cup title, and the Devils, once called a "Mickey Mouse" organization by none other than Wayne Gretzky, were on the verge of erasing the last vestige of their often humiliating past. All the experts agreed this would be a long, hard-fought series. Alas, they were wrong.

Claude Lemieux broke a 1-1 tie early in the third period of Game One

to give the Devils the opening match in Detroit. For Lemieux, who had struggled all season and spent a fair amount of time in the coach's doghouse, it was his 12th goal of the playoffs. Coming up big in the clutch, the feisty Lemieux already had two other game-winners to his credit.

In Game Two, seldom-used winger Jim Dowd broke a 2-2 tie with only 1:24 to play in the third period, and Stephane Richer added an empty-netter, to give New Jersey a 4-2 win and a two-game advantage heading back to the Meadowlands.

Bruce Driver and Lemieux scored their very last goals as Devils to open Game Three, and Neal Broten scored the eventual game-winner early in the second period, as New Jersey built a 5-0 lead before Detroit answered with a pair of meaningless goals with less than four minutes to play.

If the start to this season seemed unlikely, with a labor dispute and 103 days of inactivity, the end was just as surprising. The Red Wings had been favored to win the Cup. Now, they not only faced a four-game elimination, they could not figure out a way to stop the bleeding.

After the Red Wings took a 2-1 lead in the first period of Game Four, the Devils tied it up before the intermission, then sent out their veteran Mr. Everything, Broten, to finish the job. Broten, a long-time member of the North Stars, was acquired from Dallas during the regular season to provide checking, some offensive spark, and leadership. In the second period of Game Four, he beat Mike Vernon with his seventh goal of the playoffs, and the Red Wings never recovered. Broten's goal was the Cup-clincher as Detroit went down in a four-game sweep.

Lemieux's 13 playoff goals earned him the Conn Smythe Trophy, although some felt goalie Martin Brodeur, who finished with a spectacular 1.67 GAA and three shutouts in 20 games, was just as deserving. Lemieux would be traded to Colorado before the start of the next season, and long-time Devil Driver would sign with the rival Rangers.

With more franchise movement in the air, a grass-roots upheaval stalled the departure of the Winnipeg Jets (for at least one year), but nothing could keep the Nordiques from leaving Quebec. Marc Crawford, who was named coach of the year, shrugged as his team prepared for a move to Denver.

Good news from the Mario Lemieux camp: Feeling revitalized, No. 66 announced his intention to return to the NHL for the 1995-96 season. The only question was: Could he be the same old Super Mario?

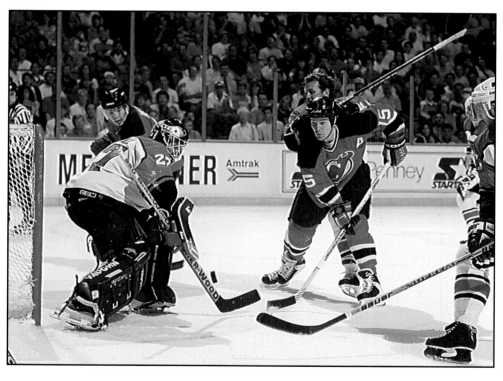

Flyers goalie Ron Hextall and Devils winger John MacLean duel it out in the 1995 Eastern Conference finals. The road team won the first five games of this series before New Jersey clinched it at home in Game Six.

After netting just six goals in the regular season, New Jersey's Claude Lemieux potted 13 in the 1995 playoffs and won the Conn Smythe Trophy.

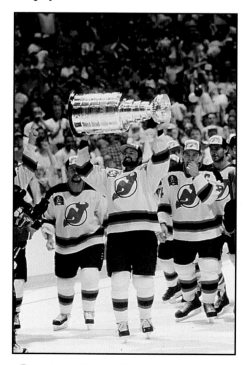

Bruce Driver hoists the Devils' first Cup in their 13-year history.

Avalanche Shock the Wings, Crush the Panthers

1 9 9 5 - 9 6

Recovering quickly from its public-relations nightmare of 1994-95, the NHL—with increased TV coverage and expansive marketing—made up all of its lost ground and enjoyed one of its most exciting and record-breaking years in 1995-96. Both on and off the ice, new standards were set for excellence.

Four new buildings opened, as the Bruins left Boston Garden for the Fleet-Center, the Canucks transferred from Pacific Coliseum to General Motors Place, the Senators moved from the Ottawa Civic Centre into the glittering new Palladium, and the Canadiens tearfully bid adieu to the Montreal Forum for their new digs at Le Centre Molson. And additional new arenas, replete with crucial income-generating executive suites, were underway in Buffalo, Philadelphia, and Florida.

Meanwhile, irony swirled in Winnipeg and Minnesota. Fans in Manitoba, who had staged an astonishing grassroots effort to keep the Jets in town for the 1995-96 season after it seemed all but certain they would leave (for the Twin Cities), ultimately lost their bid to retain their beloved team. The Jets were sold to Minneapolis businessman Richard Burke, who immediately announced his plans to have the team play in Phoenix—not the Twin Cities—beginning in 1996-97.

In Hartford, the Whalers played their "last" season in Connecticut for the umpteenth time, waiting for off-season ticket sales to boost their dwindling financial base. Same story in Edmonton.

On the ice, the action was fast and furious, the thrills in abundance. Mario Lemieux returned to the

 Colorado celebrates its 1-0 triple-O.T. victory over Florida in the decisive Game 4 of the 1996 Cup finals.

354

Pittsburgh Penguins after a yearlong hiatus, in which he recuperated from the effects of radiation cancer therapy and a chronic bad back. Not only did Lemieux play well, he recaptured all the glory of his earlier days. Despite a valiant charge from his superstar teammate Jaromir Jagr, Lemieux collected the Hart Trophy as well as his fifth career scoring title with 69 goals and 161 points in 70 games. Along the way, he scored his 500th career goal with a hat trick against the Islanders on October 26.

Lemieux was just one of four NHL veterans to reach the 500-goal plateau in 1995-96. New York's Mark Messier came next, with a hat trick against Calgary on November 6. Messier, a Hart Trophy finalist, was on his way to a 50-goal, 100-point season when a rib injury knocked him out of the lineup late in the season. He finished with 47 goals and 99 points.

On January 17, Detroit's Steve Yzerman, long rumored to be on his way out of Detroit, lifted a backhander past Colorado goalie Patrick Roy for his 500th career goal. Two weeks later, Dale Hawerchuk, skating for St. Louis, scored his 500th before a crowd of family and friends at Toronto's Maple Leaf Gardens.

On December 13, Detroit's Paul Coffey skated the length of the ice in a typical offensive rush, then left a clever drop pass for Igor Larionov. Larionov fired the puck home and earned Coffey his 1,000th career assist, the most ever by an NHL defenseman.

While records were being shattered on the ice, it was an astonishing year for player movement. Not only was there an inordinate number of trades, but some of the biggest of the big-name superstars shifted cities, led by the February deal that saw Wayne Gretzky seek and finally gain his

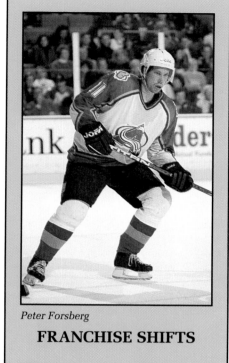

Peter Forsberg

FRANCHISE SHIFTS

Expansion wasn't the only tool by which the NHL changed its face during the 1990s. Three historic hockey hotbeds found themselves without NHL teams when economics and personal crises dictated movement to new environs.

In Minnesota, the North Stars went from Stanley Cup finalists (1991) to nomads (1993) when owner Norm Green moved the team to Dallas. Green's move came in the wake of sexual harassment charges by a former employee. Green claimed he couldn't make money in Minnesota without huge concessions that the local sports council was unwilling to give him. Many felt he ran in humiliation more than in poverty.

In Quebec, the Nordiques rebuilt themselves into playoff contenders, only to be sold and then moved to Colorado (as the Avalanche) following the 1994-95 season. And, even more shockingly, the Quebec citizenry hardly made a peep about it.

The beleaguered Winnipeg Jets were sold to Minnesota businessman Richard Burke. But instead of moving to the Twin Cities, Burke found a more welcoming community in Phoenix, where the team was expected to set up shop in 1996-97.

Mario Lemieux *(left)* and Ron Francis combined for 280 points while leading Pittsburgh to the Northeast title.

release from Los Angeles in favor of St. Louis, where he joined Brett Hull. Before the season even began, Buffalo shuffled Alexander Mogilny, their one-time 76-goal scorer, to Vancouver, where he was slated to play alongside childhood buddy Pavel Bure. But Bure was felled by torn knee ligaments, leaving Mogilny to fend for himself. All he did was score 55 goals in a brilliant season.

Midway through the year, the Jets jettisoned Teemu Selanne, whom they'd assured was not on the block, to Anaheim. The fabulous Finn teamed with Paul Kariya and lifted the Mighty Ducks to within a couple points of a playoff berth. After giving up nine goals to Detroit in December,

Roy walked out on the Canadiens, claiming coach Mario Tremblay had humiliated him, and was traded to Colorado. Hawerchuk, who had left Buffalo for St. Louis in the off-season, was traded to Philadelphia.

Wendel Clark was traded twice—from Colorado to the Isles to Toronto. Phil Housley was shipped from Calgary to New Jersey to help the goal-hungry Devils defend their Stanley Cup title. Jari Kurri left the Kings on Gretzky's heels and headed for the Big Apple (along with Marty McSorley and Shane Churla) for the Rangers' playoff run.

Claude Lemieux, winner of the 1995 Conn Smythe Trophy, was twice deported: from New Jersey to the

Islanders to Colorado. Kirk Muller, who walked out on the Isles early in the season, finally found his way to Toronto via trade. Joe Nieuwendyk, who similarly had opted not to rejoin his team, the Flames, sat out until a deal could be worked that landed him in Dallas.

Owen Nolan, who led Quebec in goals in 1994-95, was dealt to San Jose. Goalie Bill Ranford was traded back to Boston, his original NHL team. Fifty-goal scorer Ray Sheppard was traded twice, from Detroit to San Jose to Florida. Kevin Stevens, who left Pittsburgh for his hometown Bruins before the start of the season, was a bust in Boston and found himself traded to L.A. for Rick Tocchet. In all,

Though they featured hockey greats Grant Fuhr, Wayne Gretzky, and Brett Hull *(third, fourth, and fifth from left)*, the Blues had trouble scoring and barely made the playoffs.

Ron Hextall regained his old form in 1995-96, tying for the league lead in GAA (2.17) and helping the Flyers soar to the Atlantic title.

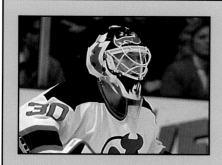

MARTIN BRODEUR

During the 1994 Stanley Cup playoffs, the New Jersey Devils were a very good team. Thanks to their rookie goalie, Martin Brodeur, they often played like a great team. In fact, with a postseason goals-against average of 1.95, Brodeur nearly took them to the finals all by himself.

Selected in the first round of the 1990 draft from St.-Hyacinthe, the Quebec junior star spent a year in the AHL before taking over as the Devils' No. 1 goalie in 1993-94, replacing Chris Terreri. He won 27 games, pitched three shutouts, and posted the second-best GAA in the NHL (2.40). Though his playoff performance didn't count in the voting, he won the Calder Trophy anyway.

During the lockout-shortened 1994-95 season, Brodeur's Devils finished only fifth among eight playoff-bound teams in the Eastern Conference, but once the postseason began the second-year netminder was back to genius level.

With Brodeur in goal for all 20 playoff games, the Devils thrashed Boston, Pittsburgh, and Philadelphia before handing the Red Wings a shocking four-game sweep in the finals to win the Stanley Cup. Brodeur narrowly missed MVP honors, which went to teammate Claude Lemieux.

⬆
Vancouver's Alexander Mogilny led all non-Penguins in goals with 55.

◀

After hearing that Florida's Scott Mellanby shot a rodent, like a puck, against a wall, Panthers fans began showering the ice with plastic rats.

more than 150 NHL players—recognized regulars, not farm-team fringe players—changed sweaters.

Interestingly, the team that made the fewest changes (just two trades all year) was Detroit, winner of its second consecutive Presidents' Trophy. The Red Wings iced a potent attack featuring their five-man Russian unit (Sergei Fedorov, Slava Kozlov, and Larionov up front with Slava Fetisov and Vladimir Konstantinov on defense). They also boasted the finest puck-stopping tandem in the league with veteran Mike Vernon and future superstar Chris Osgood, the latter of whom joined Ron Hextall as just the

second goalie in NHL history to score a true goal (on March 6 against Hartford). Ironically, the Red Wings' two top scorers, Fedorov and Yzerman, were co-finalists for the Selke Trophy as the best defensive forward.

Though nobody could catch him for the scoring championship, Lemieux had some fine company at the top of the scoring chart, including teammates Jagr and Frank Selke Trophy finalist Ron Francis, who finished second and fourth overall, respectively, with 149 and 119 points. Colorado's Joe Sakic, who would emerge as a playoff hero, edged into third place overall with

120 points, while his teammate, Peter Forsberg, finished fifth (116).

Brian Leetch of the Rangers led all NHL defensemen in scoring with 85 points, ahead of fellow Norris Trophy finalist Ray Bourque (82 points) and Coffey (74). Chicago's Chris Chelios wound up winning the Norris. Meanwhile, Ottawa's Daniel Alfredsson led all rookies with 61 points, though Chicago freshman Eric Daze had the most goals among first-year players with 30. Both were finalists for the Calder Trophy, along with Florida's brilliant rookie defenseman Ed Jovanovski. Alfredsson won the Calder in a close vote.

Philadelphia goalie Hextall, a candidate for Comeback Player of the Year, tied Detroit's Osgood for the best goals-against average in the league at 2.17. In Washington, Jim Carey was third with a 2.26 GAA and took home the Vezina Trophy. However, Carey flopped in the postseason, opening the door for backup Olaf Kolzig to establish his credentials for the future. Buffalo's Dominik Hasek battled injuries but still led the NHL in save percentage (.920), while Tampa Bay veteran netminder Daren Puppa was second (.918).

The Devils, who struggled on offense all year, became the first team since the 1969-70 Montreal Canadiens to miss the playoffs the year after they won the Stanley Cup. While the Devils watched, the NHL's two Florida-based teams—the Panthers and Lightning—enjoyed their first taste of postseason play.

GARY BETTMAN

Since the league was formed in 1917, only five men held the office of NHL president: Frank Calder (1917-43), Red Dutton (1943-46), Clarence Campbell (1946-77), John A. Ziegler (1977-92), and Gil Stein (1992-93). In 1992-93, the NHL anointed a new leader, with a new job title. Gary Bettman, a former administrator at the National Basketball Association, became the league's first commissioner.

Bettman vowed to take the game into the new century with vision and bottom-line attention to detail. Bettman got NHL games on network television in the U.S. for the first time in years, first working out a deal with ABC, then putting together a bigger pact with Fox. Bettman's appointment coincided with the announcement of two new NHL teams, Anaheim and Florida, each owned by entertainment billionaires.

Not afraid to play hardball, Bettman suspended Washington's Dale Hunter for an unprecedented 21 games after his cheap shot on Islander Pierre Turgeon in the 1993 playoffs. Bettman's hard-line approach against the players during the 1994-95 lockout led to fiscal victory for the owners.

Still a powerful presence at age 35, Mark Messier finished second in Hart Trophy balloting thanks to his 47 goals and unbeatable leadership.

Teemu Selanne *(left)* and Paul Kariya were the new darlings of Anaheim. They scored 108 points each and were both finalists for the Lady Byng.

The first round went according to plan without the drama of any major upsets. Led by Hart Trophy candidate Eric Lindros, the Philadelphia Flyers were the top team in the Eastern Conference, thanks largely to Hextall's goaltending and John LeClair's first-ever 50-goal season. They dispatched Tampa Bay in six games. In other Eastern action, the Penguins dropped two games to Washington before roaring back to win in six; the Rangers lost twice at home to open their series against Montreal, then won four straight; and Florida humiliated the Bruins in five.

In the Western Conference, the Red Wings outlasted a courageous Winnipeg club playing its final games as the Jets, winning their opening-round series in six games. Colorado played a fast and furious six-game set with Vancouver and emerged on top, and Chicago swept Calgary. In the only "upset" of the first round, the fifth-seeded Blues skated past the fourth-seeded Maple Leafs, four games to two, in a series that guaranteed to spell wholesale changes for the loser.

In the Eastern semifinals, the Panthers smothered Philadelphia with team defense and pulled off the first major upset, winning in six games as John Vanbiesbrouck outplayed Hextall in goal and the Panthers shut down Lindros and the Legion of Doom. The

⊿ Despite another heartbreaking exit in the playoffs, Steve Yzerman captained Detroit to an NHL-record 62 wins and scored his 500th goal in January.

Brothers Eric Lindros *(left)* and Brett Lindros *(right)* combined for 118 points in 1995-96—115 for Eric, three for Brett. ⊳

Penguins had little trouble with the Rangers, who couldn't stop Lemieux and Jagr, winning in five games.

Out West, Colorado and Chicago played a dramatic six-game series in which four games went to sudden-death. Game Four went to triple overtime before Sakic ended it, and the deciding sixth game went into double O.T. before Avalanche defenseman Sandis Ozolinsh ended the Blackhawks' season.

Meanwhile, the powerful Red Wings had their hands full with a Blues team that suddenly coalesced after a difficult run to the postseason. The Blues, who had lost goalie Grant Fuhr to torn knee ligaments early in their first-round series with the Maple Leafs, were recipients of a brilliant and courageous performance from Jon Casey, who spent most of the regular season in the minors after being considered all but washed up. After winning the first two games, the Wings lost three straight and had to force a seventh game on home ice. Scoreless after regulation, they finally won the game 1-0 on a double-overtime goal by their leader, Yzerman.

The Red Wings, however, were destined for a huge disappointment of their own. Widely recognized as the favorites to end the longest current Cup-less streak in the NHL (41 years), the Wings went to their conference-finals series against Colorado with a lot of work yet to do. But they lost the first two games at home, first on an O.T. goal by Mike Keane in Game One, then on a 3-0 shutout at the hands of Roy in Game Two. They were down three games to one and staved off elimination with a Game Five win on home ice, but they could not solve Roy. In Game Six, the Wings managed just one goal and lost 4-1, ending a season in which they set a league record for wins (62) but had loudly claimed that anything short of a Stanley Cup victory would be a failure.

In the Eastern Conference finals, the powerful offense of the Penguins faced its biggest challenge against the stifling Panthers and the brilliant goaltending of veteran Vanbiesbrouck. After splitting the first four games, the Pens took a three-games-to-two advantage with a Game Five victory at home, thanks to a 3-0 shutout by Tom Barrasso.

But the Panthers refused to quit. They forced a seventh game by winning Game Six at home, then staged yet another shocking upset when they beat the Pens 3-1 in Pittsburgh to clinch the series and earn their first trip to the Stanley Cup finals—in just their third year of existence. In eliminating the Pens, Florida's vastly underrated checkers held Lemieux and Jagr to just one goal apiece in the seven-game series. Afterward, Lemieux, who talked about the possibility of retiring, admitted he had never in his career played against such an effective defensive unit as Florida's.

The Stanley Cup finals, featuring two new teams and two famed goaltenders, quickly developed into a battle of masked warriors. In Game One, played in Colorado, the Avalanche spotted Florida a 1-0 first-period lead before storming back in the second period—their strongest period all year—with goals from Scott Young, Mike Ricci, and Uwe Krupp. The three goals came within four minutes and proved more than the Panthers could overcome, as they dropped the contest 3-1.

Following their intense showing against Pittsburgh in the Eastern Conference finals, the Panthers were due for a collapse, and it came in a big way during Game Two of the Cup

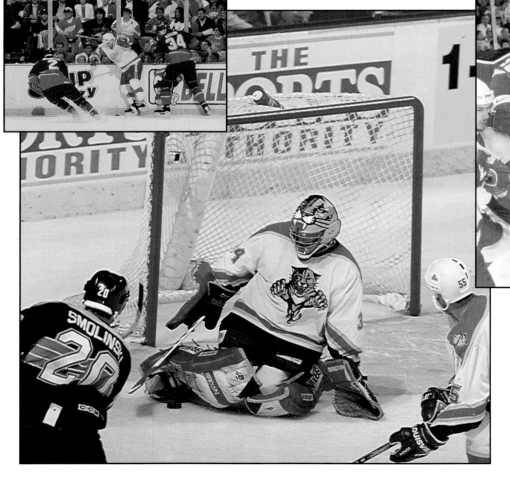

Colorado shut down Detroit's Sergei Fedorov in its Western finals upset.

In the Western semis, St. Louis pushed Detroit to the limit before losing Game Seven 1-0 in double O.T.

Florida's John Vanbiesbrouck beat Pittsburgh 3-1 in Game Seven of the Eastern finals.

finals. The Avalanche, led by Forsberg's first-period hat trick, scored four goals in the first stanza, chasing Vanbiesbrouck from the nets. The Beezer's replacement, Mark Fitzpatrick, didn't fare much better, however, giving up another four goals—including two to Jon Klemm, a defenseman playing on the wing for the first time since his childhood hockey days. Rene Corbet scored twice and Valeri Kamensky chipped in with his 10th playoff goal as Colorado declawed the Panthers 8-1.

Back in Miami for Game Three, Vanbiesbrouck, the man most responsible for the Cats even making it to the finals, was returned to the nets. And with the home crowd cheering them on, the Panthers negated an early goal by Claude Lemieux and took a 2-1 first-period lead on goals from Sheppard and Rob Niedermayer. But the Avalanche, with yet another strong second-period showing, tied the game 1:38 into the middle frame on Keane's third playoff goal. And just 1:22 later, Avalanche captain Sakic broke in alone on Vanbiesbrouck and fired a wrist shot over the Beezer's glove to give Colorado the margin of victory— and put the Panthers within one game of elimination.

In Game Four, it was Roy and Vanbiesbrouck who once again emerged as stars. In a game that was scoreless at the conclusion of regulation despite numerous chances at both ends, Roy would eventually face 63 shots, while VBK would see 56. The longest scoreless game in Stanley Cup finals history didn't end until 4:31 of triple overtime. It was defenseman Krupp, who had missed all but six games of the regular season after tearing up his left knee, whose shot from the point found its way through a screen in front of Vanbiesbrouck and snuck into the net to give the Avalanche the Stanley Cup.

Sakic, the heart and soul of the Avalanche, led all playoff scorers with 18 goals, set a new playoff record with six game-winners, and was awarded the Conn Smythe Trophy. In winning the Cup, the Avalanche became only the second team in the history of major sports to win a championship in their first season in town. The Washington Redskins, who left Boston after the 1936 season, won the NFL title in 1937.

If the NHL is looking for a dynasty, it better be patient. Colorado is the fifth team in the last five years to hoist a Stanley Cup.

DOMINIK HASEK

Known as "Dominik the Dominator," Hasek won his first Vezina Trophy in 1993-94 when he finished the season with a 1.95 goals-against average, the first GAA below 2.00 since Philadelphia's Bernie Parent finished the 1973-74 season with a 1.89 mark.

Born in Pardubice, Czecho-slovakia, Hasek was a star in the Czech senior league for nearly a decade. He was voted Czech Goalie of the Year five times and Czech Player of the Year three times. Despite being drafted back in 1983 (199th overall by the Blackhawks), he didn't make his NHL debut until 1990-91. After two mediocre seasons in the Blackhawks system, he was traded to Buffalo, where he emerged as a human brick wall.

In 1993-94, Hasek shared the Sabres' goaltending duties with Grant Fuhr, playing in 58 games and surrendering just 109 goals with a league-leading seven shutouts. Hasek's brilliant play allowed Buffalo to trade Fuhr.

During the shortened 1994-95 season, Hasek again played brilliantly, tossing five shutouts in 41 games and finishing with a league-best 2.11 GAA to capture his second Vezina Trophy. He is the only European-born goalie to win the Vezina twice.

Colorado's Joe Sakic, who won the Conn Smythe Trophy, set a playoff record with six game-winning goals. His 18 playoff red lights were one short of the mark set by Reggie Leach and Jari Kurri.

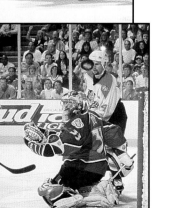

Colorado's Patrick Roy deflects the rubber against Florida in the Cup finals. In one of the great goalie performances of all time, Roy rejected all 63 shots to win the last game of the finals in triple overtime.

INDEX